Interdisciplinary Studies of the Political Order

Economy, Polity, and Society

The foundations of political economy — from Adam Smith to the Austrian school of economics, to contemporary research in public choice and institutional analysis — are sturdy and well established, but far from calcified. On the contrary, the boundaries of the research built on this foundation are ever expanding. One approach to political economy that has gained considerable traction in recent years combines the insights and methods of three distinct but related subfields within economics and political science: the Austrian, Virginia and Bloomington schools of political economy. The vision of this book series is to capitalize on the intellectual gains from the interactions between these approaches in order to both feed the growing interest in this approach and advance social scientists' understanding of economy, polity, and society.

This series seeks to publish works that combine the Austrian school's insights on knowledge, the Virginia school's insights into incentives in non-market contexts, and the Bloomington school's multiple methods real-world approach to institutional design as a powerful tool for understanding social behaviour in a diversity of contexts.

Series Editors:
Virgil Henry Storr, associate professor of economics at George Mason University and senior fellow, F. A. Hayek Program for Advanced Study in Philosophy, Politics & Economics, Mercatus Center at George Mason University
Jayme S. Lemke, senior research fellow, F. A. Hayek Program for Advanced Study in Philosophy, Politics & Economics, Mercatus Center at George Mason University

Titles in the Series:

Interdisciplinary Studies of the Market Order: New Applications of Market Process Theory, edited by Peter J. Boettke, Christopher J. Coyne and Virgil Henry Storr

Knowledge and Incentives in Policy: Using Public Choice and Market Process Theory to Analyze Public Policy Issues, edited by Stefanie Haeffele

Exploring the Political Economy and Social Philosophy of James M. Buchanan, edited by Paul Dragos Aligica, Christopher J. Coyne and Stefanie Haeffele

Exploring the Political Economy and Social Philosophy of F. A. Hayek, edited by Peter J. Boettke, Jayme S. Lemke and Virgil Henry Storr

Informing Public Policy: Analyzing Contemporary US and International Policy Issues through the Lens of Market Process Economics, edited by Stefanie Haeffele, Abigail R. Hall and Adam Millsap

Interdisciplinary Studies of the Political Order: New Applications of Public Choice Theory, edited by Donald J. Boudreaux, Christopher J. Coyne and Bobbi Herzberg

Interdisciplinary Studies of the Political Order

New Applications of Public Choice Theory

Edited by
Donald J. Boudreaux, Christopher J. Coyne,
and Bobbi Herzberg

ROWMAN & LITTLEFIELD
INTERNATIONAL

London • New York

Published by Rowman & Littlefield International, Ltd.
6 Tinworth Street, London SE11 5AL
www.rowmaninternational.com

Rowman & Littlefield International, Ltd., is an affiliate of
Rowman & Littlefield
4501 Forbes Boulevard, Suite 200, Lanham, Maryland 20706, USA
With additional offices in Boulder, New York, Toronto (Canada), and London (UK)
www.rowman.com

British Library Cataloguing in Publication Information
A catalogue record for this book is available from the British Library

ISBN: HB 978-1-7866-0980-9

Library of Congress Cataloging-in-Publication Data Is Available
ISBN 978-1-78660-980-9 (cloth)
ISBN 978-1-5381-5878-4 (pbk)
ISBN 978-1-78660-982-3 (electronic)

Contents

Introduction

New Approaches to Public Choice: Interdisciplinary Studies of the Political Order

Donald J. Boudreaux, Christopher J. Coyne, and Bobbi Herzberg[1]

The chapters in this volume explore and engage the key thinkers and ideas of the Austrian, Bloomington, and Virginia schools of economics in order to better understand various aspects of the political process and political order. The political process focuses on the ways that people come together to engage in collective decision making in a variety of contexts. The central elements of the political process include the formation of rules (both emergent and designed), the subsequent interactions that take place within those rules, and the evolution of rules over time. Together, these dynamics constitute the political process that produces a political order.

Our purpose in this introductory chapter is twofold. First, we provide background on the key themes that constitute the political process and political order. We do so by considering the central insights of the Austrian, Bloomington, and Virginia political economy traditions. In some cases, the themes are shared across the three schools. In others, they are unique to a single school of thought but complement the other schools in delineating the scope of the political process and order. Our goal in providing this overview is to establish the necessary foundations for the contributions that follow.

Our second purpose is to provide an overview of each of the subsequent contributions. Each chapter contains original research that explores and engages various aspects of the political process and political order. This interdisciplinary research makes the continuing relevance of the Austrian, Bloomington, and Virginia schools of thought for understanding the political process and political order clear.

THE POLITICAL PROCESS AND POLITICAL ORDER

Those in the Austrian tradition emphasize four important concepts necessary to understand the political process and order.[2] The first is methodological individualism, which means that the individual is the unit of analysis. The complex social phenomena that we seek to understand as social scientists are ultimately grounded in the purposive actions of people pursuing their disparate goals. While this perspective recognizes and appreciates that people belong to a variety of groups and organizations, it emphasizes that all phenomena, including the political process and political order, ultimately, emerge from the purposes and plans of individuals. An appreciation for this point directs one's focus to how people act, and interact, within certain environments in the pursuit of their goals. Different behaviors in different contexts will influence the evolution of the political process and political order that emerges.

A second theme is the focus on process as compared to a final, end state (Hayek 1948; Kirzner 1997). Instead of focusing on equilibria and end states, those in the Austrian tradition emphasize the importance of evolution and change in an open-ended system. While an end state indicates a final state of rest, the process approach stresses the importance of constant change in the face of uncertainty, error, experimentation, and learning. The term "process" is meant to capture this ongoing change and evolution to the various orders—economics, political, and social—which characterize human life. Various orders exist, but they are not final. Instead, they are constantly evolving and changing as the participants in the order learn and act.

A third theme is the importance of spontaneous, or emergent, order (Hayek 2014b, 2014c, 2014d). Order refers to the coordination or integration of activities. Order can come from two sources. It can be planned using human reason, or it can emerge spontaneously. Spontaneous orders are the result of purposive human action, but not the result of human design. That is, each individual within a system, pursuing their own ends, contributes to a broader order, which was not their intended purpose. Examples of emergent orders include language, norms, culture, customary law, and the economy.

An appreciation for emergent orders leads to a final theme of those working in the Austrian tradition—an appreciation for the limits of human reason (Hayek 1988, 2014a). One of the defining features of spontaneous order is that it is abstract. Since the order is not the result of human design, its complexity extends beyond what human reason could possibly imagine and grasp. This places limits on the ability of people to fully understand the nuances of the order and, hence, their ability to intervene to bring about a preferable state of affairs. Appreciating the limits on human reason is cause for humility when considering intervening in complex systems.

Scholars in the Bloomington School—most notably, Elinor and Vincent Ostrom—have emphasized four important concepts for understanding the political process and political order.[3] The first is the distinction between "rules in form" and "rules in use" (E. Ostrom 2005, 2010). The rules in form refer to codified rules, while the rules in use refer to the rules that people actually follow in their daily lives. This distinction is important because it is, ultimately, the rules in use that govern how people interact with others. The rules in form and rules in use can align, but in many contexts they diverge. This suggests that to understand various aspects of the political process and political order requires an appreciation for the rules in use because it is these rules that influence how people behave and the type of order that emerges.

The second key insight from the Bloomington school is the emphasis on the ability of individuals to shape and improve the institutional environment in which they live (E. Ostrom 1990, 2010). Contrary to the view that people often become "stuck" in suboptimal situations, those in the Bloomington tradition emphasize that people are creative and purposeful actors who have the ability to shape and improve the rules that govern the political process and generate the political order. This emphasis opens up space for entrepreneurship, experimentation, and innovation in the political process and subsequent order. Instead of being passive actors in the political process, those involved are active agents of choice and change.

Third, scholars working in the Bloomington tradition note the importance of polycentric orderings for producing value-added political outcomes (Polanyi 1951; V. Ostrom 1972, 1991; E. Ostrom 1999, 2005, 2010; Wagner 2005; McGinnis and Walker 2010; Aligica and Tarko 2012; Boettke and Candela 2015). A polycentric order, in contrast to a monocentric order, is one where there are numerous decision-making units. Polycentrism offers five benefits as a system of political organization. First, decentralized decision making allows actors to take advantage of local and context-specific information. Second, it also permits greater competition, experimentation, and flexibility compared to centralized control. Third, the multi-units that constitute the overall polycentric orders allow for the satisfaction of a diversity of preferences. Fourth, polycentrism disperses risk since there is no single point of failure. Finally, polycentric orders disperse power since no single unit possesses monopoly control over decision making.

An appreciation of polycentrism is important for the political process because it creates an environment whereby the participants can act entrepreneurially in discovering and changing political rules that generate a desirable political order. The idea of polycentricism is closely connected to the concept of spontaneous order discussed above. The interactions between the numerous decision-making units in a polycentric order contribute to a broader spontaneous order that is not centrally designed.

Finally, those in the Bloomington tradition move beyond the standard dichotomy between "state" and "market" to emphasize the importance of civil society (E. Ostrom 2010). In this regard, the Bloomington school is building off of the work of Alexis de Tocqueville ([1835/1839] 1969), who stressed the importance of associations for a free society. For Tocqueville, these associations emerge from the voluntary actions of private individuals and served as an important middle ground between the atomism of markets and coercive power of government. Those working in the Bloomington tradition appreciate Tocqueville's insight and place voluntary collective action at the heart of their understanding of a free, democratic society (V. Ostrom 1997; Wagner 2005). They also emphasize that voluntary cooperation is a typically overlooked, yet highly effective, mechanism for solving a variety of collective action problems, such as the tragedy of the commons (E. Ostrom 1990). An appreciation for the space between markets and politics offers the opportunity for a broader conception of the political process and political order.

Scholars in the Virginia political economy tradition—for example, James Buchanan—emphasize the importance of applying the tools of economics to nonmarket settings, including politics and civil society, which involves interactions between people who must act in groups (Buchanan 1979a, 2003).[4] These tools are used to understand both the formation of political rules—constitutional political economy—and the subsequent play within those rules—public choice. A key aspect of constitutional political economy entails comparative institutional analysis to consider the potential outcomes of a range of possible political arrangements. Public choice is focused on understanding how existing political institutions influence the knowledge and incentives that face those who operate within those institutions. This is important because the outcomes emerging from political institutions contribute to human welfare, for better or for worse.

Like those working in the Austrian and Bloomington schools, Virginia political economy scholars emphasize that individuals, with their purposes and plans, are crucial to understanding economic, social, and political phenomena. In contrast to a holistic view, which treats the "state" as a single, homogeneous entity that makes decisions as a collective, those in the Virginia school adopt an individualistic view, which focuses on the fact that individuals are embedded in an array of institutions that shape their behavior (Buchanan 1949, 1979b).

Related to this appreciation of individuals and institutions is an emphasis on exchange between individuals. For Buchanan, and others in this tradition, life is fundamentally about interaction and exchange with others (Buchanan 1979b). Exchange is relevant on a variety of margins. For example, people must cooperate and compromise in the formation of rules (Buchanan and Tullock 1962; Buchanan 1975; Munger and Munger 2015). Subsequently, people must coordinate and exchange within the rules once they are established (Buchanan 1979b). Exchange is typically associated with economics narrowly understood, but those in the Virginia political economy tradition stress that exchange also takes place in nonmarket settings where people must continually coordinate and cooperate with others to achieve their goals.

A third theme is the focus on the nature of order as an emergent process. As Buchanan (1982) put it, order is defined in the process of its emergence, meaning that order does not exist absent the process that generates that outcome. This process involves interactions between individuals as emphasized by scholars across all three schools of thought. Like those in the Austrian tradition, focus is placed on the emergence of order in an open-ended, ongoing process. And like those in the Bloomington school, stress is placed on the ability of people to shape, influence, and change their environment through their choices and actions.

Together the insights of these three schools of thought constitute the political process and political order. The key insights and themes can be summarized in the following list of propositions.

1. Only individuals choose. All phenomena can ultimately be traced back to the actions and choices of individuals.
2. People are capable of shaping and improving the world in which they live through their actions and choices, both over the rules and within the rules.
3. Interactions between people are fundamentally about exchange. Interactions with others allow people to accomplish their goals. Interactions require exchange on a variety of margins—compromise over the rules of interaction, agreements on terms of exchange, and so forth.
4. The various orders that characterize life—economics, political, social—are the result of an ongoing process. Focus should be on understanding this process as compared to final end states.
5. Many of the orders that allow for widespread cooperation and flourishing are emergent in nature. These spontaneous orders are the result of human action, but not human design.
6. Polycentric orders allow for learning and experimentation through decentralized decision-making units.
7. Human reason is limited in its ability to fully understand complex systems and in the ability of people to use their reason to construct a desired state of affairs.
8. Human life is a game played within rules. The rules that people follow—the "rules in use"—will determine economic, social, and politi-

cal outcomes for better or worse. Focus should be on understanding the rules in use, which may, or may not, align with the rules in form.
9. The standard dichotomy between "the market" and "the state" is too simplistic and neglects the importance of civil society as a mechanism as a voluntary solution for a variety of collective action problems.

The chapters that follow draw upon these insights to offer different perspectives on the political process and political order.

AN OVERVIEW OF THE VOLUME

The remainder of the volume consists of nine chapters, split into two parts, which advance various aspects of the political process and political order. Part I of the volume, Interdisciplinary Foundations, consists of five chapters, and part II, Interdisciplinary Applications, consists of the remaining four chapters.

The chapters in the first part of the volume explore various conceptual foundations of the political process and political order. In the first chapter, Malte Dold develops a constructive critique of some of James Buchanan's first principles by contrasting them with Amartya Sen's reconstruction of Adam Smith's moral philosophy. He identifies and discusses the normative "core" of Buchanan's constitutional contractarianism: specifically, (1) the role of unanimity as a decision rule; (2) the priority of procedures over outcomes; and (3) the relevance of closed impartiality, in other words, the confinement of arguments at the constitutional stage to the perspectives of the contracting agents. Since Sen criticized social contract theories on all three issues, the chapter utilizes Sen's arguments as a point of departure for a discussion of Buchanan's first principles.

Dold considers the way in which Sen positions Adam Smith's "impartial spectator" as an alternative to Buchanan's contractarianism which is built upon the ideas of "unanimity" and the "veil of uncertainty." He argues that the main advantage of the Smithian framework lies in its comparative nature that offers a more pragmatic heuristic to concrete issues of injustice, such as capital punishment in the United States. Buchanan's contractarianism, in contrast, leads to an underdetermined (i.e., transcendental) starting point for normative reasoning, which narrowly focuses on institutional procedures that can lead to parochial solutions. Dold also discusses how this "controversy" between Buchanan and Sen has the potential to enrich content and tone of current academic debates among various "camps" of liberalism.

In chapter 2, Sarah Wilford begins with the recognition that modern democratic societies continue to draw upon and revisit the wisdom of Alexis de Tocqueville and his theory of associationalism. Wilford suggests that if we are going to continue to look to Tocqueville as an authority to strengthen democracy, we are better served by a deep understanding of his theory. Her chapter offers a deeper understanding of Tocqueville by drawing on four key, yet underappreciated, themes in Tocqueville's theory. She uses these themes to evaluate the three conversations in political and social science related to matters of community, association, and localism. Robert Putnam represents the study of social capital, Elinor and Vincent Ostrom represent the study of polycentricity, and Robert Nisbet represents the study of communitarianism.

Wilford argues that for Tocqueville, the domestic sphere (gender roles and family life) is crucial. Rootedness and long-standing loyalty to locality is relevant to habit formation that serves associative life. Tocqueville's interest in associations is related to this other-regarding virtue. Finally, Tocqueville's associationalism itself was supported by a *unified* habit applied across a range of associations. These themes largely relate to the home, the most immediate and proximate association for the democratic individual that teaches citizens moral habits.

The main implication is that modern social science projects that deal in "Tocquevillian" themes ought to attend comprehensively key themes related to the domestic sphere in Tocqueville's thought: family and gender roles, love of local community, and other-regarding mores. Wilford's chapter shows that a critique of social sciences agendas from a wholeheartedly Tocquevillian perspective suggests a new set of open avenues for social scientific inquiry.

In the subsequent chapter (chapter 3), Alexander Schaefer addresses F. A. Hayek's ambivalent stance on state intervention. Despite his image as an uncompromising advocate of laissez-faire, Schaefer notes that Hayek endorses various types of government involvement in the economy, an involvement ranging from health regulations to antitrust laws. Yet, in his critique of state intervention, Hayek rebukes aspirational social planners with an array of powerful warnings. To harmonize Hayek's advocacy of government programs, on the one hand, with his arguments against state intrusion into the economy, on the other, Schaefer examines Hayek's writings through the lens of his theory of complexity.

After reviewing Hayek's most salient arguments against government intervention, Schaefer turns to passages where Hayek advocates a variety of government programs. He finds that having presented the puzzle of understanding Hayek's views on intervention, a solution emerges in the form of a unifying concern, one that underlies Hayek's arguments against interventionism as well as his advocacy of certain government interventions. This unifying concern is the complexity of social systems. In short, the government actions that Hayek opposes are those that undermine our ability to cope with the complexity of the Great Society, while those that he advocates enhance that ability. By emphasizing the properties, problems, and responses associated with complex adaptive systems, Schaefer's chapter makes an important contribution by clarifying a Hayekian theory of interventionism.

In chapter 4, Jan Vogler develops a theory of entangled public bureaucratic institutions. He begins by noting that scholars of public administration apply different perspectives to understand bureaucratic institutions. Numerous studies consider the influence of bureaucracies on one aspect of their environment, like politics, society, culture, or the economy. Alternatively, scholars sometimes analyze the impact of one of these factors on public administration. However, Vogler argues that the recent literature on institutional entanglement demonstrates that relationships between social institutions are often *mutually* constitutive, meaning that their interaction is not one directional.

Building off these insights regarding entanglement, Vogler develops a synthesized perspective of how public bureaucracies interact with their broader environment, including the social, cultural, economic, and political context in which they operate. Through a number of empirical examples, he shows how useful this view can be for understanding the characteristics of public bureaucracies. Multiple lessons can be drawn from his analysis.

When scholars design theories explaining bureaucratic structures or behaviors, they should always ask themselves how social, political, or economic factors may affect the specific dimension under consideration—and what the causal relationship to the environment is. Even though it cannot be ruled out that it is appropriate to claim and investigate one-directional relationships (like when the nascent public administration emerged), Vogler's chapter shows that a two-directional interaction is much more commonplace. Moreover, one practical/political lesson we may draw from Vogler's contribution is that the creation, modification, or abolishment of bureaucratic structures should be conducted with great care. Given the complex interaction of public bureaucracies with politics, society, and the economy, any such plans should be crafted with a keen eye toward the multifold consequences they may have.

In the final chapter of part I (chapter 5), Charles Delmotte explores the nuances of Optimal Tax Theory. He begins by noting that a core tenet of Optimal Tax Theory is the defense of a rigorous tax code that engages in various discriminatory rate policies. Theorists like George Akerlof, Joseph Bankman, and Daniel Shaviro argue for a regime of differentiated tax rates tailored to match the different value and substitutability of various forms of consumption goods, income, or talents. In doing so, this standard economic approach wishes to decrease loss in aggregated social welfare caused by taxation.

Delmotte's chapter explicitly engages not only with this concrete proposal but equally with the conception of the political process on which it rests. It shows how the general framework of optimal tax theory relies on the assumption that (1) taxation is outside the decision process it aims to regulate; (2) the people that populate this process are benignly motivated; and (3) knowledge on how to maximize welfare lies within reach of the fiscal authorities. Building on the research program known as robust political economy, Delmotte investigates whether the proposal of differentiated tax rates for varying goods or sorts of income remain acceptable under a more realistic conception of the political process. He argues that the proposal of discriminatory rate policies become unfeasible under the realistic assumption that the political process will be populated by (partly) self-interested persons with limited knowledge.

He concludes that the opposite proposal seems to flow from the "robustness" test that political economy places on normative tax theory. As suggested by James Buchanan and Richard Epstein, a flat tax avoids fiscal exploitation by self-interested agents. Delmotte discusses how the constraint of one tax rate applicable on all income can also be understood as an answer to the problem of limited knowledge. Moreover, as flat taxes respect the relative positions between pretax prices, they are therefore more compatible with the knowledge-generating function of the price system.

Part II, Interdisciplinary Applications, consists of the remaining four chapters and demonstrates the historical and contemporary relevance of the political process and political order for cooperation, conflict, and human well-being in a variety of contexts and settings. In chapter 6, Bob Kaminski draws on the literatures on budgetary commons and on common-pool resource (CPR) management to analyze the relationship between communities' boundary rules and welfare provision through the lens of seventeenth- and eighteenth-century Massachusetts towns' settlement rules and localist poor-relief systems.

He discusses how in colonial and early national New England, townships straddled the boundary between governmental and associational models of organization. They bore a responsibility to aid "deserving" residents who fell on hard times. A substantial portion of their tax revenues went toward this "poor relief." Thus, managing relief expenses was central to towns' efforts to manage their budgetary commons. At the same time, towns possessed the power to limit settlement by outsiders by "warning" them. "Warning out" started as an informal practice that advised a newcomer to leave town or be physically removed. By 1701, it had evolved into a legal ritual that disavowed a town's future obligation to the newcomer, but rarely demanded that he or she actually leave. As austere Puritan norms limited controversy over who qualified as members of the "deserving" poor and access to relief in a town was predicated upon legal "settlement" there, Kaminski argues that enforcing boundary rules with warnings served as towns' primary way to manage their relief-fund CPRs.

He goes on to discuss how towns faced a trade-off between the two fundamental concerns of CPR management—appropriations and provisions problems—which called them to limit potentially costly admissions to the community and expand its tax base, respectively. With individuals enjoying heterogeneous endowments of human and financial capital, towns—like later mutual-aid societies—screened would-be settlers on a pseudo-actuarial basis. While this strategy was sufficient to manage towns' budgetary CPRs, it—in the absence of interjurisdictional cooperation—would have left the unsettled but "deserving" poor unaided. Consequently, Massachusetts towns took advantage of nested institutions to coordinate solutions. Initially, this meant coordinating settlement for the unsettled but "deserving" poor and fashioning rules minimizing their presence. Later, wartime refugee crises undermined these measures, established provincial poor relief, and thereby created a fiscal-commons situation—eventually leading to the abolition of towns' control over settlement rights. Kaminski's chapter demonstrates how private parties can overcome some of the key challenges associated with the management of common-pool resources.

In chapter 7, James Heilman explores the literature on polycentricity and the literature on transnational environmental governance and considers the answers to two central questions that arise from these literatures. The first question is whether transnational environmental governance is just a mess with a diversity of governing units or, instead, if it is a polycentric system. The second question is whether the mechanisms of institutional change that are present in the literature on polycentricity, and in the public choice literature, are present in the literature on institutional change in environmental governance.

Heilman finds evidence in the international relations (IR) literature that issue areas in environmental governance do display properties of polycentricity. He also finds that competitive mechanisms do drive institutional change but that other factors, not typically considered in the polycentricity or public choice literatures, are also present. By comparing IR, polycentricity, and public choice literatures, Heilman's chapter opens up questions for future research, such as What are the features of club economies as opposed to public economies? What are the constitutional constraints that could exist at the transnational level of governance? What effect does issue linkage have in a polycentric system? And what drives preference formation within a polycentric system?

In the subsequent chapter (chapter 8), Inu Manak offers a public choice approach to understanding dispute avoidance through international regulatory cooperation. She begins by noting that traditional trade barriers, such as tariffs, have been on the decline. In contrast, nontariff barriers, such as regulatory measures that restrict trade, have increased. Despite this increase in opaque protectionism, she highlights that the number of formal disputes filed at the World Trade Organization (WTO) challenging these measures is small. Manak's chapter examines how the institutional design of regulatory cooperation in the WTO's committees provides a forum for dispute avoidance. She argues that industry groups in particular are able to push for the resolution of potential disputes through this institution and, in doing so, provide a welfare-enhancing outcome.

Manak's chapter has three main implications. First, the design of institutions for regulatory cooperation affects who can participate. Second, while the public choice literature generally sees interest groups as reducing social welfare by concentrating benefits on their members at the expense of non-group members, her analysis shows that, counterintuitively, interest group pressure can be welfare enhancing by pushing governments to avoid lengthy disputes and to adjust potentially trade restrictive regulations. Third, regulatory cooperation provides another way of thinking about dispute settlement more broadly, moving away from more judicial models. In fact, it highlights the continued relevance of diplomacy in the WTO, suggesting alternative paths forward for the organization as the future of the formal dispute settlement system is increasingly called into question.

In the final chapter (chapter 9), Jozef Andrew Kosc analyzes the case of postconflict constitution making in occupied Iraq (2003–2005) using Roger Koppl's theory of expert influence and failure. Koppl's framework is the latest in a long-standing political economy debate on "expert" involvement in institutional design and decision making. As Kosc notes, the Iraqi constitution was a technocratic dream, inspired by international expertise, drawing heavily from the academic literature on postconflict constitutional design. It was the most expert-influenced constitution in recent history. And yet the consociational settlement is also deemed a policy failure. Kosc employs Koppl's framework to shed light on the conditions and circumstances that led to a "thin" account of expert failure (one in which the views of the majority of nonexpert Iraqis were not reflected), drawing broader lessons for when and how expert involvement in postconflict constitution making is likely to contribute to failure. In addition to offering insight into constitution making in Iraq, Kosc's chapter also contributes to the broader, ongoing debate on the appropriateness of different schools of postconflict constitutional design.

Taken together, the chapters in this volume demonstrate the interdisciplinary relevance of research—both conceptual and applied—on various aspects of the political process and political order. There is much additional work to be done in exploring, extending, and applying the insights from the Austrian, Bloomington, and Virginia political economy traditions in these areas. Our hope is that this volume will encourage an ongoing interdisciplinary discussion to generate mutual gains from intellectual exchange in establishing a more complete understanding of the political process and political order.

NOTES

1. Donald J. Boudreaux (dboudrea@gmu.edu), Christopher J. Coyne (ccoyne3@gmu.edu), and Bobbi Herzberg (bherzberg@mercatus.gmu.edu).
2. For more on the Austrian tradition, see Vaughn 1994; Kirzner 2001; Caldwell 2004; Hulsmann 2007; Boettke, Coyne, and Newman 2016; and Dekker 2016.
3. For more on the Bloomington tradition, see Aligica and Boettke 2009 and Tarko 2017.
4. For more on the Virginia political economy tradition, see Reisman 1990; Meadowcroft 2011; and Wagner 2017.

REFERENCES

Aligica, Paul Dragos, and Peter J. Boettke. 2009. *Challenging Institutional Analysis and Development: The Bloomington School.* New York: Routledge.
Aligica, Paul Dragos, and Vlad Tarko. 2012. "Polycentricity: From Polanyi to Ostrom and Beyond." *Governance* 25 (2): 237–62.
Boettke, Peter J., and Rosolino A. Candela. 2015. "Rivalry, Polycentricism, and Institutional Evolution." *Advances in Austrian Economics* 19: 1–19.
Boettke, Peter J., Christopher J. Coyne, and Patrick Newman. 2016. "The History of a Tradition: Austrian Economics from 1871 to 2016." *Research in the History of Economic Thought and Methodology*, 2016, 34A: 199–243.
Brennan, Geoffrey, and James M. Buchanan. 1985. *The Reason of Rules: Constitutional Political Economy.* New York: Cambridge University Press.
Buchanan, James M. 1949. "The Pure Theory of Public Finance: A Suggested Approach." *Journal of Political Economy* 57 (6): 496–505.
———. 1975. *The Limits of Liberty: Between Anarchy and Leviathan.* Chicago: University of Chicago Press.
———. 1979a. "Politics without Romance: A Sketch of Positive Public Choice Theory and Its Normative Implications." Inaugural lecture, Institute for Advanced Studies, Vienna, Austria. IHS Journal, Zeitschrift des Instituts für Höhere Studien 3: B1–B11.
———. 1979b. *What Should Economists Do?* Indianapolis, IN: Liberty Fund, Inc.
———. 1982. "Order Defined in the Process of Its Emergence." *Literature of Liberty* 5 (4): 5.
———. 2003. *Public Choice: The Origins and Development of a Research Program.* Fairfax, VA: Center for Study of Public Choice, George Mason University.
Buchanan, James M., and Gordon Tullock. 1962. *The Calculus of Consent: Logical Foundations of Constitutional Democracy.* Ann Arbor: University of Michigan Press.
Caldwell, Bruce. 2004. *Hayek's Challenge: An Intellectual Biography of F. A. Hayek.* Chicago: Chicago University Press.
Dekker, Erwin. 2016. *The Viennese Students of Civilization the Meaning and Context of Austrian Economics Reconsidered.* New York: Cambridge University Press.
Hayek, F. A. 1948. *Individualism and Economic Order.* Chicago: Chicago University Press.
———. 1988. *The Fatal Conceit: The Errors of Socialism.* Chicago: Chicago University Press.
———. 1989. "The Pretence of Knowledge." *American Economic Review* 79 (6): 3–7.
———. 2014a. "The Errors of Constructivism." In Bruce Caldwell (ed.), *The Collected Works of F. A. Hayek, Volume 15: The Market and Other Orders.* Chicago: Chicago University Press, pp. 338–56.
———. 2014b. "Notes on the Evolution of Systems of Rules of Conduct." In Bruce Caldwell (ed.), *The Collected Works of F. A. Hayek, Volume 15: The Market and Other Orders.* Chicago: Chicago University Press, pp. 278–92.
———. 2014c. "The Results of Human Action but Not of Human Design." In Bruce Caldwell (ed.), *The Collected Works of F. A. Hayek, Volume 15: The Market and Other Orders.* Chicago: Chicago University Press, pp. 293–303.

———. 2014d. "The Theory of Complex Phenomena." In Bruce Caldwell (ed.), *The Collected Works of F. A. Hayek, Volume 15: The Market and Other Orders*. Chicago: Chicago University Press, pp. 257–77.

Hulsmann, Jörg Guido. 2007. *Mises: The Last Knight of Liberalism*. Auburn, AL: Ludwig von Mises Institute.

Kirzner, Israel M. 1997. "Entrepreneurial Discovery and the Competitive Market Process: An Austrian Approach." *Journal of Economic Literature* 35 (1): 60–85.

———. 2001. *Ludwig von Mises: The Man and His Economics*. Wilmington, DE: ISI Books.

McGinnis, Michael D., and James M. Walker. 2010. "Foundations of the Ostrom Workshop: Institutional Analysis, Polycentricity, and Self-Governance of the Commons." *Public Choice* 143 (3/4): 293–301.

Meadowcroft, John. 2011. *James M. Buchanan*. New York: Continuum International Publishing Group, Inc.

Munger, Michael C., and Kevin M. Munger. 2015. *Choosing in Groups: Analytical Politics Revisited*. New York: Cambridge University Press.

Ostrom, Elinor. 1990. *Governing the Commons: The Evolution of Institutions for Collective Action*. New York: Cambridge University Press.

———. 1999. "Polycentricity, Complexity, and the Commons." *Good Society* 9 (2): 37–41.

———. 2005. *Understanding Institutional Diversity*. Princeton, NJ: Princeton University Press.

———. 2010. "Beyond Markets and States: Polycentric Governance of Complex Economic Systems." *American Economic Review* 100 (3): 641–72.

Ostrom, Vincent. 1972. "Polycentricity (Part 1 and 2)." In Michael D. McGinnis (ed.), *Polycentricity and Local Public Economics*. Ann Arbor: University of Michigan Press, pp. 57–138.

———. 1991. *The Meaning of American Federalism: Constituting a Self-Governing Society*. San Francisco, CA: ICS Press.

———. 1997. *The Meaning of Democracy and the Vulnerability of Democracies: A Response to Tocqueville's Challenge*. Ann Arbor: University of Michigan Press.

Polanyi, Michael. 1951. *The Logic of Liberty*. London: Routledge.

Reisman, David. 1990. *The Political Economy of James Buchanan*. London: Palgrave Macmillan.

Tarko, Vlad. 2017. *Elinor Ostrom: An Intellectual Biography*. New York: Rowman & Littlefield International.

Tocqueville, Alexis de. 1835/1839 [1969]. *Democracy in America*, edited by J. P. Mayer, translated by George Lawrence. New York: Doubleday & Company, Inc.

Vaughn, Karen I. 1994. *Austrian Economics in America: The Migration of a Tradition*. New York: Cambridge University Press.

Wagner, Richard E. 2005. "Self-Governance, Polycentricism, and Federalism: Recurring Themes in Vincent Ostrom's Scholarly Oeuvre." *Journal of Economic Behaviour and Organization* 57(2): 173–88.

———. 2017. *James M. Buchanan and Liberal Political Economy: A Rational Reconstruction*. Lanham, MD: Lexington Books.

Part I

INTERDISCIPLINARY
FOUNDATIONS

Chapter One

A Smithian Critique of James M. Buchanan's Constitutional Contractarianism

Malte F. Dold[1]

TWO ECONOMISTS WHO EMBRACE NORMATIVE REASONING

At the methodological intersection of economics and philosophy stand two Nobel prize–winning economists, James M. Buchanan and Amartya K. Sen. Over the course of many decades, they both developed an enormous body of work in which they frequently transcended the economic profession's narrow engagement with aggregation and formalism and, instead, delved into reflections on moral and political philosophy. In their work, Sen and Buchanan understand that ethics and political philosophy are inherent parts of economics. They do not bring these disciplines back into economics, but rather emphasize that economists should recognize the ubiquity of ethical and philosophical issues in their discipline. Moreover, in their work, Sen and Buchanan show a deep concern for a democratically embedded economy. They know that a democracy can take many institutional forms, whose quality crucially depends on an open-ended debate about economic principles, issues of institutional design, and moral values.

In this chapter, I will carve out the normative kernel of Buchanan's "constitutional contractarianism" (Brennan 2013) by contrasting his position with Adam Smith's moral philosophy. In recent years, Amartya Sen (2006, 2009) has advocated Smith's account of normative reasoning as a viable alternative to social contract theories. Sen's prowess as an economist is evidenced by his many original contributions to the field, ranging from formal matters in social choice theory and welfare economics to policy issues, such as inequality, famines, and poverty (Morris 2010). Although he does not subscribe to the public choice tradition, he nevertheless possesses a deep familiarity with the political philosophy of contractarianism in general and Buchanan's work in particular. Sen refers to Buchanan in multiple papers and books throughout his long and prolific academic career. He appreciates Buchanan's contribution to the field and credits him with the introduction of discussions surrounding ethical values and legal–political institutions into economic theory. Sen states: "I think Buchanan is very impressive in terms of the breadth of his interest. In my judgement, he has done more than most to introduce ethics, legal political thinking, and indeed social thinking into economics. I have the greatest respect for Buchanan, even though I may disagree with him on a particular point" (Sen in Swedberg 1990, 263). Buchanan, in turn, praises Sen's work for its "analysis back toward a straightforward calculus of interest and away from nonindividualistic attributes of either goods or actions" (Buchanan 1990, 5).

Both scholars unite in their critique of the foundations of welfarism and their attempt to put forward an alternative approach that could fill the place of Samuelsonian welfare economics (Sugden 1993).[2] They share their admiration for the intellectual project of the European Enlightenment that seeks "a society in which reasoning, rather than faith, would be supreme, and in which public reasoning would be one of the principal aspects of human interaction" (Sen 2011, 367). Both consider the roots of their normative accounts in philosophical liberalism and find their "intellectual and moral compatriots in those thinkers who must be defined as moral equalitarians" (Buchanan 2005, 106). Furthermore, Buchanan and Sen share their methodological concern for a simplistic model of the economic agent as a rational, self-interested utility maximizer. Sen famously criticized the homo economics as a "rational fool" (Sen 1977), and Buchanan developed the idea of economic agents as self-constituting "artifactual" individuals (Buchanan 1979b).

One of the first major intellectual disputes between Sen and Buchanan dates back to the debate about the implications of Arrow's impossibility theorem (1951) and Sen's subsequent introduction of the "liberal paradox" in 1970.[3] In supporting Arrow's arguments, Sen claimed to prove that the Pareto criterion conflicts with principles of "minimal liberalism," which in turn sparked Buchanan's critique of Sen's arguments (Buchanan 1996). In this chapter, I will not delve into this more technical debate. Rather, I will focus on three broader and interrelated issues that represent the normative "core" of Buchanan's constitutional contractarianism: (1) the transcendental nature of the constitutional stage and the role of unanimity as a decision rule; (2) the priority of procedures over outcomes and the respective focus on institutional design; and (3) the relevance of closed impartiality (i.e., the confinement of arguments at the constitutional stage to the perspectives of the contracting agents). In doing so, this chapter has three aims. First, in distilling Sen's critique of the Buchananite political philosophy, it offers a more nuanced tone to the current debate on the significance and legacy of Buchanan's normative visions.[4] Rather than reviewing this debate, the chapter seeks to illustrate how one might develop a professional critique of Buchanan's work by considering the normative content and factual consequences of his analytical arguments. Second, this chapter aims to introduce Smith's moral philosophy to those public choice scholars who are mostly familiar with his writings on economics. Indeed, this might lead to a reevaluation—or more robust defense—of some foundational assumptions of Buchanan's constitutional contractarianism. Third, this chapter contributes to an assessment of the history of economic thought in the twentieth century by tracing fundamental differences between the normative frameworks of two of the discipline's most original thinkers. Upon review of the existing literature, there has not yet been an attempt to carve out the differences in the normative approaches of Buchanan and Sen.

I would like to add three caveats at the outset. First, this chapter will focus on a critique of Buchanan's political philosophy and not deal with his positive political economy. In doing so, the chapter focuses on the "normative core" of Buchanan's research program. This is helpful in identifying some inherent indeterminacies at the heart of his contractarianism. A comprehensive treatment of the "protective belt" of Buchanan's research program lies beyond the intended scope of this chapter. Second, the chapter purposefully ignores Sen's early work on capabilities (Sen 1985, 1993), understood as a person's freedom to achieve various lifestyles she has reason to value. Sen clarifies that his "capability approach points to an *informational focus* in judging and comparing overall individual advantages" (Sen 2009, 232). It puts forward an alternative notion of well-being to Rawls's focus on primary goods and the criterion of preference satisfaction in neoclassical welfare economics. In spite of its practical influence on poverty measures and development policies, Sen (2009, 232f.) acknowledges that the capability approach is mostly a conceptional contribution that aims at broadening the informational base of welfare analyses. This chapter will deal with Sen's later, more philosophical reflections on normative reasoning and justice and sidestep the debate on the merits and pitfalls of the capability approach. Third, contrary to what some readers might expect, the arguments elaborated in this chapter are not about different policy conclusions (e.g., the role of the state vis-à-vis the market in providing "public goods," such as education or social insurance). I believe that this is not a fruitful point for discussion of the generic differences between Buchanan's and Sen's line of reasoning. Both argue that the proper scope of state activities can ultimately be answered by public reasoning only, rather than by the armchair philosophizing economist.[5] The crucial difference in their normative frameworks lies at the level of first principles and the choice of their respective historical–philosophical reference points, namely, Thomas Hobbes in the case of Buchanan and Adam Smith in the case of Sen. While Buchanan draws explicitly on Smith's understanding of exchange and the market when he conceptualizes the political arena, he neglects Smith's account of normative reasoning developed in *The Theory of Moral Sentiments* (1759). Essentially, Buchanan is a Smithian in terms of his positive understanding of economics and politics, but he is a Hobbesian in terms of his contractarian political philosophy (Gaus 2018).

In the next section, I will sketch the main features of Buchanan's political philosophy. Subsequently, I will describe Sen's reconstruction of the alternative Smithian framework. This, in turn, will serve as a template for the critique of Buchanan's contractarianism. Finally, I will outline how this "controversy" between Buchanan and Sen has the potential to enrich the content and tone of current academic discussions on the normative foundations of liberal societies.

A SKETCH OF BUCHANAN'S POLITICAL PHILOSOPHY: HOBBESIAN CONTRACTARIANISM

Buchanan's political–philosophical ideas spring from his commitment to radical subjectivism and his distaste for utilitarian welfare economics. Buchanan (1949) argues that the utility-maximizing framework of welfare economics assumes misleadingly that preference orderings are stable over time and measurable by an outside observer. Buchanan rejects this methodological starting point. He argues that benefits and costs are highly subjective, while preferences can be dynamically evolving and endogenous to the choice situation (Buchanan 1954b, 1979a). In his view, economic agents construct their preferences in the moment of choice rather than maximizing preexisting utility functions. An individual's preference ranking (and, for that matter, her utility function) must therefore be seen as the consequence of her choice, rather than the determinant (Buchanan 1991). Since utility functions are not stable, they cannot be accurately estimated. Consequently, they cannot be the basis for welfare economic calculations of the universal net benefits of given policy proposals. This radical subjectivism is the reason why Buchanan believes that economists have only one method to identify net benefits in social interactions, to wit, through the observation of *mutual agreements* (Congleton 2014).

These methodological insights in economic theory are the basis for Buchanan's philosophical ventures. In general, Buchanan's political philosophy is rooted within a wider framework of classical liberalism (Brennan 2013). For Buchanan, classical liberalism starts with the assumption that the overwhelming majority of individuals are capable of governing themselves and enjoy doing so (i.e., freedom from external coercion is a "quasi-universal desire") (Buchanan 2005, 69). Normatively, his subjectivism leads to a *contractarian approach*, in which the legitimacy of any social arrangement is said to arise from its underlying voluntary contractual nature. Practically, this framework supports a market economy since it provides the institutional structure in which individuals govern themselves to their mutual advantage (Buchanan 2005, 12).

According to Buchanan, the logic of voluntary exchange pervades all human interaction (Brennan 2012). He argues that mutually beneficial exchanges are not only possible in the marketplace but also in politics (i.e., Buchanan does not conceptualize political processes as a coercive enterprise, but as a cooperative endeavor). Buchanan rejects anarchy as a viable framework for human exchange, but argues that there are issues—such as law enforcement, public goods, and externality problems—where substantial mutual gains can be fully realized only through state actions (Buchanan 1954b). Simultaneously, Buchanan always emphasized that social scientists have to analyze "politics without romance" (i.e., start with the factual observation that people hold the same self-interested motivational profile in politics as they do in markets) (Buchanan 1979b).

Assuming this behavioral symmetry, the crucial question for Buchanan becomes how citizens (the "principal") can secure governmental bureaucrats (the "agent") to act in the "public interest" and not just maximize their private utilities. In this context, his political philosophy embraces a *constitutional approach* (sometimes coined "Comprehensive Hobbesianism"; see Gaus 2018), which attempts to reason about social arrangements from a hypothetical original position (the constitutional stage), in which rational agents think about ideal legal–political rules that constrain both theirs and the state's future interactions (the postconstitutional stage).[6] At this imagined constitutional stage, Buchanan argues that agents would be distanced from their narrowly defined self-interests since they face a "veil of uncertainty" about their exact future positions under alternative rules (e.g., they don't know their future personal level of wealth or the general economic conditions). Due to this uncertainty, Buchanan posits that even purely self-interested agents come to unanimous agreements about future rules that order social interaction and select among alternatives in accordance with some generalizable criteria, such as "justice" or "efficiency" (Buchanan and Congleton 2006, 6–7). In this framework, "justice" emerges as a property of the rules that agents at the constitutional stage agree upon and "[just] conduct consists of behavior that does not violate rules to which one has given prior consent" (Brennan and Buchanan 1985, 97). More broadly, the "ideal of unanimity" becomes the decisive criterion for evaluating the "justness" of all rules that govern political (public and constitutional law) and private (civil and criminal law) interactions. However, due to decision costs of collective choices at the postconstitutional level, Buchanan emphasizes that agents at the constitutional stage would unanimously agree on qualified majorities as decision rules for most issues in day-to-day politics (Buchanan and Tullock 1962).[7]

Unlike many other classical liberals who start off with some notion of inalienable, individual moral rights that define the sphere of individual liberty, Buchanan starts off with the collective exercise of jointly working out the rules of the social, economic, and political game by the two-stage decision structure (Kliemt 2014).[8] In doing so, he assigns all agents at the constitutional stage a complete right of veto over which rules will be established.[9] The rules that emerge can be considered as "perfectly just" *because* they are the outcome of the ideal decision procedure of unanimous choice. The exact content of those rules (e.g., the delineation of the private and the public sphere, the specification of property rights, the tax scheme for redistribution) cannot be known *a priori*, but it depends *inter alia* on the typically divergent preferences of agents at the constitutional stage (e.g., for efficiency, risk aversion, or procedural fairness). Buchanan's "purpose is to see how far we can rationally discuss criteria for social change on the presumption that no man's values are better than any other man's" (1977, 83). Furthermore, Buchanan (1975) acknowledges that individuals at the constitutional stage might not only differ in their values and preferences, but also in their material resources, talents, or luck. Consequently, bargaining at the constitutional stage may lead to a wide spectrum of possible political–legal institutions (essentially anything *between* anarchy and Leviathan is consistent with Buchanan's contractarian constitutionalism). Practically, Buchanan's approach makes a case for *rule-based policies* that clarify boundaries of permissible actions at the outset. In doing so, Buchanan argues that resources at the postconstitutional stage would be freed from wasteful conflict (e.g., in the form of rent-seeking and short-term investments) to more productive use (e.g., in the form of iterated cooperation and long-term strategies).

SEN'S ALTERNATIVE STARTING POINT: ADAM SMITH'S COMPARATIVISM

Sen's political philosophy is rooted in the tradition of the Scottish Enlightenment. Contrary to Buchanan, Sen's moral–philosophical reference point is Adam Smith rather than Thomas Hobbes. This leads Sen down a different path of pursuing normative reasoning (presented in this section) from which one can distill a critique of the Buchananite framework (discussed in the next section).

Sen (2009, 5) identifies a substantial dichotomy in the Enlightenment tradition between two different lines of reasoning. The first approach considers the characterization of impartial institutions to be the primary task of political philosophy. This line of reasoning utilizes an elaborate fiction in order to arrive at their notion of impartiality in which agents are meant to choose rules in a hypothetical "original position" that shall separate them from knowledge of their own individuating features. This "fairness exercise" (Sen 2006, 217) is aimed at identifying perfectly just rules and principles and at establishing the institutional structure for a society. Sen calls this approach "transcendental institutionalism" since it pairs an idealized decision situation (decisions behind a veil of ignorance) and an ideal decision procedure (consensual contract) to justify existing or future institutional arrangements. Its focus is not on comparing different societies, which fall short of the ideals of perfection, but instead attempts to identify social characteristics that cannot be transcended in terms of justice. Sen (2006, 6) summarizes this tradition as an "inquiry [that] is aimed at identifying the nature of 'the just,' rather than finding some criteria for an alternative being 'less unjust' than another." He sees the work of Thomas Hobbes as the primary source for this tradition. This contractarian approach has been the dominant strand in political philosophy of the twentieth century, mainly because of its revitalization through the work of John Rawls.[10]

In contrast, Sen identifies a radically different line of thinking within the Enlightenment tradition that does not take the route of ideal theorizing, but shares a common interest in analyzing concrete social circumstances in a comparative perspective driven by a concern with social realizations (resulting from the working of actual institutions, people's actual behavior, and their observed interactions). Rather than searching for arguments that would describe perfectly just institutions, this tradition instead asks whether we can get "reasoned agreement" on removing what can be identified as apparent injustices (e.g., widespread hunger, the subjugation of women, or gross medical neglect). Sen identifies Adam Smith as the primary source for this line of thinking.[11]

According to Sen (2009, 44), the decisive heuristic in this philosophical tradition is Smith's idea of the "impartial spectator." The impartial spectator is an imagined observer of a particular state of affairs whose impartiality does not stem from a hypothetical veil of ignorance or uncertainty, but from being a disinterested bystander. Smith introduces this idea in *The Theory of Moral Sentiments*, as the moral requirement "to examine our own conduct as we imagine any other fair and impartial spectator would examine it" (1759, III.1.2, 110). Different from the Hobbesian tradition, Smith's impartial spectator is typically invoked for contrasting alternatives to shed light on specific issues in a comparative way without the aim to distill an ideal institutional setup or invoke an idealized decision situation (Sen 2006, 230). The Smithian approach admits a certain degree of imprecision and invites us to trust our individual capacities to identify injustice when we "remove ourselves, as it were, from our own natural station, and endeavour to view them as at a certain distance from us" (Smith 1759, III.1.2, 110). Sen highlights that Smith deploys the notion of the impartial spectator to initiate discourse about a specific issue, rather than to find a definitive, ideal answer by means of a purely formal decision criterion. Smith's "comparativism" requires the need for a public debate about values and beliefs, in which reasoned arguments are expressed "with oneself and with others, in dealing with conflicting claims, rather than for what can be called 'disengaged toleration'" (Sen 2009, x).

Sen (2009, 124–35) argues that there is another fundamental difference in the two traditions with regard to the views that should be considered in order to reach just agreements. In the social contract tradition, the only voices that must be heard come from those individuals who count as parties to the hypothetical social contract. In doing so, the contractarian tradition tends to restrict the discussion to members of a closed community or nation-state (given the nation-by-nation structure of our world). Sen (2009, 131) calls this "closed impartiality" and contrasts this view with Adam Smith's arguments in favor of "open impartiality" (i.e., the necessity to include the views of individuals "from far as well as near" when reasoning about justice).[12] One of the main motivations underlying the idea of the impartial spectator was for Smith to broaden the reach of normative reasoning beyond ethical conventions of a certain group or community. Smith (1759, III.3.38, 110) states:

> In solitude, we are apt to feel too strongly whatever relates to ourselves. . . . The conversation of a friend brings us to a better, that of a stranger to a still better temper. The man within the breast, the abstract and ideal spectator of our sentiments and conduct, requires often to be awakened and put in mind of his duty, by the presence of the real spectator: and it is always from that spectator, from whom we can expect the least sympathy and indulgence, that we are likely to learn the most complete lesson of self-command.

Following this line of reasoning, Smith not only admits but also requires the integration of the views from outsiders when assessing the normative value of alternative social arrangements.

Sen follows Smith's plea for open impartiality and comparative normative reasoning. He dismisses the idea that political philosophers (and economists) should try to find justifications for ideal institutional solutions by means of perfectly just procedural rules (the *arrangement-focused view*). In contrast, Sen favors Smith's *realization-focused approach*, which assesses alternative social states in a comparative perspective with the goal of reducing concrete injustice. The next section will have a closer look at Sen's arguments.

A SMITHIAN CRITIQUE OF BUCHANAN'S CONSTITUTIONAL CONTRACTARIANISM

The arguments presented in this section draw partially upon Sen's brief discussion of Buchanan in his books *Collective Choice and Social Welfare* (1970a) and *Rationality and Freedom* (2004b). Yet they are mainly based upon Sen's critique of "transcendental institutionalism," specifically in its Rawlsian version, developed by Sen in his opus magnum, *The Idea of Justice* (2009). Sen's critique applies equally well to Buchanan's notion of constitutional contractarianism. Buchanan himself often highlighted the great affinity between his contractarian approach and the Rawlsian project of "justice as fairness" (see, e.g., Buchanan 2005, 41; Buchanan 2003). Buchanan's and Rawls's political philosophies are built upon the same fundamental elements: a normative commitment to the decision rule of unanimous agreement as legitimizing social outcomes, their respective notions of the "veil" play a parallel role at the moment of constitutional choice, and they both focus on the issue of finding the "right" legal–political institutions for a cooperative society (Meadowcroft 2014). Consequently, both the means (a hypothetical social contract) and the ends (finding institutions that allow individuals to cooperate productively and peacefully) are similar in Rawls's and Buchanan's political philosophy.[13]

Transcendental Contractarianism

Following Sen's categorization, Buchanan's account can be called "transcendental" in that it focuses on producing "impartial" institutional arrangements *by means of* an ideal choice situation (veil of uncertainty) and an ideal decision criterion (unanimity). Sen (2009, 10) argues that such an idealized nature of the social contract is *unhelpful* in yielding comparative rankings and *unnecessary* in order to judge the relative injustice in the world.

Sen believes that transcendental conceptualization is *unhelpful* since the normative baseline of unanimous agreement is utopian. Even in collective decision situations with a relatively thick veil of uncertainty (where agents know only their preferences and talents but have no idea about their future economic positions),[14] a consensus might not be conceivable when agents are assumed to hold competing or incompatible sets of first principles. Sen (2009, 13) illustrates that conflicts of first principles are hard to eradicate, even in idealized decision situations. He offers the following stylized example: Imagine three children, A, B, and C, who are quarreling over the fate of a flute. Child A claims the flute since she is the only one who can play it (the others confirm this); child B claims it because she is the only one who does not possess any toys (the other two concede); child C claims it because she made the flute (the others do not deny this). There is no intuitively plausible reason for giving the flute to any one of the children: utilitarians might favor child A; egalitarians, child B; and libertarians, child C. There is no obvious way one can assume a clear answer as to how individuals with different moral values would come to a consensual agreement to resolve this issue, even if we assume a relatively thick veil of uncertainty.[15]

Furthermore, if one lifts the veil and allows for the heterogeneity of agents' level of information and negotiating capacities at the moment of constitutional choice, the Pareto principle turns into a dubious criterion even if agreements are to be achieved. Sen (1970, 26) argues that these agreements would be highly contingent upon individuals' relative bargaining power at the constitutional stage. Furthermore, Sen points out that the Pareto criterion suffers from an inherent "stability bias" toward status quo preferences.[16] In principle, one individual with antisocial preferences could impose her costs on all others by blocking a vote for change. Sen asserts (somewhat ironically) that "Marie Antoinette's opposition to the First Republic would have saved the monarchy in France" (Sen 1970, 25). It is therefore possible for an outcome to be Pareto efficient and yet substantially unfair since "illegitimate" starting conditions or crude antisocial preferences dictate the set of potential Pareto improvements. This challenge still occurs if one applies the Pareto criterion at the levels of rules, as Buchanan (1962) suggests. In the absence of a morally acceptable baseline, Sen argues that there is little ground to use the Pareto criterion as a necessary condition for "good" social rules.

Buchanan's account does not allow for any external criterion to judge the justness of the preconstitutional starting conditions or the final terms of the social contract. Therefore, consensual agreement is a purely procedural criterion designed to constitute the goodness of the outcome, such that whatever principle or rule it generates is, by the fact of its generation, "just."[17] Buchanan does not provide any practical guidance on how to establish the necessary preconstitutional prerequisites for "just" consensual negotiations nor how to elicit information about what a consensual outcome would look like at the postconstitutional stage. The approach is purely procedural and conceptually underdetermined and might lead to unattractive outcomes. Buchanan "overtheorizes" the social contract and "underhistorizes" the way in which conflict-reducing rules can actually come about (Boettke 2013).

One might defend Buchanan's account by saying that his contractarian approach still gives us rankings of rules in terms of comparative distances from the perfectly just baseline. Sen (2006, 219) argues that this strategy fails since there are different features involved in identifying distance (e.g., the extent that a social vote differed from unanimous agreement or the degree agents are exposed to a "thinner" veil of uncertainty) and it is not clear how to relatively weigh these imperfections. The identification of a perfectly just agreement does not yield any means to arrive at a ranking of departures from transcendence (i.e., the identification of the best combination of decision situation and decision procedure does not tell us much about how to compare two nonbest alternatives). Sen (2009, 16) illustrates this point with an analogy: "if we are trying to choose between a Picasso and a Dali, it is of no help to invoke a diagnosis (even if such a transcendental diagnosis could be made) that the ideal picture in the world is the Mona Lisa." Furthermore, descriptive closeness to an ideal state is not necessarily a criterion for valuation proximity (Sen 2009, 16). A person who prefers the policy program of a center-left candidate A to the program of a center-right candidate B may prefer either program to a coalition solution {A', B'}, even though the coalition may well be in a descriptive sense closer to the optimal state. The reason could be the possibility that a policy solution at the center of the ideological spectrum might lead to a widespread perception among citizens of a watered-down compromise of the political establishment, which, in turn, could lead to a renunciation of the mainstream and the rise of a populist far-right candidate C. If Sen is correct on these points, then Buchanan's account does not provide sufficient means for the comparative assessments of the merits of non-transcendental (i.e., nonunanimously agreed upon) institutional arrangements.

Sen (2006, 221) further argues that the identification of an ideal of procedural justice is *unnecessary* in order to rank any two alternatives in terms of their relative justness. We do not need to know the outcome of an ideal decision procedure to be able to identify blatant injustices, such as the persistence of frivolous torture. We may acknowledge that we do not know the best (i.e., unanimously agreed upon) rules against torturing, but still strongly urge that sadistic torture would be an unjust violation of liberty that calls for its immediate removal (Sen 2006, 224). Consequently, a partial ordering of social arrangements might be possible and useful without the need to invoke any transcendental identification of the best institutional solution.

Institutionalism and the Priority of Procedures over Outcomes

In Buchanan's framework, rules that emerge consensually from the social contract are prior to any understanding of the notion of "justice" (i.e., rules define the terms of justice, rather than the reverse). Brennan and Buchanan (1985, 97) note:

> Our specific claim is that justice takes its meaning from the rules of the social order within which notions of justice are to be applied. To appeal to considerations of justice is to appeal to relevant rules. Talk of justice without reference to those rules is meaningless.

According to Brennan and Buchanan (1985, 111), justice is not a "primary" concept, rather:

it is derived from two logically prior notions: first, that agreements carry moral
obligations to abide by the terms of those agreements; and second, that appeals
to justice take place within an institutional context that serves to assign justice
its meaning.

Consequently, the Buchananite notion of justice presupposes a cluster of
institutions to apply the rules identified in the social contract. Buchanan's
normative theory does not apply when the procedural and institutional preconditions cannot be met.

In doing so, Buchanan's framework sets natural limits to the exercise of
public reasoning about justice because of (1) Buchanan's insistence on linking justice with the format of constitutional choice and (2) the practical
limitations for the emergence of institutions. Sen (2006, 226) argues that this
is unfortunate since a normative theory should still be able to identify means
to reduce injustice even without the possibility of setting up institutions. He
refers to blatant cruelties happening in many places around the world where
formal institutions are absent and informal institutions are defective. Even
without the possibility of setting up consensually agreed upon institutions,
Sen argues that it might be possible to advance justice to a considerable
extent. If one accepts the fundamental value of Smith's proposal of reasoning
from "a distance," the question about the reduction of injustice becomes part
of a deliberative framework of public reasoning, which does not become
inoperative—albeit in some situations less effective—when institutional or
procedural preconditions cannot be met (Sen 2006, 228).

In its narrow interpretation, Buchanan's institutionalism is exclusively
concerned with the identification of "just institutions," rather than the actual
societies that would ultimately emerge. The unanimity rule applies to decisions about the rules of the game, which in turn depend on the outcomes that
the agents *expect* from those rules. It does not apply to the actual outcomes
that will emerge since they cannot be fully known at the constitutional stage
due to the veil of uncertainty. Therefore, Buchanan (1987, 1435) states:
"There is no criterion through which policy may be directly evaluated. . . .
The focus of evaluative attention becomes the process itself, as contrasted
with end-state or outcome patterns."

Sen (2004b, 263) acknowledges Buchanan's reasoned questioning of the
idea of a "social or collective rationality" and his emphasis on procedural
judgments. However, Sen doubts whether normative economics should abandon altogether any consequence-based evaluation of social states. Sen criticizes that, in its pure form, Buchanan's procedural approach focuses on the
"right institutions" independently from "good" outcomes. Sen (2004b, 264)
remarks that this leads to the characterization of rights in procedural terms
without considering the actual level of individual freedoms and opportunities
that emerge at the postconstitutional stage. These freedoms could be severely

impaired by unequal power relations, information asymmetries, or a lack of access to health care and education. It is important to note that Sen is not making a point against the significance of institutions for social cooperation. Rather, he is concerned with the exclusive identification of justice *via* institutional procedures.

At its core, Buchanan's skepticism about a shared "moral good" might lead to a consequence-independent understanding of procedural justice in which there is no place for justice beyond establishing "just rules" or "just institutions." This, however, could lead to corner solutions in which "just institutions" generate terrible social outcomes (i.e., "catastrophic moral horror," to use Nozick's phrase) without violating agreed upon rules or rights (Sen 2009, 85). Such a solution would stand at odds with what individuals actually perceive as just—which is usually a combination of procedural and outcome-based concerns (Dold and Khadjavi 2017; Frohlich and Oppenheimer 1992; Konow 2003). Consequently, individuals might perceive institutions as crucial since they promote the realization of just outcomes, rather than—as it is the case in the Buchananite framework—treating the institutions themselves as manifestations of justice.

Furthermore, Buchanan's account presupposes that people appropriately comply with the rules at the postconstitutional stage. For him, the ideal situation is one in which agents have unanimously agreed on the constraints and rationale of their future society. Then, if they behave correctly, they follow these rules *ad infinitum*. This is a very static notion of agency, which underestimates the evolving nature of preferences, the dynamics of knowledge, and the reflexivity between the individual and its socioeconomic environment. In line with Buchanan (and contrary to the neoclassical textbook opinion), Sen argues that the institutional environment shapes our individual preferences. One of Sen's favorite passages from Buchanan, referenced in each of his last three major books, *Development as Freedom* (1999), *Rationality and Freedom* (2004b), and *The Idea of Justice* (2009), is that Buchanan identifies democracy as "'government by discussion,' which implies that individual values can and do change in the process of decision-making" (Buchanan 1954b, 120).[18] However, if we accept the endogeneity of the preference formation process, then the constitutional moment suddenly loses its normative uniqueness. Which preferences should we take as the agent's "true preferences"—those revealed at the constitutional moment behind the veil of uncertainty or those developed at a later stage in light of experienced choices and new (and better) information? Buchanan needs to explain why evolving agents with new preference sets at the postconstitutional stage—and who are presumed to be predominantly self-interested—should comply with the previously agreed upon rules. He does not provide an answer to the question of normativity of multiple preference sets (Read 2006). Yet this conundrum must be addressed; otherwise, a purely contractarian approach to institutions might suffer from an inherent instability. Moulin (1995, 38) shows that there is no stable ex ante agreed upon procedural rule that fails to incorporate ex post distributional concerns. Consequently, in order to implement *self-enforcing* contracts at the constitutional stage, agents have to consider their (potentially) dynamically evolving preferences at the postconstitutional stage. Due to the veil of uncertainty, this is naturally very difficult to realize in the Buchananite framework.

CLOSED IMPARTIALITY OF CONTRACTUAL AGREEMENTS AND PROCEDURAL PAROCHIALISM

Buchanan's contractarianism restricts agents' knowledge of future personal circumstances in moments of constitutional choice through the veil of uncertainty; yet it does not restrict the degree of agents' shared beliefs or group norms at the constitutional stage. In addition, Buchanan's approach is built on a notion of "closed impartiality" (i.e., the unanimity rule applies only to a locally defined political community [typically within a nation state]).[19] Both points imply the confinement of arguments about "just" rules to the—actual or counterfactual—interests, knowledge, and perspectives of the contracting agents at the constitutional stage.

In contrast, the Smithian model demands that agents "must put in an effort to examine how their own practices and conventions would look to others, including people who are informed about, but not entirely reared in, that society" (Sen 2006, 231). The impartial spectator does not need to be a member of the society that faces a collective decision. As a disinterested bystander, she helps to bring in the perspective of someone who may have had a different cultural and institutional experience in solving a particular collective decision problem. According to Sen, there are at least two main arguments for the Smithian account of "open impartiality": (1) the relevance of other people's *interests* and (2) the pertinence of other people's *knowledge* and *perspectives*.

Regarding argument (1), Buchanan defines "just" institutions as the product of a unanimous contract between agents of a closed community. Yet this may well neglect the legitimate interests of noncontractors (e.g., foreigners, future generations, perhaps nature itself) who may be affected by the established rules (e.g., in the case of trade, terrorism, global warming, or epidemics). Admittedly, one can debate the general extent to which our concerns and positionality can be plausibly extended onto others. However, it seems hard to justify a notion of local justice that is exclusively concerned with in-group fairness when we acknowledge the manifold interdependences of communities by mutual economic, social, and political relations. Put differently, "There are few non-neighbors left in the world today" (Sen 2009, 173).

Appreciating the interdependence of interests in a globalized world might also acknowledge the fact that injustice (e.g., in the form of the violation of basic human rights) in one country can affect the lives and freedom in others via "domino effects." As Dr. Martin Luther King Jr. famously wrote, "Injustice anywhere is a threat to justice everywhere." One might defend Buchanan and argue for a cosmopolitan version of the constitutional stage in which all current and future people of the world are regarded as the constituents of the social contract. Admittedly, this would mitigate the closed impartiality of the collective decision (in Buchanan's parlance, the "external costs"), but at the same time aggravate the transcendental character of the social contract. The indeterminacy of the contractarian exercise would increase considerably. Furthermore, this solution might not be feasible at all in the Buchananite framework since the idea of a social contract presupposes the possibility of institutional structures that cannot exist on the global level—at least in the near future.

With respect to argument for the Smithian account of "open impartiality," Buchanan's closed impartiality produces the danger of considering only views and classes of questions that stabilize local preconstitutionally shared beliefs at the expense of neglecting reasonable arguments that would challenge the contracting agents' convictions *in the interest of informational objectivity*. Sen (2009, 71) notes that ethical judgments are often built upon false factual presumptions that are not questioned in culturally homogeneous milieus. Moreover, parochial convictions are often the result of a lack of knowledge of what turned out to be feasible in other people's experiences (Sen 2006, 234). Since Buchanan allows the hypothetical agents' views at the constitutional stage to be fully entrenched in their communities' (moral, religious, and ideological) beliefs, his approach does not provide any strong check on locally held prejudices.

In contrast, the Smithian model of normative reasoning demands that people who face a collective decision problem ought to examine how their own conventions would be perceived by informed but disinterested bystanders. Smith (1759, V.2.1, 210) vividly illustrates how moral and political reasoning confined within a local society can be fatally biased by parochial understanding:

> the murder of new-born infants, was a practice allowed in almost all the states of Greece, even among the polite and civilized Athenians. . . . Uninterrupted custom had by this time so thoroughly authorized the practice, that not only the loose maxims of the world tolerated this barbarous prerogative, but even the doctrine of philosophers, which ought to have been more just and accurate, was led away by the established custom, and upon this, as upon many other occasions, instead of censuring, supported the horrible abuse, by far-fetched considerations of public utility.[20]

A Smithian impartial spectator would welcome questions about how social problems (in this case, the custom of infanticide) are assessed in other communities around the world. Following Smith, scrutiny from "a certain distance" is absolutely crucial in order to arrive at reasoned normative judgments about collective decisions. Smith (1759, III.1.2, 110) states, "we can do this in no other way than by endeavoring to view them with the eyes of other people, or as other people are likely to view them." This exercise would have likely enriched the intellectually glorious Athenians who, at the time, were unfamiliar with societies that were able to flourish without the alleged societal necessity of infanticide.

It is important to note that the exercise of invoking the impartial spectator does not require people to accept every externally proposed argument, only that they be taken into account in their overall scrutiny of the collective decision. Indeed, one may reject many of these arguments on reasoned grounds. Yet Sen (2009, 407) believes that there is often an important subset of reasons that make communities reconsider their previously held convictions based on "global knowledge" (as it has been the case, for instance, with female suffrage or gay rights). Considering "global knowledge" means that moral judgments are built on a broader informational base of what has proved feasible experiences of other communities. The shared knowledge of people with different local backgrounds can contribute to less parochial judgments since they help to dismantle norms that are built on false or dubious factual premises. For instance, it is an important "global insight" that societies are not ending up in chaos or crisis as a result of permitting female suffrage or gay rights. Sen concludes that "[the] common standpoint that may be seen to emerge on the basis of such associative scrutiny may be far from total, and the form of the concordance need not, in many cases, go beyond noting that some social arrangements are seriously unjust in a way that can be remedied" (2006, 235–36). It is self-evident that even the most vigorous of "associative scrutiny" can leave us with conflicting arguments. However, the plurality of preferences and beliefs will then be the result of critical public reasoning, not of "disengaged toleration" with an intellectually complacent resolution as "de gustibus non est disputandum."

Sen's interpretation of Smith's impartial spectator is built on a different understanding of normative reasoning than Buchanan's "presumption that no man's values are better than any other man's" (1977, 83). In the Smith–Sen story, the value of a "man's values" is qualified as a function of his knowledge about other "men's" perspectives and interests. Sen would agree with Barry (1980, 97) that:

> [it] is rather strange that "rational discourse," for Buchanan, entails jettisoning everything that might normally be thought of as constituting rational discourse (e.g., arguments about the justice or injustice of alternative arrangements) in

favor of the comparison of brute preferences, however prejudiced or misguided, whether based on true or false ideas about the world.

A Practical Example

Rather than summarizing Sen's entire approach here, I will briefly mention
an example of how the different frameworks might play out in a practical
case. Consider the debate regarding the abolishment of capital punishment in
the United States. We would hardly obtain a satisfying answer if we tried to
reason normatively with Buchanan's transcendental contractarianism. How
would current American citizens decide behind a veil of uncertainty given
their real-life disagreements? What would they know about themselves and
the world at the constitutional stage? The answers depend on complex
counterfactuals. If Sen is right, then Buchanan's normative approach is an
underdetermined thought experiment that would specify which rules to follow if we had information that we actually cannot obtain. It is difficult to
imagine a "just solution" in which individuals would unanimously agree on
the "rules of the game." Due to the transcendental character of his approach,
it does not produce substantive information on how to handle the "justness"
of capital punishment.

In contrast, Smith's impartial spectator might provide a feasible heuristic
to think comparatively about the case by broadening our understanding and
widening the scope of our normative inquiry. It invites us to ask concrete
questions, for example, how could the public discourse in the United States
be enriched by bringing in perspectives of real-life people "from a distance"
(e.g., from Europe or Latin America)? What might the United States learn
from other societies' experiences of abolishing the death penalty (e.g., in
terms of changes in crime rates or the cost of the prison system)? How did
the abolishment of capital punishment affect the level of perceived justice/
injustice of their judicial systems (e.g., by preventing false positives)? Above
all, it might be an essential insight for the American discourse to see that
abolitionist societies have not been crumbling into chaos as a result of banning capital punishment.

FINDING THE NORMATIVE FOUNDATIONS OF
FREE AND OPEN SOCIETIES

A full assessment of the Smith–Sen framework lies beyond the scope of this
chapter. This realization-focused comparative approach has sparked apprai-
sal, but also substantial criticism.[21] In this chapter, I illustrated the ways in
which Sen's arguments based on Smith's moral philosophy help to detect the
normative "core" of Buchanan's constitutional contractarianism and reveal
some of its critical features. If the arguments of this chapter hold true, Bucha-

nan's attempt at identifying just institutions by means of idealized concepts—the unanimity rule and the hypothetical veil of uncertainty—is neither particularly helpful nor necessary to solve concrete problems of injustice. Instead, a comparative approach that is built upon a notion of open impartiality and not confined to the identification of perfectly just institutions or ideal decision procedures might be more convincing and useful in practical policy matters.

Continuing this "Buchanan–Sen controversy" can offer a more nuanced tone to the current discussion of Buchanan's legacy (for an overview, see Fleury and Marciano 2018). The intellectual interaction between Buchanan and Sen is a good example of how academics can engage professionally with dissenting normative visions, namely, by considering the basic premises and factual consequences of each other's analytical arguments. While historiographic work on the lives of these two eminent philosopher–economists is undoubtedly informative, one must not forget to immerse deep into their theories to grasp the breadth and depth of their thinking.

In addition, this "controversy" between Buchanan and Sen has the potential to enrich the general debate between high liberals and classical liberals by comparatively broadening their views on the normative foundations of free and open societies. In times when populism and nationalism are on the rise, liberal thinkers of any color might benefit from an open-ended discourse that strengthens the continuous relevance of the Enlightenment project. Gerald Gaus (2016, 250) is likely correct when he states that "[political] philosophers will have far more to contribute if they abandon their citadels of certain principles and ideals, and acknowledge that they are participants in a process of collective discovery."

Future research might examine the mutual influences in the intellectual biographies of Sen and Buchanan. In spite of the similarity of questions they address at the intersection of economics and philosophy, research does not yet exist that systematically investigates the many links and differences between their works. Currently, new ideas in *behavioral* welfare economics (Bernheim 2016) are shaking up many preconceived notions in economics and philosophy in the form of alternative theoretical notions (e.g., endogenous or context-dependent preferences) or new policy proposals (e.g., nudging). Scholars in this growing research paradigm should not ignore the inherent normativity of their endeavor and the lessons they can learn from Sen and Buchanan, who were among the most outspoken critics of neoclassical welfare economics. Finally, the critique presented in this chapter is an invitation for those scholars who would like to defend the idea that Buchanan is a "comprehensive Smithian." This chapter suggests that Buchanan follows the Scotsman in his conceptualization of politics and economics, but not in his understanding of normative reasoning.

NOTES

1. This chapter benefited from discussions with Sanjay Reddy and the feedback of Geoffrey Brennan and Hartmut Kliemt at the 2018 annual meeting of the PPE society in New Orleans. I would also like to thank Ratna Behal-Dold, Charles Delmotte, John Meadowcroft, and the 2017–2018 Adam Smith Fellows for their most helpful comments and suggestions.

2. Welfarism assumes that "the judgment of the relative goodness of alternative states of affairs must be based exclusively on, and taken as an increasing function of, the respective collections of individual utilities in these states" (Sen 1979, 468). If combined with "sum-ranking," welfarism leads to outcome utilitarianism.

3. Sen's "Paradox of the Paretian liberal" is based on a series of intuitive assumptions. According to Sen, liberalism requires that people be allowed to make a number of "personal choices" (such as, for example, reading *Lady Chatterley's Lover*) undisturbed by others. Sen shows that no social decision rule exists that (1) provides a complete ordering of alternatives, (2) applies to any set of individual preferences, and (3) satisfies the weak Pareto principle and a liberalism condition saying that each person is decisive over at least one pair of alternatives. Sen shows that, when people have preferences about what other people do, the goal of Pareto efficiency can come into conflict with the goal of individual liberty. See Sen (2004b, part IV) for an overview of the debate on the "liberal paradox."

4. See Emmett (2018), Fleury and Marciano (2018), and Munger (2018) for decent summaries of the heated debate that was sparked by MacLean (2017). In her book, MacLean accuses Buchanan of being the intellectual mastermind behind a broader movement that wants to take down liberal democracy in the United States. To see how outlandish her claim is, see Congleton (2014) as well as Brennan and Munger (2014) on Buchanan's privately held views. For excellent introductions to Buchanan's work and life, see Meadowcroft (2013) and Wagner (2017).

5. As Buchanan (1979c, 36) points out, "People may . . . decide to do things collectively. Or they may not. The analysis, as such, is neutral in respect to the proper private sector-public sector mix. I am stating that economists should be "market economists," but only because I think they should concentrate on market or exchange institutions, again recalling that these are to be conceived in the widest possible sense. This need not bias or prejudice them for or against any particular form of social order."

6. Buchanan (1975, xvii) attributes the distinction between these two stages of decision making, one that concerns the selection of rules and one that concerns actions within these selected rules, to the influence of his teacher Frank H. Knight at the University of Chicago and to the discussions with his colleague Rutledge Vining during his years as a professor at the University of Virginia.

7. Buchanan and Tullock (1962, 92) clarify, "The individualistic theory of the constitution we have been able to develop assigns a central role to a single decision-making rule—that of general consensus or unanimity. The other possible rules for choice-making are introduced as variants from the unanimity rule. These variants will be rationally chosen, not because they will produce 'better' collective decisions (they will not), but rather because on balance, the sheer weight of the costs involved in reaching decisions unanimously dictates some departure from the 'ideal' rule."

8. Congleton (2014, 63) notes, "There may be no 'natural rights' according to Buchanan, but there are nonetheless some obvious rights, procedures, and policies that would be agreed to in a world of equals. Among these are well-defined areas in which people are free to choose."

9. Brennan and Munger (2014, 335) note that Buchanan's "notion of consent was surprisingly nearly literal. He really meant consent, unanimous consent, giving each person a veto over any alterations to the status quo. He was willing to relax this rule to 'near unanimity,' but he was equally willing to privilege the status quo in ways that strike many observers as fetishistic. His reasoning was that only with unanimous consent can truly voluntary participation in the social process be assured. No consensus on any change? No change."

10. Sen also counts John Locke, Jean-Jacques Rousseau, and Immanuel Kant to this Enlightenment tradition. Alongside Rawls, modern philosophers of this tradition are, according to Sen, Robert Nozick, David Gauthier, and Ronald Dworkin. All of them draw in one way or another

on the idea of the social contract and concentrate their effort on the search for ideally just institutions.

11. In this tradition of (post-)Enlightenment, Sen also identifies Marquis de Condorcet, Jeremy Bentham, Mary Wollstonecraft, Karl Marx, and John Stuart Mill.

12. Sen traces Smith's arguments in favor of "open impartiality" back to *The Theory of Moral Sentiments*, but he also emphasizes that the comparative understanding of justice is equally present in *The Wealth of Nations*. Paganelli (2017) supports this view. She argues that, even in the *Wealth of Nations*, Smith was primarily driven by questions of justice: "Adam Smith asks: poverty brings unjust sufferings to the weakest of society, poverty kills unjustly, especially the weakest. How can we get out of it?" (2017, 14). She argues that Smith wanted to "understand wealth *because* wealth is what gives us the means to live, and to live relatively longer, better, and freer lives . . . inquire into the nature and causes of the wealth of nations, Smith inquires also into the nature and causes of justice" (2017, 15).

13. For an in-depth treatment of the difference between Rawls's and Buchanan's political theory, see the excellent dissertation by Cowen (2016).

14. For an in-depth discussion of the consequences of the move from a thick to a thin veil of uncertainty for the conceptualization of the "moral point of view," see Gaus and Thrasher (2015).

15. An early paper that expresses Sen's skepticism toward the plausibility of unanimous judgments in "original positions" is Runciman and Sen (1965). According to Sen, another problem of the procedural logic of social contract theory is "inclusionary incoherence": if one aims to give every current and future agent that is affected by a certain rule a voice in the hypothetical deliberation, one might never be able to settle the demarcation of the focal group (Sen 2002). This enhances the transcendental nature and indeterminacy of contractarianism.

16. The Pareto Criterion excludes *interpersonal* and *intertemporal* comparisons of individual levels of welfare. At various points in his work, Sen argues that this is an unnecessary strong constraint on normative reasoning (see, e.g., Sen 2004b, chapter II). On this point, see also Barry (1980).

17. Since "contractual consent" is used as a source of justification of institutions and moral principles, Buchanan puts his own classical liberal views at risk; many different social states and ethical norms can be rationalized as the outcome of a Buchananite social contract (Kliemt 2014).

18. See also Buchanan (1954a). Sen traces this line of reasoning back to Buchanan's teacher Frank Knight, who notes (1947, 280) that values "are established or validated and recognized through discussion, an activity which is at once social, intellectual, and creative." In doing so, Sen (2009, chapters 15–17) acknowledges the crucial role of institutions in facilitating our ability to scrutinize our values and priorities through opportunities for public discussion (e.g., freedom of speech and right to information).

19. Buchanan is quite vague on the question of how to find the "ideal" demarcation for a membership in a social contract. In all three of his major books on contractarianism, *The Calculus of Consent*, *The Limits of Liberty*, and *The Reason of Rules*, Buchanan hints at a "natural" perspective that invites a demarcation along the lines of nation-states. The reason is a pragmatic one (1975, xv): "We start from here, from where we are, and not from some idealized world peopled by beings with a different history and with utopian institutions." He adds later in the book that nation-states must be seen "as the effective coalitions of persons" (1975, 139).

20. The title of the chapter speaks for itself: *Of the Influence of Custom and Fashion upon the Sentiment of Moral Approbation and Disapprobation*. Smith points out that even Plato and Aristotle supported the established practice of infanticide.

21. For critical reviews, see, e.g., Brown (2010), Freeman (2010), Hinsch (2011), O'Neill (2010), and Satz (2011). See Gaus (2016, 154–65) for an excellent discussion of Sen's contribution to nonideal political theory.

REFERENCES

Arrow, Kenneth J. 1951. *Social Choice and Individual Values*. New York: Wiley.

Barry, Brian. 1980. "Review of 'The Limits of Liberty' and 'Freedom in Constitutional Contract' by James M. Buchanan." *Theory and Decision* 12: 95–106.

Bernheim, B. Douglas. 2016. "The Good, the Bad, and the Ugly: A Unified Approach to Behavioral Welfare Economics." *Journal of Benefit-Cost Analysis* 7, no. 1: 12–68.

Boettke, Peter. 2013. "Comment on 'Brennan, G., Liberty Matters: James Buchanan: An Assessment.'" Indianapolis, IN: Liberty Fund. Accessed March 28, 2018. http://oll.libertyfund.org/titles/2518.

Brennan, Geoffrey. 2012. "Politics-as-exchange and The Calculus of Consent." *Public Choice* 152, no. 3–4: 351–58.

———. 2013. "Liberty Matters: James Buchanan: An Assessment." Indianapolis, IN: Liberty Fund. Accessed March 28, 2018. http://oll.libertyfund.org/titles/2518.

Brennan, Geoffrey, and Buchanan, James M. 1985. *The Reason of Rules: Constitutional Political Economy*. Cambridge: Cambridge University Press.

Brennan, Geoffrey, and Michael Munger. 2014. "The Soul of James Buchanan?" *The Independent Review* 18, no. 3: 331–42.

Brown, Chris. 2010. "On Amartya Sen and the Idea of Justice." *Ethics & International Affairs* 24, no. 3: 309–18.

Buchanan, James M. 1949. "The Pure Theory of Government Finance: A Suggested Approach." *Journal of Political Economy* 57: 495–505.

———. 1954a. "Individual Choice in Voting and the Market." *Journal of Political Economy* 62, no. 4: 334–43.

———. 1954b. "Social Choice, Democracy, and Free Markets." *Journal of Political Economy* 62, no. 2: 114–23.

———. 1962. "The Relevance of Pareto Optimality." *Journal of Conflict Resolution* 6, no. 4: 341–54.

———. 1975. *The Limits of Liberty: Between Anarchy and Leviathan*. Chicago: University of Chicago Press.

———. 1976. "Taxation in Fiscal Exchange." *Journal of Public Economics* 6, no. 1–2: 17–29.

———. 1977. *Freedom in Constitutional Contract: Perspectives of a Political Economist*. College Station: Texas A&M University Press.

———. 1979a. "Natural and Artifactual Man." In *The Collected Works of James M. Buchanan, Volume 1: The Logical Foundations of Constitutional Liberty*, 246–59. Indianapolis, IN: Liberty Fund, Inc., 1999.

———. 1979b. "Politics without Romance: A Sketch of Positive Public Choice Theory and Its Normative Implications." *IHS Journal, Zeitschrift des Instituts für Höhere Studien* 3, B1–B11.

———. 1979c. *What Should Economists Do?* Indianapolis, IN: Liberty Press, Inc.

———. 1986. *Liberty, Market and State: Political Economy in the 1980s*. Brighton: Wheatsheaf Books.

———. 1987. "The Constitution of Economic Policy." *Science* 236, no. 4807: 1433–36.

———. 1990. "The Domain of Constitutional Economics." *Constitutional Political Economy* 1, no. 1: 1–18.

———. 1991. "The Foundations of Normative Individualism." In *The Collected Works of James M. Buchanan, Volume 1: The Logical Foundations of Constitutional Liberty*, 281–29. Indianapolis, IN: Liberty Fund, Inc., 1999.

———. 1996. "An Ambiguity in Sen's Alleged Proof of the Impossibility of a Pareto Libertarian." *Analyse & Kritik* 18, no. 1: 118–25.

———. 2003. "Justice Among Natural Equals: Memorial Marker for John Rawls." *Public Choice* 114, no. 3–4 (March): iii–v.

———. 2005. *Why I, Too, Am Not a Conservative: The Normative Vision of Classical Liberalism*. Cheltenham, UK: Edward Elgar.

Buchanan, James M., and Roger D. Congleton. 2006. *Politics by Principle, Not Interest: Towards Nondiscriminatory Democracy*. Cambridge: Cambridge University Press.

Buchanan, James M., and Gordon Tullock. 1962. *The Calculus of Consent*. Ann Arbor: University of Michigan Press.

Congleton, Roger D. 2014. "The Contractarian Constitutional Political Economy of James Buchanan." *Constitutional Political Economy* 25, no. 1: 39–67.

Cowen, Nick M. 2016. "Rawls Unveiled: The Robust Political Economy of Distributive Justice." PhD diss., King's College London.

Dold, Malte, and Menusch Khadjavi. 2017. "Jumping the Queue: An Experiment on Procedural Preferences." *Games and Economic Behavior* 102: 127–37.

Emmett, Ross B. 2018. "Reading the Hermeneutics of Suspicion with Suspicion: A Review Essay on Nancy Maclean's Democracy in Chains." Accessed July 28, 2018. https://ssrn.com/abstract=3187542.

Fleury, Jean-Baptiste, and Alain Marciano. 2018. "The Sound of Silence: A Review Essay of Nancy MacLean's Democracy in Chains: The Deep History of the Radical Right's Stealth Plan for America." *Journal of Economic Literature* (forthcoming).

Freeman, Samuel. 2010. "A New Theory of Justice." *The New York Review of Books* 57, no. 15: 14–27.

Frohlich, Norman, and Joe A. Oppenheimer. 1992. *Choosing Justice: An Experimental Approach to Ethical Theory*. Berkeley: University of California Press.

Gaus, Gerald. 2016. *The Tyranny of the Ideal: Justice in a Diverse Society*. Princeton, NJ: Princeton University Press.

———. 2018. "It Can't Be Rational Choice All the Way Down: Comprehensive Hobbesianism and the Origins of the Moral Order." In *Tensions in the Political Economy Project of James M. Buchanan*, edited by Peter J. Boettke, Virgil Henry Storr, and Solomon Stein. Arlington, VA: Mercatus Center.

Gaus, Gerald, and John Thrasher. 2015. "Rational Choice and the Original Position: The (Many) Models of Rawls and Harsanyi." In *The Original Position*, edited by Timothy Hinton, 39–58. Cambridge: Cambridge University Press.

Hinsch, Wilfried. 2011. "Ideal Justice and Rational Dissent. A Critique of Amartya Sen's The Idea of Justice." *Analyse & Kritik* 33, no. 2: 371–86.

Kliemt, Hartmut. 2014. "Buchanan as a Classical Liberal." *The Independent Review* 18, no. 3: 391–400.

Knight, Frank H. 1947. *Freedom and Reform: Essays in Economics and Social Philosophy*. Indianapolis, IN: Liberty Fund, Inc., 1982.

Konow, James. 2003. "Which Is the Fairest One of All? A Positive Analysis of Justice Theories." *Journal of Economic Literature* 41, no. 4: 1188–1239.

Lange, Matthew K. 2004. "British Colonial Legacies and Political Development." *World Development* 32, no. 6: 905–22.

MacLean, Nancy. 2017. *Democracy in Chains: The Deep History of the Radical Right's Stealth Plan for America*. New York: Penguin.

Meadowcroft, John. 2013. *James M. Buchanan*. New York: Bloomsbury Publishing USA.

———. 2014. "Exchange, Unanimity and Consent: A Defense of the Public Choice Account of Power." *Public Choice* 158, no. 1–2: 85–100.

Morris, Christopher W., ed. 2010. *Amartya Sen*. Cambridge: Cambridge University Press.

Moulin, Hervé. 1995. *Cooperative Micro-Economics: An Introduction*. Princeton, NJ: Princeton University Press.

Munger, Michael C. 2018. "On the Origins and Goals of Public Choice Constitutional Conspiracy?" *The Independent Review* 22, no. 3: 359–82.

O'Neill, Onora. 2010. "The Idea of Justice." *The Journal of Philosophy* 107, no. 7: 384–88.

Paganelli, Maria P. 2017. "240 Years of The Wealth of Nations." *Nova Economia* 27, no. 2: 7–19.

Read, Daniel. 2006. "Which Side Are You On? The Ethics of Self-Command." *Journal of Economic Psychology* 27, no. 5: 681–93.

Runciman, Walter G., and Amartya K. Sen. 1965. "Games, Justice and the General Will." *Mind* 74, no. 296: 554–62.

Satz, Debra. 2011. "Amartya Sen's the Idea of Justice: What Approach, Which Capabilities." *Rutgers Law Journal* 43: 277–93.

Sen, Amartya K. 1970a. *Collective Choice and Social Welfare*. Revised Edition. 2017. Cambridge, MA: Harvard University Press.

———. 1970b. "The Impossibility of a Paretian Liberal." *Journal of Political Economy* 78, no. 1: 152–57.

———. 1977. "Rational Fools: A Critique of the Behavioral Foundations of Economic Theory." *Philosophy & Public Affairs*: 317–44.

———. 1979. "Utilitarianism and Welfarism." *The Journal of Philosophy* 76, no. 9: 463–89.

———. 1985. *Commodities and Capabilities*. Amsterdam: North-Holland.

———. 1993. "Capability and Wellbeing." In *The Quality of Life*, edited by Martha Nussbaum and Amartya K. Sen, 30–53. Oxford: Oxford University Press.

———. 1999. *Development as Freedom*. New York: Knopf.

———. 2002. "Open and Closed Impartiality." *The Journal of Philosophy* 99, no. 9: 445–69.

———. 2004a. "Elements of a Theory of Human Rights." *Philosophy & Public Affairs* 32, no. 4: 315–56.

———. 2004b. *Rationality and Freedom*. Cambridge, MA: Harvard University Press.

———. 2006. "What Do We Want from a Theory of Justice?" *The Journal of Philosophy* 103, no. 5: 215–38.

———. 2009. *The Idea of Justice*. Cambridge, MA: Harvard University Press.

———. 2011. "On James Buchanan." *Journal of Economic Behavior & Organization* 80, no. 2: 367–69.

Smith, Adam. 1759. *The Theory of Moral Sentiments*. London: T. Cadell extended version 1790, republished, Oxford: Clarendon Press, 1976.

Sugden, Robert. 1993. "Welfare, Resources, and Capabilities: A Review of Inequality Reexamined by Amartya Sen." *Journal of Economic Literature* 31, no. 4: 1947–62.

Swedberg, Richard. 1990. *Economics and Sociology: Redefining Their Boundaries: Conversations with Economists and Sociologists*. Princeton, NJ: Princeton University Press.

Wagner, Richard E. 2017. *James M. Buchanan and Liberal Political Economy: A Rational Reconstruction*. Lanham, MD: Lexington Books.

Chapter Two

Toward a More "Tocquevillian" Social Science

Family, Gender, Loyalty, and Virtue in Modern Democratic Associationalism

Sarah J. Wilford

Tocqueville's relevance to modern political and social science is enduring. From opinion articles to academic scholarship, modern democratic societies continue to return to his insights. Among democrats who are interested in community, social capital, and localism, it could be said "we are all Tocquevilleans now" (Plattner and Diamond 2000, 9). If we are going to continue to look to Tocqueville as an authority to strengthen democracy, we have to look at the entirety of his theory, including the domestic sphere.

This chapter begins this process by connecting an understudied element of Tocqueville's associationalism, the domestic sphere, to twentieth- and twenty-first-century political and social science research. This chapter surveys three conversations in political and social science related to matters of community, association, and localism. Robert Putnam represents the study of social capital, Elinor and Vincent Ostrom represent the study of polycentricity, and Robert Nisbet represents the study of communitarianism. The themes of associationalism manifest in all three schools. Tocqueville is the poster child of these modern research agendas.

My intervention is based upon how Tocqueville's thought is appropriated within these circles. Tocqueville's associationalism was complex. It encompassed more than the social trust afforded to members of a group with a common purpose or the efficiency of local solutions to local problems, but when we address modern associationalism, we do not attend comprehensively to several key Tocquevillian themes. Four observations concerning Tocqueville's theory supplement the modern political and social science discourse on association. I will use these observations to evaluate the three research agendas. The domestic sphere is fundamental within Tocqueville's associationalism. Rootedness and long-standing loyalty to locality is important in the formation of associative mores. Also, Tocqueville's passion for associations related to his hope to preserve virtue. Finally, Tocqueville's associationalism itself is underwritten by a *unified* habit or social attitude exercised across various associations and social contexts. These themes relate to the home, the first school of the moral habits of associative life.

If we take him seriously—or even take him as inspiration—on matters of association, we should take him seriously on the domestic sphere. Modern social science projects that deal in Tocquevillian themes ought to attend comprehensively to key themes related to the domestic sphere in Tocqueville's thought. These themes are family and gender roles, love of local community, and other-regarding mores.

Offering a critique of these schools from a Tocquevillian perspective, I evaluate them using the themes of family, gender, love of locality, and other-regarding mores. My critique does not suggest these schools should "be more Tocquevillian" in the sense that they should adhere more strictly to Tocqueville's original thought. Rather, I suggest that these perspectives may benefit from additional recommendations found in his thought because, in their current forms, essential elements are missing, and Tocqueville has identified and suggested those essential elements. These three perspectives provide rich solutions—a focus on social capital, a return to local governance, and an emphasis on intimate community; however, they fail to interrogate the moral foundation and its place of origin (the home) that Tocqueville recognized as crucial to the democratic project. As such, they could offer democracy even better solutions.

My critique notes how the schools contrast with each other, and I affirm the importance of Tocqueville's unified habit that "drags" the citizen "out of himself." Overall, most of the criticism is leveled at Putnam and the social capital perspective, though I raise issues concerning the polycentricity perspective in terms of the tension between loyalty and exit. Nisbet proves the most "Tocquevillian," as he included the most (though still not extensive) attention to these themes that I contend could augment discussion of modern associationalism. Additionally, communitarians appear to favor the perspective of a unified habit in describing a flourishing associative life. First, I examine the three research agendas, followed by a Tocquevillian critique. The chapter concludes by sketching new avenues for a more Tocquevillian social science and by outlining some possibilities for hope in the face of the "problem" in modern democracy.

With anxieties reflective of Tocqueville's concerns for democratic society, proponents of social capital, advocates of polycentricity, and communitarians were and are motivated by an urgent sense that American democracy has a problem. Each identifies a slightly different, yet related, problem. Advocates of social capital lament "the problem" as one of civic disengagement and weakened social ties across many facets of social life. With less capital of this sort, citizens may struggle to achieve flourishing, productive lives. Political scientist Putman observed: "Americans have been dropping out in droves" from civic engagement (Putnam 2001, 64). He documented the collapse of social capital in many areas, from the formal, informal, political, civic, and religious to the bonds between colleagues and friends, volunteerism, and social trust.

The Ostroms and scholars of polycentricity, see the problem as rooted in the tension between a large centralized state and a multitude of local nodes of organization. Localism is crowded out by uniform bureaucratic solutions, creating inefficiencies for communities. The project of polycentricity identified increasing scientism and Wilsonian centralized administration as serious problems for the flourishing of a free democracy (V. Ostrom 2007, 8). Vincent Ostrom related "the contemporary malaise in American society" to "reform efforts" to consolidate the "fragmentation of authority and overlapping jurisdictions," worrying that the "benefits" formerly provided by smaller nodes of organization had gone extinct (V. Ostrom 2007, 100).

According to communitarian Robert Nisbet, "the growing sense of isolation in society" and "quest for community" reflects how our intimate relationships are "functionally irrelevant," politically and economically, and "meaningless" to our "moral aspirations" (Nisbet 2010, 43). Citizens invest in large entities, such as political parties, that cannot foster true moral character (Nisbet 2010, 28). A disjuncture between the possibility of a fulfilling, community-oriented moral life and the realities of the modern democratic state and complex economy means that Americans half-heartedly expect "the small traditional associations, founded upon kinship, faith, or locality" to provide for citizens' moral and spiritual needs—yet these small associations are increasingly irrelevant (Nisbet 2010, 45, 47). Given the tension between mass society and private life, small associations "and the whole network of informal interpersonal relationships" no longer offer substantial provision of "mutual aid, welfare, education, recreation, and economic production and distribution" (Nisbet 2010, 47).

Putnam, the Ostroms, and Nisbet all have a similar answer in mind to address the problem: the revitalization of associative life. All are aiming to draw attention to both the plight and potential of associations in modern democracies. The scholarship in all three fields touches on associations—small, large, religious, recreational, and administrative—and all three schools have a claim to the Tocquevillian legacy.

When it comes to studying modern associations from a Tocquevillian perspective, the domestic sphere, family, and gender roles are relevant to understanding the formation of social capital. This chapter criticizes modern scholarship in relation to these themes. For example, I note that rooted Tocqueville's perspective on love of home problematizes some literature on the usefulness of competitiveness between communities. While competition between localities and associations has benefits, that competition appears to be in tension with the formation of robust associations, according to Tocqueville's logic. Primarily concerned with habituating citizens to virtue, Tocqueville's associationalism was not merely addressing the decentralization of power, efficient solutions, or social cohesion, as some modern social scientists may suggest. In the domestic association and in wider associative life, Tocqueville's hopes for staving off democratic despotism related to moral themes. For him, the domestic sphere, local loyalty, and other-regarding virtue all related to the possibility of a transferrable unified social habit that is exercised across associative life, from family to wider society; modern researchers do not fully appreciate this possibility.

Alan S. Kahan has recast Tocqueville as a moralist, and, in turn, he contends that Tocqueville is relevant to sociological debates. Kahan states that Tocqueville's understanding of religion within democracies "makes Tocqueville a suitable discussion partner in debates over the place of religion today" (Kahan 2015, 195). This chapter follows his perspective that it is Tocqueville's concern for morals and virtue that enriches contemporary discussions concerning the social organization of democratic life.

More emphasis on the four areas (family, gender, love of locality, and other-regarding mores) that I highlight is appropriate to Putnam's social capital, the Ostroms' polycentricity, and Nisbet's communitarianism. These three schools address Tocquevillian subjects that were, for Tocqueville, conceptually bound up with what the domestic sphere can teach us about associationalism. A more thoroughgoing understanding of Tocqueville's associationalism may help provide a richer analysis within political and social science.

PUTNAM AND SOCIAL CAPITAL

I begin with Putnam and social capital research, which represent the "least Tocquevillian" of the three schools. Investigating measurable details of social networks, the social capital research agenda attends to associative life with a less explicitly normative bent than the other schools. With less emphasis on the value of intimate relationships over other associations, social capital research interrogates the workings of civil society or civil engagement more broadly. The work of Robert Putnam, a guest of American presidents and a preeminent researcher, is largely representative of this research agenda.

Political scientist Wendy Rahn heralded his famous *Bowling Alone* as "the De Tocqueville of our generation" (Putnam 2001, back cover).

In fact, Putnam occasionally gestured to Tocqueville's thought, but without extensive examination. He self-consciously participated in the fashionable norm of quoting Tocqueville, saying Tocqueville's "lines" about American associations "are often quoted by social scientists because they capture an important and enduring fact about our country" (Putnam 2001, 48). *Bowling Alone* and *American Grace* both feature smatterings of references to Tocqueville (Putnam 2001, 135; Putnam, Campbell, and Garrett 2012, 443). The social capital research agenda is less normatively committed to the wisdom of Tocqueville's thought than communitarianism, but it remains suggestive of Tocqueville's relevance nevertheless.

Putnam wanted to instigate a conversation about "how to renew our stock of social capital," and he acknowledged that this desire related to communitarian projects (Putnam 2001, 404). Social capital itself is about relationships and networks. Broadly, it is "capital" because of "the potential benefit accruing to actors because of their insertion into networks" (Portes 1998, 18). Putnam offered this formulation: "Just as a screwdriver (physical capital) or a college education (human capital) can increase productivity (both individual and collective), so do social contacts affect the productivity of individuals and groups" (Putnam 2001, 19).

Social capital literature benefited from "political scientists who equate social capital with the level of 'civicness' in communities such as towns, cities, or even entire countries," and Putnam was "the most prominent advocate of this approach" (Portes 1998, 18). Once this element of civic engagement took hold in the discussion, social capital analysis became bound up with the study of civil society, and the gist of this approach "goes something like this: a robust, strong, and vibrant civil society strengthens and enhances liberal democracy" (Chambers and Kopstein 2001, 837). As social capital takes on a connotation of civic engagement, "it principally describes norms and networks that exist at a societal or community-wide level," which means social capital is often understood in the context of relationships or "generalized norms of trust and reciprocity" among "people who are not well known to one another" (Meadowcroft and Pennington 2007, 21). Nevertheless, social capital that exists in familial relations is sometimes studied too.[1] Putnam contended that the trust built by common understanding becomes "generalized reciprocity," without perfect scorekeeping (Putnam 2001, 21). *Bowling Alone* focused on the decline in civic engagement, social capital, and this form of trust across a multitude of facets of American society. He included analysis of the role of women and the family within this portrait of America's plunging supply of social capital.

Putnam's research found that "[i]nformal social connections are much more frequent among women, regardless of their job and marital status"

(Putnam 2001, 95). He concluded that "women are more avid social capitalists," but he ultimately found that American "civic disengagement over the past several decades" cannot be explained by the changing position of women (Putnam 2001, 203). He also thought that "the transformation of American family structure and home life" did not play a very significant role in the national civic disengagement (Putnam 2001, 278). Unlike Nisbet's communitarianism, Putnam's social capital project does not worry that the changing nature of the family and modern womanhood are integral elements in explaining our current atomized condition.

Reminiscent of Tocqueville, social capital research explores norms and moral habits that bind citizens and make for flourishing societies. The social capital research, however, does not have an overarching moral or normative consensus that makes sense of how these various facets of social life interact or why it is morally good to enrich our stock of social capital. In this regard, the study of social capital, though reminiscent of Tocqueville, is unlike Tocqueville's project.

THE OSTROMS AND POLYCENTRICITY

Vincent and Elinor Ostrom founded the political economy research agenda, loosely termed the "Bloomington School," which investigates institutional diversity and polycentricity. Across their published writings, the Ostroms self-consciously linked their work with Tocqueville's thought.[2] Here, these two thinkers are grouped, but it must be noted that Vincent Ostrom was more philosophical and preoccupied by Tocqueville, while Elinor Ostrom primarily addressed the rules that organize groups and group behavior. Both, however, acknowledge an intellectual debt to Tocqueville. Vincent Ostrom conceived of his philosophical project as "resolv[ing] Tocqueville's puzzle about whether democratic societies are viable forms of civilization" (V. Ostrom 1997, x). Similarly, Elinor Ostrom listed Tocqueville as among those philosophers who addressed the same "questions that structure" their Bloomington Workshop (quoted in Sabetti and Aligica 2014, 3). Additionally, recent scholarship grappling with the Ostroms' legacy continue to refer to Tocqueville and to use the term "Tocquevillian" (Boettke, Lemke, and Palagashvili 2015, 313–15; Aligica and Boettke 2011, 31–32; Herzberg 2015, 97; Meadowcroft and Pennington 2007, 34). Polycentricity scholarship also claims a Tocquevillian outlook.

The project of the Bloomington School interrogates how citizens govern themselves "within systems of multiple and overlapping authorities" (Boettke, Lemke, and Palagashvili 2015, 313). Influenced by public choice economics, the Ostroms challenged the "'market' vs. 'state' dichotomy" and the "monocentric," centralized administrative solution (Aligica and Boettke

2011, 30). Their new viewpoint highlighted the possible impact of a multi-part structure of "hybrid" organizational systems (Aligica and Boettke 2011, 37). The Ostroms' project, and Elinor Ostrom's *Governing the Commons* in particular, communicated a new outlook for parsing common pool resource solutions in diverse institutional contexts (Herzberg 2015, 101). Undeniably, the Ostroms' research framework is bound up with philosophical concerns (see Aligica and Boettke 2011, 29; Boettke, Palagashvili, and Lemke 2013, 421). The Ostroms linked their love of democracy and liberty to comprehensive testing of institutions to develop a research framework that expanded the scope of public choice economics to encompass the details of social groups and communities. The study of polycentricity includes analysis of how competition between nodes of authority and organization can promote more efficient outcomes. They were also preoccupied with mores and the transmission of social rules.

Vincent Ostrom wrote that "the most fundamental source of human and social capital in any society is family households as they function in speech communities in which patterns of associated relationships are constituted in neighborhoods" (V. Ostrom 1997, 78). Though much of the research agenda of the Bloomington School is not based on how the domestic sphere relates to wider associative life and local initiatives, the Ostroms themselves nevertheless emphasized, similarly to the communitarians, the importance of family and local neighborhood in the formation of mores. At the same time, research in the Bloomington School tradition not only examines internal dynamics of groups and communities but also the competitive dynamics between groups and communities (for example, see Lemke 2016). For this reason, this research agenda differs from the schools of communitarianism and social capital, which have less emphasis on competition between groups and more emphasis on the norms, rules, and bonds internal to groups. Though the Ostroms did address richer moral linkages within groups (not merely the public services that bonded groups), such as Vincent Ostrom's work on religion, the additional emphasis on competition is an aspect of their work that is at odds with Tocqueville's perspective on associationalism (see V. Ostrom 1999, 53–68).

NISBET AND COMMUNITARIANISM

Communitarianism could be said to rest on what has been called "the Burke/ Tocqueville thesis," that family and intimate relationships of kinship matter in the formation of flourishing and moral democratic citizens (Galston 2000, 369–70; see also Stone 2001, 63). Like Tocqueville, communitarians emphasize the domestic sphere and intimate relationships. Also like Tocqueville, they contend that authority within small associations is necessary for free and flourishing democracies.

Robert Nisbet is representative of the communitarian answer to the problem of association, and he proves the most Tocquevillian of these three examples. He called for a reinvigoration of the intimate human relationships in order to bolster the fraying social ties that shape moral and political habits. Addressing contemporary concerns about community, civil society, and authority in our modern democracies, the communitarian movement is self-consciously Tocquevillian in tone. For the communitarians in Nisbet's vein, family, religion, and neighborhood are paramount (see Berger and Neuhaus 2000). These are "the small areas of association within which alone such values and purposes can take on clear meaning in personal life and become the vital roots of the larger culture" (Nisbet 2010, 62). Nisbet asserted that these associations truly refine character to the degree necessary for a flourishing society. Similar to Tocqueville, he contended that "social interdependence" of smaller, interpersonal associations alone fortifies citizens "to resist the tyranny that always threatens to arise out of any political government" (Nisbet 2010, 247). Associations shape moral order and liberty (Nisbet 2010, 248). For Nisbet, the experiences of private, religious, and communal life provide the most intimate social bonds that foster moral and political habits, and these realms must be perpetually promoted.

Family roles and the nature of authority are key themes within communitarianism (for more on authority, see Ehrenhalt 2000). Nisbet saw mid-twentieth-century American society as being pulled in two directions: toward "the historic world" of values associated with family, faith, and neighborhood and also toward a new world of "values identical with the absolute political community" (Nisbet 2010, 259). This first world offers genuine authority and meaningful social roles that can form authentic moral character, while the latter offers a form of tyranny. Citizens should be committed to "the authority and hierarchy of genuine communities, the contexts that form of true character" (Stone 2001, 145). Communitarians have no qualms about asserting the necessity of authority and social, sometimes hierarchical, roles. Nisbet concluded that the supposed disorderliness plaguing "the modern family is, in fact, simply an erosion of its natural authority" (quoted in Stone 2001, 144). Nisbet worried that modern politics and economics could make familial "membership" gratuitous, sometimes burdensome (Nisbet 2010, 52–53). In short, families are ill fitting in "a democratic, industrial age" yet necessary for perpetuating norms and morals (Nisbet 2010, 51).

Nisbet also addressed the changing position of women. He believed the shift away from defined gender-based social roles within the family structure had an impact on how the "whole family group" related to "society" (Nisbet 2010, 56). Additionally, he thought that the "psychological problems" that women face were related to the breakdown of roles and traditional authority, which instigated "historical changes in social position" (Nisbet 2010, 55). While this may strike twenty-first-century readers as old-fashioned, Nisbet's point was a simple one: in the "emancipation from clear, socially approved function and role within the institutionalized family group" and from "a social function and conceptualized role," many women experienced a sense of dislocation (Nisbet 2010, 55). Nisbet stated that these "historical changes" were precisely "the same context in which lie contemporary problems of the role of the father and the child" (Nisbet 2010, 55–56). This historical breakdown of authority and hierarchy is not solely gender specific.

Though he referred to Tocqueville elsewhere, he did not refer to Tocqueville on this particular topic. However, this was Tocqueville's perspective too: the same democratizing force affects gender roles and familial authority (Tocqueville 2010b, 1031–67). Nisbet concluded that the family had a unique social function, and therefore he saw the dismantling of social roles, hierarchy, and authority within the family as detrimental to the psychology of the individual and troublesome for the formation of community members (see Fukuyama 2000, 258).[3]

The communitarians see reliable authority, hierarchy, and social roles as undergirding the integrity of "this sphere of interpersonal relationships" and small associations (Nisbet 2000, 36). Nisbet thought that additional associations also shape citizens, "but the major moral and psychological influences on the individual's life" are forged in smaller associations (Nisbet 2010, 36). Communitarians, if we take Nisbet as largely representative, live up to the legacy of Tocqueville in two ways. They mirror him in their emphasis on the domestic sphere and the relationships closest to home. Second, they accept authority within those relationships as relevant to a thriving democratic life, which is also an essential aspect of Tocqueville's theory. Nisbet's communitarianism explicitly attends to the moral habits, intimate sphere, and associative life, which lay at the core of Tocqueville's thought.

THREE PERSPECTIVES ON ASSOCIATION: TOCQUEVILLE'S CRITIQUE AND THE UNITY OF HABIT

All of the modern perspectives have in common a Tocquevillian attitude, and they all believe in the potential of associative life to resolve the woes besetting democratic, and specifically American, society. Some commonalities unite the three projects, while notable differences make the projects foils to each other. Overall, each project may be served by a better understanding of the Tocquevillian attitude that ostensibly informs each scholarly endeavor. Tocqueville's associationalism could serve modern associationalism, or, at least, in reminding us of his historical version of associationalism, it may open new avenues for thinking about modern associationalism.

These three research agendas are un-Tocquevillian in some regards, while maintaining a superficially Tocquevillian pretense. I concede that it is possible that these scholars may have simply sought the usefulness or charm of invoking Tocqueville as an authority or historical mascot. While a mascot is unobjectionable as a stylistic flourish, I nevertheless submit that social scientists may benefit from reexamining where modern social science has misunderstood Tocqueville or identifying where it would profit from his insight. This offers the beginning of a new framework for studying associationalism. In this section, noting points of tension between the three perspectives, I address the themes of family, gender roles, rooted love of locality, other-regarding virtue, and the unified habit of sociability. The Tocquevillian outlook on these themes complements our modern discussion of associationalism, provoking interpretations or new questions that may be overlooked when making use of Tocqueville only as a mascot.

Consider family and gender roles. From a strict Tocquevillian perspective that attends to gender roles, Putnam's presentation of the changing position of women and the decline in traditional family cohesion would be subject to criticism. Putnam's conclusions contrast with Nisbet's handling of gender roles, which, though not extensive, did account for the effects of the changing position of women on community life. Putnam noted in *Bowling Alone* that women are "avid social capitalists" and that the entry of women into the workforce meant "fewer educated, dynamic women with enough free time to organize civic activity, plan dinner parties, and the like" were able to foster civic engagement (Putnam 2001, 95, 203). As these types of women disappeared, "the rest of us, too, have gradually disengaged" from civic life (Putnam 2001, 203). Putnam characterized the "movement of women out of the home into the paid labor force" as "the most portentous social change of the last half century" (Putnam 2001, 194). Concurrently, Putnam contended that women's entry into paid work is not "*the* primary cause of civic disengagement over the last two decades" because "civic engagement and social connectedness have diminished almost equally for both women and men, working or not, married or single, financially stressed or financially comfortable" (Putnam 2001, 203). He did not elaborate *why* widespread disengagement, irrespective of gender or marital status, explains that the changing position of women does not account for a significant portion of the decline.

Putnam himself hinted that, because women no longer plan dinner parties, "the rest of us" opt out too. Of course, we do—there are fewer dinner parties to attend. Putnam's justification here is far from being what he deems a "central exculpatory fact" that relieves the changing role of women from the burden of guilt in the sad story of civic decline that he paints. The fact that all of us—male, female, married, unmarried, employed or not—have opted out could possibly demonstrate the precise opposite of Putnam's conclusion. It could indicate the immense influence that these women "with time" for social activism and party planning had over their communities, as facilitators of networks that instill in "the rest of us" the habits of sociability, neighborliness, and civic engagement. Missing this possibility is at odds with Tocqueville's perspective on gender roles. Putnam quotes Tocqueville on American associations as a neat opener to a new section of his book (Putnam 2001, 48). He demonstrates little interest, however, in making further use of Tocqueville's insights. Tocqueville's understanding of American associationalism was deeply bound up with the position of women *inside the home* (Tocqueville 2010b, 1041–67). Understanding the historical weight of women as "makers of mores" through domestic life may have led to a less definitive conclusion on Putnam's part (Tocqueville 2010b, 1041).

Margaret Talbot heavily criticized Putnam's perspective on women's participation in the workforce in her review of *Bowling Alone*. Sardonically, she wondered how television could account for so much of the problem and "suburban sprawl and the time crunch for working women and their families" so little (10 percent each) (Talbot 2000). She asked, "how could the movement of women into the paid labor force possibly matter that little in this particular social equation?" (Talbot 2000). She accused Putnam of shying away from "focusing on women's paid labor as a drain on civic engagement" (Talbot 2000). This did not add up: "if the women who led community efforts in the past are busy elsewhere, and those efforts fall into desuetude as a result, that reduces everyone else's opportunities to participate in one too" (Talbot 2000). She rightly mused that it may be more fashionable to shame television and "couch potato-ism" rather than "the expansion of autonomy and opportunity for women" (Talbot 2000). A more Tocquevillian social science would not shy away from observing how gender roles related to the production of social capital.

Likewise, Putnam was eager to absolve the changing nature of family solidarity and authority from "much" impact. While Putnam observed that "the loosening of family bonds is unequivocal" and "[t]he traditional family unit is down (a lot)," he maintained that "apart from youth- and church-related engagement, *none* of the major declines in social capital and civic engagement that we need to explain can be accounted for by the decline in the traditional family structure" (Putnam 2001, 277–79). In Putnam's analysis, "the transformation of American family structure and home life over the last thirty years (fewer marriages, more divorces, fewer children, more people living alone)" accounts for "not that much" of the downturn in civic engagement (Putnam 2001, 278). Putnam could "find no evidence that civic disengagement is among" the reasons to maintain "traditional family values," though he had some (unelaborated) reasons of his own (Putnam 2001, 279). According to Putnam, "[f]amily instability" is not relevant to the story of the "critical period" when the decline began because the decline "began with the children of the maritally stable 1940s and 1950s" (Putnam 2001, 267). Corre-

spondingly, "working mothers are exonerated" because "the plunge in civicness among children of the 1940s, 1950s, and 1960s happened while mom
was still at home" (Putnam 2001, 267). Perhaps this provides "an ironclad
alibi" for the parents of that particular generation, in that particular moment
in time, but that boomer generation is described elsewhere by Putnam as
particularly negligent in terms of civic engagement (Putnam 2001, 258).
Where is the alibi for *their* parenting and family norms?

Putnam compared the wartime culture to the carefree, beatnik culture of
the subsequent generation. One generation, which was "a cohort of men and
women whose values and civic habits were formed during a period of heightened civic obligation," was replaced "with others whose formative years
were different" (Putnam 2001, 272). Indeed, culture shapes habits, and something as momentous as world war leaves an impression on the culture of that
generation. But this subsequent generation also influenced the making of the
new culture, which in turn shaped habits. Putnam cannot disentangle the
continued decline in civic engagement after the boomer generation from the
family instability associated with the boomer generation simply because the
boomers' parents were married. Generational replacement may be the central
explanatory factor, but only insofar as we acknowledge that the boomer
generation greatly transformed a host of American cultural norms. At that
point, however, we have to explain how *those* norms affect civic engagement. Family norms may be among those new cultural norms. It seems
unlikely that "the maritally stable 1940s and 1950s" explain or exculpate as
much as Putnam assumes.

Again, I contend that a Tocqueville's thought would benefit Putnam's
analysis here. Tocqueville emphasized the role of a bonded, affectionate
family life in the formation of habits (Tocqueville 2010b, 1031–40). By
keeping Tocqueville in mind as we observe this type of evidence, we may
expect family instability to explain part of the problem. Of course, if the
evidence does not indicate this, the family should be set aside as a variable in
deciphering this social change, but Putnam's conclusion remains puzzling.
He seems to have suggested that the family stability and the stay-at-home
mothers of the baby boomers' childhoods could "exonerate," "exculpate," or
provide an alibi for *later* family instability and *later* two-income households
in terms of civic disengagement.

Turning now to matters of familial authority and rooted love of locality, a
wholeheartedly Tocquevillian outlook would also problematize the project of
polycentricity. Conversely, the communitarians reflected Tocqueville on
these topics. The communitarian perspective on authority and loyalty is at
odds with the freedom of choice implicit in the competitive aspect of the
polycentric order (on choice and community, see Ehrenhalt 2000, 252). The
liberalism of the Ostroms is thornier than we may first assume. The Ostroms
valued the community. They also valued competition between communities,

but this complicates the integrity of the communities. The communitarianism emphasis on authority likewise problematizes a more liberal approach to family and self-sacrificing social care. The traditionally involuntary nature of the family habituated—perhaps coercively—individuals to caring responsibilities and habits of communal life, and the liberal language of "rights" and choice cannot adequately describe the community realities of caring duties (Elshtain 2000, 110; Himmelfarb 2000, 96). The free choice we associate with a liberal project, like the Ostroms', is not as straightforwardly valuable in *all* institutional arrangements. Communitarians complicate the more straightforward vision presented by social capitalists and polycentrists.

Additionally, the Ostroms and Bloomington School scholarship heavily emphasize competition between nodes of power, jurisdictions, or means of social organization. The value of institutional diversity is bound up with an experimental and competitive outlook. Because this scholarship self-consciously operated in the legacy of Tocqueville, it is worth highlighting that Tocqueville did not indicate that the real value of associations or localism lay in competitive diversity. Tocqueville did not admire the plethora of American associations because they could compete. He admired the fact that there *was* a plethora, which built up the moral habits of self-governance. This plethora indicated that people could actively exercise their liberty, and the associations they formed could have a moral effect. While he admired American freedom, he was not inspired by associations because of the variety of choices that they afforded citizens. For Tocqueville, the payoff of associations was the habit-forming, moral component of associations. The efficiency-seeking competition, or the meeting of diverse preferences, implied by free choice did not compel him, but rather he admired the moral aspect of associations that worked contra individualism.

Also, he admired American federalism because it allowed America to be "free and happy like a small nation, glorious and strong like a large one" (Tocqueville 2010a, 263). These benefits were accrued, he thought, because federalism allowed "provincial patriotism" to flourish and attention "turned toward internal improvements" of each state (Tocqueville 2010a, 260–61). Communities and smaller jurisdictions flourish, according to Tocqueville, based on a love of home. The longevity and perpetuation of mores also relies on loyalty to a given community.

The mores developed by Tocqueville's localism required habituation over time, through repetition. He referred to the commitment of the citizen to town life, the engagement with free institutions, the exercise of local liberties, and the practice of association as learning processes concerned with building artificial habits (Tocqueville 2010a, 114, 162; 2010b, 891–92, 900–902). His discussion connotes a sense of maturation and acclimatization. These are processes that take time and commitment to a given locality or group. For instance, his admiration of New England, "where society" is "already old and long settled," demonstrates his belief that older mores fared better in taming democracy (Tocqueville 2010a, 319). Tocqueville contrasted this with the South, "where the social bond is less ancient and less powerful" (Tocqueville 2010a, 319). For Tocqueville, social attachments and participation in a long-standing legacy are important for the cultivation and perpetuation of the mores that shape associative life. Localities with transient or new social links are not as instructive as those where intergenerational cultural links are deeply embedded. Tocqueville suggested that newly formed social attachments were not as useful in forming the habits of associative life. It may be possible that associations formed entirely by choice (rather than the seeming coercion of traditional communities) allow for deeper bonds over shared interests. Tocqueville's perspective, however, may give us pause. Agendas that emphasize competition and exit may well discover higher levels of trust in competing and freely entered communities, but I suggest this is a less obviously Tocquevillian feature. "Voting with our feet" and making use of "exit options" is in tension with this aspect of Tocqueville's associationalism that prioritizes "old and long settled" attachments (see Lemke 2016).

In some ways, the Ostroms' work captured this insight, even though the theme of competition seems to define the spirit of their corpus. For example, Vincent Ostrom wrote that "intergenerational continuities" are essential to "intergenerational transmission of knowledge and skill" (V. Ostrom 1997, 146). This hints at the Tocquevillian insistence upon intergenerational regard that provides for authority behind the transmission of mores. Indeed, peer culture can put community norms at risk. However, in addition, too much emphasis on intercommunity and interjurisdictional competition can also undermine the rootedness necessary for communities to successfully cooperate on matters of administration and developing mores. The work of the Ostroms was Tocquevillian because it stressed how variations in local social norms and mores meant local administration could be more effective. Tocqueville thought that centralized governments have a "uniform character that does not allow for the diversity of places and mores," but he did not favor associative life because smaller communities could compete (Tocqueville 2010a, 260). While Tocqueville admired free movement for the sake of enterprise within the United States, from a wholly Tocquevillian perspective, the concept of "a mobile citizenry" voting with their feet might raise concerns, much as the unmoored frontiersman fascinated and worried Tocqueville (see Lemke 2016, 310; for more on exit and loyalty, see Hirschman 1970). Hirschman has investigated these tensions in his 1970 work, but he reminds us that loyalty is not an oppressive burden; as a "barrier to exit . . . loyalty is of finite height" (Hirschman 1970, 79).

Next, modern social science research agendas ought to consider Tocqueville's hope for a virtuous habit in democracies that could "drag" citizens out of themselves (Tocqueville 2010b, 745–46, 889). The social capital literature struggles with the problem of how what is useful and effective intersects with what is self-sacrificing and virtuous. Sacrifice in the social capital literature is usually associated with long-term benefits for the self or the group, not virtue for virtue's sake. The notion of "moral grandeur" is not among the set of virtues, such as trustworthiness, cooperativeness, and accountability, often discussed in scholarship concerning social capital, polycentricity, and modern associative life (Tocqueville 2010a, 24; Kahan 2015, especially 49–67). Most scholars agree that "social networks can affect economic performance" (Arrow 2000, 3). Coleman explained that "social capital is productive, making possible the achievement of certain ends that in its absence would not be possible" (Coleman 2000, 16). However, social capital is also *not* like other forms of capital. Social capital is enriched through a practice of useful habits that often blends with virtuous habits. Families, friendships, and volunteerism often rely on a moral spirit that is far removed from ideas about economic production, effective administration, and calculations about how to "make us healthy, wealthy, and wise" (Putnam 2001, 287).

Contrastingly, the communitarians are more aligned with Tocqueville on this theme. The communitarian emphasis on morality and personal virtue problematizes the liberal understanding of how social capital is formed and the liberal emphasis on individualism. Participation in the moral process of developing social norms is much more complex and precarious than "other forms of human capital" that can be acquired "through a rational investment decision" (Fukuyama 2000, 260). These moral communities that provide for trust are based on "shared ethical values," and they "do not require extensive contract and legal regulation" (Fukuyama 2000, 259). The formation of this kind of "capital" requires an organic, historical community that is both nebulous and reliable. It requires a set of relationships that are more complex than the minimal relationships of trust necessary for the transactional acquisition of capital.

Putnam advocated a regeneration of social capital to benefit Americans because evidence suggested that civic engagement and "social capital makes us smarter, healthier, safer, richer, and better able to govern a just and stable democracy" (Putnam 2001, 290). Putnam quoted Tocqueville in his discussion of how social capital relates to the functioning of democracy. Putnam partly understood Tocqueville's message about associationalism and democracy. He aptly noted how Tocqueville observed that "local civic activity served as the handmaiden of their national democratic community" whether or not that activity is "self-consciously or only indirectly political" (Putnam 2001, 337–38). Putnam captured the Tocquevillian assertion that associations foster the internal development of "habits of cooperation and public-spiritedness" and "practical skills necessary to partake in public life" (Putnam 2001, 338). Using Tocqueville's phrase "schools for democracy," Putnam noted that "voluntary associations" teach "how to run meetings, speak in public, write letters, organize projects, and debate public issues with civility" (Putnam 2001, 338–39). This seems to suggest that associations are useful to the end of developing skills needed for political action and, in this way, they serve democracies. This is true, but it is not the whole picture or, at least, not Tocqueville's whole picture.

Tocqueville's admiration of American associationalism ran deeper than getting along with neighbors and forming administrative capabilities. Indeed, these transferrable skills are necessary in terms of political action and well-being, but they are also significant to democratic life for other reasons. Putnam did not emphasize other aspects of Tocqueville's admiration for associations beyond being schools that teach skills. For Tocqueville, associations are schools that benefit Americans in the immediate sense that they produce effective outcomes for a local community and, in turn, they establish local administration as the norm, rather than intervention from the centralized state. Most importantly, they are schools that attended to Tocqueville's deepest concern for democracies—moral mediocrity. The habits of associative life guide the instinctively morally mediocre democratic citizen toward virtue, not simply toward political action, good health, wealth, and education. The maintenance of virtue in a democracy related to the maintenance of liberty, according to Tocqueville. Civic connections mattered to democratic flourishing primarily because of how they related to virtue and liberty, rather than the development of skills for daily activities. Putnam said social capital is good for us and for our democracies. Tocqueville would say that it *makes* us good and, thereby, it is good for our democracies.

Economist Kenneth Arrow in fact wanted to abandon "the metaphor of capital" in large part because "[t]he essence of social networks is that they are built up for reasons other than their economic value to the participants" (Arrow 2000, 4). They are "habits of the heart," not habits of the bank account, however much they may ultimately benefit the bottom line. Unsurprisingly, Nisbet and his fellow communitarians highlight this moral aspect of associations more often than other scholars of civil society and associations (for example, see Wolfe 2000, 61; Fukuyama 2000, 264; Krishna 2000, 89). The moral and communal aspect must come first. If it does come first, associations can be truly profound, and *then and only then*, in turn, can associations make us "healthy, wealthy, and wise."

From religion to free institutions, Tocqueville's forces for moderating democracy all related to his hope to "drag" citizens "out of contemplation of" or "away from looking at themselves" (Tocqueville 2010b, 745–46, 889). Though democratic peoples tend to find virtue "useful," Tocqueville's attention to the problem of self-sacrifice within democracies can augment our understanding of modern democracies. The value of an other-regarding habit, for Tocqueville, related to much more than cohesion, cooperation, and trust for the sake of efficient societal outcomes. The value of this habit, for Tocqueville, was that it preserved virtue in the face of a social state that inherently encouraged individualism and selfishness.

Most importantly, Tocqueville's associationalism was defined by a *unified* habit of outward-looking virtue, expressed and developed in a range of contexts. A truly Tocquevillian attitude would address the unity of moral habits and the links between the environments in which they are expressed. Communitarians emphasize a unity of habits within associationalism, while advocates of social capital and polycentricity emphasize a plurality of habits in associationalism. Nisbet wrote of a "union of family, local community, and religion," highlighting how religious observance contributes to the "fusion" of religious life and other aspects of associative life (Nisbet 2010, 225). Religion supports and is supported by other "*associative* purposes" (Nisbet 2010, 225). The ethical habit of the heart, based on trust and other-regarding virtue, is reliable, transferrable, and generalizable between different social contexts. In their alertness to the possibility of a *unified* moral habituation, the communitarians are particularly Tocquevillian. This theme of unified habits may be especially significant to the area of scholarship on the potential "dark side" of associations (E. Ostrom 2000, 176–77; Satyanath, Voigtländer, and Voth 2017; van Deth and Zmerli 2010). Perhaps, further investigation is needed into whether our associations are less likely to become "dark" when they are embedded within a set of associations and institutions that express the "bright side" of associative life.

The social capital literature often works with different types of social capital in order to codify and measure the benefits of types of bonds and networks in different contexts. For example, scholarship makes distinctions between "bonding" social capital and "bridging" social capital. Bonding is "narrower," usually relating to the local and intimate connections that sustain individuals, whereas bridging broadens the individual's network, usually relating to the wider connections of reciprocity that profit individuals (Putnam 2001, 22–23). Bonding finds you friends; bridging finds you a job (see Putnam 2001, 363).

The concern of some social capital literature about the "misguided" communitarian emphasis on "the relationships necessary to sustain the social fabric" (family, church, community) indicates a liberal position at odds with the holistic communitarian perspective. This concern over small moral associations betrays the liberal expectation that "generalized trust or bridging social capital" is the primary form of social capital, and it suffices in the maintenance of an associationalism that serves the "social fabric" (Meadowcroft and Pennington 2007, 31–33). Bridging social capital allows citizens to develop "rules of interaction which enable them to go about their separate purposes" (Meadowcroft and Pennington 2007, 34). Again, I question whether such a division between the habits of the intimate and the habits of the public is truly Tocquevillian. Scholars of social capital sometimes elaborate the transferrable skills learned in a family because the family can be "a bridge between the 'micro-order' of the small group and the 'macro-order' of the wider society"; however, this literature does not insist upon the necessity of family solidarity, like the communitarians (Meadowcroft and Pennington 2007, 47).

If the success of the wider networks relies, in part, on skills learned in more intimate contexts, then perhaps it is worthwhile to advocate, with the communitarians, for family solidarity and intergenerational regard. Whatever the knowledge, skills, and habits of a given culture, strong family bonds and parental authority produce intergenerational transmission of knowledge, skills, and habits. Without these bonds, the child has no reason to listen to, and *learn* from, the parent. As noted, Vincent Ostrom knew this, but seemed to overlook how competition intersects with community loyalty. Advocates of social capital shy away from advocating the precise way to embolden the family to have a meaningful impact on the macro-order—insisting on a rich family life that prizes bonds, authority, and intergenerational regard. The hesitation is an example of how social capital scholarship wavers, or is blind, regarding the possibility of unified habits.

Perhaps because of the problem of "fashion" raised by Talbot concerning his gloss on gender, Putnam clearly fell prey to this blind spot. Intriguingly, Putnam came close to establishing, empirically, a sense of unified social habits and transferrable skills or other-regarding attitudes. This is particularly obvious in his discussion of religious practice. Like Tocqueville, all three perspectives on association take religion seriously in terms of both the meaning it gives the lives of individuals as well as the role it plays in the formation of associative life.[4] Putnam concluded that "religious involvement is a crucial dimension of civic engagement" and that "trends in civic engagement are closely tied to changing patterns of religious involvement" (Putnam 2001, 69). He saw the church as an "incubator for civic skills" (Putnam 2001, 66). He noted "churchgoers are substantially more likely to be involved in secular organizations, to vote and participate politically in other ways, and to have deeper informal social connections" (Putnam 2001, 66). He concluded that both "social ties embodied in religious communities" and "religious beliefs" contributed to "volunteerism and philanthropy" among religious people (Putnam 2001, 67; Putnam, Campbell, and Garrett 2012, 444). Overall, he estimated that "religious Americans are up to twice as active civically as secular Americans" and children raised in religious contexts are more involved with "philanthropy and good works" and are higher achieving "academically and nonacademically" than their nonreligious peers (Putnam, Campbell, and Garrett 2012, 454; Putnam 2015, 224). This research begins to point to generalizable habits, but Putnam was hesitant to assert such an explicit and interdependent relationship between church and community, as Nisbet did.

Despite his empirical research sometimes flirting with the idea of a unified other-regarding social attitude, as in the example of religion, elsewhere, Putnam overlooked this possibility. Puzzlingly, he emphasized the role of time as a resource that underwrites social ties. Because informal socializing is "higher among single and childless people," Putnam wrote, "we might have expected the real-life equivalent of *Cheers* and *Friends* to take the place of civic organizations and dinner parties" since "conventional family life has become rarer" (Putnam 2001, 108–109). I question why we *would* expect that, and, indeed, he finds a decline in traditional family life is not accompanied by "a compensating increase" in informal socializing among peer communities in bars or cafés (Putnam 2001, 108–109). He mused that "to some extent the decline in family obligations ought to have freed up time for more social and community involvement" (Putnam 2001, 279). Perhaps, if time is a key factor, this would be our expectation, but if the habits of family solidarity relate directly to general habits of sociability and responsibility, we may expect otherwise. Indeed, if we expected that, then the evidence might be on our side because *both* are in decline. In fact, he concluded that time and money are not large explanatory factors. The largest is "generational change" followed by "electronic entertainment," including television (Putnam 2001, 283).

Generational change may explain the decline in civic engagement, but because this encompasses an entire generational culture, it serves more as a catchall for the social norms and habits of a noncivic generation. If the wartime generation is "the first actor in our civic morality play" and the baby boomers are the second, this raises the question: What was the nature of the "civic morality" of the previous generation? (Putnam 2001, 257). Additionally, Putnam's presentation as to what "killed" American social capital seems to unbundle time management, financial wherewithal, and electronic entertainment from generational change. American social norms around those three areas are also linked with cultural generational norms. This betrays a lack of appreciation for the possibility of a coherent *unified* set of virtues, habits, or attitudes that could be relevant to the production of social capital.

From the Tocquevillian perspective, the key to a flourishing democracy is to "drag man out of himself" so that the democratic citizen can become habituated to other-regarding virtue. Once so inclined, the benefits are more likely to accrue across all avenues of social interaction, from—to use Putnam's phrase—"'do good' civic activities" to "informal connecting" (Putnam 2001, 115). Social capital scholarship seems to understand that there might be a relationship between different forms of social capital, but, once it has been pulled apart, dissected, and measured, the social capital perspective struggles to put it back together again. This unity matters, however. In democracies, virtue is a habit. Elinor Ostrom herself offered the essential insight: "[s]ocial capital does not wear out with use but rather with disuse" (E.

Ostrom 2000, 179). A thoroughly Tocquevillian perspective would add: *habituated virtue* wears out with disuse and, for this reason, must be exercised on all social fronts.

For our modern democracies, there is no consensus on how to get associationalism right. Communitarians are deemed "misguided" in their moralism and focus on small associations from the perspective of classical liberal social capitalists, while Putnam contends the breakdown of the traditional family is not that significant in terms of the breakdown of social capital (Meadowcroft and Pennington 2007, 31–32, 101; Putnam 2001, 278). The communitarian perspective on caring duties complicates the liberal polycentrist's preference for free choice. While all of these Tocquevillian schools are motivated by a "problem" in civil society and hope to enrich associationalism, ideological tensions remain between the various schools. A thoroughgoing Tocquevillian attitude may help in getting associationalism right.

Though these research agendas lay claim to the spirit of Tocqueville, a more faithful Tocquevillian outlook finds several details to criticize in the study of modern associationalism. Putnam's handling of the family, the social capitalists' emphasis on utility, and the polycentrists' inattentiveness to the tension between competition and community are all examples of overlooking or neglecting key insights from Tocqueville. Likewise, social capital research hesitates to suggest that a unified habit of virtue may play an important role in fostering widespread investment in social capital. They miss Tocqueville's paramount insight about associationalism. Across a range of human activity and relationships, associationalism provides a key service: it fosters the opposite of individualism.

Democratic citizens are free and flourishing not because their local association fixes a pothole instead of a central power or because they have the choice to join a different community that is better at fixing potholes. Primarily, democratic citizens are free and flourishing because they are not alone. They are not alone in fixing potholes. They are not alone on the "public road," at church, or at home (Tocqueville 2010a, 303). Therefore, the unifying feature of Tocqueville's associationalism is the other-regarding virtue that allows the citizen to escape solitude by offering a deeply rooted, robust, and well-habituated alternative to atomism, from the home to the local community. Much of the scholarship on modern associationalism overlooks the depth of Tocqueville's moral perspective.

I do not propose a ban on the use of historical mascots in modern social science research; I merely suggest that a deeper understanding of our mascots can open up new approaches, raise important questions, and alert us to old explanations. For example, researchers grappling with the role of the family and the changing position of women in society may benefit from understanding Tocqueville's thought on the role of the domestic, and this may offer the beginning of an explanation for new trends. Advocates of a polycentric order may benefit from understanding Tocqueville's emphasis on rooted local norms and community spirit, and this may provoke questions about the impact of competition. Scholars of social capital may benefit from understanding the underlying unity of Tocqueville's associationalism, and they may develop a new approach for looking for patterns across the different forms of relationships that they investigate. These suggestions are not to scold political and social scientists, but rather these suggestions aim to point us toward a broader scope of inquiry. If Tocqueville and his associationalism truly matter to modern scholars and democratic societies, it is worth gleaning more than snippets and slogans from his thought.

TOCQUEVILLE'S HOPE AND OUR MODERN DEMOCRACIES

Tocqueville knew he had much to fear and hope for in democratic society (see Tocqueville 2010a, 28; 2010b, 1284). The worries of the scholars discussed in this chapter—the decline in associative life and the growth of the administrative state—were certainly among Tocqueville's fears for democratic society during the nineteenth century. He was not without hope, however, and he was optimistic that democrats could forge the mores of the future while respecting the wisdom of their communities. Modern democracies need not despair as long as they remain alert to the need for meaningful associative life. We may dispute and discuss what constitutes *meaningful* associative life, but as long as we hold fast to this important conservation, we, like Tocqueville, can remain hopeful. We need social scientists to continue this debate because, as Alan Wolfe reminds us, "[f]or all their tendency toward jargon and abstraction, the ideas of social scientists remain the most common guideposts for moral obligation in a secular, nonliterary age" (Wolfe 2000, 56). Democracy cannot do without guideposts.

If mores underpin associationalism, then it follows that we need to understand where these mores come from and what they are for. I suggest that these social science debates, which lay claim to Tocqueville, ought to continue to look to Tocqueville for more answers. For Tocqueville, women make mores in the domestic sphere. Contemporary sensibilities about gender have shifted, but I contend that gender roles and family must be a component of a thoroughgoing evaluation of associations. Unfortunately, research into the decline of social capital overlooks the impact of family life and gender roles, as evidenced by Putnam in particular. I also contend that our admiration for the benefits of competition between localities or associations, as exemplified by the Ostroms, should not distract us from the value of faithfulness to a particular locality, community, or group. Both loyalty to locality and the longevity of social norms within a particular locality are valuable to the making of mores in Tocqueville's associationalism. Finally, I suggest the work of mores to drag citizens out of themselves aims at a more profound moral goal than much literature on social capital and polycentricity currently suggests. On the whole, Nisbet's communitarian perspective appears the most Tocquevillian. Other traditions that conceive of themselves as Tocquevillian may continue to benefit from investigating the themes that Tocqueville raised.

Features such as technological change and market shifts may be ultimately inconsequential in the grand scheme of civil society in our modern democracies because, though they may be detrimental to some types of social capital, they may also breed unforeseen "forms of associational life" (Meadowcroft and Pennington 2007, 55).[5] Communitarians of Nisbet's ilk may dispute such optimism that older, small forms of social capital are so readily replaceable with new forms that can offer the same social value. Nisbet himself, however, was not overly nostalgic. He wrote that "[n]either science, nor technology, nor the city is inherently incompatible with the existence of moral values and social relationships which will do for modern man what extended family, the parish, and the village did for earlier man" (Nisbet 2000, 48). Our associations do not need to be inappropriately "antiquarian," but they do need to serve us as "traditional" ones have (Nisbet 2000, 36). In the meantime, Nisbet thought it worthwhile to adjust, with moderation, the forms of associative life that we already know can serve us well, rather than obliterate these forms through democratic passion or simple negligence. Wolfe concluded similarly that if modern society implies "a withering away of such institutions as the tight-knit family and the local community that once taught the moral rules of interdependence, modern people must simply work harder to find such rules for themselves" (Wolfe 2000, 66).

This may be a burdensome call to action considering the moral weightiness and intense intimacy of older forms of association. This conversation moving forward has to face difficult questions about our values. The position of women is the prime example. My critique from a Tocquevillian perspective forces us to question: Can we have Tocqueville's associationalism without Tocqueville's gender roles and traditional family life? Gender is an essential theme within his associationalism, and Tocqueville would contend that women, as makers of mores, are integral to a flourishing associative life. Perhaps, the only way moderns can have Tocqueville's associationalism without his gender roles is if we address very carefully the work that the gender roles were doing within his system. We must ask ourselves the stark question: Have modern democracies taken up this work, or have we let it fall by the wayside?

Because liberal democrats now tend to value equality of opportunity for women, we may simply have to acknowledge a social shift. An old way of operating, which strikes us as partly bad (because we value equality) and partly good (because we value a rich associative life), is lost. Talbot in her critique of Putnam concluded that this "trade-off may be worth it" when it comes to the loss in social capital due to women's empowerment (Talbot 2000). She called on men and women to work together to compensate. If we identify shifts, trade-offs, and new modes of association, if we understand how older forms of association served individuals, and, finally, if we call for mores that serve a free and flourishing future, then we *can* call ourselves truly "Tocquevillian."

At the end of *Democracy in America*, Tocqueville concluded that democracies cannot try to hold on to the "particular advantages" of aristocratic society and that the task of the modern age is to guarantee "the new advantages" of democratic society (Tocqueville 2010b, 1283). He wrote: "[w]e must not aim to make ourselves similar to our fathers, but to work hard to attain the type of grandeur and happiness that is appropriate to us" (Tocqueville 2010b, 1283). When it comes to gender roles, we no longer live by the standards of "our fathers," but we can "work hard" to provide, if by different means, a rich family and associative life.

We may ask ourselves what can replace gender roles and still fulfill the necessary work for a flourishing associative life. Steven Horwitz addresses the distinction between the "form" and "function" of the family in his work, highlighting the changing nature of the modern family in terms of gender roles and LGBTQ families (Horwitz 2015, 101–36). The most immediate solution in replacing gender roles appears to be an egalitarian division of childcare and domestic work between two parents who also operate in the public sphere. Men and women ought to equally divide the responsibilities of the private sphere so they can both enjoy equal status in the public sphere. Even though this may be our instinct, studies show that women, even after mass entry into the paid workforce, still assume responsibility for the majority of domestic duties (see Horne et al. 2017; "Women Shoulder the Responsibility of 'Unpaid Work'" 2016). As women are attempting to fulfill most of a private role as well as a public role, even among the most well-meaning and caring working mothers, it seems possible that the private role may become thinned. The moral work taking place at home may be at risk. This indicates that our modern democracies are still working on establishing new mores and modes of providing sufficiently for childcare and a rich family life. Future democracies may rethink their expectations of men and women, better divide domestic responsibilities between men and women, or, as grandparents increasingly live longer and in good health after retirement, establish a generational division of labor. The new norms remain malleable, and it is clear we live in a period of transition. Those who think of themselves as Tocquevillian should take care not to lose sight of these mores. Tocqueville's hope for democracy is hard work, but his thought can be a guide for political and social scientists undertaking this hard work as we examine our norms and make our mores.

I suggest that modern social science projects can benefit (even more than they already have) from the themes raised by Tocqueville's associationalism. My suggestion leaves us with a set of important questions. To the advocates of social capital and polycentricity, we may ask, can we move beyond the idea that Tocquevillian localism is simply efficient? In the face of social atomization and permissive exit options, can associations and localities that lack loyalty endure and continue to provide norms and social purpose? To the likes of Putman, we may ask, can we acknowledge the trade-off between an older form of associative life and women's participation in the public sphere? And to the future researchers of social capital, how do men and women share the burden of forming moral norms and social networks? Can we draw to the fore the idea of virtue, over efficiency, in considering social capital? Can we make mores "appropriate" to our age? In short, can we do the hard work? It is my hope that a thorough understanding of Tocqueville's associationalism, which raises additional themes beyond the simple efficiency of localism, can offer these vital questions to social science.

NOTES

1. For example, Coleman's analysis of how social capital within the family relates to children's educational attainment, see Coleman 2000.
2. See V. Ostrom 1997, 2014, 240; Sabetti and Aligica 2014, 3; V. Ostrom 2007, 147.
3. Francis Fukuyama has highlighted similar themes. He examines the role that authority and hierarchy play in the formation of trust and moral norms, reminding readers that without authority and hierarchy, a community has little power or clout in promoting ethical norms.
4. For religion and associative life, see Nisbet 2010, 225; Putnam 2001, 66–69; for religion and philanthropy, see Putnam, Campbell, and Garrett 2012, 444–54; for religion and the attainment gap, see Putnam 2015, 224; and for religious norms and the formation of American federalism, see V. Ostrom 1999, 53–68.
5. See also Putnam 2001, 180. For more on adaptation and technological change, see Munger 2018.

REFERENCES

Aligica, Paul Dragos, and Peter Boettke. 2011. "The Two Social Philosophies of Ostroms' Institutionalism." *Policy Studies Journal* 39: 29–49.
Arrow, Kenneth J. 2000. "Observations on Social Capital." In *Social Capital: A Multifaceted Perspective*, edited by Partha Dasgupta and Ismail Serageldin, 3–5. Washington, DC: The World Bank.
Berger, Peter L., and Richard John Neuhaus. 2000. "To Empower People: From State to Civil Society." In *The Essential Civil Society Reader: Classic Essays in the American Civil Society Debate*, edited by Don E. Eberly, 143–81. Lanham, MD: Rowman & Littlefield.
Boettke, Peter J., Jayme S. Lemke, and Liya Palagashvili. 2015. "Polycentricity, Self-Governance, and the Art & Science of Association." *The Review of Austrian Economics* 28: 311–35.
Boettke, Peter, Liya Palagashvili, and Jayme Lemke. 2013. "Riding in Cars with Boys: Elinor Ostrom's Adventures with the Police." *Journal of Institutional Economics* 9: 407–25.

Chambers, Simone, and Jeffrey Kopstein. 2001. "Bad Civil Society." *Political Theory* 29: 837–65.

Coleman, James S. 2000. "Social Capital in the Creation of Human Capital." In *Social Capital: A Multifaceted Perspective*, edited by Partha Dasgupta and Ismail Serageldin, 13–39. Washington, DC: The World Bank.

Ehrenhalt, Alan. 2000. "The Lost City: The Case for Social Authority." In *The Essential Civil Society Reader: Classic Essays in the American Civil Society Debate*, edited by Don E. Eberly, 239–55. Lanham, MD: Rowman & Littlefield.

Elshtain, Jean Bethke. 2000. "Democracy on Trial: The Role of Civil Society in Sustaining Democratic Values." In *The Essential Civil Society Reader: Classic Essays in the American Civil Society Debate*, edited by Don E. Eberly, 101–22. Lanham, MD: Rowman & Littlefield.

Fukuyama, Francis. 2000. "Trust: The Social Virtues and the Creation of Prosperity." In *The Essential Civil Society Reader: Classic Essays in the American Civil Society Debate*, edited by Don E. Eberly, 239–55. Lanham, MD: Rowman & Littlefield.

Galston, William A. 2000. "Individualism, Liberalism, and Democratic Civic Society." In *The Essential Civil Society Reader: Classic Essays in the American Civil Society Debate*, edited by Don E. Eberly, 353–72. Lanham, MD: Rowman & Littlefield.

Herzberg, Roberta Q. 2015. "Governing Their Commons: Elinor and Vincent Ostrom and the Bloomington School." *Public Choice* 163: 95–109.

Himmelfarb, Gertrude. 2000. "The Demoralization of Society: What's Wrong with Civil Society." In *The Essential Civil Society Reader: Classic Essays in the American Civil Society Debate*, edited by Don E. Eberly, 95–99. Lanham, MD: Rowman & Littlefield.

Hirschman, Albert O. 1970. *Exit, Voice, and Loyalty: Responses to Decline in Firms, Organizations, and States.* Cambridge, MA: Harvard University Press.

Horne, Rebecca M., Matthew D. Johnson, Nancy L. Galambos, and Harvey J. Krahn. 2017. "Time, Money, or Gender? Predictors of the Division of Household Labour across Life Stages." *Sex Roles* 78.

Horwitz, Steven. 2015. *Hayek's Modern Family: Classical Liberalism and the Evolution of Social Institutions.* New York: Palgrave Macmillan.

Kahan, Alan S. 2015. *Tocqueville, Democracy, and Religion: Checks and Balances for Democratic Souls.* Oxford: Oxford University Press.

Krishna, Anirudh. 2000. "Creating and Harnessing Social Capital." In *Social Capital: A Multifaceted Perspective*, edited by Partha Dasgupta and Ismail Serageldin, 71–93. Washington, DC: The World Bank.

Lemke, Jayme S. 2016. "Interjurisdictional Competition and the Married Women's Property Acts." *Public Choice* 166: 291–313.

Meadowcroft, John, and Mark Pennington. 2007. *Rescuing Social Capital from Social Democracy.* London: Institute of Economic Affairs.

Munger, Michael C. 2018. *Tomorrow 3.0.* Cambridge: Cambridge University Press.

Nisbet, Robert. 2000. "'The Quest for Community': A Study in the Ethics of Order and Freedom." In *The Essential Civil Society Reader: Classic Essays in the American Civil Society Debate*, edited by Don E. Eberly, 33–49. Lanham, MD: Rowman & Littlefield.

———. 2010. *The Quest for Community: A Study in the Ethics of Order and Freedom.* Wilmington, DE: Intercollegiate Studies Institute.

Ostrom, Elinor. 2000. "Social Capital: A Fad or a Fundamental Concept." In *Social Capital: A Multifaceted Perspective*, edited by Partha Dasgupta and Ismail Serageldin, 172–214. Washington, DC: The World Bank.

Ostrom, Vincent. 1997. *The Meaning of Democracy and the Vulnerabilities of Democracies: A Response to Tocqueville's Challenge.* Ann Arbor: University of Michigan Press.

———. 1999. *The Meaning of American Federalism.* San Francisco: ICS Press.

———. 2007. *The Intellectual Crisis in American Public Administration.* Tuscaloosa: University Alabama Press.

———. 2014. "A Conceptual-Computational Logic for Federal Systems of Governance." In *Choice, Rules and Collective Action: The Ostroms on the Study of Institutions and Governance*, edited by Paul Dragos Aligica and Filippo Sabetti, 227–41. Colchester, UK: ECPR.

Plattner, Marc F., and Larry Jay Diamond. 2000. "Introduction." *Journal of Democracy* 11: 5–10.

Portes, Alejandro. 1998. "Social Capital: Its Origins and Applications in Modern Sociology." *Annual Review of Sociology* 24: 1–24.

Putnam, Robert. 2001. *Bowling Alone: The Collapse and Revival of American Community.* New York: Simon & Schuster.

Putnam, Robert D. 2015. *Our Kids: The American Dream in Crisis.* New York: Simon & Schuster.

Putnam, Robert D., David E. Campbell, and Shaylyn Romney Garrett. 2012. *American Grace: How Religion Divides and Unites Us.* New York: Simon & Schuster.

Sabetti, Filippo, and Paul Dragos Aligica. 2014. "Introduction: The Ostroms' Research Program for the Study of Institutions and Governance: Theoretical and Epistemic Foundations." In *Choice, Rules and Collective Action: The Ostroms on the Study of Institutions and Governance*, edited by Paul Dragos Aligica and Filippo Sabetti, 1–19. Colchester, UK: ECPR.

Satyanath, Shanker, Nico Voigtländer, and Hans-Joachim Voth. 2017. "Bowling for Fascism: Social Capital and the Rise of the Nazi Party." *Journal of Political Economy* 125 (March): 478–526.

Stone, Brad Lowell. 2001. *Robert Nisbet: Communitarian Traditionalist.* Wilmington, DE: Intercollegiate Studies Institute.

Talbot, Margaret. 2000. "Who Wants to Be a Legionnaire? Review of Bowling Alone: The Collapse and Revival of American Community." *The New York Times Review of Books*, 25 June 2000. www.nytimes.com/books/00/06/25/reviews/000625.25talbott.html?mcubz=3.

Tocqueville, Alexis de. 2010a. *De La Démocratie En Amérique Vol. 1, Democracy in America: Historical-Critical Edition of De La Démocratie En Amérique: A Bilingual French-English Edition.* Edited by Eduardo Nolla. Translated by James T. Schleifer. Indianapolis, IN: Liberty Fund.

———. 2010b. *De La Démocratie En Amérique Vol. 2, Democracy in America: Historical-Critical Edition of De La Démocratie En Amérique: A Bilingual French-English Edition.* Edited by Eduardo Nolla. Translated by James T. Schleifer. Indianapolis, IN: Liberty Fund.

van Deth, Jan W., and Sonja Zmerli. 2010. "Introduction: Civicness, Equality, and Democracy—A 'Dark Side' of Social Capital?" *American Behavioral Scientist* 53: 631–39.

Wolfe, Alan. 2000. "Whose Keeper? Social Science and Moral Obligation." In *The Essential Civil Society Reader: Classic Essays in the American Civil Society Debate*, edited by Don E. Eberly, 51–67. Lanham, MD: Rowman & Littlefield.

"Women Shoulder the Responsibility of 'Unpaid Work.'" 2016. Office for National Statistics. 10 November 2016. https://www.ons.gov.uk/employmentandlabourmarket/peopleinwork/earningsandworkinghours/articles/womenshouldertheresponsibilityofunpaidwork/2016-11-10.

Chapter Three

Coping with Complexity

A Theory of Hayekian Interventionism

Alexander Schaefer

Before he had finished speaking to his paper, [Thatcher] reached into her briefcase and took out a book. It was Friedrich von Hayek's *The Constitution of Liberty*. . . . "This," she said sternly, "is what we believe," and banged Hayek down on the table.

—John Ranelagh (1991)

Margaret Thatcher was interrupting a member of the Conservative Research Department who was advocating a policy approach that blended free-market conservatism with progressive economic controls. This vignette, whether true or not, underscores a common misperception about Hayek's stance on economic intervention. Contrary to widespread opinion, F. A. Hayek supported active governmental involvement in the economy. In fact, according to Hayek, the principle of laissez-faire has likely "done more harm to the liberal cause" than any other idea (Hayek 2007, 71; see also Hayek 1980e, 110). When it comes to concrete policy proposals, Hayek's writings suggest ambivalence toward government programs, and he sometimes supports even programs that are vehemently opposed by other advocates of limited government.[1] In the more abstract areas of governmental activity, the creation of laws for example, Hayek's view is highly nuanced, recommending the use of both "spontaneous ordering forces," and direct legislative intervention (Hayek 1983, 89).

Nevertheless, Hayek deserves his credentials as an advocate of free markets and limited government. His enthusiasm for the market order, or *catallaxy*, persists as a common theme throughout his massive oeuvre. What makes the catallaxy a "marvel," according to Hayek, is its ability to solve the

fundamental problem of economics: utilizing knowledge that is widely dispersed, often inarticulable, and therefore inaccessible to any individual or
organization (Hayek 1980c, 77–91). Moreover, Hayek also recognizes the
existence of other such "spontaneous orders," for example, law and morality.
Intervention disrupts spontaneous order—at least in some narrow sense of
intervention—undermining the use of decentralized mechanisms of coordination, such as the catallaxy.

On the one hand, therefore, Hayek views intervention into decentralized
orders, such as the catallaxy, as inimical to their healthy functioning (Hayek
1980c, section VI). On the other hand, he envisions an important role for
government in managing a successful economy and, perhaps, by extension, a
successful society.[2] Reconciling these two aspects of Hayek's thought poses
an interesting challenge, one that runs into various contemporary debates
regarding the interpretation of Hayek's position.

Rejecting the claim that Hayek was careless and inconsistent in his dual
advocacy of spontaneous order and active government, this paper aims to
provide a reading that reconciles these two aspects of Hayek's thought.
While several passages in Hayek pose a challenge to interpreting his stance
on intervention, recognizing Hayek's theory of complex systems as a foundational element of his social and political thought harmonizes a great deal of
apparently conflicting claims. It thereby clarifies a Hayekian theory of intervention. Hayekian interventions are those that take full account of the epistemic challenges posed by complex systems, such as society. By contrast, the
interventions that Hayek most vehemently opposes exhibit a naive hubris
with regard to the management of such systems by treating them as if they
were similar to simple or "unorganized" systems (i.e., closed systems that
contain either few parts or low levels of interdependence between the parts).[3]
The aim of this chapter is not to defend Hayek's position in all of its particulars or to point out its shortcomings. Rather, I aim to shed light on one
fundamental aspect of his approach, his theory of complexity. This aspect
resolves certain tensions in Hayek's position and thus reveals a coherence in
Hayek's view that might otherwise go unnoticed.

In the next section, I will identify three of Hayek's arguments against
intervention, which I take to be his central objections to intervening in decentralized orders. The third section then presents some textual evidence that
Hayek supported interventions of various kinds and clarifies the puzzle of
reconciling spontaneous order with active intervention. Beginning in the
fourth section, I develop a complexity reading of Hayek's stance on intervention, first arguing that Hayek's arguments against active intervention are
grounded in his theory of complex systems and then showing that Hayek's
support for interventions of certain types also has a basis in his theory of
complexity. In particular, the fifth section proceeds by presenting close parallels between Hayek's remarks on policy reform and the policy approaches

advocated by contemporary complexity theorists. Before concluding, the sixth section applies these complexity considerations, revealing a coherent solution to the puzzle of section III, that is, the puzzle of Hayekian intervention.

HAYEK CONTRA INTERVENTION:
THREE CENTRAL ARGUMENTS

"Intervention" is used broadly in this chapter. It includes any conscious effort to affect emergent, system-level properties. Governmental central planning of production and consumption is a form of intervention since it supersedes the prices and decisions that emerge from the market process in order to achieve a particular result on a systemic scale. "Central planning" within firms is not intervention, at least so long as the goal is to maximize firm profits rather than to affect some property of the social order as a whole. The distinction is not between public and private: judge-made law is not intervention when judges restrict themselves to articulating the rules of a preexisting order, and firms might engage in intervention when they lobby for special legislation, such as tariffs or subsidies, that will affect the social order as a whole or even when they fund private campaigns that aim to alter the social order in some significant way.[4]

Hayek levels many objections against interfering in the voluntary activities of individuals and organizations within society in order to achieve system-level goals. These objections are often related by key themes in Hayek's work, such as the dispersal of information or the requirements of spontaneous order. The three arguments presented here provide one way to sort out Hayek's most salient objections to intervention. While this categorization is clarifying, its artificiality becomes apparent in the tight connections between these arguments. In fact, as section IV will argue, all three find support in Hayek's theory of complexity, which is, on my reading, the logical foundation of Hayek's views on intervention.

The Argument from Diversity and Authority

General rules allow cooperation among a diverse populace that could not agree on reasons for intervening that violate these rules. This argument, which constitutes the core of the *Road to Serfdom*,[5] turns on a contrast between systems based on centralized planning and systems based on unplanned orders, which emerge spontaneously from general rules, both formal and informal. In *The Road to Serfdom*, Hayek develops an impossibility proof, seeking to demonstrate an incompatibility between the values affirmed by socialist planners and the methods they propose to achieve those values. Without denying that their goals are laudable, Hayek claims that the methods they propose to attain these goals are unacceptable, not just to the opponents of socialism, but to socialists themselves. To be more specific, Hayek's socialist affirms the freedom and equality of each individual, on the basis of which he or she advocates a planned society that could ensure a just distribution of economic surplus. However, central planning requires, by definition, centralized direction of production and consumption. It thus removes such decisions from the sphere of personal choice and relocates them to an official body that will determine which purposes are worthy to receive support and funding and which are not. Consequently, such a system manages people and their productive energies as resources for the achievement of purposes, which they may or may not recognize. When economic decisions are to be made by a central body, then it is this body, rather than individuals, that must determine the relative importance of diverse and incompatible ends. This, Hayek argues, entails a rejection of freedom and an affirmation of unequal partiality (Hayek 2007, 128, 130).

Notice the role of diversity in this argument: individuals have diverse and incompatible preferences, yet in order to bring about its ends, a planning authority must "reduce the diversity of human capacities and inclinations to a few categories . . . and . . . disregard minor personal differences" (Hayek 2007, 130).[6] Modern, large-scale societies are full of individuals with diverse dispositions and competing values. Among individuals in such a society, "there will exist no agreement on the relative importance of their respective ends," and consequently, there is no agreed-upon criteria by which to evaluate social outcomes (Hayek 1978, 3; see also, Hayek 1997, 201–202).[7] Tellingly, Hayek suggests that, when society faces an existential threat, such as a major war with an aggressive and powerful opponent, the shared and overriding interest of survival softens the moral predicament of central planning (e.g., Hayek 1997, 122, 168). Our individual differences are superseded by a single goal. And when we are told to produce more guns and consume less butter in order to serve this goal, we will not object that we are being used for the purposes of others.

Encapsulating this argument, Hayek asserts that (1) socialist planners value freedom and equality but that (2) carrying out socialist plans (which dictate production and consumption decisions) is incompatible with respecting these values. Therefore, (3) society must choose between either entrusting some authority to determine the use of social resources or upholding the kind of freedom and equality that is possible only when individuals make their own decisions about how to use the resources that they produce or acquire.[8]

The Knowledge Argument

Knowledge is dispersed and tacit yet necessary for rational and efficient coordination, and only a spontaneous order is able to leverage such knowledge. Hayek is pointing to the sheer difficulty of acquiring the knowledge necessary to produce a rational economic plan for society (i.e., one that satisfies feasibility and efficiency). In particular, he draws our attention to the nature of the information that would be required to determine the relative trade-off ratios (viz. prices) between various goods and services. In essence, Hayek's argument is that the data required to determine rational trade-off ratios—data about the beliefs and preferences of individuals as well as of special skills of production and of resource availabilities—are always dispersed throughout society, often unknown to any single individual, and (most importantly) often lie tacit and inarticulable in their possessor. Moreover, the subjective data are constantly in flux, since interactions between individuals within the market process shape their beliefs and preferences (Hayek 1961). Consequently, the data can never be gathered and entered into the equations that would allow us to calculate equilibrium prices and quantities.[9]

The error of the prospective planner lies partly in the hubristic effort to supersede the existing rules, which constitute tacit knowledge (Hayek 2011, 77). It lies also in the implied subordination of dispersed centers of decision making to the decisions of the planning authority. Such subordination reduces the amount of knowledge available in making plans to the limits of a single consciousness (or to the limits of a planning board). Due to the dispersed and tacit nature of the data, these limitations are severe; economic planning conducted in this manner will be underinformed and, consequently, irrational (Hayek 1980c).

The Argument from Predictive Difficulty

Society is unpredictable and thus uncontrollable. Hayek's third argument against central planning rests on a distinction, first expressed in his 1955 "Degrees of Explanation," that marks a major advance in his thought between simple phenomena and complex phenomena.[10] Simple phenomena are systems composed of relatively few parts with relatively weak connections between these parts. Phenomena of "organized complexity," on the other hand, are systems containing a large number of connected and interdependent elements.[11] The character of such phenomena depends not only "on the properties of the individual elements of which they are composed, and the relative frequency with which they occur, but also on the manner in which the individual elements are connected with each other" (2014g, 365). Such systems exhibit strong feedback relations between their elements, resulting in special properties, such as sensitivity to initial conditions, network structures, and path dependencies. These properties undermine the possibility of precise predictions. For example, the relative benefits of a given phenotypic expression of a gene depend upon a massive number of other factors: the traits exhibited by other members of the same species, the traits exhibited by species inhabiting the same environment, the structure of interactions between various organisms, and even random events that affect organisms' fitness. Moreover, one organism's response to its environment constitutes part of the environment to which connected organisms must respond. When the relative fitness of traits exhibit such interdependencies, it is impossible to locate an optimal set of traits for an organism to exhibit, for by the time such an optimal set of traits is attained, the environment will have changed, likely rendering such a set suboptimal. In the terms of modern complexity theory, the fitness landscape is "dancing" (Page 2011, 93–94). It is thus impossible to predict the precise set of traits toward which a species will gravitate since this depends upon the massive number of reactive adjustments made along the way by other organisms inhabiting the same environment.

Although scientists recognize that it would be hopeless to apply the theory of evolution with the hopes of predicting the future genetic makeup of a given species, Hayek believes that economists fall into a similar error when they attempt to use economics to make precise predictions about society. As a phenomenon of organized complexity, a social system gives rise to events that "depend on so many concrete circumstances that we shall never in fact be in a position to ascertain them all" (Hayek 2014c, 269). Economists, in Hayek's view, ignore the complexities of social systems and, consequently, treat them as simple or unorganized systems, importing inappropriate methods from the physical sciences that lead them into serious errors.[12] This error leads social scientists to believe that they can predict and control social systems—yet, if societies are complex as Hayek argues, the supposed knowledge that prediction and control require is mere pretense.

To summarize the argument from predictive difficulty: (1) Only simple or unorganized systems are amenable to successful (precise) prediction. (2) Society is not a simple or unorganized system; it exhibits organized complexity. (3) Society is thus not amenable to successful (precise) prediction. (4) Successful (precise) control implies (precise) prediction. Therefore, (5) society cannot be successfully (precisely) controlled.

At this point, two caveats are in order. First, Hayek does not claim that *all* prediction is impossible in systems of organized complexity and, therefore, does not claim that all control is impossible. Rather, we are restricted to what he calls "pattern predictions," or equivalently, explanations in terms of general principles. Therefore, only interventions that depend on the accuracy of precise or long-term predictions are ruled out by his argument. This will become important when we turn to developing a theory of Hayekian intervention.

Second, unpredictability does not imply undesirability. Suppose, for example, that intervening into the normal functioning of social rules or the market process causes a brilliant scientist to direct her efforts toward developing a new technology that produces clean, renewable energy at stunningly low cost. Without such an intervention, imagine that she would have developed a new superweapon, instead, or perhaps a new shoe polish. Of course, we could imagine exactly the opposite scenario, in which intervention sacrifices the energy source for the shoe polish, but if interventions can produce incredibly good or incredibly bad results, then why the presumption *against* such interventions?

One response is simply to say that, if there is little to no prospect of achieving one's aim, then there is no point in incurring the costs of intervention. However, there is another response to this caveat, one that rests on Hayek's notion of spontaneous order. Like the organisms in an ecosystem, human beings and their various plans exhibit strong interdependencies. Mutual expectations and joint compatibility of diverse actions constitute a delicate equilibrium resting on a set of formal and informal rules of conduct. [13] Furthermore, the effectiveness of any given rule depends upon the other rules in place, just as the adaptiveness of any given species trait depends upon the traits of other organisms within the ecosystem. Altering social rules is thus disruptive in multiple ways. First, it disrupts the balance between expectations and actions in the same way that removing or adding a species to an ecosystem will disrupt the balance of the ecosystem. Second, it may alter or abrogate rules that contribute to the effectiveness of the other rules in place. Although it is certainly possible that intervening will leave an ecosystem intact, or even healthier, the fact that many species depend upon the continued, predictable activities of other organisms in their environment implies that altering ecosystems is generally harmful. Similarly, altering or abrogating rules generates confusion and disequilibrium, justifying Hayek's presumption against intervention in the absence of reliable predictions.

We have now completed our survey of Hayek's most salient arguments against intervention. It remains to catalog the various interventions he advocates (section III) and to consider how we might reconcile Hayek's aversion to intervention with the various interventionist measures he advocates.

THE PUZZLE OF HAYEKIAN INTERVENTION

As we have seen, Hayek presents a battery of challenges to the prospective central planner who wishes to control society by interfering in the lives and activities of individuals. Doing so clashes with our basic values of equality and liberty among a diverse populace, presumes the possession of unattainable information, and naively posits the ability to make precise predictions about the operation of complex systems. Arguments such as these support a typical reading of Hayek in which, as one commentator puts it, Hayek "directs his objections not only against attempts to 'organise' in a total or 'utopian' way but also against more modest 'interferences' with the order, which he alleges, always disrupt it" (Vernon 1979, 64). If this is correct, then as James Buchanan puts it, Hayek's view implies that "any 'constructively rational' interferences with the 'natural' processes of history are . . . to be studiously avoided. The message seems clear: relax before the slow sweep of history" (Buchanan 2001, 312; see also, Buchanan 2000, 211).

Yet, as I have already asserted, and as Buchanan recognized, Hayek's view is not so simple. In his most anti-interventionist work, *The Road to Serfdom*, Hayek complicates his image as a libertarian crusader in various passages. For instance, he rejects the terminology and the policy of "laissez-faire," he accepts regulation of various industries (citing concerns with safety and sanitation), and he even goes so far as to claim that free-market competition is compatible "with an extensive system of social services—so long as the organization of these services is not designed in such a way as to make competition ineffective over wide fields" (Hayek 2007, 86–87). Some might read Hayek as pandering to centrist readers since *The Road to Serfdom* was an attempt to influence public opinion. Hayek did, after all, dedicate it to "socialists of all parties." However, Hayek goes even further in his 1947 address to the Mont Pelerin Society, a venue that attracted an antisocialist audience. In this address, Hayek entertains or endorses a surprising array of government programs: sanitation and health services, monetary management (ideally via automatic mechanisms), welfare provision for the unemployed, city planning, intellectual property, antitrust laws and regulations on the size of corporations, temporary restrictions or regulations on international trade, and an inheritance tax to support social mobility (Hayek 1980e, 109–18). Some of these policies may be regarded as unfortunate concessions that Hayek makes in order to pursue the greater task of advancing an agenda of liberty. This address might be read as a pragmatic policy approach, rather than an outline of an ideally free society. Yet, even in his abstract and thoroughly unpragmatic work on political order, work that involves highly idealized accounts of the formation of laws and the operation of society, Hayek provides wide scope for intervention. Chapter 2 of *Law, Legislation, and Liberty* contains what may be the most challenging passage in all of Hayek's work for the anti-interventionist reading. Though long, it is worth quoting in its entirety:

> The fact that law that has evolved [spontaneously] has certain desirable properties does not prove that it will always be good law or even that some of its rules may not be very bad. It therefore does not mean that we can altogether dispense with legislation.

There are several reasons for this. One is that the process of judicial development of law is of necessity gradual and may prove too slow to bring about the desirable rapid adaptation of the law to wholly new circumstances. Perhaps the most important, however, is that it is not only difficult but also undesirable for judicial decisions to reverse a development, which has already taken place and is then seen to have undesirable consequences or to be downright wrong. The judge is not performing his function if he disappoints reasonable expectations created by earlier decisions. Although the judge can develop the law by deciding issues which are genuinely doubtful, he cannot really alter it, or can do so at most only very gradually where a rule has become firmly established; although he may clearly recognize that another rule would be better, or more just, it would evidently be unjust to apply it to transactions which had taken place when a different rule was regarded as valid. In such situations it is desirable that the new rule should become known before it is enforced; and this can be effected only by promulgating a new rule which is to be applied only in the future. Where a real change in the law is required, the new law can properly fulfill the proper function of all law, namely that of guiding expectations, only if it becomes known before it is applied.

The necessity of such radical changes of particular rules may be due to various causes. It may be due simply to the recognition that some past development was based on error or that it produced consequences later recognized as unjust. But the most frequent cause is probably that the development of the law has lain in the hands of members of a particular class whose traditional views made them regard as just what could not meet the more general requirements of justice. . . . But such occasions when it is recognized that some hereto accepted rules are unjust in the light of more general principles of justice may well require the revision not only of single rules but of whole sections of the established system of case law. This is more than can be accomplished by decisions of particular cases in the light of existing procedures. (Hayek 1983, 88–89)

At first glance, this passage is astonishing. How can the operation of spontaneous order be consistent with intentional and direct alteration of *whole sections of the established system of case law*? And if these are inconsistent, then how will such intervention not raise the issues that Hayek identifies in his arguments against intervention? Hayek appears to reject the gradual and evolutionary development of law—because it is *too slow* or is *recognized as unjust*—in favor of large-scale legislative interventions that exhibit all the serious failings of interventionist policies, some of which Hayek points out in the very same work.

In order to grasp the contours of this puzzle and the difficulties involved in developing an adequate interpretation of Hayek's position, it may help to encapsulate and review the key claims involved, resulting in two propositions that appear inconsistent at first face:

1. *Interventions cause great harm*: Interventions trammel on the freedom of citizens and deny their equal status; they prevent the use and coordination of vast stores of dispersed and tacit information; and, in the absence of reliable predictions and feasible control, they generate unpredictable consequences.
2. *Interventions of various sorts are compatible with or necessary for a healthy society*: Hayek entertains the desirability of various centrally administered regulations, welfare programs, and public services. He also asserts that spontaneous, judge-made law may evolve too slowly and it may require changes too extensive—due to mistakes or systemic injustice—to rely upon the quasi-evolutionary process by which law may arise spontaneously.

Between claims (1) and (2), there exists a clear tension, but is it an outright contradiction? This pair of propositions fixes the challenge for a theory of Hayekian intervention: *How do we avoid the pitfalls of intervention that Hayek established in arguments (i)–(iii) while also permitting the possibility of centrally administered policies and of direct legislative overhaul of the legal framework? How do we separate out those interventions that undermine society from those that support it?*

COMPLEXITY: THE UNIFYING CONCERN

To make sense of Hayek's stance on intervention, that is, to understand why he views certain interventions as salutary while others as disastrous, we must look closely at his reasons for opposing intervention. Although I have already laid out Hayek's most salient arguments against intervention (section II), there is an underlying theory that unifies these arguments and points toward a principled account of Hayekian intervention. I am referring to the theory of complex systems.

Hayek made pioneering contributions to the study of complex systems starting in 1955 with the publication of "Degrees of Explanation," and he continued to write on the topic throughout the following decades, most notably in "The Theory of Complex Phenomena" and "The Pretense of Knowledge." Hayek's characterization of complexity—as several commentators have noted (e.g., Vaughn 1999; Lewis 2017; Lewis and Lewin 2015)—mirrors contemporary characterizations of complexity. According to Scott Page, for example, complex systems are characterized by connected, interdependent, adaptive (or rule-following), and diverse entities (Page 2011, 25, 38). In virtue of their interdependencies, such systems exhibit network structures, feedback mechanisms, emergent properties, and path dependence. In his various writings on complexity, Hayek mentions every single one of these features. Although the theory of complex systems is currently a live research program and continues to undergo important developments, invoking this theory is therefore not anachronistic.

In what follows, I will argue that complexity theory constitutes a unifying thread between Hayek's three arguments against intervention. The point of doing so is to justify the approach of understanding Hayek's theory of intervention in terms of his theory of complexity. Accordingly, in the following section, I apply the complexity framework to develop a theory of Hayekian intervention. Our new focus on the problem of complexity will allow us to better explain both Hayek's general opposition to intervention and his advocacy of interventions of various types. The ultimate aim is to reconcile the apparently conflicting views that Hayek expresses toward interventions.

Hayek's first argument against intervention turns on the existence of diversity in society—in particular, diversity of purposes, preferences, beliefs, and other subjective data. If we all share a common goal, as Hayek seems to think we do when facing an existential threat, then the diversity in our respective ends diminishes significantly. Consequently, each individual becomes willing to accept his or her ascribed role in an organized plan of action. In such situations, the leader overrides peoples' individually chosen actions without forcing large numbers of individuals to sacrifice their ends for the ends of others because, in such rare and dire situations, individuals actually share a "common end," namely, survival.[14] A necessary condition for Hayek's conclusion in *The Road to Serfdom*, therefore, is a certain level of diversity and disagreement among individuals.

Where does this diversity come from and why is it so endemic to modern society? Contemporary complexity theorists, such as Brian Arthur, have argued that complexity actually *generates* diversity (Arthur 1994, 66–69). The phenomenon of complexity occurs when several interacting elements, tightly bound by what Hayek and others have called "feedback relations," interact and adapt to one another. As this interaction unfolds, new opportunities, or "niches," arise, allowing for the entry of new and different entities—different strategies, for example. These new entrants, by interacting with already established entities, generate yet further niches and so on, all coalescing into an upward spiral of diversity. Hayek outlines the proliferation of novel products and technologies as well as consumer preferences and beliefs in his essays on the market process. For Hayek, the key to understanding this process is to grasp that "[t]he problem becomes one of how the 'data' of the different individuals on which they base their plans are adjusted to the objective facts of their environment (which includes the actions of other people)" (1980d, 93). Crucially, the subjective data—preferences and beliefs—are in a state of constant flux due to "the acquisition of new knowledge by the different individuals or of changes in their data brought about by the contacts between them" (Hayek 1980d, 93–94). Thus, for Hayek, as for

Arthur, the interdependencies between individuals contribute to the emergence of novel beliefs, preferences, and strategies (including production methods) that drive the increasing diversity of our complex society.[15]

Diversity is not merely a consequence of complexity, but is also a contributing factor of complexity.[16] Contemporary complexity theorists have explored this connection, producing various models to illuminate the effect of diversity on complexity (Page 2011, 33–41).[17] Though Hayek never developed this relationship in detail, he does mention that complexity arises when the "the number of significantly connected variables *of different kinds*" is high (Hayek 2014b, 195, emphasis added). He also expresses awareness of it in his writings on market competition. In "The Meaning of Competition," for example, Hayek makes two points that, together, link diversity and complexity: (1) competition is most important under conditions of complexity, where the outcome is unpredictable (1980d, 93–94),[18] and (2) when various producers of a given commodity yield homogeneous products using similar methods—and, consequently, consumers have accurate and homogeneous beliefs regarding these products—"there is little need or scope for competitive activities" (1980d, 102–103). Putting (1) and (2) together suggests that we require competition in order to cope with situations where products and subjective data are diverse because such situations are more complex than situations characterized by greater homogeneity. Complexity and diversity thus exhibit a mutually reinforcing relationship for Hayek, and for this reason, complexity constitutes an important feature of his first argument against intervention.

Complexity also plays an important role in Hayek's second objection to intervention, the knowledge argument. Recall that this argument relies on the idea that important knowledge is dispersed and tacit (i.e., that individuals know their local environments and subjective data quite well but lack information regarding the environment and subjective data of others). What would prevent a central planner from acquiring this knowledge and using it to coordinate the plans of individuals from afar? In contrast to scientific knowledge, the knowledge informing economic decisions is often particular, rather than general; it is based on "temporary opportunities" and "circumstances of the fleeting moment" (Hayek 1980c, 80), which cannot possibly be collected, disseminated to, and processed by a planner in a timely fashion. Often, such knowledge is skill based, rather than theoretical, involving an intuitive sense of how to proceed under various contingencies and how to quickly acquire information that one does not yet possess. Consequently, the utilization of such knowledge depends upon leaving the relevant decisions to its possessor or making them with her active participation (Hayek 1980c, 80).

Hayek grants that achieving a *complicated* task, such as fighting a war or building a spaceship, poses little difficulty for an interventionist planner. The difficulty is when the task is not merely complicated, but *complex*. A paradigm example is that of achieving coordination or equilibrium among a vast number of individuals possessing diverse and interdependent knowledge, beliefs, and preferences. For Hayek, this task requires "the combination of fragments of knowledge existing in different minds [to] bring about results which, if brought about deliberately, would require a knowledge on the part of the directing mind which no single person can possess" (1980a, 54). Positing that centrally planned coordination faces insurmountable epistemic difficulties that arise due to the vast number of interdependent plans is tantamount to positing that the complexity of the situation—the large number of interdependent variables—renders the task of planned coordination impossibly difficult. As we have seen, in a relatively small or homogeneous group of independent individuals, the knowledge problem does not arise.[19] According to Hayek, it is under an extensive division of labor, in which individuals' plans "require corresponding actions on the part of other individuals" (1980a, 38), that we face the difficult challenge of coordinating the beliefs and behaviors of diverse individuals. It is the complexity of modern society that gives birth to the knowledge problem.

The connection between complexity and Hayek's third argument against intervention is the most direct of the three. The central premise is that, when dealing with society, our predictive powers face severe limitations. Society is a complex system, and predicting the behavior of complex systems requires vast amounts of information:

> The multiplicity of even the minimum of distinct elements required to produce (and therefore also of the minimum number of data required to explain) a complex phenomenon of a certain kind creates problems that dominate the disciplines concerned with such phenomena and gives them an appearance very different from that of those concerned with simpler phenomena. The chief difficulty in the former becomes one of, in fact, ascertaining all the data determining a particular manifestation of the phenomenon in question, a difficulty that is often insurmountable in practice and sometimes even an absolute one. (Hayek 2014c, 263)[20]

When systems exhibit high levels of interdependence between a large number of elements, predicting their behavior requires ascertaining a massive amount of information about the "initial and marginal conditions" (Hayek 2014c, 259). Obtaining such information is often beyond the realm of the feasible (Hayek 2014g, 370).

If we are limited in prediction, then we are limited in control. Pretending that we may manipulate society as if it were a simple system will lead to "deplorable effects" (Hayek 2014g, 368) since the attempt to control society will "impede the functioning of those spontaneous ordering forces by which, without understanding them, man is in fact so largely assisted in the pursuit of his aims" (Hayek 2014g, 371). The spontaneous order, Hayek's alternative to central planning, is essentially a method—accidentally discovered, unwittingly employed—for coping with complexity. By undermining the spontaneous ordering forces of society, intervention by a planning authority undermines our ability to deal effectively with the complexities arising from a diversified and highly interdependent society.

Understood this way, Hayek's view of society and intervention are fundamentally rooted in his theory of complexity. Diversity is its condition and its consequence. Coordinating a diverse and heterogeneous set of individuals, each of which possesses important, though inaccessible, knowledge is essentially a problem of complexity—that is, a problem that requires solving various connected, interdependent equations without having full access to the information such a solution would require. Furthermore, the paradigm of prediction-and-control breaks down when applied to society simply in virtue of its prediction-limiting complexity. We will now see that understanding the fundamental problem as one of complexity allows us to make sense of Hayek's position on intervention and allows us to reconstruct a theory of Hayekian intervention with deep affinities to the approach proposed by contemporary complexity theorists.

HAYEKIAN INTERVENTION AS A COMPLEXITY APPROACH

In the previous section, I argued that Hayek's theory of complexity is fundamental to his opposition to intervention. All three major arguments that Hayek levels against active intervention have some basis in his analysis of society as a complex system. Intriguingly, Hayek's theory of complexity also illuminates why Hayek finds certain types and methods of intervention less objectionable. Complexity-based issues present a hurdle to effective policy. Overcoming this hurdle, though not sufficient, provides a necessary check on interventionist proposals.[21] Contemporary complexity theorists, though their focus tends to be narrower, share Hayek's awareness that complexity constrains the feasible set of effective policy interventions. To better understand why Hayek accepts some interventions as, at least, worthy of consideration while viewing others as objectionable in principle, it is valuable to examine how these complexity theorists approach policy reform and how this approach parallels Hayek's in several ways. Although the complexity approach to policy remains underdeveloped (Colander and Kupers 2014, 6, 53), many complexity theorists have begun to explore the policy implications of viewing society as a complex adaptive system (Wilson and Kirman 2016; Colander and Kupers 2014; Axelrod and Cohen 2000). Like Hayek, these theorists emphasize the unpredictability of intervening in society and the importance of drawing on local knowledge and adjustments to bring about benefits for society as a whole. And, like Hayek, these theorists tend to emphasize the process of social evolution over the desirability of particular equilibrium states.[22]

The recognition that a complex society is unpredictable and dynamic has clear affinities with Hayek's way of thinking about society and intervention. The approach to intervention and public policy that follows from this picture of society reveals further similarities between Hayek and contemporary complexity theorists. Such similarities suggest that, at base, it is Hayek's theory of society as a complex system that gives rise to his particular views on intervention.

The remainder of this section will elaborate on some key themes in contemporary approaches to policy from a complexity framework. It will then show how these themes figure into Hayek's claims about proper and improper interventions, establishing Hayek's theory as one fundamentally concerned with the challenges and opportunities that complex systems pose for interventions of various sorts.

Key Themes in Contemporary Complexity Policy

One way of conceptualizing the nature of a complex system is to view it as a set of *epistatically* linked (i.e., interdependent) elements, different combinations of which facilitate different functionalities, or *service characteristics*, to different degrees.[23] A noncomplex problem lacks strong epistatic relationships between its variables or else has very few variables. For example, as Fredrick Taylor famously demonstrated, designing an ideal shovel is a simple problem: starting very small, as the shovel gets larger (as we change its elements), its capacity to move materials (its service characteristic) increases, peaks, and then steadily declines as size continues to grow. The problem of designing the optimal shovel generates a "Mount Fuji landscape"—one in which the parameters are unitary, or nonepistatic, resulting in an easily discoverable optimum. By contrast, society involves millions of variables that interact in various ways. Limiting our attention to the economy, various goods and services form an interconnected web of inputs and outputs, and consequently, the actions of each firm and of each consumer impinge upon the optimization problems of the others. Modifications to consumption patterns will affect the preferences, beliefs, and future behavior of consumers and producers. Tracing out the long-term effect of particular changes is impossible. Unlike simple problems, the landscape resulting from a complex problem is constantly shifting—as we change the values of certain variables in order to approach an optimum, this change in variables affects other variables both by altering the values they may take and by altering the contribution to service characteristics that these variables make. In the terminology of complexity theory, the result is a "dancing landscape." In the work of complexity theorists who address these sorts of problems, there are several recurring themes. To demonstrate the strong affinity between contemporary complexity policy and Hayek's views on intervention, I focus on three such themes.

(1) Contemporary theorists often recommend an incrementalist and experimental approach to reform. Imposing large changes on the complex system will yield wildly unpredictable results. Consequently, making global changes is tantamount to playing roulette with the functionality of the social order. Far better is to make marginal changes to existing policy to see how they affect the functionality of the current order or to conduct small-scale experiments on rule changes before introducing them on a larger scale. Smaller interventions minimize risk by generating smaller effects and by exhibiting greater reversibility.[24]

In the realm of complexity policy, the incrementalist approach finds wide expression. Charles Lindblom's famous essay, "The Science of Muddling Through," contains a classic statement of the incrementalist approach to policy, or what he calls the "branch method." According to Lindblom, there are too many important factors with too many interdependencies to engage in an exhaustive search for the globally optimal policy. Instead, we must be content with a procedure of "successive limited comparisons" (i.e., of marginal changes, the effects of which we evaluate according to provisional standards) (Lindblom 1959). More recently, evolutionary biologist and complexity theorist David Wilson has written:

> Selecting complex systems for group-beneficial outcomes is especially fraught with difficulties because interventions are likely to produce unintended consequences. According to some estimates, over half of change efforts in the business world make things worse rather than better (Schaffer and Ashkenas 2007). Given the pervasiveness of unintended consequences and cascading effects of interventions in complex social systems, there is no alternative to conducting careful experiments and scaling up practices that work. (Wilson 2016, 45)

Changes are likely to be disruptive in unpredictable ways. To protect ourselves from disaster, we must undertake only minor changes or else take steps to isolate the effects of these changes to subsections of the system.

This approach to intervention in complex systems faces important limitations. First, it applies only to systems characterized by *moderate* complexity, rather than *maximal* complexity or chaos (Gaus 2018). In a maximally complex system, each element has a strong connection to every other element. Consequently, even a small change to just one of the elements will generate dramatic changes at the system level. The result is radical uncertainty as to the effect of even the most minor reforms. Furthermore, since the small change will have altered the state of all elements in the system, rolling back the reform is not feasible. The experimental approach under such conditions has little to recommend it. By contrast, in a moderately complex system, small alterations of the elements lead to relatively small perturbations of the remaining elements. There is a strong correlation between the system state before and after a minor change. In such a system, marginal tinkering and experimentation are far more feasible.

In addition, the path dependence exhibited by complex systems can generate a second, almost opposite, limitation: an *inability* to perturb the system. Due to the possibility of becoming stuck as suboptimal local equilibria, marginal changes may be insufficient to dislodge a system from its current, undesirable state. How do complexity theorists propose to deal with the prospect of suboptimal equilibria that may require a more heavy-handed approach to reform? The answer to this question constitutes a second major theme in complexity approaches to policy.

(2) When large interventions are required to shift a complex system to a new equilibrium, we come up against the problem of predictability. Unless there is some way to quarantine the effects of changes in certain elements of the system, we can have little confidence that an intervention will make things better rather than worse. The idea of isolating effects of policy changes to subsections of the system points toward a second common theme in complexity-inspired policy theory: the idea of modularity (Simon 1962; D'Agostino 2009). Even if complex systems are made up of large numbers of epistatically linked elements, there may be a way to partition the system into relatively self-contained subsystems, or *modules*. Such a system exhibits *decomposability*. For example, the many parts of a car are, obviously, quite interdependent. A larger engine requires a chassis that can bear greater weight, the size of seats is limited by the interior space of the cabin, and so on. Nevertheless, it is not necessary to design all the parts together. We can have a team that designs and assembles the radio and that does so quite independently of the team that designs and assembles the engine. Each team has a much simpler problem to solve than a team that needs to consider the vehicle as a whole and can therefore proceed much more quickly to the optimal solution. As D'Agostino explains this approach, the trick "is not to attack such a problem head-on, but, rather, to divide it into parts, allocate the parts to teams, allow the teams to solve the resulting sub-problems, and then assemble the solutions discovered by these teams to provide an overall solution to the problem in question" (2009, 109).

The modularity approach is by no means a panacea. Even in relatively decomposable systems, such as our automobile, interdependencies between the modules may prove important (Axelrod and Cohen 2000, 107). Suppose, for example, that the ideal radio for the vehicle requires an electric current of 20 amps, but the ideal battery cannot produce this current—at least, not if we implement the proposed ideal headlights, wipers, wiring, GPS system, and vehicle weight. If the teams all go ahead and put their "ideal" modules together, the result will be a completely dysfunctional car.[25] Importantly, this means that certain elements within each module set limitations on the elements within other modules (or vice versa).

Despite these challenges, if a system is relatively decomposable, interdependencies between its modules can be addressed by imposing *design rules*. Design rules limit the search space *within* modules by fixing the variables that determine functionality *between* modules. So, for example, if one of the variables that the radio team must decide upon is the number of amps required, a design rule may fix this variable at a reasonable 14, while fixing the corresponding variable in the car battery at some number greater than or equal to 14. If each team observes these design rules as they go about searching for the optimal design of their module, then when we assemble the various modules we will, at least, have a functioning vehicle. And the existence of this solution is important. For, as Marengo and Dosi put it, "problem solving by boundedly rational agents must necessarily proceed by decomposing any large, complex and intractable problem into smaller sub-problems which can be solved independently" (quoted in D'Agostino 2009, 109).

(3) Echoed by many complexity theorists is the idea of addressing society as an organic, evolving entity, rather than a designed artifact (Colander and Kupers 2014, 55–58; D'Agostino 2009, 120–22; Gowdy et al. 2016, 327; Axelrod and Cohen 2000, xvi, 155). Attempts to achieve precise results or execute a detailed plan by manipulating individuals within society ignores the fundamental fact that individuals are unpredictable and that they interact in unpredictable ways. Although society cannot be effectively controlled, as one might control a computer program, there may be ways in which we can positively influence society by altering the conditions in which it evolves. A common metaphor is to compare the role of the policymaker to that of the cultivator, in contrast to that of the engineer. Policymaking, like gardening, is most effective when it leaves the organism (society) free to grow as its internal principles direct it, exerting influence only on the environment in which that growth occurs. In gardening, this means paying attention to soil, fertilizer, water, and sun. In society, this means paying attention to the incentive structures that individuals face with an eye toward the effect of their actions on the whole order.

Perhaps the clearest statement of this idea, one which brings it beyond mere analogy, emerges from David Wilson's distinction between two ways in which complex systems adapt and evolve: (1) CAS1, which refers to macro-level adaptations of the system as a whole, and (2) CAS2, which refers to the adaptive behaviors or strategies employed by the parts of the system (Wilson 2016, 31). Wilson, along with several coauthors, leverage this distinction in explaining the role of a policymaker when dealing with complex systems. Rather than disregarding CAS2 in an attempt to control CAS1 characteristics, the task is to align adaptation on both levels so that the adaptive behaviors of individuals, CAS2, actually lead to CAS1 adaptations, thus yielding benefits on the system level (Gowdy et al. 2016, 328, 330, 340). When this alignment occurs, the independent and often myopic behaviors of various individuals serve a purpose beyond their immediate aims, contributing to a flourishing society that benefits all. In short, the task of the policymaker is to tweak the institutions and the incentives they offer so as to actualize Adam Smith's proverbial invisible hand, in which each individual is "led . . . to promote an end which was no part of his intention" (Smith 1981, 456). Or, as expressed by two contemporary complexity theorists: "In the complexity policy frame, it is the result of a conscious attempt to develop an ecostructure without a central controller that is adequate to coordinate individuals' actions" (Colander and Kupers 2014, 59).

Hayekian Interventionism

Our examination of themes in complexity theory has revealed that approaching policy with social complexity in mind tends to promote skepticism about the policymaker's ability to *control* society without promoting skepticism about the policymaker's ability to *influence* society. Hayek's approach to interventions exhibits these same tendencies. In fact, his approach to intervention expresses many of the same central themes as contemporary complexity theorists.

(1) Consider, first, Hayek's version of incrementalism. In his presentation of the idealized evolution of law and of social reform more generally, Hayek posits that changes to rules should be gradual. Large changes in the rules will disrupt the ability of individuals to develop reliable expectations and thus to coordinate their actions. Accordingly, law should typically emerge from a judge whose main concern is not "what any authority wants done in a particular instance, but with what private persons have 'legitimate' reasons to expect, where 'legitimate' refers to the kind of expectations on which generally his actions in that society have been based" (Hayek 1983, 98). The judge, then, primarily seeks to understand an existing order so that she might determine what the most reasonable set of expectations would be within this order. In this sense, the judge is often not a creator of rules, but merely a student and an articulator of preexisting rules, which she formulates as explicit legal precedents. When situations arise where there is no preexisting rule that would determine whether one set of expectations is more reasonable than another, the judge is tasked with creating a new one. In such a situation, however, the change to the rules underlying the spontaneous order is relatively minor—it aims merely to fill in a gap in the existing rules and to do so in the least disruptive manner possible (Hayek 1983, 101).[26] The role of the judge, as Hayek's preferred source of laws and legal reform, is that of "mov-

ing within an existing system of thought" and to employ a method "of piece-meal tinkering" (Hayek 1983, 118).

The idea of *piecemeal tinkering* also appears in Hayek's account of moral reform. For example, in "The Errors of Constructivism," Hayek outlines what he takes to be a nonconservative but still responsible approach to moral reform:

> The proper conclusion from the considerations I have advanced is by no means that we may confidently accept all the old and traditional values. Nor even that there are *any* values or moral principles, which science may not occasionally question. The social scientist who endeavours to understand how society functions, and to discover where it can be improved, must claim the right critically to examine, and even to judge, every *single* value of our society. The consequence of what I have said is merely that we can never at one and the same time question *all* its values. (Hayek 2014f, 352)

By affirming or rejecting values in isolation, and doing so only in light of their compatibility with the rest of our values, we maintain the integrity of our current order and avoid drastic changes yielding unpredictable results.[27]

(2) Hayek assigns a special term, *immanent criticism*, to the method of evaluating particular rules or values only in light of their coherence within the total system of rules and values. The purpose of immanent criticism is "to make the whole more consistent both internally as well as with the facts to which the rules are applied" (Hayek 1983, 118), and in this capacity, immanent criticism points toward the way in which Hayek's interventionism exhibits a second major theme of complexity-based policy: modularity. Immanent criticism suggests that, when altering rules, we do not simply intuit what rule would be best, nor do we apply a simple criteria, based on a narrow set of concerns (as primitive versions of act utilitarianism would recommend). Rather, we take a system-level perspective and consider the connections between the rules we wish to modify and the other rules within the system. In complex systems, large changes yield unpredictable results, but as we have seen in discussing D'Agostino's work on modularity, if systems are relatively decomposable, large changes can be made within subsystems so long as design rules are in place to maintain compatibility between these subsystems. Does this idea find expression in Hayek's writings on intervention?

In Hayek's view, institutions and rules are at least somewhat decomposable in the sense explained above: there are subsets of rules that exhibit strong interdependencies among one another and weaker connections to elements in other subsystems.[28] As Hayek characterizes the *Great Society*, it is comparable to "a nucleus, or several nuclei, of more closely related individuals occupying a central position in a more loosely connected but more extensive order" (1983, 47). These loose partitions are made up of distinct but overlapping subsets of individuals and are also governed by different sets of rules. For example, the rules of a military are distinct from the rules of citizens, but because individuals are members of both categories, these sets of rules are not entirely independent.

This version of modularity provides a clue for making sense of Hayek's nonincremental interventions. For instance, when Hayek discusses nonincremental changes in the law undertaken by legislators, he is careful to emphasize the system-level perspective. These changes are desirable only in considering the incoherence between subsets of rules and the undesirable "dead end" to which inevitably path-dependent rule evolution can lead. Just as D'Agostino points out about *design rules*, when functionality considerations lead us to fix rules that connect two subsystems, this may create a path dependency by restricting searches to sets that satisfy this design rule. The law will not *evolve* in such a way that could alter this design rule since doing so in an effective manner would require a systematic or nonincremental alteration in the rules. As Hayek explains, "The development of case-law is in some respects a sort of one-way street: when it has already moved a considerable distance in one direction, it often cannot retrace its steps when some implications of earlier decisions are seen to by clearly undesirable" (Hayek 1983, 88). Legislation, when the suboptimal equilibrium is sufficiently obvious, can correct these path-dependent lock-ins because, unlike judge-made law, legislation is not confined to piecemeal tinkering. Notably, Hayek explicitly mentions that legislators should strive to understand the properties and requirements of the system as a whole and that this systemic perspective should influence their judgments; legislators must decide cases "in a manner appropriate to the function which the whole system of rules serves" (1983, 116; see also Mack 2006, 279–80).

Consider a difficult example for Hayek's conception of law: slavery. If the institution of slavery becomes entrenched in a society, the gradual evolution of judge-made law is unlikely to dislodge it. Too many expectations depend upon the persistence of this institution. In many countries, though not the United States, legislative intervention succeeded in abolishing the institution while minimizing the disappointment of expectations. The rules surrounding the ownership of slaves can be seen as a somewhat modular subsection of property law, which itself is a subsection of law in general, with important connections to other modules within the system of rules, including moral rules.[29] As moral rules and values evolved, slavery became increasingly incompatible with common opinion regarding basic rights and interpersonal rules of conduct.[30] Since laws emerge together, however, there existed tight connections between various laws (Hayek 1983, 65); case law had produced a lock-in effect, or path dependency, which was impossible to undo through *piecemeal tinkering*. Too many interests depended on the persistence of slavery. Too many plans had been laid on the assumption of its continued existence. And too many other laws (and legal precedents) depended on and supported the institution of slavery. Instead of piecemeal tinkering, a less gradualist intervention, one based on *immanent criticism*, was required. Thus, when Hayek advocates "the revision not only of single rules but of whole sections of the established system of case law," he is best understood as advocating a form of system-level or modularity thinking in which the compatibility between various subsets of values drives moral and legal reform.[31] This focus on immanent criticism explains why, when discussing the creation of new legislation, Hayek often points out that these reforms do not occur in a vacuum, but rather that "hereto accepted rules are unjust *in the light of more general principles of justice*" (1983, 89) (i.e., in light of other values and rules within the system or within connected systems). The legislator, just like the judge when he must create new rules, is focused on the system as a whole and on the order that it generates. In doing so:

> the only standard by which we can judge particular values of our society is the entire body of other values of that same society. More precisely, the factually existing, but always imperfect, order of actions produced by obedience to these values provides the touchstone for evaluation. (Hayek 2014f, 354)

(3) As for the third theme—that of cultivating, rather than controlling— Hayek advances a vision of intervention in perfect alignment with the viewpoint of modern complexity theorists. Just as contemporary complexity theorists criticize policy approaches that fail to take account of social complexity, ascribing labels such as "state control policy" (Colander and Kupers 2014, 44) or pointing out an undue focus on "allocation" rather than "formation" (Gowdy et al. 2016, 328), Hayek also criticizes more common ways of understanding the role of policy as a means of control (2014a, 163). Because we possess only knowledge of the principles of how complex systems operate and are thus limited to mere "pattern predictions," policymakers cannot predict and thus cannot control a complex system like society (Hayek 2014g, 365). Nevertheless, the policymaker may be in a position to support the ability of individuals to coordinate with one another and to pursue their respective ends. As Hayek explains in "Degrees of Explanation":

> Even if we cannot control the external circumstances at all, we may adapt our actions to them. And sometimes, though we may not be able to bring about the particular results we would like, knowledge of the principle of the thing will enable us to make circumstances more favourable to the kinds of events we desire. . . . An explanation of the principle will thus often enable us to create such favourable circumstances even if it does not allow us to control the outcome. Such activities in which we are guided by a knowledge merely of the principle of the thing should perhaps better be described by the term *cultivation* than by the familiar term "control"—cultivation in the sense in which the farmer or gardener cultivates his plants, where he knows and can control only some of the determining circumstances, and in which the wise legislator or

statesman will probably attempt to cultivate rather than to control the forces of the social process. (Hayek 2014b, 210)[32]

The main method that Hayek proposes for *cultivating* a successful society is to promote general, equal, and predictable laws, or what Hayek labels the *Rule of Law*. With such laws in place, the spontaneous order is likely to emerge from the interactions between individuals. The requirements of generality, equality, and certainty still leave ample room for variety. The policymaker should aim, within these constraints, to determine which policies best promote the capacity of individuals to interact in beneficial and predictable ways.

To borrow Wilson's terms, Hayek believes that the task of the policymaker is to set up conditions under which the behavioral adaptations of individuals, the CAS2 adaptations, promote positive change on the social level (i.e., generate positive CAS1 adaptations). But this requires understanding the nature and conditions of individuals' self-organizing capacities: "our main task must be to adjust our rules so as to make the spontaneous forces of society work as beneficially as possible. The first need in order that we should be able to do so is that we learn to understand the working of those forces" (Hayek 2014a, 192).

Hayek's comments on intervention therefore bear a striking resemblance to more contemporary views that approach policymaking from a complexity perspective. This resemblance appears in various forms; I have emphasized three key themes that characterize Hayek's viewpoint as well as that of more contemporary theorists. From a complexity perspective, incremental changes are typically better than large-scale ones. Yet, path dependency and lock-in may demand exceptions, and when exceptions must be made, complexity requires system-level thinking. Accordingly, policymakers must pay attention to any potential for decomposability within the system. Otherwise large-scale interventions are likely to severely disrupt the social order and to unleash a host of unintended consequences. Finally, the approach recommended by the complexity perspective is that of *cultivating* a successfully evolving order, of reconciling adaptations on the CAS1 and CAS2 levels, rather than attempting to *control* CAS1 characteristics directly. I have already suggested how complexity considerations may shed light on Hayek's seemingly oxymoronic position on intervention. Before concluding, the ability of complexity theory to reconcile Hayek's claims about intervention must be made more explicit.

ADDRESSING THE PUZZLE

Having seen that Hayek's theory of complexity sheds light on both his opposition to and his advocacy of interventionist measures, it remains to be seen if this new understanding can also aid in reconciling these two strands in Hayek's writings. Recall the two claims presented in section III that give rise to a perceived tension in Hayek's stance on intervention: (1) *Interventions cause great harm.* (2) *Interventions of various sorts are compatible with or necessary for a healthy society.* Taking (1) as given, how can Hayek endorse (2)? To examine this issue, consider two different types of intervention that Hayek discusses: governmental programs and legal or institutional reform. Reading Hayek as a complexity theorist provides the key to resolving the tension that arises with regard to both types of intervention.

First consider particular governmental programs, such as a social safety net or the provision of public goods. Whether or not such programs create harmful disturbances in a complex system may depend on how they are implemented and how they interact with currently existing laws and norms. Hayek has relatively little to say about the implementation of these programs, but his comments on the importance of piecemeal tinkering as well as imma-nent criticism suggest that a Hayekian intervention would refrain from im-posing large-scale programs or regulations that would be both disruptive and unpredictable. Instead, small changes or small-scale implementation better fits the Hayekian vision of policy aimed at facilitating reliable expectations and interpersonal coordination under conditions of complexity.

Even with this approach to implementation, however, certain policies are simply off the table for Hayek. As Hayek explains in his Cairo lectures, "all laws and institutions which offend against the ideal of the Rule of Law are objectionable in principle, while any law which conforms to it will have to be judged on its individual merits" (Hayek 2014a, 178). A necessary condition for any policy or rule change is that it satisfy three conditions of the Rule of Law: generality, equality, and certainty (Hayek 2014a, 172). Although there are many ways in which a law or policy can be harmful, if interventionist activities are restricted by generality, equality, and certainty, then the indi-vidual retains the ability to respond to a reasonably predictable environment, one insulated from the whims of authority (Hayek 2014a, 178).[33] The thought is that, given the unpredictability of complex systems, restricting laws in this manner is necessary in order to "make the world around us a more familiar world in which we can move with greater confidence that we shall not be disappointed because we can at least exclude certain eventual-ities" (Hayek 2014b, 209–10).[34]

Admittedly, this account places a heavy burden on a somewhat dubious distinction—interferences that satisfy the Rule of Law and those that do not. Hayek claims that price-fixing, for example, cannot satisfy the Rule of Law (2014a, 180). Yet price-fixing might be applied in a manner that is general (applying to all cases that are relevantly similar), equal (applying equally to all citizens), and certain (predictably applied). Given that the policy implica-tions of complexity theory are still being explored and debated, it is perhaps unsurprising that Hayek's early treatment falls short of perfection. Still, it would be rather scandalous if Hayek's theory lacked the resources to distinguish between the interventions he entertains and those he claims are simply out of the question.

A more helpful distinction than that between laws that do and laws that do not satisfy the Rule of Law is the distinction between principle and expedience. Although this distinction appears briefly in the Cairo lectures (Hayek 2014a, 180), Hayek develops it further in volume one of *Law, Legislation, and Liberty*. Principles are inchoate rules, delimiting which concerns do and which do not permit a change in the laws (Hayek 1983, 55). Their purpose is to supersede case-by-case assessment of particular actions or policies, which would lead to myopic decision making, taken in the heat of the moment.[35] Expedience, on the other hand, focuses not on the sorts of considerations that may justify a rule change but on the desired outcome to be achieved (Hayek 2014a, 180). In Hayek's view, principles lead to predictable "interventions," consistent with the functioning of a spontaneous order in complex systems, while decisions based on expediency are unpredictable and thus undermine the formation of spontaneous order. Recalling the third theme of the complexity approach, we see that *expedience*, in virtue of its specific goals, leads to attempts at control, rather than cultivation. Principle-based policy, on the other hand, lacks *specific* purposes for particular persons, seeking instead to facilitate an "order of actions," which promotes the ability of individuals to pursue their own diverse plans.

This distinction clarifies how many economic controls, such as price-fixing, fall outside the realm of acceptable interventions. If we are constrained to apply rules only in light of principles, not considering immediate expedience, then price controls lack appeal. For why would one endorse a policy of price control if not to benefit a particular group at a particular time (i.e., on the basis of *expedience*)?[36] A price control may help a select group of sellers, but it does so at the expense of other prospective sellers, of consumers, and ultimately of economic efficiency.[37] The only reason to institute such a policy is to achieve a particular purpose at a particular time—but, as we have seen, such endeavors are incompatible with facing the challenges of social complexity since they undermine the expectations of interacting individuals. While ruling out many of the interventions that Hayek opposes, this *principle–expedience* distinction seems to allow for many toward which Hayek is more ambivalent: for example, a social safety net and the provision or regulation of public goods. As Hayek recognized, exactly which interventions are or are not justified by principles is debatable. Where Hayek is confident is in his assertion that, when evaluating the acceptability of a policy on the basis of a principle, complexity considerations play a central role. In order to function under conditions of complexity, society must facilitate accurate expectations and interpersonal coordination. It cannot do so when expediency, rather than principle, drives policy.

Hayek's theory of complexity also suggests a reconciliation between his support for both spontaneous order and direct legislative intervention. A crucial point, which has been implicit, is that a spontaneous order is distinct and separable from the spontaneous origin of the laws that give rise to it: "while the rules on which a spontaneous order rests may also be of spontaneous origin, this need not always be the case . . . it is at least conceivable that the formation of a spontaneous order relies entirely on rules that were deliberately made" (Hayek 1983, 45).[38] This is why Hayek need not rule out legislative intervention: rules are not good or bad in virtue of their *source*, but rather, in virtue of their *form*. Do they or do they not allow us to cope with complexity by enabling individuals to develop accurate expectations and to succeed in coordinating their activities? Importantly, Hayek does not say that laws or legislation are incompatible with spontaneous order; he says that *commands* are:

> It is advisable . . . not to confuse laws and commands. . . . The important difference between the two concepts lies in the fact that, as we move from commands to laws, the source of the decision on what particular action is to be taken shifts progressively from the issuer of the command or law to the acting person. (Hayek 2011, 218)

While commands are appropriate for organizations in which members are directed by a central authority and work toward a single goal, they cannot engender a spontaneous order of actions in which individuals pursue their own ends and are coordinated by formal rules that do not specify particular ends.[39] The legislator who finds it necessary to correct an evolutionary "dead end" in case law need not issue commands and therefore need not undermine the spontaneous order or mold society as a whole into the form of an organization. Instead, the legislator can restrict new rules to the form of laws. Combined with the complexity considerations covered in section V—specifically, the system-level thinking of immanent criticism and the potential for focusing on modules within the system of rules—this distinction between commands and laws reveals how legislative reform of "whole sections of the established system of case law" is less drastic and disruptive than it sounds. By isolating these "sections" into relatively self-contained modules while also focusing on important connections these modules have to other sections of the system of law, the legislator can maintain or even enhance the ability of individuals to form expectations and to coordinate, at least so long as the legislator issues bona fide laws and avoids the temptation to issue commands.

On the flip side, it is precisely due to complexity that such heavy-handed interventions sometimes become necessary. Complex systems are characterized, in part, by positive feedbacks and path dependence (Arthur 2014, 13–14; Marengo and Dosi 2005, 310). For this reason, Hayek explains, "spontaneous process of growth may lead into an impasse from which it cannot extricate itself by its own forces or which it will at least not correct quickly enough" (Hayek 1983, 88; see also Vaughn 1999, 249). In correcting such undesirable directions of growth, a prevailing concern is to maintain society's ability to spontaneously order itself; policy is to be "directed toward the securing of an abstract overall order" (Hayek 1978, 114). Hayek's concern with this order of actions, so crucial to interpersonal coordination in a complex system, again motivates his emphasis on principle over expediency. Aiming at particular outcomes, as expediency dictates, would yield policies and rules incompatible with the requirements and limitations presented by complex systems. Laws based on principle, on the other hand, are better suited to decentralize decision making to dispersed actors, thereby supporting the spontaneous forces that give rise to the order of actions.

Hayek the laissez-faire marketeer is an urban legend. Yet his writings express a strong anti-interventionist streak. Concerns with diversity, with knowledge, and with predictability lead him to conclude that interventions are often harmful and unjustified. To focus only on this aspect of his position, however, is to mistakenly view his stance on intervention as one of unequivocal opposition. In fact, there are many interventions that Hayek believes are worth considering, interventions that cannot be ruled out on principle. To understand Hayek's views on intervention requires that we search out exactly what divides those interventions that one can rule out on principle from those that must stand or fall on the basis of a consideration of their particular merits. To this end, I have suggested that we pay closer attention to Hayek's theory of complexity and how his understanding of society as a complex system underlies his stance on intervention. Complexity provides insight into why certain interventions—those that do not disrupt spontaneous order—are permissible. Whether or not Hayek's complexity approach to intervention is fully satisfactory, considering his position in light of complexity certainly contributes to our understanding of statements that otherwise appear capricious or contradictory. The restrictions Hayek places on intervention closely track restrictions on successful intervention into a complex society. Those he allows are those that maintain our capacity to cope with complexity.

NOTES

1. Ayn Rand criticizes Hayek for making excessive concessions in a letter she wrote to the founder of the magazine *The Freeman*, claiming that he, along with other "compromisers,"

does "more good to the communist cause" than to the case for laissez-faire (see Rand 1995, 299). Walter Block (1996) has criticized Hayek's *Road to Serfdom* on similar grounds. Hans Hermann-Hoppe is another prominent member of this group.

2. Given Hayek's rejection of an overarching goal for society, exactly what counts as "success" is a controversial question. Eric Mack suggests that Hayek provides a "telic" justification of rules and institutions in which they aim at an abstract order of actions, as opposed to a concrete outcome. Success would then mean the successful facilitation of this spontaneous order (see Mack 2006).

3. Though I lack the space to discuss this, understanding Hayekian intervention also sheds light on interpretive difficulties concerning spontaneous orders. Spontaneous orders provide a means of coping with complexity, and in this capacity resides their desirability. Accordingly, we can better understand the notion of a spontaneous order by focusing on Hayek's theory of complexity, which clarifies the social function of such orders.

4. There are tricky questions here that I pass over. Doesn't order sometimes arise spontaneously on a local or micro level? If so, then why wouldn't attempts to control these small-scale, nonsystemic orders qualify as intervention? Some macro-level properties, such as the organization of national defense, seem to be systemic but not spontaneous. Attempts to control such systems are not Hayek's concern and should not be seen as "interventions." While exploring these issues in greater depth would surely aid in understanding Hayek's position, answering them is outside the purview of this paper.

5. Hayek offers a distinct argument that relies on premises so similar that I regard it as a second version of the argument just canvassed. This argument occurs in *The Constitution of Liberty*, and it concerns the difficulty of reconciling authority with diversity or, more precisely, of reconciling the authority of law with the freedom of individuals to pursue their diverse ends. This argument differs from the first variant in its more central use of the key concepts of law, command, and Rule of Law. Similarly to the first variant, however, diversity of ends and interests plays an important role in vindicating the premises (Hayek 2011, 217–19, 221).

6. Notice that Hayek usually speaks in terms of values or inclinations, rather than preferences. The term "preferences" has the advantage of avoiding the psychological or ethical baggage that Hayek's terms lug with them.

7. For an excellent discussion on this issue, see Mack 2006, 261, 271, 274. See also Gaus 2018, 5.

8. To complete the argument, Hayek spends much of the book presenting reasons to prefer this kind of freedom and equality to the ends that socialist planning might successfully achieve. One such reason is the difficulty that a planner would have in actually achieving these ends, meaning that our freedom and equality will have been sacrificed for comparatively little. This aspect of the argument is discussed under the third category of arguments, the "prediction-control argument."

9. As Hayek (2014g) explains: "It is true that their systems of equations describing the pattern of a market equilibrium are so framed that *if* we were able to fill in all the blanks of the abstract formulae, that is, *if* we knew all the parameters of these equations, we could calculate the prices and quantities of all commodities and services sold. But as Vilfredo Pareto, one of the founders of this theory, clearly stated, its purpose cannot be 'to arrive at a numerical calculation of prices,' because, as he said, it would be 'absurd' to assume that we could ascertain all the data" (366).

10. For a brief history of this turning point, see Bruce Caldwell, "Introduction," in *The Market and Other Orders*, ed. Bruce Caldwell (Chicago: University of Chicago Press, 2014), pp. 14–15.

11. Hayek identifies a third category of phenomena, those of "unorganized complexity," which, though comprised of many entities, can be analyzed purely in terms of (1) the properties of the entities the phenomena comprise and (2) "the relative frequency" of these entities. Such phenomena can be studied using standard statistical methods (Hayek 2014g, 365).

12. Hayek refers to this as the error of "scientism," which "involves a mechanical and uncritical application of habits of thought to fields different from those in which they have been formed" (Hayek 2010, 80).

13. "The spontaneous order arises from each element balancing all the various factors operating on it and by adjusting all its various actions to each other, a balance which will be destroyed if some of the actions are determined by another agency on the basis of different knowledge and in the service of different ends" (Hayek 1983, 51).

14. This is not to claim *full* homogeneity of ends. Obviously, there are still pacifists, and some individuals will bear greater burdens than others.

15. As Hayek explains elsewhere, "the tastes of man, as is also true of his opinions and beliefs and indeed much of his personality, are shaped in a great measure by his cultural environment" (1961, 347).

16. Hayek claims that society is a complex system of the elements of which are complex systems. See Hayek 1952, 19, 43ff, 185ff, and Lewis, forthcoming.

17. Page discusses a prisoner's dilemma model that becomes complex with the addition of diverse players. The model is developed in Nowak and May (1993).

18. Hayek does not use the word "complex" in this discussion since it predates his use of that terminology. Nevertheless, he points to the concept that he will later call complexity by referring to the "contacts between" individuals resulting in a "process of continuous change" in those interacting individuals. He also introduces complexity into the discussion in his later essay on the market process (Hayek 2014e).

19. Hence, Hayek postulates (perhaps incorrectly) that small, tribal societies are run like organizations rather than relying on spontaneous orders, like larger societies that exhibit deep division of labor (1983, 77).

20. See also Hayek 2014b, 211: "the more we move into the realm of the very complex, the more our knowledge is likely to be of the principle only, of the significant outline rather than of the detail. Especially where we have to deal with the extreme complexity of human affairs, the hope of ever achieving specific predictions of particulars seems vain."

21. Showing that the ideal policy is consistent with societal complexity does not show that such a policy is likely to emerge from the political process. Indeed, Hayek was a forerunner of public choice economics, often pointing out the perverse incentives that government actors face. In *The Road to Serfdom*, for example, Hayek argues that an ample sphere of government action will lead to interest group conflicts and will attract unsavory character types into government positions. We must therefore recognize that policy formulation and implementation are subject to the influence of interest group lobbying and to that of politicians with little to no regard for public welfare. For a discussion of Hayek and public choice, see Leeson and Boettke 2003.

22. Especially interesting in this respect is Brian Arthur's pioneering work on "complexity economics," which is replete with Hayekian themes. See, for example, Arthur 2014, 16.

23. This terminology is borrowed from Fred D'Agostino (2009).

24. The danger of making systemic changes under conditions of complexity has been expressed in various disciplines. The economic historian Robert Allen, for example, blames the failure of Soviet planning largely on the severity of its mistakes, which were not isolated to a single firm but were applied on a system-wide scale (Allen 2009).

25. As D'Agostino explains, "It cannot be guaranteed, in other words, that a composite object formed from four subsystems which were optimized locally would itself be either technically feasible or globally optimal in its service characteristics" (2009, 112).

26. An additional way in which judges improve the law in an incremental fashion is simply by messing up: errors in articulating the rules that undergird the order of society function like random genetic mutations in a species. Those that are beneficial will tend to stick around; those that are not will tend to dissipate (D'Agostino 2009, 78).

27. Importantly, "values" is a term that Hayek uses *very* broadly. It refers also to what we would call rules, rights, and duties. See Hayek 2014f, 343.

28. Hayek expresses the idea of modularity in a very different context while discussing complex systems: "What we single out as wholes, or where we draw the partition boundary will be determined by the consideration whether we can thus isolate recurrent patterns of coherent structure of a distinct kind which we do in fact encounter in the world in which we live. . . . The coherent structures in which we are mainly interested are those in which a complex pattern has produced properties which make self-maintaining the structure showing it" (2014b, 362).

29. The qualification "somewhat" is important in this sentence. The rules surrounding slavery had important cultural, economic, and political connections to other rules in the system. I thank Gerald Gaus for calling attention to this important fact.

30. This is not to claim that increased moral awareness was the sole, or even the primary, factor that caused the abolition of slavery, though it does seem to have been a necessary condition or, at least, contributing factor in many places.

31. Notably, Hayek explicitly mentions that judges should strive to understand the properties and requirements of the system as a whole and that this systemic perspective should influence their judgments in controversial cases: the judge must decide cases "in a manner appropriate to the function which the whole system of rules serves" (1983, 116). See also Mack 2006, 279–80.

32. Hayek (2007) also uses this metaphor in *The Road to Serfdom*: "The attitude of the liberal toward society is like that of the gardener who tends a plant and, in order to create the conditions most favorable to its growth, must know as much as possible about its structure and the way it functions" (71).

33. Although this leaves room for "objectionable forms of oppression," policies that are oppressive without violating the Rule of Law must be opposed on grounds distinct from the fact that they intervene in the actions of individuals.

34. See also Lewis and Lewin 2015, 27–29.

35. See Mack 2006, 275–76.

36. The connection between principles and general or impartial benefit helps to explain why Hayek endorses the veil of ignorance construction employed by John Rawls (Hayek 1978, xiii). From an ex ante position characterized by uncertainty, individuals would choose principles that work well on average, rather than the approach of making decisions on a case-by-case basis (Hayek 1978, chapter 10). See also Mack 2006, 282.

37. For an analysis of the costs of price controls that goes beyond typical textbook treatments, see Colander et al. 2010 or Coyne and Coyne 2015.

38. Even some of Hayek's best students seem to miss this important point. See, for example, Mack 2006, 262, 264, 280.

39. Organizations can, however, exist within spontaneous orders. Thus, a spontaneous order may have many commands operating, even though these commands are not the rules that facilitate its emergence.

REFERENCES

Allen, Robert. 2009. "The Soviet Climacteric." In *Farm to Factory: A Reinterpretation of the Soviet Industrial Revolution*, 189–211. Princeton, NJ: Princeton University Press.

Arthur, Brian. 2014. "Complexity Economics: A Different Framework for Economic Thought." In *Complexity and the Economy*, 1–30. Oxford: Oxford University Press.

———. 1994. "On the Evolution of Complexity." In *Complexity: Metaphors, Models, and Reality*, edited by G. Cowan, D. Pines, and D. Meltzer, 65–77. Boulder, CO: Westview Press.

Axelrod, Robert, and Michael D. Cohen. 2000. *Harnessing Complexity*. New York: Basic Books.

Block, Walter. 1996. "Hayek's Road to Serfdom." *Journal of Libertarian Studies*, vol. 12, no. 2: 339–65.

Buchanan, James. 2001. "Cultural Evolution and Institutional Reform." In *Federalism, Liberty, and the Law*, 302–25. Indianapolis, IN: Liberty Fund, Inc.

———. 2000. *The Limits of Liberty*. Indianapolis, IN: Liberty Fund, Inc.

Colander, David, Sieuwerd Gaastra, and Casey Rothschild. 2010. "The Welfare Costs of Market Restrictions." *Southern Economic Journal*, vol. 77, no. 1 (July): 213–23.

Colander, David, and Roland Kupers. 2014. *Complexity and the Art of Public Policy: Solving Society's Problems from the Bottom Up*. Princeton, NJ: Princeton University Press.

Coyne, Christopher, and Rachel Coyne. 2015. *Flaws & Ceilings: Price Controls and the Damage They Cause*. London: IEA.

D'Agostino, Fred. 2009. "From the Organization to the Division of Cognitive Labor." *Politics, Philosophy & Economics*, vol. 8, no. 1: 101–29.

Gaus, Gerald. 2018. "Hayekian 'Classical' Liberalism." In *The Routledge Handbook of Libertarianism*, edited by Jason Brennan, Bas van der Vossen, and David Schmidtz, 34–52. New York: Routledge.

Gowdy, John, Mariana Mazzucato, Jeroen C. J. M. van den Bergh, Sander E. van der Leeuw, and David S. Wilson. 2016. "Shaping the Evolution of Complex Societies." In *Complexity and Evolution: Toward a New Synthesis for Economics*, edited by David S. Wilson and Alan Kirman, 327–51. Cambridge, MA: MIT Press.

Hayek, Friedrich. 2014a. "The Political Ideal and the Rule of Law." In *The Market and Other Orders*, edited by Bruce Caldwell, 119–94. Chicago: University of Chicago Press.

———. 2014b. "Degrees of Explanation." In *The Market and Other Orders*, edited by Bruce Caldwell, 195–212. Chicago: University of Chicago Press.

———. 2014c. "The Theory of Complex Phenomena." In *The Market and Other Orders*, edited by Bruce Caldwell, 257–77. Chicago: University of Chicago Press.

———. 2014d. "Notes on the Evolution of Systems of Rules of Conduct." In *The Market and Other Orders*, edited by Bruce Caldwell, 278–92. Chicago: University of Chicago Press.

———. 2014e. "Competition as a Discovery Procedure." In *The Market and Other Orders*, edited by Bruce Caldwell, 304–13. Chicago: University of Chicago Press.

———. 2014f. "The Errors of Constructivism." In *The Market and Other Orders*, edited by Bruce Caldwell, 338–56. Chicago: University of Chicago Press.

———. 2014g. "The Pretense of Knowledge." In *The Market and Other Orders*, edited by Bruce Caldwell, 362–72. Chicago: University of Chicago Press.

———. 2011. *The Constitution of Liberty: The Definitive Edition*. Edited by Ronald Hamowny. Chicago: University of Chicago Press.

———. 2010. "Scientism and the Study of Society." In *Studies on the Abuse and Decline of Reason*, edited by Bruce Caldwell, 77–168. Chicago: University of Chicago Press.

———. 2007. *The Road to Serfdom: Text and Documents*. Edited by Bruce Caldwell. Chicago: University of Chicago Press.

———. 1997. "Freedom and the Economic System." In *Socialism and War: Essays, Documents, Reviews*, edited by Bruce Caldwell, 189–211. Chicago: University of Chicago Press.

———. 1983. *Law, Legislation, and Liberty Volume 1: Rules and Order*. Chicago: University of Chicago Press.

———. 1980a. "Economics and Knowledge." In *Individualism and Economic Order*, 33–36. Chicago: University of Chicago Press.

———. 1980b. "The Facts of the Social Sciences." In *Individualism and Economic Order*, 57–76. Chicago: University of Chicago Press.

———. 1980c. "The Use of Knowledge in Society." In *Individualism and Economic Order*, 77–91. Chicago: University of Chicago Press.

———. 1980d. "The Meaning of Competition." In *Individualism and Economic Order*, 92–106. Chicago: University of Chicago Press.

———. 1980e. "Free Enterprise and Competitive Order." In *Individualism and Economic Order*, 107–118. Chicago: University of Chicago Press.

———. 1978. *Law, Legislation, and Liberty Volume 2: The Mirage of Social Justice*. Chicago: University of Chicago Press.

———. 1961. "The Non Sequitur of the 'Dependence Effect.'" *Southern Economic Journal*, vol. 27 (April): 346–48.

Leeson, Peter T., and Peter J. Boettke. 2003. "An 'Austrian' Perspective on Public Choice." In *Encyclopedia of Public Choice*, edited by Charles Rowley and Friedrich Schneider, 27–31. New York: Kluwer Academic Publishers.

Lewis, Paul. Forthcoming. "An Analytical Core for Sociology: A Complex, Hayekian Analysis." *Review of Behavioral Economics*.

———. 2017. "The Ostroms and Hayek as Theorists of Complex Adaptive Systems: Commonality and Complementarity." In *The Austrian and Bloomington Schools of Political Economy*, edited by Paul Dragos Aligica, Paul Lewis, and Virgil H. Storr, 49–80. Bingley, UK: Emerald Publishing Limited.

Lewis, Paul, and Peter Lewin. 2015. "Orders, Orders, Everywhere . . . On Hayek's *The Market and Other Orders.*" *Cosmos + Taxis*, vol. 2, no. 2: 1–17.

Lindblom, Charles. 1959. "The Science of Muddling Through." *Public Administration Review*, vol. 19, no. 2 (Spring): 79–88.

Mack, Eric. 2006. "Hayek on Justice and the Order of Actions." In *The Cambridge Companion to Hayek*, edited by E. Feser, 259–86. Cambridge: Cambridge University Press.

Marengo, Luigi, and Giovanni Dosi. 2005. "Division of Labor, Organizational Coordination and Market Mechanisms in Collective Problem Solving." *Journal of Economic Behavior and Organization*, vol. 58 (August): 303–26.

Nowak, M. A., and R. M. May. 1993. "The Spatial Dilemmas of Evolution." *International Journal of Bifurcation and Chaos*, vol. 3, no. 1: 35–78.

Page, Scott. 2011. *Diversity and Complexity*. Princeton, NJ: Princeton University Press.

Rand, Ayn. 1995. *Letters of Ayn Rand*. Edited by Michael S. Berliner. New York: Plume Publishing.

Ranelagh, John. 1991. *Thatcher's People: An Insider's Account of the Politics, the Power, and the Personalities*. Glasgow: HarperCollins.

Simon, Herbert. 1962. "The Architecture of Complexity." *Proceedings of the American Philosophical Society*, vol. 106, no. 6 (December): 467–82.

Smith, Adam. 1985. *The Theory of Moral Sentiments*. Edited by D. D. Raphael and A. L. Macfie. Indianapolis, IN: Liberty Fund, Inc.

———. 1981. *An Inquiry into the Nature and Causes of the Wealth of Nations: Volume II*. Edited by R. H. Campbell and A. S. Skinner. Indianapolis, IN: Liberty Fund.

Vaughn, Karen. 1999. "Hayek's Theory of the Market Order as an Instance of the Theory of Complex, Adaptive Systems." *Journal des Économistes et des Études Humaines*, vol. 9, no. 2/3: 241–56.

Vernon, Richard. 1979. "Unintended Consequences." *Political Theory*, vol. 7, no. 1: 57–73.

Wilson, David S. 2016. "Two Meanings of Complex Adaptive Systems." In *Complexity and Evolution: Toward a New Synthesis for Economics*, edited by David S. Wilson and Alan Kirman. Cambridge, MA: MIT Press.

Wilson, David S., and Alan Kirman, eds. 2016. *Complexity and Evolution: Toward a New Synthesis for Economics*. Cambridge, MA: MIT Press.

Chapter Four

The Entanglement of Public Bureaucratic Institutions

Their Interactions with Society, Culture, Politics, and the Economy

Jan P. Vogler

There are many excellent studies regarding the effects of public administrations on their environment, including their impact on economic growth (Evans and Rauch 1999), legal traditions, and the quality of public institutions (Charron, Dahlström, and Lapuente 2012) as well as long-term political development (Lange 2004).[1] Alternatively, other studies show the effect of environmental factors on the bureaucracy, including the influence of the political–legal framework (Huber and Shipan 2002), administrative procedures (McCubbins, Noll, and Weingast 1987), and socioeconomic interest groups (Vogler 2018c). Even though these studies have delivered insights into how bureaucracies function, they typically do not thoroughly explore the possibility of a two-directional *inter*action and *inter*dependence between environmental factors and the institutions of public administrations. This means that there is significant space for future research because recent contributions to the field of political economy have highlighted the usefulness of a perspective of "institutional entanglement," which refers to the mutual impact of and complex interplay between institutions from two or more spheres of social life (Smith, Wagner, and Yandle 2011; Wagner 2016).[2]

For example, Smith, Wagner, and Yandle (2011) show that we cannot fully separate political structures and processes from economic structures and processes. They argue against the traditional perspective, according to which the economy can be studied in isolation from politics. Network connections between political and economic entities mean that an equilibrium achieved in one dimension also affects the other dimension and vice versa. Accordingly, the dense interaction between political institutions and the economy makes the traditional view misleading.[3] Moreover, Wagner (2016) expands on this perspective by presenting a comprehensive overview of the entanglement of political and economic institutions. He illustrates the dense interplay between economic and political actions through analyses of electoral competition, the welfare state, and economic regulation, among others.

Similar to other institutions, the character and performance of public administrations may *simultaneously shape and be shaped by* society, culture, or the economy. However, the relative importance that is attributed to social, economic, and cultural factors for explaining bureaucratic institutions and behavior is comparatively low even in the most thorough and most prominent studies of administrative organization. For instance, Huber and Shipan (2002) explain cross-sectional variations in the relationship between legislature and bureaucracy in the lawmaking process mainly through political circumstances and the overarching political–legal framework, including the structure and capacity of the legislature. While they include a proxy for political culture and a dummy variable for corporatism in some of their regressions, sociocultural factors receive significantly less theoretical and empirical attention than political–legal characteristics. Similarly, in his cross-country study of bureaucratic organization, Silberman (1993) primarily focuses on macro-political variables, such as uncertainty about leadership succession and the structure of political networks, to explain the emergence of professional versus organizational public administrations.[4]

Why do many scientific contributions on cross-national variation not explore the impact of culture, society, or the economy on public administrations? In many cases, practical space and scope limitations mean that a perspective of entanglement cannot be applied or explored in detail. Yet this opens many new possibilities for research, primarily, because cross-country and cross-regional differences in bureaucratic institutions may be related to variations in the social, cultural, or economic spheres.

The relevance of studying these dimensions is highlighted by the fact that they could have both a direct and *indirect* influence on public administrations. In particular, those factors could be causally prior to the impact of the political–legal system. For example, there is some evidence that economic interest configurations have historically shaped electoral laws and thus the political–legal framework (Cusack, Iversen, and Soskice 2007).[5] Accordingly, from a historical perspective, the utility of a perspective of entanglement may be especially high.

Even authors who acknowledge and describe the interdependence between public administration, society, and economy often do not take the next step, by explaining *differences* in bureaucracies based on sociocultural factors. For example, although Weber (1978, Ch. 11)—in his landmark studies on the development of bureaucratic systems—acknowledges several social and economic factors that lead to bureaucratization, he treats bureaucratization as a uniform development process. Economic development, social progress, and democratization are seen as leading to a modern, rational bureaucratic administration characterized by high levels of specialization, hierarchy, meritocracy, and adherence to written rules (Pierson 1996, 20–22; V. Ostrom 2008, 68–69). This perspective does not leave much room for explaining lasting variations in the structure of modern bureaucracies among postindustrial societies that may be due to persistent differences in culture, society, or economic structures.

Interestingly, the common scholarly perspective on bureaucracies as separated from their socioeconomic and cultural context also corresponds with popular concerns about bureaucrats, including views that they are inaccessible, alienated, and culturally or intellectually detached from society (Raadschelders forthcoming; Peters 2001, Ch. 1) or simply a representation for "what is wrong with the country" (Peters 2001, 29). As a response to both the scholarly and the public point of view described above, I argue that there often is a dense interaction and connectedness between societies and bureaucracies. Thus, understanding their mutual influence is relevant for explaining the functioning of administrative systems.

It is important to note here that, due to this chapter's focus on the interaction between bureaucracies and their environment, we cannot discuss the *internal* organization of administrative systems in detail. However, the internal dimension of public bureaucracy has been thoroughly analyzed by a number of authors, including Simon (1997), who studies internal decision making; Tullock (2005), who (among others) discusses consequences of hierarchical bureaucratic structures; and Niskanen (1971), who presents a formal model of bureaucratic operation.

As touched upon above, sometimes, the exclusion of the broader socioeconomic and cultural context, which we observe even in the most excellent studies of public bureaucracies, may be due to space constraints—such as length limitations on journal articles—and for practical reasons, for example, to keep an argument clear and simple. However, both our understanding of public administrations and our ability to explain cross-national/regional differences in bureaucracies could be enhanced by considering the complex interaction with their environment to a greater extent.

Thus, I proceed as follows: After the introduction—based on the most recent research in the field of public administration—I develop a theory of *bureaucratic entanglement* focused on the complex interdependence between public administrative organizations and their environment. Here, I consider four dimensions of interaction: (1) the embeddedness of bureaucracies in society at the time of their creation, (2) the complex and multifaceted principal–agent relationship with the political leadership, (3) the interdependence with social structures and culture, and (4) the mutual influence of economic developments and bureaucratic organization. At the end of the theoretical section, I combine insights from all four dimensions to a joint theory of bureaucratic entanglement, which represents the core of the chapter. In the following section, I discuss a multitude of examples of and empirical evidence for the suggested interaction between public administrations and their environment. Specifically, this part covers (1) a comparison of public bureaucratic structures and service provision in Germany and the United States, (2) variation of entanglement within America, (3) the role of crises in shaping bureaucratic entanglement, and (4) how persistence in culture may affect administrative organization over long time periods. I generally find strong support for the notion that bureaucracies simultaneously shape *and* are shaped by their political, social, cultural, and economic environment. I close with suggestions and recommendations for future research based on the perspective of bureaucratic entanglement.

A THEORY OF BUREAUCRATIC ENTANGLEMENT

Below, I outline four key dimensions of connections between public administrations and the context in which they operate, specifically (1) "politics," (2) "culture," (3) "the economy," and (4) "society." We may understand these dimensions as "function systems" as suggested by Luhmann (1996). Luhmann develops a framework that allows us to distinguish between these different subsystems, which each follow their own internal logics. Even though there may be additional function systems, such as "art" (Luhmann 2000), the discussion of the interaction of bureaucracies and the following four systems/dimensions can be the foundation for an overarching theory of bureaucratic entanglement.

What follows are definitions that provide the foundation of the subsequent discussion. Since no definition can be perfectly applied in all contexts, the following items should be seen as *working definitions* with some degree of flexibility.

1. "Politics" are defined as all processes and structures within a country that are engaged in the making/passing of legally authoritative decisions, rules, and regulations.
2. "Culture" is defined as the collection of norms, values, and recurring patterns of behavior among the citizens of a polity.
3. "The economy" is defined as all activities and institutions controlled by private actors that lead to the production of goods or the provision of services. (Please note that this definition is intentionally limited to private actors because we aim to analyze the interaction between the

public administration and other spheres of social organization. If we include publicly provided goods and services in this definition, the interaction between the public administration and the economy becomes tautological.)

4. "Society" is defined as the networks, groups, and relationships that are constituted by persons within a country. Membership in certain groups and access to certain networks may give individuals access to informational, emotional, or financial resources, which may be labeled "social capital" (Storr, Haeffele-Balch, and Grube 2017, 449–50).

The connections between bureaucracies and politics (dimension II) have received by far the most attention in the political–economy literature on public bureaucracy. The other three dimensions have received some attention, but there is significant space for expanding upon existing studies. The four categories discussed here are by no means the only dimensions of entanglement, but for analytical and practical reasons it is desirable to keep a limit on them.[6]

Dimension I: The Critical Impact of Society during the Period of Bureaucratic Emergence and the Long-Term Consequences

The first dimension is the impact of socioeconomic conditions during the formative period of bureaucratic emergence. In the Western world, prior to the nineteenth century, public administrations were extremely limited in their capacities. Aristocratic rulers often had a small staff surrounding them and little control over society beyond the collection of taxes and the extraction of wealth (Raadschelders forthcoming; Raphael 2000). In the middle ages, even less control was required due to the very decentralized system of feudalism, in which local lords monitored economic activity and extracted resources from the peasants (Blaydes and Chaney 2013). In Europe, for many centuries, it was not the state but the church that administrated the lives of people, among others, by collecting taxes; organizing public services; and administering records on birth, marriage, and death (Southern 1978). State bureaucracies were often highly developed only in the military domain. Since the fifteenth century, advancements in technology and administrative capabilities made the creation of large-scale armies possible and revolutionized the conduct of war (Doyle 1992, Ch. 11).

When societies transformed in the nineteenth century due to industrialization and international commerce, the modern state with a significantly larger number of tasks came into being (Raadschelders forthcoming). This process was associated with the creation of massive bureaucratic apparatuses that provided a large number of public services, including infrastructure, education, and social insurance systems (Mann 1993, Ch. 11–13). During this formative period, when the fundamental organization of bureaucracies was determined (Raadschelders and Rutgers 1996), socioeconomic conditions and interest groups had the most far-reaching impact on the design of bureaucratic institutions (Skowronek 1982).

Three social groups sought to shape the nascent modern bureaucracy based on their own interests: the landed elites wanted to maintain high levels of political control through nondemocratic institutions and a socially selective recruitment system. Meanwhile, the middle classes pushed for an education-based meritocratic recruitment system and the protection of the public administration from political influence. Finally, the working class was interested in control through democratic institutions, anticipating that they would dominate in numbers. The relative influence of each group significantly affected the final structures of the public administration (Vogler 2018c).[7]

By contrast, in countries that were subject to foreign rule, imperial powers shaped administrative structures, often by imposing their own bureaucratic systems on the ruled territories. This practice frequently fueled resistance against the external administrative institutions (Becker et al. 2016; Lange 2004; Vogler 2018a, 2018b).

There is a large body of empirical evidence for the intertemporal persistence of bureaucratic organization, highlighting the necessity to study these historical developments for understanding present-day configurations (Becker et al. 2016; Goetz 2011, 47; Mann 1993, Ch. 11–14; North, Wallis, and Weingast 2009, 220; Painter and Peters 2010; Raadschelders and Rutgers 1996, 34–35; Raphael 2000; Silberman 1993; Tocqueville 2011; Wunder 1986, Ch. 4). Accordingly, variations in administrative institutions that were historically implemented can still explain some cross-national differences in bureaucratic organization.

Figure 4.1 provides a graphical illustration of the social embeddedness of bureaucratic institutions during the formative period of modern bureaucracies. We observe the following developments in this graphic: industrialization and steeply increasing levels of (international) commerce in the eighteenth and nineteenth centuries had three effects, which ultimately led to the creation of modern bureaucratic systems in the nineteenth and early twentieth centuries. First, they were associated with rising socioeconomic complexity, which traditional forms of public administration were overwhelmed by. This made the creation of modern bureaucratic institutions necessary. Second, they gave rise to a number of new social groups that were interested in shaping this modern bureaucracy according to their own preferences (in countries that enjoyed domestic political autonomy). Third, the wealth generated by these two developments gave imperial powers a stronger foundation to effectively rule a large number of non-European peoples and force them to adopt some of their administrative institutions.

Dimension II: The Political Steering of Bureaucratic Systems and the Influence of Bureaucracies on Politics

The most widely studied way in which bureaucratic institutions are entangled with their environment is their relationship to political principals—often discussed in terms of the infamous principal–agent problem (Cook and Wood 1989; McCubbins 2014; Tullock 2005; Weingast 1984). It is noteworthy that bureaucratic agents embedded in a complex institutional web may have multiple political principals and might also have to account for the interests of additional outside groups in their decision-making process (Ferejohn 1987).

How can political actors shape the discretionary power of bureaucracies? Politicians who are in charge of making authoritative decisions can delegate some decision-making power to bureaucrats who typically have superior expertise in the respective area of interest.[8] However, bureaucrats may use this power for advancing their own interests rather than the preferences of their political principals. There are many different mechanisms through which political supervision and the delegation of authority can take place.

The extremes of political control are the proactive monitoring of bureaucrats through specifically created institutional bodies (which has been labeled "police patrols") and a more decentralized system of "fire alarms" that relies on the voluntary and more spontaneous input of social actors affected by

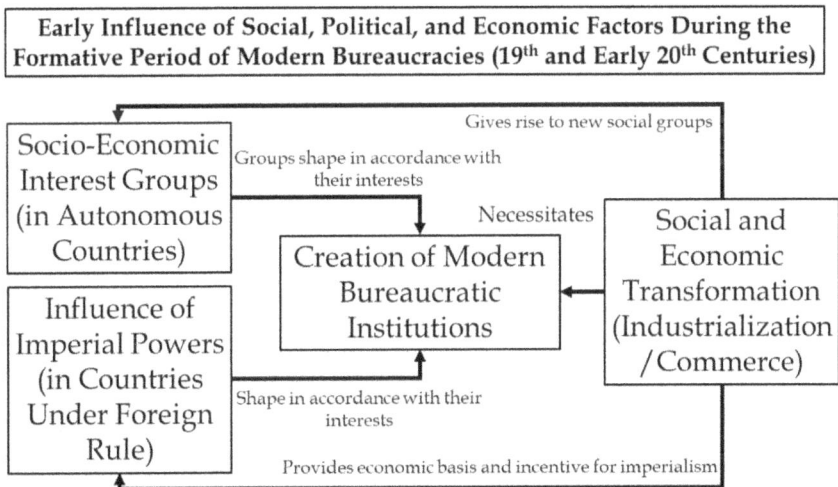

Figure 4.1.   Early Influence of Social, Political, and Economic Factors during the Formative Period of Modern Bureaucracies (Nineteenth and Early Twentieth Centuries)

bureaucratic decisions. The latter is the more cost-effective and more widely implemented option (McCubbins and Schwartz 1984). If politicians want to shape the behavior of bureaucrats, they can—among others—do so by changing administrative procedures and administrative law. Manipulating administrative law is a subtle yet powerful mechanism to put limits on the behavior of bureaucrats (Calvert, McCubbins, and Weingast 1989; McCubbins, Noll, and Weingast 1987).

An alternative method to control the behavior of bureaucrats is the use of political appointments, the effects of which have been widely studied by scholars of public administration and political science (Gallo and Lewis 2012; Gilmour and Lewis 2006; Hollibaugh, Horton, and Lewis 2014; Krause and O'Connell 2016; Krause, Lewis, and Douglas 2006; Lewis 2003). If the government can appoint bureaucrats, it can choose actors that are closely aligned with its own agenda and thereby increase political influence over bureaucratic agencies (Wood and Waterman 1991). However, higher politicization may also have negative effects on the performance of agencies, such as the placement of incompetent candidates for patronage purposes (Hollibaugh 2017) or slower response times to FOIA requests as shown by Wood and Lewis (2017).

A third way of limiting the discretion of bureaucracies in the lawmaking process in particular is the passing of highly specific bills that do not leave much space for variation in implementation (Huber and Shipan 2002). This would imply a reduction in the legislative–political power of bureaucrats. Finally, one of the most extreme (and lasting) ways to limit the discretion of bureaucrats is agency termination. The subsequent reallocation of material and human resources means that political actors gain significant power over the future course of policies in the respective domain (Holmgren 2018; Lewis 2002).

In addition to these *strategies* regarding political processes that politicians can use to limit the discretion of bureaucrats, the institutional setup of the government may also affect the performance of public administrations. For instance, Kogan, Lavertu, and Peskowitz (2017) show that mechanisms of direct democracy can increase administrative transaction costs—among others by introducing greater uncertainty about policies—and reduce the effectiveness of public administrations at delivering public services.

But could bureaucrats influence politics or political agendas? The first and most obvious channel of influence is through the lawmaking process. Using the American bureaucracy as his example, Workman (2015) shows that public administration officials not only implement what politicians want them to. Instead, bureaucrats act as experts who highlight areas of concern and shape the legislative agenda of the American Congress. With their expertise, bureaucrats are often much more aware of problems within their respective fields that require fixing. Thus, from the perspective of Workman, there is a process of *mutual influence*, in which Congress and the bureaucracy jointly determine the policy agenda.[9]

The impact of bureaucracies on the policy agenda may be affected by the share of "administrative professionals" (employees with a professional administrative background, primarily engaged in public management and advisory roles), which could have a positive effect on the number and diversity of issues, and the degree of participation in the legislative process by politicians, which could have a negative effect on the power of bureaucrats (Baekgaard, Mortensen, and Bech Seeberg 2018).

Furthermore, the public administration has decisive impact on the extent and properties of public goods and services (Yazaki 2018). The quality of their provision, especially in the areas of health care and education, directly affects crime rates and economic growth prospects (Baum and Lake 2003; Lochner and Moretti 2004; Machin, Marie, and Vujić 2011). Because these factors are important for the quality of life of citizens, they might influence approval ratings for governments—and ultimately the outcome of elections. Yazaki (2018) argues that, if there is a conflict between politicians and bureaucrats, the latter may actively reduce/limit public goods provision to worsen the electoral chances of the former. In turn, politicians may seek ways to hold bureaucrats accountable when they underperform at the delivery of public services (Nielsen and Moynihan 2017). Thus, the quality of public administrations has an indirect effect on the configuration of governments via the quality of public goods.

The indirect impact of public administrations on the fortunes of countries exists also in developing countries with poor quality of public services. The clientelistic distribution of bureaucratic positions among specific social groups can have a mobilization effect on those groups during elections (Kitschelt and Wilkinson 2007). Thus, the quality and recruitment procedures of public administrations can have an impact on the satisfaction of specific citizen groups that may be able to decisively influence the outcome of electoral contests.

All the contributions above highlight the extent to which there is a mutual influence and interconnectedness between political principals and bureaucratic agents. Even the lawmaking process is not as one-directional as it might seem. Instead, bureaucrats often have decisive influence even on the policy agenda.

Dimension III: Shaping Social Structures and Recruiting Citizens— The Interdependence of Society and Bureaucracy

The third dimension of entanglement is the intimate connection that bureaucracies have to (parts of) society by shaping social structures and through the recruitment of personnel. Before bureaucrats become bureaucrats, they are members of society. Formal institutions are a critical aspect of bureaucratic organizations, but so are the people who work there. Accordingly, who gets recruited into a bureaucracy and under what circumstances affects the administrative culture (Jamil and Dangal 2009), the representation of social interests (Aberbach, Putnam, and Rockman 1981), and performance of administrative organizations, including corruption levels (Dahlström and Lapuente 2017; Dahlström, Lapuente, and Teorell 2012).

The degree of entanglement with society depends to some extent on how broad administrative recruitment is and at which level new recruits can enter the bureaucracy. If administrators are recruited from a limited number of social groups, then social representativeness is relatively low. The representativeness of bureaucratic recruitment can not only affect perceptions of the public administration's performance (Andrews et al. 2005) but also trust in and cooperation with governmental authorities (Riccucci and Van Ryzin 2017). Furthermore, when citizens interact with bureaucrats, they might be treated differently based on their social status and affiliation. In particular, minority groups might have different experiences with and perceptions of public administrations due to a potentially greater administrative burden (Nisar 2018).[10]

In addition to the general sociocultural background of bureaucrats (Jamil and Dangal 2009), a set of prosocial values related to public service motivation (PSM)—such as altruism—has been found to be a key factor in determining individuals' efforts, performance, and innovative behavior in public organizations (Christensen, Paarlberg, and Perry 2017; Miao et al. 2018; Ritz, Brewer, and Neumann 2016).[11] Research also shows that even perceptions of their (work) environment can affect the motivation and performance of public employees, likely affecting overall organizational effectiveness (Jacobsen and Jakobsen 2018). Besides their background and personality traits, the process of organizational socialization of new bureaucrats can also have a significant impact on their behavior at work (Sobral, Furtado, and Islam 2017).

Furthermore, some general insights with respect to organizations, including businesses, could transfer to public bureaucracies: Cyert and March (1963) argue that different groups within firms can have diverging interests with respect to the businesses' operation (this also explicitly applies to governmental organizations). In a comparable fashion, perceptions, values, and interests of employees and stakeholders can affect the conduct of business. Research shows that, even in competitive market environments with great external pressures, factors such as the political ideology of board members (Gupta and Wowak 2017) or personal traits of CEOs (Chen and Nadkarni 2017) can affect the governance of organizations. Similarly, based on their background and interests, public administrators at various levels of the administrative hierarchy may have diverging preferences or display diverging behavioral patterns that likely affect the organization's performance and effectiveness.

While society may shape administrative culture, the provision of specific public services through the bureaucracy can also affect social structures. For example, the utilization of social capital may be affected by the character of services provided by the state. Communities at all levels of the administrative hierarchy (local, regional, and national) have strong incentives to acquire resources provided by the state through lobbying. Thus, changes in the availability of public resources may affect the use of social capital (Chamlee-Wright and Storr 2011).

Similarly, if specific services are made available to society through the public bureaucracy (such as transportation), the incentives for the private provision of those services will be reduced. For instance, the creation of public transportation in a city may constitute a natural monopoly that prevents private actors from entering the market. Or, if any of these services had previously been supplied, social structures associated with the private provision of these services (such as social knowledge or networks) may disintegrate. Vice versa, the *nonprovision* of public services creates incentives for their private provision. Thus, private social knowledge and private social networks centered on the provision of these services may arise if there is no public option. Accordingly, even the mere *absence* of public bureaucratic structures in specific dimensions can affect social structures.[12] The most extreme example of this might be the legal–judicial bureaucracy of the state, which is crucial for enforcing the state monopoly on violence. If the legal–judicial bureaucracy is unable to fulfill this function, citizens may seek ways to enforce rules themselves (Ellickson 1994; Stringham 2015).

A third alternative to the full provision and nonprovision of services through the state is a process of "coproduction," in which members of society participate in the delivery of public goods. Such coordination and cooperation between the state and citizens could contribute to greater efficiency and/or effectiveness in the supply of education, infrastructure, and other services (Nabatchi, Sancino, and Sicilia 2017; E. Ostrom 1996; Ostrom and Ostrom 1977). Citizens may have diverse motivations to engage in the coproduction of public services, such as civic attitudes or the identification with or desire to improve one's own environment (O'Brien et al. 2017). Accordingly, there are a large number of possibilities for the interaction of society and public administrations.

Dimension IV: The Effects of Bureaucratic Institutions and Actors on Economies and Vice Versa

The final dimension of entanglement of bureaucratic institutions is the connections with the economy that were briefly mentioned in the introduction.

Bureaucracies strongly affect markets through various supervisory functions, including the monitoring of business conduct, antitrust measures, and the implementation of economic regulations (Vogel 1996, 2018). The potentially strongest impact that public bureaucracies have on economic growth is through the provision of public services (Evans and Rauch 1999).[13] As pointed out above, the quality of health care and education can decisively influence the economic prospects of a country (Baum and Lake 2003).

In general, the character of the public administration is seen as highly relevant for economic development. For instance, Evans (1995) argues that two kinds of bureaucracies are bad for development: (1) bureaucracies that represent only the interests of the (authoritarian) state and (2) bureaucracies that are entirely captured by special interests. Instead of these two extremes, an intermediary level of interconnectedness to society is preferable. The state may collaborate with firms to some extent, but should not exclusively serve their particular interests. Such coordination between businesses and public bureaucracies is particularly important for firm performance in periods of economic reform when uncertainty about future market structures and modes of exchange is high (Haveman et al. 2017). The necessity of some degree of bureaucratic autonomy from the political leadership in particular is also highlighted by Johnson (1987, 151–56). He illustrates the positive effects that result from the depoliticization of economic decision making with the cases of Japan, South Korea, and Taiwan.

Bureaucracies can also be detrimental to economic growth by extracting resources from society or placing a financial burden on the economy (Raadschelders forthcoming). A historical example is the bureaucracy of the Austro-Hungarian Empire, which often meant a financial burden for the territories ruled by the Habsburgs. The poorly developed region of Galicia (in present-day Poland), for instance, suffered heavily from the taxes that were needed to finance the Austro-Hungarian public administration (Wandycz 1975, 71). Particularly, if corruption is a widespread practice among public officials, it can have a strongly negative effect on investment and ultimately economic growth (Zakharov 2018).

Even for the wealthiest states, such as the United States, large-scale military bureaucracies can be very costly. Beyond the expenditures for research, equipment, and weapons, the administration of armies by itself often already places a heavy financial burden on countries. For instance, according to NPR (2011), Gates, the American defense secretary at the time, said that "[t]he Defense Department runs the risk of the fate of other corporate and government bureaucracies that were ultimately crippled by personnel costs."

Interestingly, mere expectations toward public administrations can have a real impact on the interaction between the broader public and bureaucracies. Theoretical expectations about bureaucratic strategies and actions affect the economic behavior of citizens, who may act themselves if they expect inaction from the public bureaucracy (Chamlee-Wright and Storr 2010). If bureaucrats anticipate specific patterns of behavior, it might also affect their own actions/inactions. Insofar, there could be a mutual reinforcement of bureaucratic behavior and citizen expectations toward the public administration.

The long-term health of the economy has an extremely important feedback effect on the development of public bureaucracies. By providing the tax basis for state development, the economy ultimately also decides how much bureaucrats can be paid and the quality of technology that is available to them. In this respect, a certain level of economic development can greatly benefit the development of state capacity. Thus, it is not only the state that puts a burden on the economy, but also the economy that can unleash and enable the development of state capacity.

Additionally, technological change in the economy could have an impact on public management practices. Bodrožić and Adler (2018) show that waves of technological revolution had an impact on the dominant management paradigm in private organizations. For instance, the emergence of the steel industry and electric power led to the rise of unitary and centralized organizational structures, which were associated with the rise of Taylorism and an approach of organizational management focused on standardization. In a similar fashion, technological change could also affect public bureaucracies. For example, the most recent advancements in information technology are likely to have an impact on government services and might even affect the degree of control that political authorities have (Ahn and Bretschneider 2011).

SUMMARY

There are at least four crucial dimensions of interdependence between public bureaucracies and their environment. Social factors have not only shaped public administrations historically (through the influence of socioeconomic interest groups), but continue to influence the quality and structures of the public administration. Vice versa, the provision or nonprovision of public services can shape the structures of society and influence election outcomes. Additionally, bureaucrats may shape political agendas by using their intimate knowledge of issue areas to alter the politician–bureaucrat relationship. There is no simple one-directional relationship between political principals and bureaucratic agents. Instead, we have to consider their relationship as one of *mutual influence*. Finally, with respect to the economy, there is a complex interaction between public administrations and private actors. Economies provide the tax basis for the development of state capacity, and the latter's intervention into economic affairs can significantly alter growth prospects.

Figure 4.2 provides a graphical illustration of dimensions II, III, and IV of my theory of bureaucratic entanglement. The actors and institutions of the public bureaucracy are at the center of the framework and, therefore, at the center of this graphic. They are entangled with their environment in a number of ways. By determining the quality of public services and policy implementation, they shape social structures and affect the performance of the economy. Changes in social structures may cause new challenges to the public administration, and the performance of the economy determines the tax base, which is the financial foundation of their operation. The performance of the economy also directly affects the electoral prospects of the bureaucracy's principals: politicians. The latter's ability to delegate tasks to and modify the discretionary power of bureaucrats can affect the public administration's autonomy and effectiveness. However, bureaucrats are not powerless: they can use their more intimate knowledge of certain issues to influence the policy agenda. Additionally, the quality of public services directly affects the prestige of the bureaucracy, which has an impact on self-selection into civil service careers. Last but not least, recruitment patterns may influence internal administrative culture. The key takeaway is that there is no simple one-directional relationship between bureaucracies and their environment. Instead, there is a continuous mutual impact between all these factors and public administrations.

It is important to acknowledge that the degree of centralization or decentralization of political–economic systems may affect the depth and quality of bureaucratic entanglement (and other forms of entanglement) (Wagner 2016). In more decentralized systems, interactions between the public administration and local actors may be more frequent and associated with fewer transaction costs. When there are many units with autonomous decision-making power and overlapping authorities in a more decentralized political–economic structure, we can also speak of a "polycentric system" (Andersson and Ostrom 2008; E. Ostrom 2010a, 2010b). While interactions with the environment may have a higher degree of depth in such systems, the monitoring, supervision, and control of public administrations and their actions may enjoy economies of scale in more centralized systems, which could also affect the character of entanglement. However, considering the complex consequences of political–economic centralization and decentralization on bureaucratic entanglement likely requires a comprehensive separate line of theoretical argument and empirical illustration.

In the following sections, I discuss multiple examples of the entanglement of public bureaucratic structures with their environment. These examples are meant to highlight how useful a perspective of bureaucratic entanglement can be for understanding the operation of public administrations.

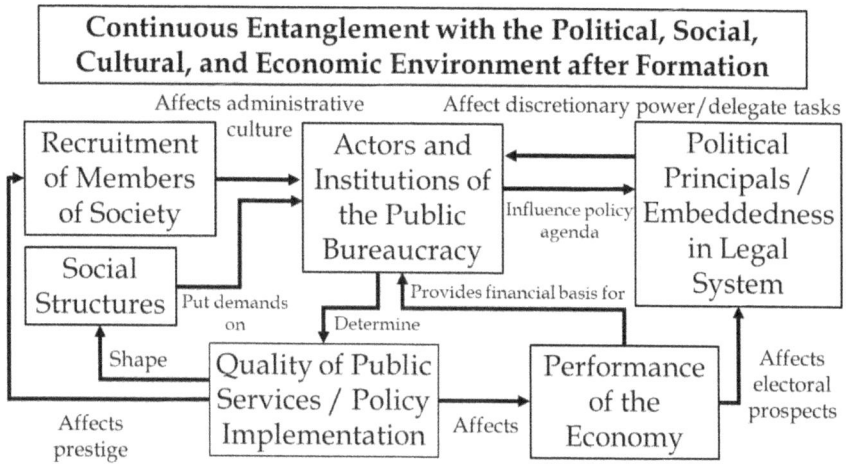

Figure 4.2. Continuous Entanglement with the Political, Social, Cultural, and Economic Environment after Formation.

EXAMPLES AND ILLUSTRATIONS OF BUREAUCRATIC
ENTANGLEMENT

The United States and Germany — The Interdependence of Bureaucracies and Societies

The mutual feedback loop between bureaucratic structures and society can be illustrated by comparing the provision of public services in the United States and Germany. In Germany, the provision of services through public bureaucracies, especially in the areas of social insurance, unemployment benefits, education, and health care, is significantly more extensive than in the United States. These differences in the comprehensiveness of public services are historically deeply rooted. In Germany (and most of Western Europe), the welfare state was not only introduced earlier but also expanded over time, meaning that European states continuously held the upper position when it came to the level of state intervention (Flora and Heidenheimer 1981). In America, the relative absence of public bureaucratic structures providing these social services has led to greater private initiative when it comes to social welfare and the emergence of private organizational structures filling the void (Alesina, Glaeser, and Sacerdote 2001; Esping-Andersen 1990; Hacker 2002).

To illustrate this greater relevance of private actors in the provision of certain services in the United States compared to Germany, a comparison of the two countries in relevant areas would be helpful. According to data by the

World Bank (2018), in the United States, the share of private expenditures among all health care expenditures was 8.9 percent of GDP in 2014, which is up from 7.2 percent in 1995. In comparison, Germany's private health care expenditures accounted for only 2.6 percent of GDP, up from 1.8 percent in 1995. Considering the relatively high average quality of health care in both countries, these differences are remarkable.

Moreover, according to data by the OECD (2018), the differences in private expenditures for education are similarly striking. In 2014, while private spending on education (primary to tertiary) accounted for 6.2 percent of GDP in the United States, in Germany they accounted for only 4.3 percent of GDP. While these variations appear small in the dimension of percentage points, if the United States had private expenditures at Germany's level, private spending would have been US $330 billion lower (based on an overall GDP of 17.39 trillion in 2014).

As we can see from the above numbers, the relative absence of services provided by public bureaucracies has led to the emergence of private organizations and private social networks that organize many of the above services. For example, while most health insurance companies in Germany are public organizations (public-law entities), major health insurance companies in the United States are often private for-profit organizations (such as United-Health Group).[14] It is noteworthy that, similar to the American political system, the American system of health care is also characterized by a high degree of decentralization, which leads to greater regional variation in prices and the quality of health care than in other advanced industrialized countries (*The Economist* 2018).

The more extensive provision of services through private actors in the medical field is not limited to the domain of health insurance. There are also many more private hospitals and schools in the United States than in Germany. This is perfectly exemplified by the intersection of health care and education: university clinics are nearly exclusively run by public universities in Germany but often by private universities in the United States. This includes the leading university hospitals in America. Beyond education and health care, in the United States, private organizations and networks, such as churches or volunteer associations, were and are often providers of services to poor or unemployed people (although we observe intertemporal variation in the relative levels of public vs. private service delivery) (Esping-Andersen 1990; Kramer 1981, Ch. 3).

The social structures centered on the private provision of health care and education that have emerged in the United States could arise to this extent only because of the absence of public bureaucratic structures in the respective domains. Vice versa, the presence of public bureaucratic structures in Europe has likely "crowded out" the provision of the respective services through private actors (Alesina, Glaeser, and Sacerdote 2001, 203).

As a result of decades of development, societies in Europe have come to expect the public provision of these services, while it is considered normal in the United States for them to be privately organized. This is reflected by attitudes toward the welfare state, which differ remarkably between both countries: people in Germany have significantly more positive views of governmental action in the provision of jobs, reducing inequality, and providing a basic income (Andreß and Heien 2001; Blekesaune and Quadagno 2003).

Applying a different perspective, Americans—on average—highly value private enterprise and individualism (McClosky and Zaller 1984). In Europe, the public preference for the provision of services through the state makes it difficult for private actors to establish themselves as competitors. Thus, there is a direct interaction between public bureaucracies, the provision of services through them, the attitudes of citizens toward the welfare state, and the prospects of private businesses to enter the respective markets. The factual presence or absence of services shapes sociocultural expectations toward the state, and those expectations in turn shape the continued provision or nonprovision of services by public versus private organizations.

Variation within the United States—The Connections of Society, Political Actors, and the Bureaucracy

The above comparison between America and Germany reveals that there are significant cross-national differences in the interaction between public bureaucracies and societies. Additionally, there is significant intertemporal and cross-regional variation in the United States itself.

For example, after Hurricane Katrina (2005), there was an expansion of public services in the affected areas: US $133 billion of federal funds were transferred to the region. Those funds were—among others—used for disaster relief efforts and for the reconstruction of crucial infrastructure, including "healthcare facilities, schools, and libraries" (Chamlee-Wright and Storr 2011).

The massive increase in federal assistance also had an effect on social structures. Chamlee-Wright and Storr (2011) present evidence, based on a series of surveys and interviews with affected citizens, that social capital (potentially available for mutual assistance within communities) was utilized to form new interest groups, aiming to capture as great a share of federal assistance as possible. Once the social structures created for lobbying efforts existed, some turned into permanent bodies that sought additional federal funding for other projects. Thus, the financial assistance provided by federal agencies had a long-term impact on the use of social capital and social structures.

Looking at a similar phenomenon, but from a slightly different perspective, Dutta (2017) shows that the ability of communities to organize after natural disasters is affected by the diversity of existing voluntary associations. Using data from communities in California (1991–2010), he finds that communities with greater diversity in such organizations are more capable of responding to such exogenous shocks. This implies that the ability of communities to respond to disasters can depend on the extent to which they had previously engaged in the autonomous organization of their social life. Similarly, Storr, Haeffele-Balch, and Grube (2017) show that high levels of social capital (resulting from existing associations) greatly contribute to postdisaster recovery because they are associated with more effective communication and collective action in the face of unforeseen circumstances. [15]

The interaction between bureaucracies and society can also go beyond mere rent seeking. As discussed in the theoretical section, cooperation and coordination between public administration officials and residents could contribute to the more efficient or effective provision of public services (Nabatchi, Sancino, and Sicilia 2017; E. Ostrom 1996; Ostrom and Ostrom 1977). In this respect, Boettke, Lemke, and Palagashvili (2016) argue that the centralization and militarization of the police in the United States has made it increasingly difficult for citizen groups to voice their interests and affect police behavior. This might have contributed to alienation between communities and police forces, potentially making the latter less effective at providing security—an essential public good. Accordingly, the character of the interaction between citizens and public officials, and the extent to which they can cooperate, has important implications for crucial aspects of social organization, such as public safety.

Analyzing the circumstances of coproduction is of great relevance because, for various reasons—including tight public budgets—the delivery of public services often depends on citizen cooperation. In this regard, Uzochukwu and Thomas (2018) investigate the determinants of citizen participation in public service delivery in Atlanta, Georgia, and find that, contrary to existing views, people with lower incomes and minority backgrounds may be more likely to engage in coproduction.

Coordinating with the public and taking multiple interests into account when delivering public services could generally have an impact on the operation of public administrations. In particular, the extent to which public managers consult with their social environment may have a significant impact on organizational performance. Jimenez (2017) shows that networking of bureaucrats with a number of stakeholders, including business groups, neighborhood associations, unions, and others can have an impact on the fiscal health of city governments after the Great Recession (2008–2009). He points out that interaction with a range of actors, such as banks, businesses, and nonprofit organizations, can introduce innovative strategies to public managers, make them aware of previously unknown possibilities to deal with current problems, and access new institutional capacities in joint projects with external organizations, among others. However, at the same time there are opportunity costs to networking, and coordination with private actors can delay decisions so the effect of networking may not be exclusively positive. Accordingly, in his empirical analysis, Jimenez finds that some interaction with social actors is beneficial but very high levels of connectedness are associated with increasingly negative effects on the fiscal health of local governments.

An aspect of public administration that has been discussed in the theoretical section—but for which no empirical example has been provided yet—is the reputation of government agencies among the broader public. In this respect, Teodoro and An (2018) argue that federal agencies, such as the US Department of Agriculture (USDA) or the Environmental Protection Agency (EPA), care about their public (brand) image. If agencies are perceived positively, they experience multiple positive consequences: First, they are considered more legitimate. Furthermore, both citizen satisfaction with the respective public services and even citizen trust in the agency increase. These findings about the importance of agency reputation are in line with the theory of bureaucratic entanglement, which highlights that positive images of public bureaucracies are likely to lead to the self-selection of highly qualified applicants to public positions.[16]

Finally, in the theoretical section, we discussed a contribution by Workman (2015) highlighting the complex interaction between bureaucrats and politicians in terms of the lawmaking process. In this respect, Boushey and McGrath (2017) show that, in many American states, the balance of power between legislatures and bureaucracies has shifted in favor of the latter due to increasing bureaucratic professionalization. By acquiring more expertise in their respective areas, public administrators (1) create incentives to the legislature to transfer discretionary power and (2) gain a reputation for competence, which can also be the foundation for greater bureaucratic autonomy. As part of this process, since the mid-twentieth century, bureaucrats were able to increase their salaries and take significantly greater initiative in the lawmaking process. Thus, for many decades, bureaucracies have been becoming increasingly politically influential. This supports the notion that thinking of the relationship between bureaucrats and politicians in a one-directional fashion simply misses important aspects of their interaction.

All these examples clearly demonstrate that there is a complex interaction between bureaucracies and society. Therefore, even within a single country, intertemporal and cross-regional variation in the relationship between bureaucracies and their environment is significant. The discussed interplay between public administrations and citizens is not one-directional: bureaucracies are used and abused by citizens. Their image plays an important role for their legitimacy and citizen satisfaction with their public services, which in turn may shape their attractiveness to highly qualified candidates. Moreover, the presence or absence of bureaucratic structures can inhibit or enhance the ability of communities to self-organize. The effectiveness and efficiency of the state and providing social services can vary based on the level of coordination with citizens. Bureaucracies are not powerless actors though: through increasing professionalization, they may gain additional political power, especially vis-à-vis state legislatures.

The Impact of Economic Crises on the Bureaucracy and the Responses of Public Administrations

As stated earlier, economic crises can amplify the interaction between the political and the economic dimension of social life (Smith, Wagner, and Yandle 2011). Could the same be true for bureaucratic institutions? Do economic crises amplify the interaction between public administrations and their broader environment?

There is evidence that they do. The financial crisis and "Great Recession" of 2008–2010 may serve as an ideal background for such an investigation. The recession had devastating consequences (Keech 2013), including long-term reductions in economic output (Ball 2014), rising unemployment rates (Bentolila et al. 2012), and disproportionately negative labor-market effects on young people (Bell and Blanchflower 2011). Since inefficient public sectors were seen as exacerbating existing economic problems, the calls for their reform were widespread, especially in the most strongly affected countries and regions.

In this respect, Asatryan, Heinemann, and Pitlik (2017) investigate the effects of the Great Recession on public administrations. They find that the economic circumstances at the time indeed meant strong incentives for public sector reform. However, they also observe that in countries with powerful bureaucracies, there was substantial resistance against restructuring or reorganization. Where bureaucrats are numerous and politically influential, they were able to thwart attempts of public sector reforms that contradicted their interests.

Accordingly, the study by Asatryan, Heinemann, and Pitlik highlights two aspects of bureaucratic entanglement. First, similar to the entanglement between politics and the economy, crises indeed amplify interaction between both dimensions. Second, the findings of the study are a perfect example of the mutual influence between environmental factors and the bureaucracy. While economic downturns can create political incentives to reform the bureaucracy, the public administration is not a neutral actor—especially when they expect negative consequences for themselves, bureaucrats may seek to shape political agendas and stop public sector reform.

It is noteworthy that economic crises are not the only type of "extreme event" that bureaucracies may be subject to—in the twenty-first century, possible challenges include "earthquakes, severe weather, disease outbreaks, power outages, social movements, technical break-downs and cyber-attacks" (Zhang, Welch, and Miao 2018, 371). Therefore, the ability to maintain the provision of public services when facing such severe circumstances is becoming ever more relevant. According to Zhang, Welch, and Miao (2018), the accurate perception and anticipation of such risks is a crucial component of "adaptive capacity building," which in turn enables swift organizational responses and the maintenance of operations in the event of a crisis.

The Enduring Interactions between Culture, Society, and Bureaucratic Structures in Poland and Romania

The interaction between bureaucracies and their environment does not only take place in the economically most advanced societies, like the cases of Germany and the United States that were discussed above. Societies at low or intermediary levels of economic development are also affected by bureaucratic entanglement. A series of interviews that were conducted by the author in May and June 2017 in Poland and Romania for the research project *The Political Economy of Public Bureaucracy: The Emergence of Modern Administrative Organizations* support the notion that there is an intimate connection between public administrations and their sociocultural environment. Interviews with a total of twenty-four experts were conducted in six Polish and two Romanian cities. Participants were (1) scholars of public administration and closely related fields (such as administrative law), (2) scholars of sociology, (3) employees of public administrations, and (4) local politicians.

The main goal of the interviews was to identify mechanisms responsible for the inter-temporal transmission of bureaucratic characteristics in Poland and Romania. Even though this was the primary focus of the interviews, their content also allows us to learn about the interactions of societies, culture, and public administrations (for example, through the channel of recruitment). Thus, these interviews can also be used to assess the extent to which bureaucracies are entangled with other cultural, political, and social institutions. In particular, the impact that the general culture of a country or a region within a country has on administrative culture would be worth investigating.

One important result of the interviews is that regional differences in (1) culture, (2) social structures, and (3) views of the public administration still affect state-society interactions and bureaucratic structures. For example, in the Western parts of Poland, formality, anonymity, and adherence to written rules and regulations are more highly valued than in the Eastern parts of Poland. Civil servants do not simply forget their cultural background when they enter the public administration. If they have internalized certain patterns of behavior, values, and norms, they are unlikely to completely suppress them at work. Thus, their cultural background likely still affects their behavior in office. This could explain higher levels of bureaucratic meritocracy and efficiency in Poland's Western parts as compared to Poland's East (Vogler 2018b).

Similarly, regional variation in social structures could affect the performance of public bureaucracies. To give an example, for decades in the Eastern parts of Poland communities have been more tight-knit and personal relationships have been more highly valued. Thus, both cultural and social factors could contribute to and explain why we find higher levels of patronage recruitment in the Eastern parts of Poland (Vogler 2018b).

The dense interaction with the sociocultural environment is not limited to Poland. In Romania, the inhabitants of the north-western region of Transylvania maintain a social memory that is different from the inhabitants of Moldavia and Wallachia. They see themselves as more civilized and their public institutions as more reliable (Vogler 2018a). A study by Becker and others (2016) provide similar evidence: historically formed views of public administrations persist and shape citizen perceptions for decades. Such striking differences in public perceptions could affect the attractiveness of working at the public administration, influencing the number and quality of applicants to positions. Ultimately, if a public administration has more qualified applicants, it can deliver better public services and reinforce existing beliefs about the quality of its personnel. Thus, there is likely a self-reinforcing, enduring feedback loop between culture, perceptions of public institutions, and the quality of public services delivered.

To summarize, the interviews conducted for the research projects described above show that we cannot completely ignore sociocultural factors when analyzing differences in the institutions or performance of bureaucracies across regions and countries. On the contrary, a comprehensive analysis of cross-regional and cross-national differences in bureaucratic organization should take these factors into account.

CONCLUSION AND SUGGESTIONS FOR FUTURE RESEARCH

There are many excellent studies on bureaucratic organization. A large number of them investigate the (one-directional) effect of public administrations on society, the economy, or politics—or vice versa. However, the recent literature on "institutional entanglement" shows us that social relationships are often two-directional or mutually constitutive. Thus, in this chapter, I have used the vast existing literature on public administration—including some of the most recent research in the field—to create a synthesized theoretical perspective of how bureaucracies interact with their social, economic, cultural, and political environment. I have used a number of empirical examples to demonstrate how useful such a perspective can be for our understanding of administrative organizations.

Which implications and suggestions for future research can we derive from this chapter? First, when scholars design theories explaining bureaucratic structures or behavior, they should always ask themselves the following questions. Which factors in their broader environment affect the specific dimension of public administration under consideration? This chapter may serve as a starting point for such an investigation. Second, when scholars have identified the relevant factors, the next question that needs to be answered is, what is the causal direction? Even though it cannot be ruled out that it is appropriate to claim and investigate one-directional relationships (like when the nascent public administration emerged), this chapter has shown that a two-directional interaction is much more commonplace. Third, even when authors are not able to fully explore the interaction between bureaucracies and their environment due to practical limitations, it would nevertheless be worthwhile for them to highlight that potential future research could uncover this interaction. This would open new opportunities for research on the entanglement of bureaucracies and their environment.

One political lesson we may draw from this chapter is that the creation, modification, or abolishment of bureaucratic structures should be conducted with great care. Given the complex interaction of public bureaucracies with other parts of society, such plans should be crafted with a keen eye toward the multifold consequences they may have. Additionally, in any such process, all social actors who may be affected by bureaucratic reorganization should be able to voice their concerns and those should be considered to arrive at a final decision.

Considering the possibility of varying degrees of bureaucratic entanglement, we could also ask the normative question: Which level of interaction between public administrations and their broader environment is *desirable*? We might interpret Evans (1995) as suggesting that an intermediary level of entanglement has positive consequences for economic growth. However, one might also argue that bureaucracies that are completely embedded into society will most likely be perceived positively by citizens due to their closeness to the people. A high level of embeddedness could also contribute to the coproduction of public services and may be more easily achieved in democratic societies, in which citizens have a multitude of opportunities for political participation. Authoritarian rulers may be more likely to shield bureaucratic systems from the influence of social actors that are excluded from the political system. However, we cannot make conclusive judgments on these normative issues yet as they will require more in-depth investigations in the future.

Thus, even though we have gained new insights through the analysis at hand, many opportunities for further research remain and should be more comprehensively addressed in future contributions. In addition to a more nuanced exploration of the normative implications, we may expand the theory of bureaucratic entanglement by more systematically considering the complex linkage to monocentric versus polycentric systems[17] (Andersson and Ostrom 2008; E. Ostrom 2010a, 2010b) or to quasi-markets (Boettke, Coyne, and Leeson 2011; Glennerster 1991). Of course, these are only two of many options for further research, and dozens more are likely to arise in the future.

NOTES

1. Helpful comments have been provided by Mathew McCubbins, Jos Raadschelders, Katherine Spruill, and Virgil Storr. Moreover, I am grateful to the participants of seminars at Duke University and the Adam Smith Fellowship research sequence.

2. While socioeconomic and cultural factors are often ignored, some aspects of the entanglement of bureaucracies with the environment have been studied in detail. Specifically, there is a thorough treatment of the principal–agent problem in the politics of bureaucracy literature (Gailmard and Patty 2007, 2012; Weingast 1984).

3. These claims are illustrated by Smith, Wagner, and Yandle (2011) through two examples—the Troubled Assets Relief Program (TARP) and the New Deal's National Recovery Administration. Economic crises (and responses to them) are particularly useful to illustrate connections between the economy and the political system because they amplify interaction between both spheres.

4. Similarly, Hollyer (2009) explains the introduction of meritocratic recruitment in nineteenth- and early twentieth-century bureaucracies purely based on rational cost-benefit calculations by governments without reference to the broader transformation in socioeconomic conditions that created the political interest in administrative reform.

5. For a critical response to Cusack, Iversen, and Soskice (2007), see Kreuzer (2010).

6. Future scholarly contributions could explore further dimensions of entanglement.

7. Please note that thinking in terms of groups—both in this specific context and more generally—often is a theoretical simplification (Vogler 2018c) and there are wide-ranging debates regarding the appropriateness of framing social theories in terms of groups versus individuals (Hodgson 2007; Sarker and Valacich 2010; Udehn 2002).

8. It is a standard assumption in the principal–agent literature that bureaucratic agents are more familiar than their political principals with the narrow issue area on which they work. Political principals often need to simultaneously gain knowledge on multiple topics and are thereby prevented from specializing in a single issue. Despite the commonality of this assumption, there have been diverging viewpoints regarding the role and reliability of expertise in both public bureaucracies and society more generally (Ericsson and Smith 1991; Koppl 2018; Levy and Peart 2016; Nichols 2017; Tullock 2005).

9. Similarly, Aberbach, Putnam, and Rockman (1981) show that, in many democracies, the role of bureaucrats in the lawmaking process is greater than was forecast by Max Weber.

10. Recent findings with respect to police behavior suggest that discrimination against minority groups in the interaction with bureaucrats may be reduced by improving the representation of these groups in the public administration (Hong 2017a).

11. However, an exclusive emphasis of PSM in recruitment may not result in higher-quality applicants because citizens with high levels of PSM might apply to public sector jobs regardless. In order to reach a broader pool of applicants and increase diversity in public administrations, it may be necessary to highlight career benefits and other positive aspects of public employment opportunities (Linos 2018). Furthermore, the effects of PSM may be conditional

on both contextual factors, such as national setting (Harari et al. 2017), and individual factors, such as the tenure of civil servants (Jensen and Vestergaard 2017).

12. A similar hypothesis regarding the crowding out of private charitable donations to nonprofit organizations through government spending has been subject to much debate and received mixed evidence (de Wit and Bekkers 2017).

13. Similar arguments regarding the quality of public institutions, including bureaucracies, and their impact on economic growth are made by Di Liberto and Sideri (2015).

14. Alternatively, other insurance companies are organized as public welfare organizations (such as Blue Shield of California or Blue Cross and Blue Shield of North Carolina).

15. Similarly, Storr, Grube, and Haeffele-Balch (2017) show that polycentric orders with the private supply of services are capable of dealing with multifold challenges in a postdisaster environment.

16. Agency reputation could also be shaped by organizational performance. In this respect, Olsen (2017) shows that Danish citizens evaluate the performance of public administrations against both historical reference points and the performance of other organizations. This means that performance evaluations are inherently relative. Moreover, Marvel (2016) demonstrates that deeply rooted—and possibly unconscious—views of public sector organizations are often highly relevant for performance evaluations by individuals, even when concrete positive performance information about the institution was provided.

17. For instance, Kogan (2017) explores the effects of administrative decentralization versus centralization on the responsiveness of bureaucracies. Furthermore, Hong (2017b) considers how accountability mechanisms differ between local and central administrative organizations. The level of decentralization is closely associated with the degree of polycentrism. Thus, these studies might be a good point of departure for analyzing the relationship of polycentrism and entanglement.

REFERENCES

Aberbach, Joel D., Robert D. Putnam, and Bert A. Rockman. 1981. *Bureaucrats and Politicians in Western Democracies*. Cambridge, MA: Harvard University Press.

Ahn, Michael J., and Stuart Bretschneider. 2011. "Politics of E-Government: E-Government and the Political Control of Bureaucracy." *Public Administration Review* 71(3): 414–24.

Alesina, Alberto, Edward Glaeser, and Bruce Sacerdote. 2001. "Why Doesn't the United States Have a European-Style Welfare State?" *Brookings Papers on Economic Activity* 2001(2): 187–254.

Andersson, Krister P., and Elinor Ostrom. 2008. "Analyzing Decentralized Resource Regimes from a Polycentric Perspective." *Policy Sciences* 41(1): 71–93.

Andreß, Hans-Jürgen, and Thorsten Heien. 2001. "Four Worlds of Welfare State Attitudes? A Comparison of Germany, Norway, and the United States." *European Sociological Review* 17(4): 337–56.

Andrews, Rhys, George A. Boyne, Kenneth J. Meier, Laurence J. O'Toole Jr., and Richard M. Walker. 2005. "Representative Bureaucracy, Organizational Strategy, and Public Service Performance: An Empirical Analysis of English Local Government." *Journal of Public Administration Research and Theory* 15(4): 489–504.

Asatryan, Zareh, Friedrich Heinemann, and Hans Pitlik. 2017. "Reforming the Public Administration: The Role of Crisis and the Power of Bureaucracy." *European Journal of Political Economy* 48: 128–43.

Baekgaard, Martin, Peter B. Mortensen, and Henrik Bech Seeberg. 2018. "The Bureaucracy and the Policy Agenda." *Journal of Public Administration Research and Theory* 28(2): 239–53.

Ball, Laurence. 2014. "Long-Term Damage from the Great Recession in OECD Countries." *European Journal of Economics and Economic Policies: Intervention* 11(2): 149–60.

Baum, Matthew A., and David A. Lake. 2003. "The Political Economy of Growth: Democracy and Human Capital." *American Journal of Political Science* 47(2): 333–47.

Becker, Sascha O., Katrin Boeckh, Christa Hainz, and Ludger Woessmann. 2016. "The Empire Is Dead, Long Live the Empire! Long-Run Persistence of Trust and Corruption in the Bureaucracy." *The Economic Journal* 126(590): 40–74.

Bell, David N. F., and David G. Blanchflower. 2011. "Young People and the Great Recession." *Oxford Review of Economic Policy* 27(2): 241–67.

Bentolila, Samuel, Pierre Cahuc, Juan J. Dolado, and Thomas Le Barbanchon. 2012. "Two-Tier Labor Markets in the Great Recession: France versus Spain." *The Economic Journal* 122(562): F155–F187.

Blaydes, Lisa, and Eric Chaney. 2013. "The Feudal Revolution and Europe's Rise: Political Divergence of the Christian West and the Muslim World before 1500 CE." *American Political Science Review* 107(1): 16–34.

Blekesaune, Morten, and Jill Quadagno. 2003. "Public Attitudes toward Welfare State Policies: A Comparative Analysis of 24 Nations." *European Sociological Review* 19(5): 415–27.

Bodrožić, Zlatko, and Paul S. Adler. 2018. "The Evolution of Management Models: A Neo-Schumpeterian Theory." *Administrative Science Quarterly* 63(1): 85–129.

Boettke, Peter J., Christopher J. Coyne, and Peter T. Leeson. 2011. "Quasimarket Failure." *Public Choice* 149(1–2): 209.

Boettke, Peter J., Jayme S. Lemke, and Liya Palagashvili. 2016. "Re-Evaluating Community Policing in a Polycentric System." *Journal of Institutional Economics* 12(2): 305–25.

Boushey, Graeme T., and Robert J. McGrath. 2017. "Experts, Amateurs, and Bureaucratic Influence in the American States." *Journal of Public Administration Research and Theory* 27(1): 85–103.

Calvert, Randall L., Mathew D. McCubbins, and Barry R. Weingast. 1989. "A Theory of Political Control and Agency Discretion." *American Journal of Political Science* 33(3): 588–611.

Chamlee-Wright, Emily, and Virgil Henry Storr. 2010. "Expectations of Governments Response to Disaster." *Public Choice* 144(1): 253–74.

———. 2011. "Social Capital, Lobbying and Community-Based Interest Groups." *Public Choice* 149(1–2): 167–85.

Charron, Nicholas, Carl Dahlström, and Victor Lapuente. 2012. "No Law without a State." *Journal of Comparative Economics* 40(2): 176–93.

Chen, Jianhong, and Sucheta Nadkarni. 2017. "It's about Time! CEOs' Temporal Dispositions, Temporal Leadership, and Corporate Entrepreneurship." *Administrative Science Quarterly* 62(1): 31–66.

Christensen, Robert K., Laurie Paarlberg, and James L. Perry. 2017. "Public Service Motivation Research: Lessons for Practice." *Public Administration Review* 77(4): 529–42.

Cook, Brian J., and B. Dan Wood. 1989. "Principal-Agent Models of Political Control of Bureaucracy." *American Political Science Review* 83(3): 965–78.

Cusack, Thomas R., Torben Iversen, and David Soskice. 2007. "Economic Interests and the Origins of Electoral Systems." *American Political Science Review* 101(3): 373–91.

Cyert, Richard M., and James G. March. 1963. *A Behavioral Theory of the Firm.* Upper Saddle River, NJ: Prentice-Hall.

Dahlström, Carl, and Victor Lapuente. 2017. *Organizing Leviathan: How the Relationship between Politicians and Bureaucrats Shapes Good Government.* Cambridge: Cambridge University Press.

Dahlström, Carl, Victor Lapuente, and Jan Teorell. 2012. "The Merit of Meritocratization: Politics, Bureaucracy, and the Institutional Deterrents of Corruption." *Political Research Quarterly* 65(3): 656–68.

de Wit, Arjen, and Ren Bekkers. 2017. "Government Support and Charitable Donations: A Meta-Analysis of the Crowding-Out Hypothesis." *Journal of Public Administration Research and Theory* 27(2): 301–19.

Di Liberto, Adriana, and Marco Sideri. 2015. "Past Dominations, Current Institutions and the Italian Regional Economic Performance." *European Journal of Political Economy* 38: 12–41.

Doyle, William. 1992. *The Old European Order, 1660–1800.* Oxford: Oxford University Press.

Dutta, Sunasir. 2017. "Creating in the Crucibles of Nature's Fury: Associational Diversity and Local Social Entrepreneurship after Natural Disasters in California, 1991–2010." *Administrative Science Quarterly* 62(3): 443–83.

Ellickson, Robert C. 1994. *Order without Law.* Cambridge, MA: Harvard University Press.

Ericsson, K. Anders, and Jacqui Smith. 1991. *Toward a General Theory of Expertise: Prospects and Limits.* Cambridge: Cambridge University Press.

Esping-Andersen, Gosta. 1990. *The Three Worlds of Welfare Capitalism.* Hoboken, NJ: John Wiley & Sons.

Evans, Peter B. 1995. *Embedded Autonomy: States and Industrial Transformation.* Cambridge: Cambridge University Press.

Evans, Peter B., and James E. Rauch. 1999. "Bureaucracy and Growth: A Cross-National Analysis of the Effects of 'Weberian' State Structures on Economic Growth." *American Sociological Review* 64(5): 748–65.

Ferejohn, John A. 1987. "The Structure of Agency Decision Processes." In *Congress: Structure and Policy.* Edited by Mathew D. McCubbins and Terry Sullivan, 443–45. Cambridge: Cambridge University Press.

Flora, Peter, and Arnold Joseph Heidenheimer. 1981. *The Development of Welfare States in Europe and America.* Piscataway, NJ: Transaction Publishers.

Gailmard, Sean, and John W. Patty. 2007. "Slackers and Zealots: Civil Service, Policy Discretion, and Bureaucratic Expertise." *American Journal of Political Science* 51(4): 873–89.

———. 2012. "Formal Models of Bureaucracy." *Annual Review of Political Science* 15(1): 353–77.

Gallo, Nick, and David E. Lewis. 2012. "The Consequences of Presidential Patronage for Federal Agency Performance." *Journal of Public Administration Research and Theory* 22(2): 219–43.

Gilmour, John B., and David E. Lewis. 2006. "Political Appointees and the Competence of Federal Program Management." *American Politics Research* 34(1): 22–50.

Glennerster, Howard. 1991. "Quasi-Markets for Education?" *The Economic Journal* 101(408): 1268–76.

Goetz, Klaus H. 2011. "The Development and Current Features of the German Civil Service System." In *Civil Service Systems in Western Europe.* Edited by Frits M. van der Meer, 37–65. Cheltenham, UK: Edward Elgar.

Gupta, Abhinav, and Adam J. Wowak. 2017. "The Elephant (or Donkey) in the Boardroom: How Board Political Ideology Affects CEO Pay." *Administrative Science Quarterly* 62(1): 1–30.

Hacker, Jacob S. 2002. *The Divided Welfare State: The Battle over Public and Private Social Benefits in the United States.* Cambridge: Cambridge University Press.

Harari, Michael B., David E. L. Herst, Heather R. Parola, and Bruce P. Carmona. 2017. "Organizational Correlates of Public Service Motivation: A Meta-analysis of Two Decades of Empirical Research." *Journal of Public Administration Research and Theory* 27(1): 68–84.

Haveman, Heather A., Nan Jia, Jing Shi, and Yongxiang Wang. 2017. "The Dynamics of Political Embeddedness in China." *Administrative Science Quarterly* 62(1): 67–104.

Hodgson, Geoffrey M. 2007. "Meanings of Methodological Individualism." *Journal of Economic Methodology* 14(2): 211–26.

Hollibaugh, Gary E. 2017. "The Incompetence Trap: The (Conditional) Irrelevance of Agency Expertise." *Journal of Public Administration Research and Theory* 27(2): 217–35.

Hollibaugh, Gary E., Gabriel Horton, and David E. Lewis. 2014. "Presidents and Patronage." *American Journal of Political Science* 58(4): 1024–42.

Hollyer, James R. 2009. "Meritocracy or Patronage? The Choice of Bureaucratic Appointment Regimes." Working Paper. Accessed July 16, 2018. http://jameshollyer.com/.

Holmgren, Mikael. 2018. "Partisan Politics and Institutional Choice in Public Bureaucracies: Evidence from Sweden." *Journal of Public Administration Research and Theory* 28(3): 355–70.

Hong, Sounman. 2017a. "Black in Blue: Racial Profiling and Representative Bureaucracy in Policing Revisited." *Journal of Public Administration Research and Theory* 27(4): 547–61.

————. 2017b. "What Are the Areas of Competence for Central and Local Governments? Accountability Mechanisms in Multi-Level Governance." *Journal of Public Administration Research and Theory* 27(1): 120–34.

Huber, John D., and Charles R. Shipan. 2002. *Deliberate Discretion? The Institutional Foundations of Bureaucratic Autonomy*. Cambridge: Cambridge University Press.

Jacobsen, Christian Bøtcher, and Mads Leth Jakobsen. 2018. "Perceived Organizational Red Tape and Organizational Performance in Public Services." *Public Administration Review* 78(1): 24–36.

Jamil, Ishtiaq, and Rameshwor Dangal. 2009. "The State of Bureaucratic Representativeness and Administrative Culture in Nepal." *Contemporary South Asia* 17(2): 193–211.

Jensen, Ulrich Thy, and Christian Fischer Vestergaard. 2017. "Public Service Motivation and Public Service Behaviors: Testing the Moderating Effect of Tenure." *Journal of Public Administration Research and Theory* 27(1): 52–67.

Jimenez, Benedict S. 2017. "When Ties Bind: Public Managers Networking Behavior and Municipal Fiscal Health after the Great Recession." *Journal of Public Administration Research and Theory* 27(3): 450–67.

Johnson, Chalmers. 1987. "Political Institutions and Economic Performance: The Government-Business Relationship in Japan, South Korea, and Taiwan." In *The Political Economy of the New Asian Industrialism*. Edited by Frederic C. Deyo, 136–64. Ithaca, NY: Cornell University Press.

Keech, William R. 2013. *Economic Politics in the United States*. Cambridge: Cambridge University Press.

Kitschelt, Herbert, and Steven I. Wilkinson. 2007. *Patrons, Clients and Policies: Patterns of Democratic Accountability and Political Competition*. Cambridge: Cambridge University Press.

Kogan, Vladimir. 2017. "Administrative Centralization and Bureaucratic Responsiveness: Evidence from the Food Stamp Program." *Journal of Public Administration Research and Theory* 27(4): 629–46.

Kogan, Vladimir, Stéphane Lavertu, and Zachary Peskowitz. 2017. "Direct Democracy and Administrative Disruption." *Journal of Public Administration Research and Theory* 27(3): 381–99.

Koppl, Roger. 2018. *Expert Failure*. Cambridge: Cambridge University Press.

Kramer, Ralph M. 1981. *Voluntary Agencies in the Welfare State*. Berkeley: University of California Press.

Krause, George A., David E. Lewis, and James W. Douglas. 2006. "Political Appointments, Civil Service Systems, and Bureaucratic Competence: Organizational Balancing and Executive Branch Revenue Forecasts in the American States." *American Journal of Political Science* 50(3): 770–87.

Krause, George A., and Anne Joseph O'Connell. 2016. "Experiential Learning and Presidential Management of the US Federal Bureaucracy: Logic and Evidence from Agency Leadership Appointments." *American Journal of Political Science* 60(4): 914–31.

Kreuzer, Marcus. 2010. "Historical Knowledge and Quantitative Analysis: The Case of the Origins of Proportional Representation." *American Political Science Review* 104(2): 369–92.

Levy, David M., and Sandra J. Peart. 2016. *Escape from Democracy: The Role of Experts and the Public in Economic Policy*. Cambridge: Cambridge University Press.

Lewis, David E. 2002. "The Politics of Agency Termination: Confronting the Myth of Agency Immortality." *Journal of Politics* 64(1): 89–107.

————. 2003. *Presidents and the Politics of Agency Design*. Palo Alto, CA: Stanford University Press.

Linos, Elizabeth. 2018. "More than Public Service: A Field Experiment on Job Advertisements and Diversity in the Police." *Journal of Public Administration Research and Theory* 28(1): 67–85.

Lochner, Lance, and Enrico Moretti. 2004. "The Effect of Education on Crime: Evidence from Prison Inmates, Arrests, and Self-Reports." *American Economic Review* 94(1): 155–89.

Luhmann, Niklas. 1996. *Social Systems*. Palo Alto, CA: Stanford University Press.

———. 2000. *Art as a Social System*. Palo Alto, CA: Stanford University Press.

Machin, Stephen, Olivier Marie, and Sunčica Vujić. 2011. "The Crime Reducing Effect of Education." *The Economic Journal* 121(552): 463–84.

Mann, Michael. 1993. *The Sources of Social Power, vol. 2. The Rise of Classes and Nation-States 1760–1914*. Cambridge: Cambridge University Press.

Marvel, John D. 2016. "Unconscious Bias in Citizens' Evaluations of Public Sector Performance." *Journal of Public Administration Research and Theory* 26(1): 143–58.

McClosky, Herbert, and John Zaller. 1984. *The American Ethos: Public Attitudes toward Capitalism and Democracy*. Cambridge, MA: Harvard University Press.

McCubbins, Mathew D. 2014. "Common Agency? Legislatures and Bureaucracies." In *Oxford Handbook of Legislative Studies*. Edited by Shane Martin, Thomas Saalfeld, and Kaare Strøm, 567–87. Oxford: Oxford University Press.

McCubbins, Mathew D., Roger G. Noll, and Barry R. Weingast. 1987. "Administrative Procedures as Instruments of Political Control." *Journal of Law, Economics, and Organization* 3(2): 243–77.

McCubbins, Mathew D., and Thomas Schwartz. 1984. "Congressional Oversight Overlooked: Police Patrols versus Fire Alarms." *American Journal of Political Science* 28(1): 165–79.

Miao, Qing, Alexander Newman, Gary Schwarz, and Brian Cooper. 2018. "How Leadership and Public Service Motivation Enhance Innovative Behavior." *Public Administration Review* 78(1): 71–81.

Nabatchi, Tina, Alessandro Sancino, and Mariafrancesca Sicilia. 2017. "Varieties of Participation in Public Services: The Who, When, and What of Coproduction." *Public Administration Review* 77(5): 766–76.

Nichols, Tom. 2017. *The Death of Expertise: The Campaign against Established Knowledge and Why It Matters*. Oxford: Oxford University Press.

Nielsen, Poul A., and Donald P. Moynihan. 2017. "How Do Politicians Attribute Bureaucratic Responsibility for Performance? Negativity Bias and Interest Group Advocacy." *Journal of Public Administration Research and Theory* 27(2): 269–83.

Nisar, Muhammad A. 2018. "Children of a Lesser God: Administrative Burden and Social Equity in Citizen-State Interactions." *Journal of Public Administration Research and Theory* 28(1): 104–119.

Niskanen, William A. 1971. *Bureaucracy and Representative Government*. New York: Aldine-Atherton.

North, Douglass C., John Joseph Wallis, and Barry R. Weingast. 2009. *Violence and Social Orders: A Conceptual Framework for Interpreting Recorded Human History*. Cambridge: Cambridge University Press.

NPR. 2011. "National Public Radio: Health Care Costs New Threat to U.S. Military." Accessed July 16, 2018. https://www.npr.org/2011/06/07/137009416/u-s-military-has-new-threat-health-care-costs.

O'Brien, Daniel Tumminelli, Dietmar Offenhuber, Jessica Baldwin-Philippi, Melissa Sands, and Eric Gordon. 2017. "Uncharted Territoriality in Coproduction: The Motivations for 311 Reporting." *Journal of Public Administration Research and Theory* 27(2): 320–35.

OECD. 2018. "Private Spending on Education." Accessed February 26, 2018. https://data.oecd.org/eduresource/private-spending-on-education.htm.

Olsen, Asmus Leth. 2017. "Compared to What? How Social and Historical Reference Points Affect Citizens Performance Evaluations." *Journal of Public Administration Research and Theory* 27(4): 562–80.

Ostrom, Elinor. 1996. "Crossing the Great Divide: Coproduction, Synergy, and Development." *World Development* 24(6): 1073–87.

———. 2010a. "Beyond Markets and States: Polycentric Governance of Complex Economic Systems." *American Economic Review* 100(3): 641–72.

———. 2010b. "Polycentric Systems for Coping with Collective Action and Global Environmental Change." *Global Environmental Change* 20(4): 550–57.

Ostrom, Vincent. 2008. *The Intellectual Crisis in American Public Administration*. Tuscaloosa: University of Alabama Press.

Ostrom, Vincent, and Elinor Ostrom. 1977. Public Goods and Public Choices. In *Alternatives for Delivering Public Services: Towards Improved Performance.* Edited by E. S. Savas, 7–49. Boulder, CO: Westview Press.

Painter, Martin, and B. Guy Peters. 2010. *Tradition and Public Administration.* New York: Springer.

Peters, B. Guy. 2001. *Politics of Bureaucracy.* London: Routledge.

Pierson, Christopher. 1996. *The Modern State.* London: Routledge.

Raadschelders, J. C. N. Forthcoming. "The Iron Cage in the Information Age: Bureaucracy as Tangible Manifestation of a Deep Societal Phenomenon." In *The Oxford Handbook of Max Weber.* Edited by Edith Hanke, Lawrence Scaff, and Sam Whimster. Oxford: Oxford University Press.

Raadschelders, J. C. N., and Mark R. Rutgers. 1996. "The Evolution of Civil Service Systems." In *Civil Service Systems in Comparative Perspective.* Edited by Hans A. G. M. Bekke, James L. Perry, and Theo A. Toonen, 67–99. Bloomington: Indiana University Press.

Raphael, Lutz. 2000. *Recht und Ordnung: Herrschaft durch Verwaltung im 19. Jahrhundert.* Fischer.

Riccucci, Norma M., and Gregg G. Van Ryzin. 2017. "Representative Bureaucracy: A Lever to Enhance Social Equity, Coproduction, and Democracy." *Public Administration Review* 77(1): 21–30.

Ritz, Adrian, Gene A. Brewer, and Oliver Neumann. 2016. "Public Service Motivation: A Systematic Literature Review and Outlook." *Public Administration Review* 76(3): 414–26.

Sarker, Saonee, and Joseph S. Valacich. 2010. "An Alternative to Methodological Individualism: A Non-Reductionist Approach to Studying Technology Adoption by Groups." *MIS Quarterly* 34(4): 779–808.

Silberman, Bernard S. 1993. *Cages of Reason: The Rise of the Rational State in France, Japan, the United States, and Great Britain.* Chicago: University of Chicago Press.

Simon, Herbert A. 1997. *Administrative Behavior.* New York: Free Press.

Skowronek, Stephen. 1982. *Building a New American State: The Expansion of National Administrative Capacities, 1877–1920.* Cambridge: Cambridge University Press.

Smith, Adam, Richard E. Wagner, and Bruce Yandle. 2011. "A Theory of Entangled Political Economy, with Application to TARP and NRA." *Public Choice* 148(1/2): 45–66.

Sobral, Filipe, Liliane Furtado, and Gazi Islam. 2017. "The Pathways That Make New Public Employees Committed: A Dual-Process Model Triggered by Newcomer Learning." *Journal of Public Administration Research and Theory* 27(4): 692–709.

Southern, Richard. 1978. *The Penguin History of the Church: Western Society and the Church in the Middle Ages.* New York: Penguin Books.

Storr, Virgil Henry, Laura E. Grube, and Stefanie Haeffele-Balch. 2017. "Polycentric Orders and Post-Disaster Recovery: A Case Study of One Orthodox Jewish Community Following Hurricane Sandy." *Journal of Institutional Economics* 13(4): 875–97.

Storr, Virgil Henry, Stefanie Haeffele-Balch, and Laura E. Grube. 2017. "Social Capital and Social Learning after Hurricane Sandy." *The Review of Austrian Economics* 30(4): 447–67.

Stringham, Edward. 2015. *Private Governance: Creating Order in Economic and Social Life.* Oxford: Oxford University Press.

Teodoro, Manuel P., and Seung-Ho An. 2018. "Citizen-Based Brand Equity: A Model and Experimental Evaluation." *Journal of Public Administration Research and Theory* 28(3): 321–38.

The Economist. 2018. "America Is a Health-Care Outlier in the Developed World." Accessed July 16, 2018. https://www.economist.com/special-report/2018/04/26/america-is-a-health-care-outlier-in-the-developed-world.

Tocqueville, Alexis de. 2011. *The Ancien Regime and the French Revolution.* Cambridge: Cambridge University Press.

Tullock, Gordon. 2005. *Bureaucracy.* Indianapolis, IN: Liberty Fund.

Udehn, Lars. 2002. "The Changing Face of Methodological Individualism." *Annual Review of Sociology* 28(1): 479–507.

Uzochukwu, Kelechi, and John Clayton Thomas. 2018. "Who Engages in the Coproduction of Local Public Services and Why? The Case of Atlanta, Georgia." *Public Administration Review* 78: 514–26.

Vogel, Steven Kent. 1996. *Freer Markets, More Rules: Regulatory Reform in Advanced Industrial Countries*. Ithaca, NY: Cornell University Press.

———. 2018. *Marketcraft: How Governments Make Markets Work*. Oxford: Oxford University Press.

Vogler, Jan P. 2018a. "The Complex Imprint of Foreign Rule: Tracking Differential Legacies along the Administrative Hierarchy." Working Paper. Accessed July 16, 2018. http://www.janvogler.net/Imperial_Differential_Effects.pdf.

———. 2018b. "Imperial Rule, the Imposition of Bureaucratic Institutions, and Their Long-Term Legacies." Working Paper. Accessed July 16, 2018. http://www.janvogler.net/Imperial_Rule.pdf.

———. 2018c. "The Political Economy of Public Bureaucracy: The Emergence of Modern Administrative Organizations." Working Paper. Accessed July 16, 2018. www.janvogler.net/PE_of_Bureaucracy.pdf.

Wagner, Richard E. 2016. *Politics as a Peculiar Business: Insights from a Theory of Entangled Political Economy*. Cheltenham, UK: Edward Elgar Publishing.

Wandycz, Piotr S. 1975. *The Lands of Partitioned Poland, 1795–1918*. Seattle: University of Washington Press.

Weber, Max. 1978. *Economy and Society: An Outline of Interpretive Sociology*. Berkeley: University of California Press.

Weingast, Barry R. 1984. "The Congressional-Bureaucratic System: A Principal Agent Perspective (with Applications to the SEC)." *Public Choice* 44(1): 147–91.

Wood, Abby K., and David E. Lewis. 2017. "Agency Performance Challenges and Agency Politicization." *Journal of Public Administration Research and Theory* 27(4): 581–95.

Wood, B. Dan, and Richard W. Waterman. 1991. "The Dynamics of Political Control of the Bureaucracy." *American Political Science Review* 85: 801–828.

Workman, Samuel. 2015. *The Dynamics of Bureaucracy in the US Government: How Congress and Federal Agencies Process Information and Solve Problems*. Cambridge: Cambridge University Press.

World Bank. 2018. "Health Expenditure, Private." Accessed February 26, 2018. https://data.worldbank.org/indicator/SH.XPD.PRIV.ZS.

Wunder, Bernd. 1986. *Geschichte der Bürokratie in Deutschland*. Berlin: Suhrkamp.

Yazaki, Yukihiro. 2018. "The Effects of Bureaucracy on Political Accountability and Electoral Selection." *European Journal of Political Economy* 51: 57–68.

Zakharov, Nikita. 2018. "Does Corruption Hinder Investment? Evidence from Russian Regions." *European Journal of Political Economy*.

Zhang, Fengxiu, Eric W. Welch, and Qing Miao. 2018. "Public Organization Adaptation to Extreme Events: Mediating Role of Risk Perception." *Journal of Public Administration Research and Theory* 28(3): 371–87.

Chapter Five

The Conception of Taxation

The Romantic versus the Realistic Point of View

Charles Delmotte

Economics has, over the past hundred years, evolved as the prime intellectual advisory board of the state when it comes to improving the *condition humaine* (Boettke 2017, 45; Heady 1993, 15). Within that discipline, mainstream doctrines (e.g., welfare economics) provide the tools of government (Salamon 2002; Hood 2007) to solve various policy questions. When it comes to the issue of tax, several economic strands can be distinguished. One stream of thinking asks the question how taxes can be raised while enhancing overall utility, expressed through a social welfare function. The standard economic tax model assumes that, before the occurrence of taxation, markets are in equilibrium. Indeed, the economic model on taxation assumes rationally optimizing self-interested actors with complete shared information acting in a world where the impersonal forces of supply and demand mold all that scattered data into a mass point: the price (Boudreaux 1986, 55). This equilibrium—to be found as a dot on the blackboard—represents the situation in which goods and services are allocated to their most valid uses (Alston, Eggertsson, and North 1996). In equilibrium, competitive prices will reflect their marginal values and are adjusted to the amount of resources the marginal buyer is willing to allocate to secure a good (Gaus 2010, 89). Within the equilibrium model, tax theorists' public role is to work out how to impute taxes while *minimizing losses* in aggregated social welfare (Stiglitz 1994, 43; Hettich and Winer 1999, 102). Because taxes raise the price for a consumer and decrease the income for the seller, both taxes will cause consumers and producers to substitute away from market activity (Myles 1995). Hence, the task of optimal tax theory is to investigate how fiscal lawmaking can maximize social welfare *despite* the occurrence of taxation (Boettke 2017, 47).

Optimal tax theorists have thus favored talent taxes (Shaviro 2000; Stark 2005; Kaplow 2008; Zelenak 2006; Logue and Slemrod 2008) as an optimal form of taxing labor and have pleaded to tax capital through a mark-to-market approach (Kwall 2011, 79; Schenk 2004, 377). When concentrating on existing tax systems in order to maximize output, policy advice typically builds on the private responses to various taxes (Boadway 2012, 34). The appropriate (re)configuration of the tax system depends on parameters such as the elasticities of supply and demand of the taxed transaction, the ability to pay of the person being taxed, and the income available for the taxpaying unit (Hamlin 2017). In their search for taxes that would be less distortive, optimal tax theorists have argued for *deferring rates* on the basis of, respectively, height (Mankiw and Weinzierl 2010); race (Akerlof, 1978, 15; Mirrlees 1971, 175); SAT score (Zelenak 2006, 1180); gender (Akerlof 1978, 15; Alesina et al. 2011); level of income (Diamond and Saez 2011; Corneo 2002); type of income (excluding capital income; see, for instance, Bankman and Shaviro 2015; Lucas 1990); and regarding the type of product purchased, for instance, "luxury goods" (Bankman and Weisbach 2006; Bennassi and Randon 2015; Ireland 1994, 2001; Micheletto 2011, 72). Though these tax scholars seem to realize that some of these ideas might be hard to bring into practice, they do valorize them as *genuine ideals*, in the sense that they will screen which kind of tax rules can practically approximate these blueprints (Mankiw, Weinzierl, and Yagan 2009).

Completeness demands that I add that not all contributions commence from markets in equilibrium. Indeed, markets typically do not correct for various negative externalities, and taxation has often been advanced as a tool to correct for these imperfections of the market. To the extent that these tax scholars are aiming to enhance aggregate social welfare, they can still be seen as optimal tax theorists, *sensu latu*. Nonetheless, it is more apt to call them "Pigouvian tax scholars," after the influential A. C. Pigou (1932). These tax scholars propose discriminatory rate structures to correct for the externality problem posed within a standard market situation (Baumol 1972; Harrison and Theeuwes 2008, 68–80; Simpson 1995). For instance, carbon taxes are intended to make taxpayers internalize the negative externalities that such emissions exert on society.

Outside the scope of (direct) social welfare maximization, economists equally take recourse to taxation to stop people from harming themselves. Indeed, economists propose sin taxes on sin goods, such as soda and fat, which harm people's health (O'Donoghue and Rabin 2003, 2006; Brownell et al. 2009; Jacobson and Brownell 2000). We can call these scholars "paternalist tax scholars" because they are screening how the fiscal instrumentarium can assist policymakers in making people refrain from harming themselves. To the extent that the damage imposes costs on other people too (for instance, because of a collectivized health insurance), sin taxes are a form of Pigouvian taxes, *sensu latu*.

Although the optimal tax theorists look for taxes that do not alter people's behavior and the Pigouvian and paternalist tax scholars typically endeavor to influence people's actions, there is one common thread in contemporary fiscal writings: the idea of discriminatory tax rates, tailored at the specific characteristics of various transactions. With regard to the optimal tax theorists, as the private responses tend to vary for different persons, goods, and services, "in theory, every distinct transaction should be taxed at a separate rate that takes into account all relevant direct and indirect effects on efficiency and distribution" (Hettich and Winer 1999, 104). With regard to Pigouvian taxes for correcting the market, Stiglitz (1994, 43) says: "A full corrective policy would entail taxes and subsidies on virtually all commodities, based on estimated demand and supply elasticities for all commodities (and all cross elasticities)." Regarding paternalist taxes, the damage done by harmful products, of course, depends on the specific product (sugar, alcohol, fat) and the individual consumer; hence, the idea of taxes differentiated for various distinct transactions appears equally here.

We are not so much interested in the discriminatory tax proposal in itself as in the *conception of the fiscal process* on which it rests. Pigouvian and paternalist tax theorists attribute another *telos* to the tax system (i.e., stopping people from harming, respectively, others or themselves); however, their discriminatory tax proposal stands on similar assumptions regarding the fiscal process. So, while this paper will interact explicitly with optimal tax theory, it addresses a basic philosophy of taxation that applies to various academic strands. The remainder of this chapter is structured as follows. First, we will make explicit the assumptions regarding the fiscal process that drives optimal tax theory and the proposal of discriminatory tax rates more broadly. The next part will pinpoint these as unrealistic ideals and replace these assumptions with a more realistic conception of the fiscal process. Building on the framework of Robust Political Economy, the following section grounds the task of normative scholars to check the repercussions of their policy proposals under nonideal scenarios and makes explicit the general research lines this generates within the domain of tax policy. The last part, then, tentatively executes the task expressed previously and will check whether conventional tax scholars' proposal for discriminatory tax rates survives under two realistic conditions, which are the challenge of incentives and of knowledge. Arguing that this is not the case, the end of the paper shows how, integrating realistic assumptions of the fiscal process, the idea of flat taxes turns into a more feasible option.

THE CONVENTIONAL CONCEPTION OF TAXATION

It is no doubt true that we *could* enhance aggregate social welfare *if* we could anticipate peoples' varying responses to taxes on their labor and consumption, as is proposed by the optimal tax theorists. If we could tax a highly talented individual who does not exploit his full market potential, he *might* be encouraged to start doing so. Surtaxes on types of luxury goods that the richest 1 percent buy might not stop their consumption, and hence, an optimal tax could target these transactions (Bankman and Weisbach 2006, 1453; Bennassi and Randon 2015). It is also conceivable that we should target labor rather than capital income because this would discourage investment and innovation and encourage capital to leave the corporate sector (Mankiw and Weinzierl 2010, 18; Lucas 1990).

That said, this chapter is not so much interested in all the things we *hypothetically* could do via the institution of taxation. What we are focusing on here is the image we make of the fisc when we propose such hypothetical measures. Rather than focusing on how the state can enhance aggregate social welfare, here, we pay more attention to the underlying assumptions regarding the machinery that will generate this enhancement. Moreover, we focus on what *qualities* mainstream economics attributes to the state and to the institution of taxation in particular.

The theory of optimal taxation thrives on the idea of a specific causal sequence between the market and politics. Taxation—and politics at large—is presented as independent of the economy (Cowen 2016, 427). The outcome generated by the pure market can be captured through a static photo, a snapshot, which delivers the first draft of an economy (Wagner 2016, 35). The economy, however, is secondary to politics, and taxation is a toolkit to repair and perfect the results of human actions that take place through market processes (Stiglitz 1994). Furthermore, two qualities undergird the traditional image that politics (and thus taxation) holds as a domain separated from the economy and that it can unilaterally determine the latter. The deeper reason lies in two qualities attributed to the political process.

First, the market and politics are assumed to be populated differently. Models of the market typically assume various self-interested agents, while tax policy is portrayed as something a single agent can choose (Buchanan 1949, 496; Brennan and Buchanan 2000b, 128). More importantly, this monolithic entity is assumed to be a benevolent actor: when fiscal competences are proposed to serve a moral goal, the policymaker is assumed to act automatically in pursuit of that goal (Brennan and Buchanan 2000a, xiii–xiv). Indeed, tax theorists assume that potential political actors will share their own genuine motivations and, thus, powers would be employed "with a single-minded dedication to follow the dictates of welfare economics" (Wagner 2016, 13; Meade 2013, 29). Empowering governments to differentiate tax rates is not subjected to any evaluation of how it deals with opportunistic behavior because political agents are presumably programmed to shape competences only according to the objective goals taxation ought to realize. Buchanan and Congleton (2006, 87) had this methodological blindfold in mind when they stated: "nowhere in the whole of this approach to taxation is there any recognition that persons and groups will invest valuable resources in the politics that may operate to produce favorable or unfavorable tax treatment."

Equally, optimal tax theorists' models imply some specific epistemological assumptions. First, when conceptualizing an equilibrium, objective values for consumption, labor, talent, or capital are imputed in the model. Indeed, these models assume that the specific values we attribute to things in our lives are objectively accessible to "the fiscal brain" (Buchanan 1949, 497). The neoclassical model assumes knowledge of what "the price" is under perfect markets (O'Driscoll and Rizzo 1985, 643). Therefore, "'utility,' or 'that which is maximized,' has presumptive existence that is independent of any exercise of choice itself" (Buchanan 2000, 281). Equally, in order to enhance the economic outcome, the specific private responses (e.g., the substitutability of a certain good or service) to a certain tax appear as a given to the political actor. For instance, when a tax authority discourages saving (e.g., by putting a wealth tax on money held in a bank account), traditional models assume knowledge of the extent to which people would turn away from saving in favor of consumption under a specific surtax. Both types of assumptions create the image that the political agent has perfect knowledge for optimizing the economic outcome. In addition, proposals for mark-to-market taxation—that is taxing capital at market values—assumes these values "exist in some objective way" (O'Driscoll and Rizzo 1985, 3). Whether dealing with the market value of one's talent, the substitutability of a specific good, or the effect of taxing capital, the neoclassical model implies full access of political agents to the data required to boost overall welfare.

TOWARD A REALISTIC CONCEPTION OF TAXATION

Because reality is too complex for the human mind, we can often grasp only parts of social life through simplifications of the issues at stake. Taxation is no exception; in order to demonstrate the potential engineering capacities of fiscal actions, theorists focus on the *economic sphere*, wherein taxation operates. In this sense, it can hardly be denied that (1) some people have more economic capacities than others, (2) the demands for and supplies of some goods are more inelastic than that of others, or (3) taxing some forms of income might create more deadweight loss than others. What is left untouched, or even ignored, is the *political sphere*, wherein prospective fiscal decisions take place. The explicit assumptions regarding the market process that taxation aims to affect can be highly advanced. The model that is implied regarding the political processes that determine taxation itself is less convincing. Filling this gap requires us to sketch a realistic conception of taxation.

To begin, the engineers that are designing the economy are not causally separate from their object of investigation. The idea of a policymaker working with an economy displayed through a mass point equilibrium feeds the idea that this policymaker is "outside of this process" (Wagner 2016, 48). However, policymakers and citizens occupy the same social space (Wagner 2016, 40–44; McChesney 1987, 104). "Tax makers" spend their lives among taxpayers, and they do not occupy a separate decision-making unit (Buchanan 1949, 498).

Furthermore, within that single social universe, there is no reason to attribute superior qualities to political actors. By this we mean two things. First, traditional tax theory has always assumed that policymakers have an alternative motivational structure and that they stand above the normal forces that drive individual action. Whereas in the market we assume people to be self-interested, the analysts who "run the lab" are modeled as benevolent individuals focused on the common good (i.e., maximizing *aggregate* social welfare). However, observations, knowledge of everyday life, and empirical reasoning insist that political actors are not less self-interested than other persons and will actually *respond* to taxpayers' opportunistic strategies when doing so serves their *own* welfare level (e.g., staying in office, winning the next election, or advancing their career in government). The analyst is, thus, not ontologically different from his object. As such, the implicit behavioral "asymmetry" implied by tax theory is not empirically or theoretically plausible (Butler 2012, 77). There is no evidence that people undergo a personality transformation when they enter the political arena. Thus, there is no reason to assume fiscal policymakers are more benevolent than common citizens (Gwartney and Wagner 1988, 7). Against the motivational romanticism of traditional tax scholars, we propose to apply the self-interestedness postulate within politics.

Second, the epistemological properties of optimal tax theory models portray the economic reality incorrectly. The value of a specific good or service or its precise substitutability is not like a runner's racing time. These are unknown elements, similar to guessing how people would value watching a running race or what they would do if the price of a particular good changed (Wagner 2016, 38). The fact that entrepreneurs engage in various costly statistical tests and marketing studies to acquire a risky, imperfect estimation of such data signals that something remarkable is going on here. Why would we assume governments to have information no single person can acquire? When it comes to the epistemic assumptions of neoclassical economics, Boettke (2012, 105) sketches the situation as follows: "Traditional economics has dealt with the problem of uncertainty by assuming that human decision making consists of choosing between alternatives that are present to the chooser with a *known utility tag* and a probability distribution." On the assumption that legislators are aware of these things, economists engage in "demonstrative reasoning" and showcase how specific policies enhance the common good. From this point on, economics becomes a purely mathematical exercise. The illustration, however, is delusionary: things do not become valuable because some third party says they do. In reality, the values we attach to goods and—connected—the way we respond to price changes (e.g., a tax) are subjective matters (Delmotte 2017, 293). Against the epistemic romanticism of traditional tax scholars, we propose "epistemic subjectivism": when it comes to the value we attach to goods or our precise reactions to switching prices, there is no certain and easily accessible knowledge. Such knowledge is often tacit and scattered over the minds of millions of people who will reveal the answers through the choices they make under specific constraints and ever-changing circumstances (Hayek 1945).

FROM IDEAL TO NONIDEAL FISCAL THEORY

Optimal tax theory's claim that authorities can enhance the aggregated welfare level by designing a complex system of incentives and disincentives stands on the following assumptions: (1) taxation is outside of the very process it aims to regulate, (2) the people who populate this fiscal process are benignly motivated, and (3) knowledge of how to maximize welfare lies within reach of the fiscal authorities. Once these foundations have been unmasked as shaky and heavily idealized, the question remains whether the policy proposals that have been constructed upon them should equally be revised. No model is perfect, and imperfect models can lead and have often led to sound policy advice. The remaining question, then, is whether policy advice engendered by optimal tax theory can survive once the romantic pillars on which it rests are taken away.

Whereas traditional contributions to taxation are based on ideal scenarios, this paper explores traditional viewpoints under nonideal circumstances. Integrating a postromantic conception of taxation, we are focused on the space that will inevitably emerge between the intention behind a policy proposal and its manifestation within political reality. The remainder of this article will focus on the intended and unintended consequences that will arise when self-interested voters and politicians with limited knowledge start acting upon the specific tax rules under scrutiny here. Indeed, we are interested in the consequences that are to be expected, for instance, once *self-interested* majorities have political power to tax some goods and not others and how they will employ these powers on those outside the ruling majority. Equally, how will/does political reality look when fiscal authorities are—just like anyone else—relatively *ignorant* of the precise value of specific goods and services, as they are of people's reactions once the prices (i.e., taxes) on those goods and services start to alter. To phrase our endeavor in the language of Mark Pennington (2011), what kind of tax policy is "robust" to deal with the imperfections of reality? The question that drives the rest of this chapter, can be unraveled into two:

1. Do the kind of policies professed by conventional tax theory hold in the light of the political realism described above, and moreover, can they survive the challenges exerted by, respectively, the self-interestedness postulate and epistemic subjectivity (Pennington 2011; Cowen 2016)?
2. In case the previous is met with negative answers, the second question involves a tentative *estimation* for the kind of fiscal policy that does meet the stress test imposed by, respectively, the self-interestedness postulate and the challenge of epistemic subjectivism.

ON DOCTORS AND BANKERS:
THE CHALLENGE OF INCENTIVES

Discriminatory Tax Rates under the Assumption of Self-Interested Political Actors

When optimal tax theorists propose to include potential income into the domain of governmental exaction, or when they argue for the power to tax different types of income differently, they do so with respect to specific behavioral assumptions. When it comes to the efficiency models of optimal tax theorists, Brennan and Buchanan (2000a, 225) sketch romanticism by means of an analogy of neighbors discussing how to restrain their dog:

> It is costly to build a fence or to purchase a chain. It is possible to prove that the no-fence, no-chain solution is more efficient than either, provided that we model the behavior of our dog in such a way that he respects the boundaries of our property. As we have put this example from personal experience, the exercise seems, and is, absurd. But is it really very different from that procedure which argues that tax structure X is more "efficient" than tax structure Y provided that we model the behavior of government in such a way that it seeks only to further efficiency in revenue collection?

Optimal tax theory reduces taxation to an entity occupied with "the maximization problem" (Buchanan 1949, 505). Within this framework, tax makers are modeled as naturally motivated to enhance our welfare; hence, the model predicts that unlimited competences will favor general welfare. The assumption is that the competence to tailor different tax rates to different kinds of persons, goods, and incomes will effectively be employed in *those ways* that enhance the general welfare. This presumes that tax makers will spontaneously execute the tax rules according to the objectives set out by economic theory. On the nonideal account, however, the assumption is that individuals and the political associations they form will invest resources to shape tax rules in those ways that yield *private* gain (Boudreaux and Pritchard 1993, 115). When there are no restraints on political actors and they are at liberty to transgress the boundaries of others' property, they indeed have the *possibility* to create the better social states that economists sketch. However, in the absence of the benevolence assumption, the other option is that the lack of boundaries will enable the dog to appropriate other people's holdings.

To understand the patterns that tax exemptions will generate under a realistic appreciation of people's intentions, we need a paradigm shift. Conventional tax theory has compared tax makers with people like doctors, people who know more and want only the best for us. On a nonideal account, the image of the state changes from an "omniscient benevolent" into something like a "peculiar investment bank" (Wagner 2016, 162; McChesney 1987, 102). Policymakers are not angels but rather bankers, albeit with the special prerogative to raise money through the use of *coercion*. Ever since the publication of the *Calculus of Consent*, political economists have set up models that focus the patterns generated by opportunistic strategies under a given rule structure (Boettke 2012, 256). The task is indeed to treat government "as a complicated network of individuals, each with an incentive to maximize its own interest" (McChesney 1987, 101). One apparent flaw of tax exemptions under majority rule is that they enable those in power to transfer the costs of public goods to those outside their membership. For a given number of constituents, fiscal exemptions under a mere majority rule may give rise to fiscal exploitation, whereby a majority (and its most powerful subgroups) exempts itself from taxation and the bulk of the burden is suffered by the minority. The potential failure of majoritarianism under the realistic assumption of self-interestedness was already Madison's concern (Padover 1953, 40–41) when he said:

> It remains to be enquired whether a majority having any common interest, or feeling any common passion, will find sufficient motives to restrain them from oppressing the minority. If two individuals are under the bias of interest or enmity against a third, the rights of the latter could never be safely referred to the majority of the three. Will two thousand individuals be less apt to oppress one thousand or two hundred thousand one hundred thousand?

Madison's proto-game theoretic insights, indeed, signal a specific danger of majoritarian democracy: any two parties can coalesce against the third.

Buchanan and Tullock (1999) and later Buchanan and Congleton (2006) have elaborated on this further and conceptualized the majoritarian problem within a game theoretical framework: while cooperation pays, cheating is encouraged. Translated to tax policy, there is an incentive for majorities to maximize profits and shift the tax burden onto the minority.[1] Figure 5.1 (Delmotte 2018) depicts the options of one-shot majoritarian coalitions.

We imagine a majority and minority, respectively. The majority can think of a cooperative scheme that distributes the fiscal shares over all constituents, represented by Cell I, on the upper left; both gain 1. Although cooperation pays, the majority can benefit the most by lowering taxes on its own group and shifting the costs of public goods onto the minority. As depicted by Cell III, the majority now gains 2 while the minority currently has -1. As high-lighted by Buchanan and Congleton (2006, 28), prospective majority coali-tions will always select the option that will generate distributional advantages for their members. The result is that legislation takes the form of a *taking*: one party wins by extracting from the other.

A Flat Tax as the Constitutional Response to the Self-Interestedness Postulate

Optimal tax theorists sketch scenarios where governments enhance utility by taxing good A at 5 percent and good B at 20 percent. Trading a romantic conception of the political process for a realistic one, we can echo Richard

Minority

	Cooperation	Tax Benefit
Majority Cooperation	1, 1	-1, 2
Tax Benefit	2, -1	0, 0

Figure 5.1. Tax Exemptions under a Majoritarian Constraint. *Source:* Delmotte, Charles. "Tax Uniformity as a Requirement of Justice" (working paper).

Wagner (2016, 36): "there is no strong reason to think that political processes would *operate* in the manner the theory *envisions*." Indeed, under the assumption of self-interested political players, there is no guarantee that majorities will pick those types of goods for exemptions that are proposed by theory. Quite the contrary, majorities are expected to exempt those kinds of goods (or income) from taxation that the majority consumes (or produces). The origin of the idea of equal treatment lies not in its utility-enhancing role per se, but in its being a constitutional remedy against misuse of power, whereby majorities benefit their own position and impose costly externalities on those outside the membership (Hayek 2011, 318). Indeed, the requirement that majorities ought to *assign equal duties or claims* throughout the constituency is a response to the challenge posed by the self-interestedness postulate (Delmotte 2018). In their sophisticated approach, the technicality of which extends the scope of this chapter, Buchanan and Congleton have outlined the idea of "generality" as eliminating the "off-diagonals," being the options that embody differential payoffs for the majority or minority (Buchanan and Congleton 2006, 35–54). In our Figure 5.2, this means that only the "symmetrical" options remain attainable:

In policy terms, the political realism animating these public choice contributions singles out optimal tax theory's proposal: differential taxation empowers majorities to maximize their revenue by shifting the burden onto others (Figure 5.1, Cell III: 2, -1). Conversely, once the public choice objection has been brought within tax policy, all other things being equal, a uniform tax—being a single rate on all income—appears as at least a feasible

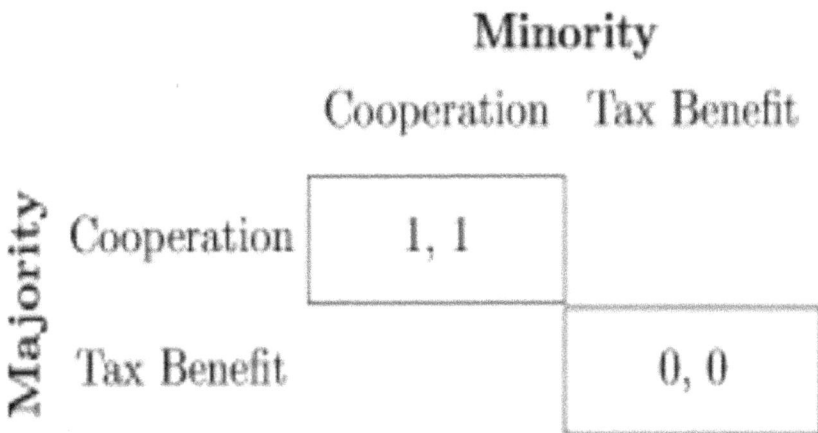

Figure 5.2. Symmetrical Outcomes under a Flat Tax. Source: Delmotte, Charles. "Tax Uniformity as a Requirement of Justice" (working paper).

candidate (Buchanan and Congleton 2006, 93). The question of which type of policy implies an equal economic *impact* and thus approximates the ideal of Cell I (1,1) the best is outside the scope of this article. However, in the wake of the dangers generated by self-interestedness and assuming the production of public goods creates an equal value for each citizen, the equal pro rata division of fiscal shares can be celebrated for its unique *incentive-aligning qualities*.[2] Once constitutionally enforced, the equal-rate requirement is an overarching rule that induces majorities to take into account the interests of those outside the realm of power (Hayek 2007, 441).[3] As Epstein (1995, 138) argues, the fact that "people know to tax their neighbors is to tax themselves" radically alters the motivational structure of the game. No ruling majority can try to put the burden onto others by means of an increase in rate (e.g., 70 percent) since this will simply mean a higher tax burden on their own goods/income.

In other terms, the constitutional requirement of a flat tax disciplines tax makers not to increase taxation to levels they themselves would not want to be subject to and, as such, precludes fiscal exploitation. Although, admittedly, fiscal opportunism is not excluded and some parties will be favorable to high rather than to low taxation, the range whereby such opportunism can take place is severely limited under a flat tax because the landscape of differential fiscal payoffs is severely restricted: all those options whereby one group can gain simply by taxing others at higher levels cease to exist.

Outside the scope of this chapter, the requirement of a flat tax equally generates a number of positive side effects. For instance, it will discourage overinvestment on the tax-spending side (Buchanan and Tullock 1999, 132–48). Under the uniform allocation of tax rates, the costs of public actions are now properly internalized by tax makers, who no longer have power to utilize those without power as the cost carriers of their decisions. This constraint will incentivize those in charge to make more rational spending decisions. Equally, one rate on all income would push current tax systems in the direction of less fiscal complexity, the latter being another often-raised problem regarding our tax systems (Fichtner and Feldman 2013). Lastly, flat taxes could also form a check upon fiscal competition between regions and countries. Moreover, such competition typically consists of specific industries and large companies acquiring tailored benefits (so-called tax expenditures). To the extent that much fiscal competition revolves around tax exemptions for mobile industries, these measures would vanish under the constitutional requirement that all income face the same rate.

To conclude, once the benevolence assumption has been exchanged for the self-interestedness postulate, uniform taxation excels through its "robustness" (Pennington 2011). Moreover, it appears relatively immune to the dangers wrought by self-interested tax makers, in the sense that a pro rata division of fiscal shares limits the range of political strategies meant to transfer the fiscal burden onto others.

FROM OMNISCIENCE TO EPISTEMIC SUBJECTIVITY: THE CHALLENGE OF KNOWLEDGE

Discriminatory Tax Rates under the Assumption of Epistemic Subjectivity

Imagine that tax makers would share the genuine intentions of the theory they are expected to execute. Then, the problem discussed under section 5 would not occur. In this section, we hypothesize that Che Guevara's "new man" was successfully invented and that the officials vested with the task of micromanaging the tax rate throughout the economy have no other intention than assisting the general interest. Taxation no doubt creates deadweight loss, but how much depends on the value of the tax base and its substitutability. In light of these data, fiscal rules could indeed anticipate what is and what isn't economically important and, even more importantly, which things are and which are not interchangeable and to what extent. Differential tax rates will apply depending on the value of the type of income (e.g., labor or capital), product (e.g., normal good or sin good), or capacity (e.g., high talent or low talent) and its substitutability, being the ease by which people can find alternatives that equally satisfy their preferences. Moreover, optimal tax models explore how omniscient legislators can shape the price of any kind of transaction and boost overall utility with great accuracy.

This framework might constitute an interesting mathematical challenge, but it does not show us much about what we can expect from legislators in the real world. Indeed, echoing Boettke (2012, 105), assuming the existence of fully informed agents "does not explain human decision making in the face of *uncertainty*." This section explores the avenue not taken by standard tax theory and estimates the role of tax rules within the nonideal scenario of epistemic subjectivism. Departing from conventional economic models, we explore how knowledge of people's values regarding economic goods or their substitutability is disclosed in reality. As mentioned before, determining the value people attach to goods or their substitutability (from now on called "economic preferences") is not like measuring how tall someone is or how fast someone runs (Wagner 2016, 38).

Imagine you had to buy a present for someone you deeply care about, yet you do not know the person very well. For instance, during Thanksgiving, a selection procedure decided that you ought to give your Uncle Bob a present. Despite the deep respect and affection you feel for your uncle, you haven't seen him for years. How could we characterize the process by which you aim to satisfy his preferences? Well, first of all, you could engage in some sort of personal inquiry. Some things are expensive and others are cheap, but you are not sure that your uncle likes expensive things. Or, alternatively, you could ask your mom what *he* likes, as an individual. Moreover, you are aware that people's preferences change (Pennington 2011, 23). Bob might have been keen on cycling in the past, but his preferences evolve in an ever-changing environment. In this way, it's relevant to find out that he now spends his days playing golf. Lastly, even when you followed the advice of your mom to give him golf clubs, you will not be at ease until you see his reaction when you give the gift. However, he might put on a smile as a form of politeness. It is possible that you will be able to deduce the value of the golf club you gave to him only through the fact that he uses it or he gives you a very nice present back. Even then, there will always remain an element of opacity regarding your uncle's preferences and his precise level of satisfaction when it comes to your gift.

This example draws us to the essential moral challenge that all human agents face: how do we find out what it is that other people want (Hayek 1945)? The three elements, personal inquiry (to find out what someone wants is essentially a question *about that person*), change (whatever preferences he has, they are subject to alteration) (see also O'Driscoll and Rizzo 1985, 37), and opacity (preferences remain subject to uncertainty), assist us in understanding epistemic subjectivism: what other people want is *encapsulated in the mindset* of those other people (O'Driscoll and Rizzo 1985, 6). This fundamental premise might sound like a no-brainer. Taking its implications seriously, however, does require some intellectual effort. Moving away from models that assume full knowledge on the value of talent X or the substitutability of product Y, the realization is that the real "scientific" answer (i.e., not assuming the problem away) to the question of which kind of good we should tax more or which kind of income we should tax less is not "out there" (O'Driscoll and Rizzo 1985, 649). Even the seemingly easy case for a surtax on soda (O'Donoghue and Rabin 2006) is simply unsolvable (Wagner 2016, 36). Knowing the precise subjective value of drinking soda for a person, the decrease in value he experiences when we replace it with something healthier, and how he will adjust his behavior to a tax is like finding out which present Uncle Bob likes the most. There is simply no way of finding out such information on millions of people.

This realization pulls policymakers back to Earth. Theoretically, they might use models and formulas that showcase how to steer a welfare function. In reality, the numbers they put in the models reflect the "contents of the human mind" that are not readily accessible (O'Driscoll and Rizzo 1985, 22). And, even moving past the subjectivity problem, aggregated welfare will equally be determined by knowledge regarding which drinks are healthy and which are not (information often gets revealed only from studies conducted years later), the precise effect that drinking less sugar has on our health, and how the industry reacts to tax exemptions (e.g., would the type of drinks developed to circumvent the surtax really be healthier?).

As O'Driscoll and Rizzo (1985, 5) propose, the recognition of subjectivity demands a shift away from the mathematical maximization models, of which optimal tax theory holds is an example. Optimal tax theory is an interesting *theory* based on the assumption that the fundamental problem of economic action—knowledge of others' preferences—does not arise (Hayek 1945). On the account that one has perfect knowledge on people's preferences, economics can be reduced as a *technological problem*, similar to something like the best bridge to connect two pieces of land (Buchanan 1964, 216). Within such an account, economics turns into a managerial science. However, it does not help us to solve genuine economic questions (Buchanan 1964), such as "what can tax rules do when governments lack the knowledge necessary to maximize aggregate social welfare?"

The Knowledge-Generating Function of the Price System

Before analyzing the type of tax policy that is acceptable on epistemic grounds, the illusionary models of optimal tax theory invite us to ask: how do we become informed of other peoples' subjective states in the first place? No society has the time or means to get into the type of uncertain inquiry we conducted to know what present Uncle Bob likes, so a genuine economic question, then, regards the "catallaxy" of knowledge: how does knowledge of people's preferences get acquired (Buchanan 1964, 217)? Surely, central planners cannot conduct the task of discovering the subjective desires of millions of people in any ways similar to what we had to do for Uncle Bob. The fundamental task of living together in peace and prosperity is finding ways to assist our fellow man in his desires, under conditions that equally promote my goals (Russel 2016). The epistemic challenge of this credo is that we have no a priori knowledge of what our fellow citizens want (Hayek 1945). One way of overcoming this barrier is the emergence and formation of small and durable groups whose members are aware of "what others are likely to want and how they are likely to respond" (Epstein 1995, 44). Small communities might be able to decrease information costs on their members' desires and engage in informal transactions. Fiscal policy, by contrast, is designed for societies of millions of people. Looking for the proper requirements for the fiscal rules in those societies, we must recognize how those (i.e., "our") societies channel knowledge of individual preferences throughout their constituent parts.

One way of understanding the use of private property rights—a system by which people can fence their holdings and trade them for others—lies not in the justice of it ("people deserve to have a right to what they made/have") nor prima facie in its direct incentive-aligning effect ("giving people property rights encourages work and cooperation"). A third way of seeing a role for property and exchange is beyond the merit or incentives of a single individual but amounts to property's *systemic and societal* role. By this, we mean that the justification of private property is not to be found in any appreciation of a single application of the right (merit/incentive) but rather in the institutional effect it bears over the whole set of applications: the price system. As we will see, this price performs a crucial epistemic role.[4]

If a thousand miles away, thousands of people desperately prefer Californian bikes above all others, this will be revealed. If tourists start to find the hotel prices in London exorbitant, they will send signals by not renting rooms in these hotels. If people are fed up with the predominant music or literature, this will produce effects in the market for cultural goods. Moreover, the cyclists, tourists, and readers will "talk" with producers/providers through the language of contracting, contracting a lot or not contracting at all. These signals generate reasons for producers and providers to increase or decrease either the price or quantity of the goods and services they have on offer. Although consumer preferences are subjective, scattered, and highly variable, the nature of the market makes sure these are communicated in the form of a single number (Delmotte 2017, 294). This is the reason Stigler (1987, 12) presents prices as "election results": everybody shapes the outcome, but the precise outcome is no one's intention. A system of property and exchange empowers consumers to gauge commercial initiatives set up by entrepreneurs, who will be evaluated through occurring profit or loss (Pennington 2011, 43).

Importantly, within this framework of communication of preferences, producers are not mere "price takers" but "talk back" to their conversation partner and share their knowledge as well (Kirzner 2013, 14–15, 24–69). They might tell them that they are paying too much and bring cheaper accommodation to the London market. Or they might convince them that, for the money they pay, they can have better bikes. Or they will convey that the books they were reading reflect an old bourgeois type of society and the time has come for something more edgy. The epistemological role for the providers and producers is twofold. First of all, entrepreneurs will often try to respond to signals from consumers by either finding cheaper ways to make a product or making improved products (Pennington 2011, 22; Kirzner 2013, 19). In fulfilling their role as either price breaker or product innovator, entrepreneurs actively integrate information about consumers within their actions and, hence, within the market (Kirzner 2013, 9–13; Pennington 2011, 35). Second, being warned about unforeseen opportunities through prices, each entrepreneur makes use of *his own* local and/or tacit knowledge (Hayek 1945; Lavoie 1986). Indeed, chances of entrepreneurs to beat their competitors will often depend on their *alertness* to employ specific insights related to their own specific circumstances and experiences (Kirzner 2013, 12). Some digital developers might have a specific sense of which technique could be used to make an innovative application. A designer who formerly worked as an artist might alter the modification of a product by transferring her aesthetic insights.

This points us toward the specific epistemic capacity of the price system generated by the institution of property and exchange. Its effects lie not so much in its direct functioning but its long-term systemic effects, being the information channels it establishes within a society over time. It installs a specific process whereby consumer preferences (and changes in them) are revealed and entrepreneurs are incentivized to respond to these alterations while making use of their unique knowledge in the light of their ever-changing circumstances. Looking back to optimal tax models, they now seem all the more remarkable. Tax theorists *demonstrate* how, for a given moment, tax rules can possibly steer the welfare function, *assuming* full information of the value of products and their substitutability. When discussing neoclassical equilibrium theory and the models of fully informed and rational agents allocating goods to their most valid use, Hayek (1948, 45) mentions:

> In the usual presentations of equilibrium analysis it is generally made to appear as if these questions of *how the equilibrium comes about* were solved. But, if we look closer, it soon becomes evident that these apparent demonstrations amount to no more than the apparent proof of what is *already assumed.*

Optimal tax theorists start their reasoning with something that is in reality the outcome of an entire process (Kirzner 2013, 5, 21). Here, we try to understand markets not as equilibria but as *equilibrating*: we try to capture the *processes* that are conducive to the people satisfying each other's preferences (Kirzner 2013, 21–23). In this regard, ab initio, the utility tags, or knowledge of the substitutability of a good or service, are not readily available. In reality, the values we attach to goods and the way we respond to price changes (i.e., a tax) are subjective matters *encapsulated in the mindset* of other people and revealed through the choices we make. One of the genuine reasons for actually having a market system lies in its knowledge-generating effect, in the sense that it detects and reveals our "utility scalars" and the substitutability of one thing for another (Kirzner 1985). In other terms, tax economists engineer a process on the basis of information that is in reality the *outcome* of that very process. Whereas economists' models work with *hypothetical* information when it comes to people's preferences and the process of giving people gifts requires a *costly* inquiry to find out what other people want, market societies employ a middle man for these tasks, one that gives *reliable information* at a *fair cost.* Specifically, the price system embodies a social mechanism whereby initially hidden and unknown knowledge, for instance, regarding preferences or the use of the external world, incrementally will reveal itself (Pennington 2011, 23). The reason we, in the world outside gifts and blackboard economics, opt for private property is because this institution creates both reliable numbers that reflect unique knowledge of other peoples' ever-changing preferences and incentives to take these numbers seriously.

The Flat Tax as an Epistemologically Feasible Tax Policy

Traffic lights are a form of intervention, a rule imposed by the state and enforced with coercion. The reason traffic lights do a fair job of enabling people to go where they want to go lies not in their intelligence but in their simplicity. The public road embodies a complex, nonsurveyable number of streams, each time constituted by people who have their own destinations in pursuit of their own individual ends. To get where they want to be, people calculate the distance and maybe pass a place at which they want to eat. People have many different destinations, and some of them change halfway. The point is, each single traffic user has a different plan, different purposes in the face of ever-changing circumstances. Enabling them to get to where they want to be, does not require a highly complex code. As Schmidtz (2010, 85) explains: "We want the most compact set of lights that enables motorists to know what to expect from each other, and thereby get from point A to point B with minimal interference."

Traffic lights are successful for two reasons in *streamlining* the complex movements of many individuals with different plans. First, they do not complicate these plans; they offer a simple rule to follow. Second, they do not tell anyone where to go. They respect the destination of each individual, in the sense that every destination is affected similarly by the rule. Theoretically, it is possible to imagine how a traffic system could make us all better off if some passengers got to their destination quicker, at the cost of others. Surely some scholars would deem some destinations more important than others. Practically, such a system would demand information on who goes where and for what reason. Traffic lights are designed with an understanding that there is an underlying network of reasons and information that determines why people want to go somewhere and everybody is better of when traffic lights facilitate traffic by means of rules that apply to each motorist in the same way.

In a similar manner, tax rules are a form of useful coercion. On a minimalist account, taxes are the middle man we need to pay to get the price system working. As mentioned by Holmes and Sunstein (1999), even property rights and freedom of contract are not free, and their enforcement requires money. On a broader account, they are a price we pay for public goods and welfare programs. Tax rules are the prerequisite to have a public road in the first place and maybe even a safety net if we happen to crash. So to have an ordered society where everybody has a chance to arrive at their destination, we also need tax rules. In pretty much the same way as with traffic lights, these tax rules cannot really "think for us." Demanding from tax rules to optimize the social welfare function would be like asking traffic lights where we need to go to. But that does not mean traffic lights are not necessary; it just means we are asking the wrong things from them.

Tax rules, then, ought to do just what traffic rules do: streamline the economic movements by applying a simple set of rules that affect each economic traveler equally. First, they ought to be simple in the sense that they impose no heavy extra cost on the economic agents (O'Driscoll and Rizzo 1985, 6). Second, tax rules that are epistemically feasible are those that respect the underlying network of information. This information is not present in rules, but in the broader social sphere, it intervenes in the emergent prices. Hence, tax rules ought to *respect prices*. Because prices offer the feedback to the rest of the economic community, the relative relation between prices needs to remain intact. This means that taxes should try to affect each price, *the storage of unique knowledge*, in an equal way. First, a flat tax respects both requirements: it holds as a simple rule that does not impose much additional computational costs. Second, a flat tax respects the underlying informational network wherein it operates. Moreover, flat taxes, by "cutting off" or "adding" an equal proportion of each transactional price, respect the relative positions of these prices. If one sort of labor costs 50 an hour pretax and another 100, a flat tax of 50 percent does not alter the relative relation: the first type of labor will still pay only half as much as the second. If one form of product requiring a huge manpower costs 1,000 and another simple digital product costs 200, a uniform tax of 20 percent will present these two products in relatively the same way to potential buyers: one product costs five times as much as the other. Exerting similar repercussions on all transactions, flat taxes roughly respect the feedback that prices will offer to economic agents. Because flat taxes do not reshuffle the effects of pretax prices on economic agents, they create a legal framework that harnesses the knowledge-generating function of the price system.

It is clear from the outset that optimal tax theory or, for instance, a system of steep progressive taxes, by virtue of being systems of differentiated taxation, are not "epistemically feasible":

> If, before taxation, a surgeon gets as much for an operation as an architect for planning a house, or a salesman gets as much for selling ten cars as a photographer for taking forty portraits, the same relation will still hold if proportional taxes are deducted from their receipts. But with progressive taxation of incomes this relation may be greatly changed. Not only may services which before taxation receive the same remuneration bring very different rewards; but a man who receives a relatively large payment for a service may in the end

be left with less than another who receives a smaller payment. (Hayek 2011, 443)

Indeed, Hayek's opposition to progressive taxation lay not so much in matters of principle or merit but in the importance of preserving the relative feedback exerted by prices before taxation. The underlying reason is that those prices are not a "manna from heaven" but contain important knowledge of people's preferences, knowledge that creates the right incentives for innovation and competition. The system of differentiated taxation, as championed by conventional tax theory, pretends to be able to *shape* the signals of the market in ways that would create desired behavioral responses. Not only do its proponents forget that this system lacks knowledge of the relative values necessary to set tax rates at theoretically desired levels, but that, by effectively applying differentiated tax rates, tax theorists make sure people in real life lack the signals they need to take each other's preferences seriously. It might be that proponents of progressive taxation are aware of the problem sketched here but argue that, due to decreasing marginal utility, it is precisely progressive (income) taxation that realizes an equal effect on income. The response here is that, as has been sufficiently argued, flat taxes could "catch" the effect of decreasing marginal utility since proportionality clearly demands more from those who have higher income flows. In other terms, the elasticity of marginal utility needs to be relatively high for it to justify progressive taxes, and many authors gauge uniform taxation to be sufficient to satisfy the equal sacrifice principle (Young 1990, 255; Samuelson 1947, 247). What should be added is that flat taxes might not always realize equal effects in the pure economic sense, meaning that they affect every transaction equally. Rather than exerting pure equal effects, the requirement to stick to a *general rule* that applies in equal proportion to any transaction appears the *least distortive option* because it leaves policymakers the least amount of discretion to re-shuffle the prices. In this regard, progressive taxation might be theoretically appealing, but there is no guarantee that policymakers would choose the rates and brackets that are theoretically "optimal." Quoting J. R. McCulloch (Hayek 2011, 433): "The moment you abandon the cardinal principle of exacting from all individuals the same proportion of their income or of their property, you are at sea without rudder or compass, and there is no amount of injustice and folly you may not commit." Hence, to proponents of progressive taxation, we could mention that taxes will always be distortive but the flat taxes are the proposal that will probably give rise to the least amount of distortion because, of all the proposals for equal taxation, it is the one that leaves the least amount of fiscal discretion.

We currently live in a world where it is possible that, due to taxation, a cheap car is presented to me as an expensive one and an expensive one can be fairly cheap. One kind of breakfast meal can be subject to 10 percent VAT while another kind is supported by subsidies. One entrepreneur pays 30 percent taxes on profits and the other 15 percent. The systematic riddles of exemptions and exceptions distort the price function and make it impossible for both entrepreneurs to fully appreciate consumer preferences and consumers to honestly evaluate producer initiatives. It is an epistemic wonder in itself why some of the most influential tax scholars have hitherto failed to take these issues seriously and, by their championing of differentiated tax rates, support Pareto-inferior policies that characterize our tax codes. Conversely, our demand for equal taxation on all prices serves as a check on government officials acting upon imperfect knowledge and integrates the challenge of epistemic subjectivism within fiscal processes. A flat tax is epistemically more robust than the prevailing alternatives because the requirement to apply one rate to all commercial transactions sensibly limits the range for governments to replace the unique knowledge-generating function of the market with fallible political estimations of the value of goods and services or their substitutability.

This chapter does not flesh out any single idea advanced by mainstream tax theory. Rather, it argues for a *Copernican turn* in our fiscal thinking. Whether optimal, Pigouvian, or paternalist, academic fiscal thinking is strongly idealized, and specific proposals are advanced on the assumption that (1) taxation is outside the very process it aims to regulate; (2) the people who populate this fiscal process are benignly motivated; and (3) knowledge of what is fair and how to maximize welfare lies within reach of the fiscal authorities. This chapter, in contrast, expounds that politics—and thus taxation—will be shaped and executed by people who are self-interested and face severe epistemological constraints to enhance the aggregated social welfare. Whereas, here, we employed this realization to debunk the general idea of discriminatory tax rates. Future researchers will need to scrutinize *specific proposals* as brought forward by conventional tax theory. Once the general assumptions that ground fiscal thinking have been unmasked as idealized, the prospective research task is indeed to confront the masses of contemporary tax proposals with realistic worries and limitations regarding the fiscal process in an in-depth analysis. Whether the proposal is to enhance people's health with a tax on soda (O'Donoghue and Rabin 2003) or to limit wealth inequality with a 100 percent rate on income above a specific bracket (Robeyns 2016, 33), traditional tax scholars need to screen whether their proposals remain viable once the twin problem of human opportunism and limited knowledge has been integrated within the field. If theorizing about a better tax system has the aspiration to actually enhance tax systems in this world, tax proposals need to be robust and deal with the challenges that mark the political process as we know it. In other words, if normative tax theory has anything to do with the real world, it needs to incorporate a realistic point of view.

NOTES

1. In the real world, there is more going on than the two group images that dominate our approach here. Various interest groups will be effective at securing legislative benefits through representation (if their votes have strategic importance) or through lobbying (if they are well organized and financially powerful). Rather than "a majority" dominating "a minority" in each majoritarian cycle and in all new fiscal legislation (e.g., a new "tax deal"), in practice, various pressure groups respond to each other's interests via logrolling until a majority coalition has been formed.

   The institution of representative democracy also complicates the model. Individuals secure their interests indirectly by trading votes for fiscal favors. These are just a few elements that point to the fact that fiscal favors will not be acquired by the majority as such, but often instead by the best organized subgroups. That said, this is just a nuance that does not touch upon the institutional essence we describe here: a majority rule absent of any extra constitutional requirements enables those in charge to offset the costs onto others (Buchanan and Tullock 1999, 85–96).

2. Assuming that the production of public goods creates an equal value for each citizen, I focus on the taxing part of the "fiscal exchange." Buchanan also isolates the funding part of the exchange from the expenditure side. For instance, Buchanan and Tullock (1999, 137) focus on spending decisions by a majority under the presumption of an equal property tax on all citizens. Nonetheless, I acknowledge the two sidedness of the fiscal account (i.e., that taxation is part of public economics, *sensu latu*, and that the justice of taxation equally depends on the production and distribution of public goods among the constituency. See, for instance, Brennan and Buchanan (2000a, 133–49).

3. On a Hayekian account, the idea of general rules that apply without any distinction to all individuals is the very meaning of the Rule of Law. In the *Constitution of Liberty*, Hayek resurrects this old definition of the Rule of Law, by pointing to one of its functions, namely, the protection it affords against misuse of power. In this regard, the flat tax can be conceptualized as the fiscal instantiation of the Rule of Law:

> That a majority, merely because it is a majority, should be entitled to apply to a minority a rule which does not apply to itself is an infringement of a principle much more fundamental than democracy itself, a principle on which the justification of democracy rests. . . . It is the great merit of proportional taxation that it provides a rule which is likely to be agreed upon by those who will pay absolutely more and those who will pay absolutely less and which, once accepted, raises no problem of a separate rule applying only to a minority. (Hayek 2007, 441)

4. As the previous lines might suggest, the following pages will isolate the issue of the *distribution* of preferences, as separate from the *production* of preferences. This might give the impression that preferences are "out there," waiting to be revealed. However, it should be clear that the system of property and exchange performs a role in both aspects; hence, markets take up their role to create preferences too.

REFERENCES

Akerlof, George. 1978. "The Economics of 'Tagging' as Applied to the Optimal Income Tax, Welfare Programs, and Manpower Planning." *The American Economic Review* 68, no. 1: 8–19.

Alesina, Alberto, Andrea Ichino, and Loukas Karabarbounis. 2011. "Gender-Based Taxation and the Division of Family Chores." *American Economic Journal: Economic Policy* 3, no. 2: 1–40.

Alston, Lee, Thrainn Eggertsson, and Douglass North. 1996. *Empirical Studies in Institutional Change: Political Economy of Institutions and Decisions*. Cambridge: Cambridge University Press.

Bankman, Joel, and Daniel Shaviro. 2015. "Piketty in America: A Tale of Two Literatures." *Tax Law Review* 68, no. 3: 453–517.

Bankman, Joseph, and David Weisbach. 2006. "The Superiority of an Ideal Consumption Tax over an Ideal Income Tax." *Stanford Law Review* 58, no. 5: 1413–56.

Baumol, William. 1972. "On Taxation and the Control of Externalities." *The American Economic Review* 62, no. 3: 307–22.

Bennassi, Corrado, and Emanuela Randon. 2015. "Optimal Commodity Taxation and Income Distribution." Quaderni Working Paper DSE No. 1001. Accessed March 22, 2018. http://dx.doi.org/10.2139/ssrn.2592385.

Boadway, Robin. 2012. *From Optimal Tax Theory to Tax Policy: Retrospective and Prospective Views*. Cambridge, MA: MIT Press.

Boettke, Peter. 2012. *Living Economics: Yesterday, Today, and Tomorrow*. Oakland, CA: The Independent Institute and Universidad Francisco Marroquin.

———. 2017. "Ian Kumekawa: The First Serious Optimist: A. C. Pigou and the Birth of Welfare Economics." *Public Choice* 173, no. 1–2: 245–48.

Boudreaux, Donald. 1986. "Schumpeter and Kirzner on Competition and Equilibrium." In *The Market Process: Essays in Contemporary Austrian Economics*. Edited by Peter Boettke and David Prychtiko, 52–61. Cheltenham, UK: Edward Elgar.

Boudreaux, Donald, and Adam Pritchard. 1993. "Rewriting the Constitution: An Economic Analysis of the Constitutional Amendment Process." *Fordham Law Review* 62, no. 1: 111–62.

Brennan, Geoffrey, and James Buchanan. 2000a. *The Power to Tax: Analytical Foundations of a Fiscal Constitution*. Indianapolis, IN: Liberty Fund.

———. 2000b. *The Reason of Rules*. Indianapolis, IN: Liberty Fund.

Brownell, Kelly et al. 2009. "The Public Health and Economic Benefits of Taxing Sugar-Sweetened Beverages." *New England Journal of Medicine* 361, no. 16: 1599–605.

Buchanan, James. 1949. "The Pure Theory of Government Finance: A Suggested Approach." *Journal of Political Economy* 57, no. 6: 496–505.

———. 1964. "What Should Economists Do?" *Southern Economic Journal* 30, no. 3: 213–22.

———. 2000. *The Logical Foundations of Constitutional Liberty*. Indianapolis, IN: Liberty Fund.

Buchanan, James, and Roger Congleton. 2006. *Politics by Principle Not Interest: Towards Nondiscriminatory Democracy*. Cambridge: Cambridge University Press.

Buchanan, James, and Gordon Tullock. 1999. *The Calculus of Consent: Logical Foundations of Constitutional Democracy*. Indianapolis, IN: Liberty Fund.

Butler, Eamonn. 2012. *Public Choice: A Primer*. London: IEA.

Corneo, Giacomo. 2002. "The Efficient Side of Progressive Income Taxation." *European Economic Review* 46, no. 7: 1359–68.

Cowen, Nick. 2016. "Introduction: Symposium on Robust Political Economy." *Critical Review* 28: 420–39.

Delmotte, Charles. 2017. "The Right to Autonomy as a Moral Foundation for the Realization Principle in Income Taxation." In *The Philosophical Foundations of Tax Law*. Edited by Monica Bhandari, 281–302. Oxford: Oxford University Press.

———. 2018. "Tax Uniformity as a Requirement of Justice." Working paper.

Diamond, Peter, and Emmanuel Saez. 2011. "The Case for a Progressive Tax: From Basic Research to Policy Recommendations." *Journal of Economic Perspectives* 25, no. 4: 165–90.

Dorling, Danny. 2014. *Inequality and the 1%*. New York: Verso Books.

Epstein, Richard. 1995. *Simple Rules for a Complex World*. Cambridge, MA: Harvard University Press.

Fichtner, Jason, and Jacob Feldman. 2013. "The Hidden Cost of Tax Compliance." Accessed July 12, 2018. https://www.mercatus.org/system/files/Fichtner_TaxCompliance_v3.pdf.

Gaus, Gerald. 2010. "The Idea and Ideal of Capitalism." In *The Oxford Handbook of Business Ethics*, edited by George Brenkert and Tom Beauchamp, 73–100. Oxford: Oxford University Press.

Gwartney, James, and Richard Wagner. 1988. *Public Choice and Constitutional Economics*. Greenwich, CT: JAI Press.

Hamlin, Alan. 2017. "What Political Philosophy Should Learn from Economics about Taxation." Accessed September 26, 2017. https://www.research.manchester.ac.uk/portal/en/publications/what-political-philosophy-should-learn-from-economics-about-taxation%28c51023ed-2e26-451c-ba15-fe1adefe6f4c%29/export.html#export.

Harrison, Jeffrey, and Jules Theeuwes. 2008. *Law and Economics*. New York: W. W. Norton & Co.

Hayek, Friedrich. 1945. "The Use of Knowledge in Society." *The American Economic Review* 35, no. 4: 519–30.

———. 1948. *Individualism and Economic Order*. Chicago: University of Chicago Press.

———. 1976. *Law, Legislation and Liberty. Vol. 3 The Political Order of a Free People*. Chicago: University of Chicago Press.

———. 2007. *The Road to Serfdom*. Chicago: University of Chicago Press.

———. 2011. *The Constitution of Liberty*. Chicago: University of Chicago Press.

Heady, Christopher. 1993. "Optimal Taxation as a Guide to Tax Policy: A Survey." *Fiscal Studies* 14, no. 1: 15–41.

Hettich, Walter, and Stanley Winer. 1999. *Democratic Choice and Taxation: A Theoretical and Empirical Analysis*. New York: Cambridge University Press.

Holmes, Stephen, and Cas Sunstein. 1999. *The Cost of Rights: Why Liberty Depends on Taxes*. New York: Norton.

Hood, Christopher. 2007. *The Tools of Government in the Digital Age*. Basingstoke, UK: Palgrave Macmillan.

Ireland, Norman. 1994. "On Limiting the Market for Status Signals." *Journal of Public Economics* 53, no. 1: 91–110.

———. 2001. "Optimal Income Tax in the Presence of Status Effects." *Journal of Public Economics* 81, no. 2: 193–212.

Jacobson, Michael, and Kelly Brownell. 2000. "Small Taxes on Soft Drinks and Snack Foods to Promote Health." *American Journal of Public Health* 90, no. 6: 854–57.

Kaplow, Luis. 2008. *The Theory of Taxation and Public Economics*. Princeton, NJ: Princeton University Press.

Kirzner, Israel. 1985. *Discovery and the Capitalist Process*. Chicago: University of Chicago Press.

Kirzner, Israel. 2013. *Competition and Entrepreneurship*. Indianapolis, IN: Liberty Fund.

Kwall, Jeffrey. 2011. "When Should Asset Appreciation Be Taxed? The Case for a Disposition Standard of Realization." *Indiana Law Review* 86, no. 1: 77–118.

Lavoie, Donald. 1986. "The Market as a Procedure for Discovery and Conveyance of Inarticulate Knowledge." *Comparative Economic Studies* 28, no. 1: 1–19.

Logue, Kyle, and Joel Slemrod. 2008. "Genes as Tags: The Tax Implications of Widely Available Genetic Information." *National Tax Journal* 61: 843–63.

Lucas, Robert. 1990. "Supply-Side Economics: An Analytical Review." *Oxford Economic Papers* 42, no. 2: 293–316.

Mankiw, Gregory, and Matthew Weinzierl. 2010. "The Optimal Taxation of Height: A Case Study of Utilitarian Income Redistribution." *American Economic Journal: Economic Policy* 2, no. 1: 155–76.

Mankiw, Gregory, Matthew Weinzierl, and Danny Yagan. 2009. "Optimal Taxation in Theory and Practice." *Journal of Economic Perspectives* 23, no. 4: 147–74.

McChesney, Fred. 1987. "Rent Extraction and Rent Creation in the Economic Theory of Regulation." *The Journal of Legal Studies* 16, no. 1: 101–18.

Meade, James. 2013. *The Just Economy*. London: Routledge.

Micheletto, Luca. 2011. "Optimal Nonlinear Redistributive Taxation and Public Good Provision in an Economy with Veblen Effects." Accessed July 12, 2018. https://doi.org/10.1111/j.1467-9779.2010.01493.x.

Mirrlees, James. 1971. "An Exploration in the Theory of Optimum Income Taxation." *The Review of Economic Studies* 38, no. 2: 175–208.

Musgrave, Richard, and Peggy Musgrave. 1989. *Public Finance in Theory and Practice*. New York: McGraw-Hill.

Myles, Gareth. 1995. *Public Economics*. Cambridge: Cambridge University Press.

O'Donoghue, Ted, and Matthew Rabin. 2003. "Studying Optimal Paternalism, Illustrated by a Model of Sin Taxes." *American Economic Review* 93, no. 2: 186–91.

———. 2006. "Optimal Sin Taxes." Journal of Public Economics 90 , no. 10–11: 1825–49.

O'Driscoll, Gerald, and Mario Rizzo. 1985. *The Economics of Time and Ignorance*. London: Routledge.

O'Neill, Martin. 2017. "Philosophy and Public Policy after Piketty." *Journal of Political Philosophy* 25, no. 3: 343–75.

Padover, Saul. 1953. *The Complete Madison: His Basic Writings*. New York: Harper & Brothers Publishers.

Peeters, Bruno, Hans Gribnau, and Jo Badisco. 2017. "Introduction." In *Building Trust in Taxation*. Edited by Bruno Peeters, Hans Gribnau, and Jo Badisco, v–vii. Cambridge: Intersentia.

Pennington, Mark. 2011. *Robust Political Economy*. Cheltenham, UK: Edward Elgar Publishing.

Pigou, Arthur. 1932. *The Economics of Welfare*. London: Macmillan and Co.

Piketty, Thomas. 2014. *Capital in the Twenty-First Century*. Cambridge, MA: Belknap Press of Harvard University Press.

Robeyns, Ingrid. 2016. "Having Too Much." In *Wealth: NOMOSLVI*. Edited by Jack Knight, and Melissa Schwartzberg, 1–44. New York: NYU Press.

Russell, Dan. 2016. "Self-Ownership as a Form of Ownership." In *The Oxford Handbook of Freedom*, edited by David Schmidtz and Carmen Pavel, 21–39. Oxford: Oxford University Press.

Salamon, Lester. 2002. *The Tools of Government: A Guide to the New Governance*. Oxford: Oxford University Press.

Samuelson, Paul. 1947. *Foundations of Economic Analysis*. Cambridge, MA: Harvard University Press.

Schenk, Deborah. 1995. "Taxation of Equity Derivatives: A Partial Integration Proposal." *Tax Law Review* 50, no. 4: 571–642.

———. 2004. "A Positive Account of the Realization Rule." *Tax Law Review* 57, no. 3: 355–96.

Schmidtz, David. 2010. "Property and Justice." *Social Philosophy and Policy* 27, no. 1: 79–100.

Shaviro, Daniel. 2000. "Inequality, Wealth, and Endowment." *Tax Law Review* 53, no. 3: 397–421.

Simpson, David. 1995. "Optimal Pollution Taxation in a Cournot Duopoly." *Environmental and Resource Economics* 6, no. 4: 359–69.

Slemrod, Joel, and Jon Bakija. 2006. *Taxing Ourselves: A Citizen's Guide to the Debate over Taxes*. Cambridge, MA: MIT Press.

Stark, Kirk. 2005. "Enslaving the Beachcomber: Some Thoughts on the Liberty Objections to Endowment Taxation." *Canadian Journal of Law and Jurisprudence* 18, no. 1: 47–68.

Stigler, George. 1987. *The Theory of Price*. New York: Macmillan.

Stiglitz, Joseph. 1994. *Wither Socialism?* Cambridge, MA: MIT Press.

———. 2012. *The Price of Inequality*. London: Allen Lane.

Tebble, Adam. 2017. *Epistemic Liberalism*. London: London: Routledge.

Wagner, Richard. 2016. *Politics as a Peculiar Business: Insights from a Theory of Entangled Political Economy*. Cheltenham, UK: Edward Elgar Publishing.

Young, Peyton. 1990. "Progressive Taxation and Equal Sacrifice." *The American Economic Review* 80, no. 1: 253–66.

Zelenak, Lawrence. 2006. "Taxing Endowment." *Duke Law Journal* 55: 1145–80.

Part II

INTERDISCIPLINARY APPLICATIONS

Chapter Six

Warning Out, Settlement Laws, and Managing Poor-Relief CPRs in the Tocquevillian Township

Bob Kaminski

In November 2016, residents of Gipf-Oberfrick voted 144 to 62 against granting Nancy Holten citizenship status in their town and, by extension, a Swiss passport.[1] Residents of the small Aargau town resented her activism for bovine welfare (especially her opposition to customary Swiss cowbells) and questioned why they should provide her citizenship "if she annoys us and doesn't respect our traditions." The American press treated this decision as an exotic curiosity—wholly foreign to the American tradition of govern-ance.[2] With international migration representing an increasingly hot-button issue, similar attitudes inform the commonplace idea that America placed no restrictions on immigration before the widely reviled Chinese Exclusion Act of 1882. But Holten's experience would have been familiar to Frances Oliver and thousands of others whom local officials "warned out" of American towns between the seventeenth and early nineteenth centuries. At the time, an individual's right to aid or "relief"—financial or in kind—from one's town when one fell on hard times was predicated upon it being recognized as one's legal "settlement." "Warning out" started as an informal practice that advised a newcomer to leave town lest he or she be physically removed. Over the seventeenth century, it evolved into a legal ritual that disavowed a town's future obligation to provide for the newcomer, but rarely demanded that he or she actually leave. These practices proved particularly prevalent in New England, where they represented a limit on individual freedom but also served useful purposes fostering community cohesion and localist poor re-lief.

Drawing on the literatures on budgetary commons (Wagner 1992; Jakee and Turner 2002; Buchanan and Yoon 2004; Lipford and Yandle 2014) and, especially, common-pool resource (CPR) management (Runge 1981; Gardner, Ostrom, and Walker 1990; Ostrom 1990; Raudla 2010), this chapter will analyze the relationship between communities' boundary rules and welfare provision through the lens of colonial and early national Massachusetts towns' settlement rules and localist poor-relief system. These towns—the purest examples of Tocqueville's ideal of localist democratic governance—represented a gray area between associational and governmental models of organization. They selectively granted would-be residents legal settlement. They enforced these boundary rules not only to protect community stability, sociocultural homogeneity, and commitment to a shared view of the good but also to manage their budgetary CPRs. In so doing, they faced a trade-off between the two fundamental concerns of CPR management—appropriations and provisions problems (Ostrom 1990), which called them to limit potentially costly admissions to the community and expand its tax base, respectively. In managing these problems, they relied heavily upon the sociocultural homogeneity and commitment to austere Puritan norms (Innes 1995) that they protected through their boundary rules, which helped them overcome the "Samaritan's dilemma" articulated by James Buchanan (1975; Skarbek 2016) by delineating a clear boundary between the "deserving" and "undeserving" poor. With different individuals enjoying heterogeneous endowments of human and financial capital, towns—like later mutual-aid societies (Beito 2000)—screened would-be settlers on a pseudo-actuarial basis, sparking interjurisdictional competition for more-promising settlers (Lemke 2016). But they required interjurisdictional cooperation to settle and relieve the less fortunate. Like many of Ostrom's (1990) appropriation communities that successfully managed large, complex CPR systems, representatives of Massachusetts towns took advantage of their province's nested institutions to do so—coordinating at the provincial level to settle the unsettled but deserving poor in appropriate towns and to fashion rules disallowing towns from harboring outsiders without granting them settlement rights.

During the late-seventeenth century, Massachusetts' poor-relief system faced a destabilizing exogenous shock—a refugee crisis brought about by a series of wars—that fell unevenly on the colony's different towns. The situation necessitated major reforms to its settlement and relief rules lest the system collapse or fail to aid fellow Massachusetts settlers rendered homeless by war. To avoid either undesirable outcome, towns' representatives in the General Court passed a series of orders spreading the burden of relief for refugees over the entire province and detaching warnings out from actual calls to vacate towns. This solution effectively took advantage of nested institutions to solve the immediate crisis yet displayed imperfect foresight—it created a fiscal-commons situation that each town grazed with increasing impunity by warning out all newcomers, shifting the burden for their relief to the provincial government. Over time, this new regime contributed to changing norms about mobility. Massachusetts' legislators eventually reflected the new norms when they changed the settlement laws to eliminate this fiscal-commons situation in 1794—displaying a mutually constitutive relationship between the iterative process of formal rulemaking and informal norm formation.

This chapter will begin by reviewing the relevant economic and historiographical literature and theorizing its relation to colonial and early national poor relief. Second, it will examine the sociocultural and economic context that defined the CPR problem of poor relief in seventeenth-century Massachusetts towns with a significant trade-off between the incentives created by the appropriation and provision problems. It will also reinterpret Massachusetts' early settlement laws codifying warning out as using the province's nested institutions to prevent the deserving poor from going unaided. The third section will deal with how towns' representatives in Massachusetts' General Court attempted to adapt these institutions in response to humanitarian crises sparked by a series of wars. By creating provincial-level relief provisions and making warnings toothless legal formalities that merely vacated towns' responsibility to relieve newcomers, these initially effective changes created perverse incentives that prompted towns to graze the provincial fiscal commons—changing norms about mobility in the process and ultimately leading legislators to craft a less-associational system with weakened boundary rules. Finally, it will conclude with a brief discussion of the chapter's theoretical takeaways and their implications for contemporary policy debates.

THEORIZING LOCALIST POOR RELIEF AS A COMMON-POOL RESOURCE

Alexis de Tocqueville famously lauded local township government—exemplified most purely in New England—as coming "directly from the hand of God" but fragile, straddling the boundary between government and voluntary association with "institutions [that] are to liberty what primary schools are to knowledge" (Tocqueville [1835/1840] 2012, 101–102). Properly cultivated, it represented the source of civic engagement and associational life that formed a bulwark against the evil of democratic despotism. Thus, it is unsurprising that references to *Democracy in America*'s discussion of townships, other associations of civil society, and the mores they foster have abounded in the social–science literature concerning the role of civil society in liberal democracy. But their engagement with Tocqueville's incisive thought has often been limited by cursory readings of his works (see Sarah Wilford's contribution to this volume). Productive engagement with Tocqueville must also recognize the disjunctures between his narrative and historical experience. *Democracy in America* and its users and abusers all reflect a nostalgia for a localist agrarian society that was already passing from the scene in New England when the Norman nobleman visited America in 1831.[3] Consequently, examining the evolution of New England townships from their foundation to the early nineteenth century not only captures the process through which these bulwarks against democratic despotism and exemplars of democratic administration emerged but also promises the clearest look at the Tocquevillian ideal in practice. In particular, focusing on the evolving relationship between settlement laws and poor relief offers insight into a thorny problem of democratic administration intimately tied to communities' boundary rules.

A handful of historians have written on settlement laws, warning out, and poor relief, taking particular advantage of the relatively rich sources on the topics' New England histories. Josiah Benton (1911) set the agenda for the field with a well-documented policy history that placed the practice within a common-law tradition and noted that New Englanders practiced warning out to police the boundaries of their communities for socioreligious and, especially, economic reasons. Depictions of parsimonious New England Puritans shrinking from the idea of supporting potentially unruly outsiders permeated a number of new social histories that have gone far toward reconstructing the experience of poverty in early America (Jones 1975; Cray 1988; Smith 1988; Herndon 2001; Loiacono 2015; Hirota 2017). Ruth Wallis Herndon's *Unwelcome Americans* (2001) stands out as the most important contribution to this tradition by using a particularly detailed portrait of warning out in Rhode Island to draw attention to racial and sexual inequities in its enforcement. However, Cornelia Dayton and Sharon Salinger's masterful *Robert Love's Warnings* (2014) redefined the historiography on the topic. Through a rich social history of warning out as practiced in Boston between the French and Indian War and American Revolution, they present a compelling reinterpretation of the policy's eighteenth-century Massachusetts manifestation: "rather than a gesture meant to exclude," they argue, "warning facilitated the province's policy of making available a larger pool of welfare funds for Britons and non-Britons . . . than existed elsewhere in the Empire."

A small but insightful literature has developed around Richard Wagner's idea that budgetary politics can be described as a tragedy of the commons "where choice is divorced from responsibility for the consequences of those choices" (1992, 107). Economists building off this insight have identified a significant source of inefficient public spending (Buchanan and Yoon 2004; Jakee and Turner 2002; Lipford and Yandle 2014). But their models have captured only part of the problem involved in budgeting commonly held funds. They deal primarily with very large populations and agency problems connected to representative government, limiting their applicability to direct democracies or small towns. More significantly, Ringa Raudla has compellingly argued that the fiscal-commons literature suffers from the same myopically unexamined assumptions that Elinor Ostrom and her confrères studying CPRs have identified with regard to the literature on natural commons.[4]

Like classic commons problems, CPR problems exist when natural or man-made resources are subtractable so that withdrawn units are no longer available, multiple appropriators exploit them, and suboptimal outcomes emerge from appropriators failing to internalize the full cost of their actions. But the key contribution that CPR scholars have made is recognizing that alternatives to this suboptimal situation—beyond pure privatization or governmental regulation—may be feasible (Gardner, Ostrom, and Walker 1990). This recognition turned their attention to analyzing appropriation communities' efforts to establish self-governing rules for CPR management. Ostrom (1990) found that CPR-management institutions that have persisted over long periods shared eight design principles: (1) clearly defined boundaries delineating the resource and the community appropriating it; (2) congruence between appropriation rules, provision rules, and local conditions; (3) collective-choice arrangements; (4) effective provisions for monitoring; (5) graduated sanctions punishing violators by seriousness and context of offenses; (6) conflict-resolution mechanisms; (7) at least minimal recognition of rights to organize from outside authorities; and—when CPR systems are large and complex—(8) nested institutions to coordinate multiple layers of organization. Five of Ostrom's design principles apply to township-based poor relief, with little complication,[5] but three require further discussion, as do her analyses of the sociocultural contexts in which they tend to flourish and the conditions that shape their development.

Though insufficient to manage CPR problems themselves, boundary rules (delimiting the CPR and its appropriation community) appear first on Ostrom's list of design principles and stood at the heart of towns' strategies for managing relief funds. That is because boundary rules were intimately tied to both the appropriations and provisioning problems for CPRs, including localist relief funds. Their bearing on the appropriations problem is obvious—limiting relief to the deserving poor and managing their number. Like Beito's (2000) voluntarist mutual-aid societies, towns did the latter by screening would-be settlers based on pseudo-actuarial principles—disallowing settlement by those with poor expected financial and bodily health. But towns provisioned their relief funds through their residents' ratable incomes, creating a trade-off between managing their appropriation problems and seeking productive new residents in a labor (and capital) starved environment. For township-based poor relief, the operative provision problem did not involve ensuring citizens' rate payments—towns possessed the power to compel them—but, instead, involved managing the size and financial health of the taxable community. The provision problem also involved managing the community's socioreligious cohesion that was connected to the social solidarity underlying willingness to support the poor-relief system and—for better or worse—remains so (Putnam 2007).

Ostrom (1990) also notes that persistent appropriation communities depended as much on noneconomic, sociocultural factors as economic incentives to support their CPR-management systems. Her persistent CPR systems all dealt with uncertain environments in which the human population was stable and socioculturally homogeneous—minimizing conflict and fostering cooperation with lengthened time horizons and norm-defined behavior. These conditions applied in colonial New England as well. Bodily and financial health was uncertain, as it always is. Towns' origins in a religious project to establish shining cities on hills and continuing enforcement of boundary rules that restricted who could settle saw to their populations' stability and homogeneity. Norms also ordered actors' priorities. They underlay New Englanders' distinction between the deserving and undeserving poor and fueled their drive to ensure that none of the former fell through the cracks— deprived of relief by lack of a legal settlement.

Applying the CPR scholarship to voluntarist disaster relief, Emily Skarbek (2014, 2016) identified the "Samaritan's dilemma" James Buchanan (1975) theorized as a central part of relief-fund managers' appropriations problem. In it, one actor is in the position of dispensing aid to another, who has the choice whether to work or not. The former has an empathetic utility function vis-à-vis the other, making him suffer watching the latter starve. But the latter would rather enjoy the Samaritan's largesse than work, creating a situation in which—barring some form of credible commitment to do otherwise—the Samaritan aids the unfortunately named "parasite" who makes little effort to work. Skarbek (2016) argued that voluntary associations could display strategic courage in the face of Buchanan's dilemma. Namely, they could dispense temporary aid without creating permanent dependence by delineating unambiguous, preestablished boundary rules channeling relief to only the deserving poor while embedding the liberal–individualist assumptions underlying these rules into self-reinforcing associational constitutions. In colonial and early national Massachusetts, different normative commitments and institutional rules similarly gave towns strategic courage in the face of a potential Samaritan's dilemma. Namely, the Protestant work ethic and lack of affluence that Buchanan (1975) mentioned as forces of strategic courage played their parts, as did a legally instantiated belief in St. Augustine's prioritization of local duties over more distant ones.

New England's poor relief—like the larger and more complex CPR systems Ostrom (1990) saw persisting—evolved within a nested system allowing cooperation between appropriation communities when necessary, such as meeting New Englanders' priority of aiding all deserving poor. As in her discussion of CPRs' institutional changes, they adapted their institutions to changing conditions through provincial-level changes in the General Court—straddling the boundary between overarching constitutional- and practical policy-level changes. These left localities with control over strategies within the overarching system—both at the policy and implementation levels. This nested institutional structure helped towns overcome perverse incentives and cooperate to meet the Good Samaritan's challenge to aid deserving strangers. Though scholars, such as Jayme Lemke (2016), have argued that interjurisdictional competition for migrants can lead to increasing individual rights, welfare provision represents a particularly thorny problem for localist models of government. Put simply, individuals enjoy heterogeneous endowments, and there is little incentive for a community to welcome an outsider who would represent a drain upon the public coffers rather than a net taxpayer. Indeed, one of the key criticisms leveled against polycentric and localist governance has involved the inclusion of socioeconomically disadvantaged groups (Boettke, Coyne, and Leeson 2011). Though adherents of Weber's Protestant work ethic, colonial New Englanders believed deeply in aiding the incapacitated (Innes 1995). Consequently, perhaps *the* key issue that they faced when attempting to manage their system of township-based poor relief was balancing localism with universality. Early on, towns' representatives in Massachusetts' General Court found this balance by crafting provincial-level rules minimizing the number of unsettled individuals at the expense of freedom of movement and interjurisdictional competition. Subsequently, it embraced provincially funded relief for them amid a wartime humanitarian crisis, allowing towns to warn out newcomers (leaving the provincial government responsible for their relief) with no requirement that they actually leave. This solution destabilized the system in the context of continued local control. Thereafter, towns followed their perverse incentives to graze the provincial fiscal commons with impunity by warning all newcomers. Nevertheless, Massachusetts' nested institutions provided the space for the development of new rules forestalling this abuse—bringing (largely) localist poor relief into the nineteenth century.

SEVENTEENTH-CENTURY MASSACHUSETTS' SOCIOECONOMIC CONTEXT, CPR PROBLEM, AND SOLUTIONS

Massachusetts' laws regulating legal settlement and poor relief evolved within a larger English tradition and a specific New England Puritan context, which shaped actors' normative priorities and their policy imaginations. In this context, they managed the CPR of poor-relief funds largely by enforcing boundary rules restricting entry into their communities that largely resembled voluntary associations. These boundary rules performed multiple functions.

Historians have long recognized that towns enforced them to protect their communities' commitment to a religiously informed vision of the common good and to limit their sociocultural heterogeneity (Benton 1911; Herndon 2001). For better or for worse, both of these functions indirectly supported their CPR-management strategy by reinforcing the in-group solidarity that underlay townspeople's willingness to fund welfare provisions. More directly, towns enforced boundary rules to manage the balance between the two central components of CPR problems—the appropriations problem of limiting relief outlays and the provision problem of expanding their ratable tax bases—by selectively admitting the more promising of heterogeneously endowed outsiders to legal settlement. The whole localist poor-relief system also depended upon clear normative boundaries between the deserving and undeserving poor, which went far toward alleviating James Buchanan's "Samaritan's dilemma" (1975). But New Englanders appreciated the moral of the parable to which Buchanan referred. Consequently, towns took advantage of their position nested within Massachusetts' provincial government to craft rules minimizing the number of souls failed by the localist relief system's disincentives to care for the least among us by strictly coordinating the settlement of the unsettled poor and enforcing boundary rules to prevent sojourners from staying anywhere without gaining legal settlement entitling them to relief.

Tocqueville numbered "an overseer of the poor, whose duty, very difficult to fulfill, is to enforce the laws relative to the poor" among the "multiplying officials" who carried out democratic administration in American townships (Tocqueville [1835/1840] 2012, 106, 117). This Jacksonian-era office fulfilled a responsibility that predated England's American colonies. Following customs that the Poor Laws of 1572, 1598, and 1601 had enshrined into law within the metropole, the towns of English colonies in the Americas were responsible for relieving their poor inhabitants (Dayton and Salinger 2014). "Inhabitants" was, however, an important term. Towns in either England, New or Old, recognized no legal responsibility to aid destitute strangers—a category that did not necessarily imply complete unfamiliarity. In the legal parlance of the day, "stranger" simply meant anyone without a legal settlement within a community. And gaining a legal settlement within a community was more complicated than simply arriving in one.

Seventeenth-century New England towns claimed substantial rights to define who could settle within their communities. Portsmouth, Rhode Island, exemplified this position when it resolved at a town meeting that "none shall be received as inhabitants . . . but such as shall be received . . . by the consent of the Bodye, and do submit to the Government that is or shall be established, according to the word of God" (Benton 1911, 100). In different towns this "consent of the Bodye" could variously mean the assent of the town's selectmen, a favorable vote at a town meeting, or some combination thereof. But regardless of these mechanics, cultural as well as economic concerns shaped towns' boundary rules.

A vision of towns as integral corporate bodies informed their right to define their boundaries. In 1679, Boston's freemen cast the assumptions behind this vision into sharp relief with a petition challenging Massachusetts' representational model. At the time, each town with twenty freemen was entitled to send two deputies to the province's General Court—in a very real sense, it was towns and not their residents that enjoyed representation in the provincial assembly. Boston's townsfolk resented how this model accorded towns of twenty freemen equal representation to their town with almost 400 freemen who bore "their full proportion of all publique charges." They presaged the more famous (and catchier) cries that would ring out in Boston a century hence with their declaration that "all townes should be allowed their priuilege proportionable to y^e. charge they beare." Yet, even in their argument for representation "proportionable to our Nomb^r of Freemen [or] at least to our Nomb^r of Churches," Bostonians left the door open to representation predicated on membership within another set of integral, organic communities—their churches (*Boston Town Records*, v. 7, 1881, 133–34).

The New England town's corporate body had a soul, which settlers sought to protect by demanding conformity to religious doctrines and the sociopolitical institutions they believed flowed from them. The founding covenant Dedham's first 126 settlers signed in 1636 was instructive. The Massachusetts townsmen pledged, "We engage by all means to keep off from our company such as shall be contrary-minded, and receive only such into our society as will . . . promote its temporal and spiritual good" (Benton 1911, 32). Such a requirement could hardly have surprised anyone five years after the colony's General Court had ordered that "noe man shalbe admitted to the freedome of this body polliticke, but such as are members of . . . the churches" (*Records of Massachusetts*, v. 1, 1853, 87). This was not just talk. Statements like "hee is . . . disfranchized & banished" or "shee shalbee gone by the last of this month" for preaching heterodox doctrines pepper the records of Massachusetts' General Court (*Records of Massachusetts*, v. 1, 1853, 189, 207, 211–12, 226, 242). And its neighbor colonies made similar demands.[6]

These thick communities imposed serious responsibilities upon their members beyond religious orthodoxy. Tocqueville's observation that "Each inhabitant is obligated, under penalty of fine, to accept these different [town] offices" was as true in the seventeenth century as it would be in the nineteenth (*Records of Massachusetts*, v. 2, 1853, 208; Tocqueville [1835/1840] 2012, 107). No more could individuals escape from their fiscal responsibilities than from public service. In 1638, Massachusetts's General Court observed individuals shirking their duty to pay taxes and tithes "in such voluntary contributions as are in vse." This situation was unacceptable. The Court "declared, that ev'y inhabitant in any towne is lyable to contribute to all charges, both in church & comõn welth." Any inhabitant who did not "contribute, pportionably to his ability . . . to all comõn charges," was now liable to legal action (*Records of Massachusetts*, v. 1, 1853, 240–41).

Poor relief was one of towns' more onerous common charges. It could take many forms. There was indoor relief, which Boston's selectmen offered Mrs. Jane Woodcock the day after a cold Little Ice Age Christmas in 1664. That day, their minutes noted that the "Widdow hath liberty of admittance into the Allme house." They also granted one of their number "Mr Petter Oliuer . . . pouer to order ye same." Not long before, Oliver had worked with the Church of Boston's deacons to make good on a number of bequests "giuen for the erecting of an Allmehouse" (*Boston Town Records*, v. 7, 1881, 7, 24). As Dayton and Salinger note (2014), Oliver's successors would increasingly make use of the almshouse, especially for impoverished strangers after Massachusetts created provisions for their relief at provincial expense in 1701.

Many legally settled individuals, however, preferred outdoor relief, which allowed them to remain in their homes—sometimes, literally, as it did for a woman who received "40^s. for the paym^t of her rent" in 1662. Outdoor relief took multiple forms. It could be monetary, in kind, or even town-sponsored health care. The latter could be quite expensive. In October 1662, Boston paid Mathew Coy "£10. out of the Towne Treasuery for his . . . healinge of William Ockington" in a year when the town collected less than £700 *"for Country, County, and Towne occasions."* Subsequently, Boston would make agreements with local surgeons to wave their rates in exchange for their "promise of attendance . . . vpon any poore, sicke or hurt in the towne" (*Boston Town Records*, v. 7, 1881, 6, 12, 51, 64, 76). Another informal form of relief was significantly cheaper—Boston's selectmen oft granted individuals, such as "Widdow Beamsely," liquor licenses as a physically manageable way to meet the "necessitye of her famely releafe" without creating dependence. Others received more conventional forms of relief—Boston's selectmen "allowed 40^s. for p^rsent supply of one good Favour Inhabitant" on Christmas Eve in 1661. They also placed individuals—both children and adults—within households and paid for their maintenance (*Boston Town Records*, v. 7, 1881, 5, 12, 15, 21, 43, 55). These various forms of relief—indoor and outdoor—represented a substantial portion of towns' outlays.

The funding mechanisms that underlay towns' relief efforts were little more formalized than their ad-hoc system of distribution. Relief funds came out of town treasuries that were restocked as needed primarily through rates assessed on property, polls, and "faculties" or income. In times of normalcy, these rates took on something resembling regularity—around midcentury, Boston's selectmen routinely voted a rate assessing taxpayers between £500 and £800 annually in late autumn. But this regularity disappeared in wartime and other periods of great expense. Crises, such as King Philip's War (1675–1678), multiplied rates' frequency and burden. And towns' selectmen always had the option of calling for additional rates to meet budgetary short-falls, making towns' provision for poor relief a peculiar variant of Richard Wagner's fiscal commons (1992) with no formal budgeting process. This fact—along with clear definitions of who was entitled to relief—pushed the key decisions involved in managing towns' relief-fund CPRs back to the time of strangers' arrivals, that is, deciding whether or not to allow them settlement.

New Englanders attempting to manage their towns' poor-relief funds faced an important trade-off tied to CPR situations' two fundamental concerns—appropriation and provision problems (Ostrom 1990). For towns with small populations—even Boston only numbered around 6,000 by the late-seventeenth century—a marginal addition to the relief rolls represented a significant expense. Managing the appropriations problem meant drawing boundaries disallowing the undeserving poor from claiming relief and limiting settlement for likely relief cases. But a larger, more economically diversified population could better handle these expenses. Thus, the provision problem gave towns the incentive to welcome (at least some) newcomers.

Dealing with Buchanan's Samaritan's dilemma represents a major part of appropriations problems for poor-relief CPR systems (Buchanan 1975; Skarbek 2016) but—setting aside questions of legal settlement—there was little controversy over who fit the bill as deserving of aid in colonial New England. Despite embracing different and changing poor laws and settlement regimes, these colonies shared a remarkably consistent definition of who qualified for relief. It invariably stated that "if by sickness, lameness or the like, he comes to want relief, he . . . shall be reputed their proper charge" wherever his legal settlement was.[7] The deserving poor looked like Boston's Moses Bartlett, "a lame man," and "Widdow Harden [who] beinge blinde [wa]s allowed 3ˢ p. weeke out of the towne treasury." They also looked like "Elizabeth Habell [who] in yᵉ time of her sickness, [lived] outt of yᵉ Townes stock" (*Boston Town Records*, v. 7, 1881, 4, 38, 43). That is, the deserving poor were permanently or temporarily incapacitated members of the community—those who could not support themselves.

Which categories of impoverished individuals did not qualify for relief by their (settled) townships was more often unsaid, particularly in the early decades of English colonization. An order by Massachusetts' General Court in 1692, however, codified earlier assumptions.[8] One group might be fully deserving of aid but saw their claim on the community superseded by a stronger claim on their families—towns were responsible for relief "unless the relations of such poor impotent person . . . be of sufficient ability." Familial responsibilities were not just a moral duty. If capable close relations shirked them, they stood subject to "forfeit twenty shillings for every month's neglect." Even in their neglect, town authorities enforced their responsibility of support—this fine was to "be imployed to the use and relief of such impotent poor person" (*Acts and Resolves*, v. 1, 1869, 67–68). In so doing, Massachusetts gave legal teeth to Saint Augustine's exhortation that, "since you cannot do good to all, you are to pay special regard to those who, by the accidents of time, or place, or circumstance, are brought into closer connection with you" (Augustine [397] 2012, 19).

The same act by Massachusetts' General Court also vividly highlighted who the truly undeserving poor were. It indicated that "any person or persons fit and able to work shall refuse so to do, but loiter and or mispend his or her time, wander from place to place, or otherwise misorder themselves" did not qualify for aid. Rather, they could "be sent to the house of correction, and at their entrance be whipped on the naked back . . . and be there kept to hard labour" (*Acts and Resolves*, v. 1, 1869, 67). In other words, the Protestant work ethic was not just a personally imposed mode of conduct or culturally normative prescription in colonial Massachusetts—it could be punitive (Innes 1995).

This principle—like the priority of familial obligations—was a common sense so obvious to New England colonists that it could go unsaid. (The easy availability of farmland for able-bodied settlers to till rendered judgments about willingness to work less ambiguous than they would become in more-proletarianized periods.) With the relief cases they recognized as deserving eliciting little controversy, nobody surpassing the Puritans as exemplars of the Protestant work ethic (Innes 1995), and no hint of the softness of modern affluence, there was little room for the Samaritan's dilemma described by Buchanan (1975) to dog them—the boundary rules delineating the deserving and undeserving poor were too clear. There was little room for them to economize on relieving the "impotent poor person" who already possessed settlement rights.

Rather, the operative boundary rules New Englanders used to manage their relief expenses involved judiciously guarding who was allowed settlement rights. Like David Beito's (2000) voluntarist mutual-aid associations, Massachusetts towns screened heterogeneously endowed would-be settlers on a pseudo-actuarial basis to deal with their appropriations and provisions problems simultaneously.

With great natural abundance and low population density, colonial America stood as a classic labor-poor environment where towns had reason to welcome new settlers to aid in handling their provision problems. As Jayme Lemke has argued (2016), unattached individuals could find themselves in enough demand to inspire interjurisdictional competition for their settlement—something Benton recognized as early as 1911 with regard to New England towns dangling settlement rights to lure desired infusions of capital and labor. For example, in 1656—the same year the town passed an order that no person be allowed to purchase land until he was admitted to settle-ment—Chelmsford admitted one newcomer, granting him land "provided he set up his trade of weaving and perform the town's work." It admitted an-other stranger and granted him land on the condition "he set us a saw-mill and supply the town at three shillings a hundred." Three years earlier Saco had made a similar deal with Roger Spencer, granting him the liberty of the town in exchange for setting up a sawmill, working cheaper for his new neighbors than outsiders, and offering preferential hiring to them (Benton 1911, 33–36). Thus, some towns that recognized economic gains to be made through an infusion of capital and labor practiced a form of township mer-cantilism in their settlement policy. Such efforts to expand their tax base represented one strategy towns embraced to manage the provisions problem of their budgetary CPRs—including fostering the economic diversity that could decrease the covariance between different townspeople's economic health by luring settlers with valuable human or physical capital to fill locally unfilled niches.[9]

Nevertheless, not every individual fit the bill as a likely contributor to a town's budgetary CPR—some instead represented likely relief cases. This fact helps explain why the definition of deserving poor who were eligible for relief near invariably included an exception for "any children or elder per-sons [who] shall be sent, or come from one Town to another, to be nursed, schooled, or otherwise Educated, or to a Physitian . . . to be cured of any disease or wound." This exception was a question of settlement and not eligibility for relief—should it be required, they were to be "relieved and maintained by the Township [from] whence they came" (Benton 1911, 54–55). But it marked an important boundary on membership within a com-munity. People sojourning in it in a state of dependency had done nothing to merit recognition as members of the community who could make a claim on its largesse—in a world of heterogeneous economic endowments, they had little to offer and were likely relief cases. And there was little economic incentive for a town to act the Good Samaritan for an unhealthy, impover-ished stranger. That is, they neither contributed to a town dealing with the provision problem nor were a good bet vis-à-vis the appropriations problem.

New England towns also managed their fiscal commons in more unsavo-ry fashions. As social scientists, such as Robert Putnam (2007), have noted, ethnic heterogeneity tends to decrease the community solidarities that under-lie welfare programs. Though they were not privy to these studies, it is a sad fact that New Englanders equaled their efforts to enforce religious homoge-neity ethnically and racially. Herndon (2001) has compellingly highlighted the sexually and racially differential experiences of warning out in Rhode Island. Not to be outdone, Bostonians could be counted upon to order that their neighbors "nott employ y^e . . . Negro" (*Boston Town Records*, v. 7, 1881, 5).

Though New England towns' efforts to police their boundaries in the first part of the seventeenth century did not follow a standard, ritualized process of warning out unwelcome sojourners, they soon would. Outsiders hoping to settle legally within a township—or often even purchase property—already required its assent. But by 1655, diverse informal processes would be formalized. That year the General Court ordered that "tounes in this jurisdicc͠on shall haue libertie to p̃vent" strangers from sojourning in them. Reflecting customary boundary rules, it declared, "all such psons as shalbe brought into any such toune w^{th}out the consent" of its selectmen "shall not be chargeable . . . where they dwell."[10] Historians have long remarked that warning out's resulting exclusionary aspects rendered colonial Massachusetts "so drab and so dry of true sympathy" (Kelso 1922, 91).

There is another side to this story that has received far less emphasis but is central to understanding the implications of New England's seventeenth-century settlement rules and localist poor-relief system. Starting in 1637, towns' representatives in Massachusetts' General Court used the province's nested institutions not only to adjudicate disputes but also to realize their normative priority that all their deserving poor receive relief. They passed a series of orders to minimize the number of individuals within the colony who could claim no legal settlement—and, therefore, no poor relief.

This legislative program began in May 1637. That month the General Court "ordered, that no towne or p̃son shall receive any stranger . . . above three weekes, except [when] such p̃son shall have alowance vnder the hands of" local officials to claim legal settlement. And—with a few reasonable exceptions—townspeople who entertained such unauthorized visitors were liable for punishment.[11] This order has been read as a simple reaffirmation that towns enjoyed the right to police their boundaries. But such an explanation can ill explain why it included a provision dictating that "ev^{r}y towne that shall give or sell any lot or habitation to any such [person], not so alowed [legal settlement], shall forfet 100s for every offence" (*Records of Massachusetts*, v. 1, 1853, 196). This provision clearly aimed not to facilitate towns' collective behaviors but to constrain them. The reason for this order becomes clearer when considered in the context of the General Court's orders dealing with unauthorized strangers and their legal disputes and employment contracts—all serving to minimize the number of unattached people within the colony who could not claim legal settlement in any town.[12] It aimed to do the same—ensuring that all Massachusetts residents had recourse to relief.

On June 6, 1639—the same day the General Court established expedited provisions for trials involving strangers—it passed an order with a far larger legacy for the colony's poor-relief system. That day, it "ordered, that the Court, or any two magistrats out of Court, shall have power to determine all differences about a lawfull setling & p̃videing for pore p̃sons, & shall have power to dispose of all vnsetled psons into such townes as they shall iudge to bee most fitt for the maintenance of such psons." Historians have typically treated this oft-cited order as an early articulation of Massachusetts' township-based system in which poor relief was predicated on legal settlement. This it was. But this interpretation ignores how the General Court structured the province's nested institutions to handle the complex CPR problem of localist relief that took seriously the lesson of the Good Samaritan. Unsurprisingly, the Court or its magistrates would adjudicate conflicts between townships. More significantly, its second clause empowered provincial officials "to dispose of all vnsetled [poor] psons into such townes as they shall iudge to bee most fit"—ensuring that they receive relief (*Records of Massachusetts*, v. 1, 1853, 264). With this order, the General Court's members recognized that a purely localist system predicated on legal settlement would not provide for the already impoverished or visibly vulnerable stranger—an unacceptable outcome given New Englanders' normative priorities.

There is danger in extending a celebration of the institutional balance Massachusetts achieved or a revisionism inspired by Dayton and Salinger's (2014) evaluation of its eighteenth-century policy too promiscuously with regard to the seventeenth century. The colonists' xenophobia and drive for religious conformity militated in the same direction as their effort to ensure that their community's poor received relief. In October 1645 "a petition of divᵣs psons, for considʳation of yᵉ lawe about new comʳs . . . & yᵉ lawe against Anabaptists" displayed this connection—as did the General Court's huffy response that the "laws mentioned should not be altered at all, *nor explained*" (*Records of Massachusetts*, v. 2, 1853, 141). Other aspects of Massachusetts' settlement policy were still more explicitly exclusionary. For example, in May 1674, the General Court, "accounting it their duty by all due meanes to provent appearance of sinn & wickedness," ordered it unlawful "for any singlewoman or wife in the absence of hir husband to enterteine or lodge any . . . sojourner" without permission from her town's selectmen. This came with the sharp "pœnalty of fiue pounds p weeke" or corporal punishment when a two-pound penalty prevailed for harboring unauthorized strangers for three weeks for other offenders (*Records of Massachusetts*, v. 5, 1854, 4)! Clearly, policing the moral boundaries of the community mattered as much to seventeenth-century New Englanders as policing their towns' boundaries for economic reasons.

Nevertheless, boundary rules were crucial to Massachusetts towns' seventeenth-century management of their relief-fund CPRs. Towns' representatives in the General Court crafted nested institutions to coordinate boundary rules and ensure that few individuals within the colony would be without a settlement and seeking support. In their case, too, it empowered county and provincial officials to make judicious decisions settling them within a town for the purposes of relief. Overall, it had designed a set of institutions that balanced—if imperfectly—commitment to local, community-oriented solutions with something like universal coverage. By the mid-1670s, however, this system would find itself in crisis.

WAR, CRISIS, AND POLICY CHANGES IN
NESTED INSTITUTIONS

The General Court commenced its November 1675 session by reflecting on its colony's sinfulness. "[T]he most wise & holy God, for seuerall yeares past, hath not only warned us by his word, but chastized us wth his rods," they resolved, "but we haue" not been "effectually humbled for our sinns to repent of them, reforme, and amend our ways." Such reflections were hardly exceptional among the wider oeuvre of the province's puritanical solons, but the events that inspired them were. In their words, "the righteous God hath . . . given comission to the barbarous to rise vp against us, and to become a . . . seuere scourge to us, burning & depopulating seuerall hopefull plantations, murdering many of people of all sorts." Manifold sins ranging from women sporting "superstitious ribbons both on hajre & apparrell" to the toleration of "open meetings of Quakers" had been a "provocation of divine jealousie against this people" in the form of King Philip's War—one of the bloodiest wars England's American colonists ever fought (*Records of Massachusetts*, v. 5, 1854, 4). Its outbreak in June 1675 marked the beginning of decades of conflict with New England's native population and, eventually, their French allies.

These conflicts were not just military crises. They also represented serious humanitarian challenges—sending streams of refugees from the colony's frontiers to its largest, most-defensible towns, especially Boston. Dayton and Salinger (2014) have rightly identified the pressure that these flows of refugees placed upon Boston as the key reason Massachusetts reorganized its poor-relief and settlement laws between 1675 and 1701. Representatives in its General Court repeatedly concluded that maintaining status-quo boundary rules would lead to unacceptable outcomes—refugees overappropriating Boston's relief-fund CPR or being driven from town unaided—and passed orders attempting to mitigate the situation. These orders typically did so—at least temporarily. But these ad-hoc responses to local crises were marked as imperfect by changing political and economic conditions, compromises that addressed immediate problems but not their causes, and representatives' imperfect foresight. Thus, further crises required additional changes, which completely transformed Massachusetts' settlement and poor-relief laws through an unplanned, iterative process. It brought about a system of provincially funded relief for its residents without legal settlement alongside the local variant—first, as an informal response to specific refugee crises but evolving into a formalized system by 1701. This change was important because the same reforms unmade the earlier rules ensuring that all residents could claim legal settlement. With warnings now merely legal rituals disavowing towns' duty to relieve a new resident in times of duress, towns increasingly wielded them indiscriminately—grazing the provincial fiscal commons without any worry that they were individuals' only source of support.

The same month that the General Court found itself examining Massachusetts' collective conscience, Boston's selectmen presented it a petition that approached the war's destruction from a far more-materialist direction. This petition concerned "those . . . who by ye Outrage of ye Enimie were bereaued of all meanes of theire subsistance or forced from theire habitations." More specifically, it was concerned with who was responsible for their relief. The selectmen were anxious that the Court devise "some generall way where by" they "may finde . . . reliefe . . . yᵗ noe particular Towne may be burdened thereby" (*Boston Town Records*, v. 7, 1881, 97). Boston had already collected an abnormal rate of £745 in July and would soon collect another "2641ˡᵈ. 11ˢ. 8ᵈ. for yᵉ occasions of yᵉ Countrie for yᵉ Indian warr." These rates blew the previous year's "£691. 2ˢ for a single rate to the Countrie and other occasions of the towne" out of the water and nearly doubled again the following year. [13] Under these pressures, the town felt ill disposed to shoulder a disproportionate burden for relieving the colony's refugees, who—though fellow Massachusetts Puritans—were strangers. Under prevailing settlement and relief laws, it had no duty to do so—unless the strangers remained there for three months without warning or after ignoring one. Boston might thus escape from relieving the refugees but only at the cost of expelling them and leaving them unaided. Not enamored by these possibilities, towns' representatives in the General Court acted fast. Only two days after Boston's plea, it "declare[d], that such persons (being inhabitants of this jurisdiction) who are so forced from their habitations and repair to other plantations for reliefe, shall not, by virtue of their residenc[e] in sajd plantations . . . be accounted or reputed inhabitants thereof . . . according to [the poor] law." Boston now could manage its budgetary CPR's appropriations problem without expelling the refugees in its midst. Rather, "where necessity requires, (by reason of inability of relations, &c.) they shall be suppljed out of the publicke treasury" of the province (*Records of Massachusetts*, v. 5, 1854, 64).

Though this order was just an ad-hoc solution to an individual crisis, it would eventually become a general rule. The General Court's responses to Boston's continuing refugee and poor-relief problems over the ensuing decades saw to that. Though peace had temporarily been restored in April 1678, by August 1679, Bostonians still found their "towne . . . fild with poore idle and profane psons" that had come "for shelter and releife in time of warr." Bostonians were anxious to change that. They instructed their deputies to the General Court to request the "powre to eject all such persons y^t. come . . . wth.out a due & orderlie admission" (*Boston Town Records*, v. 7, 1881, 135). But Boston's problems were not always concerns of other Massachusetts towns—differing priorities of towns nested within the same system limited its structural changes in response to localized problems until they became larger crises that could not be ignored. Through the 1680s, representatives of other towns could ignore Boston's woes as its CPR's appropriations problem started to get out of hand. Bostonians grudgingly witnessed poor relief take up a greater and greater share of their attention and resources. They elected their first dedicated overseers of the poor in 1691, and rates "for the occasions of this towne" became rates collected "for the poore and other occasions of this Towne."[14] With war again sending new waves of refugees, however, Boston freemen's wish for reform would finally be granted. Amidst the General Court's recodification of the province's laws in 1692, it generalized the ad-hoc step it took during the last war—it removed the requirement that towns expel warned strangers so residency after a warning no longer could serve as the basis for legal settlement (*Records of Massachusetts*, v. 4, 1854, 365). Nevertheless, Boston's woes persisted. With the town having grown "so Populous and [the strangers] shifting from place to place," by 1701 it was hard to ensure "they be Descouered" and warned in the three months before "the law makes them Inhabitants." Thus, its selectmen petitioned the General Court to make it easier to forestall—or at least avoid fiscal responsibility for—the flow of "other poor and vild persons . . . from Other Towns" (*Boston Town Records*, v. 7, 1881, 241). This time it did not take long for Boston to get its wish. The next day, the General Court passed an act extending the time towns had to warn newcomers from three months to twelve.

But this 1701 act did much more than that. Like Massachusetts' earlier restrictions on unwelcome sojourns, it required ships making port to "deliver . . . a perfect list . . . of all passengers . . . and their circumstances" to local officials. And when "any passenger . . . be impotent, lame or otherwise infirm, or likely to be a charge to the place," the ship's captain was required to carry the person away "or otherwise to give sufficient security . . . to . . . keep the town from all charge for . . . relief and support." The new law recognized two exemptions reflecting the community's boundaries and responsibilities—the person who "was, before, an inhabitant of this province, or [the case] that such impotence, lameness, or other infirmity befel . . . him or her during the passage." The former's claim to admission was obvious— he or she already possessed legal settlement—but the latter is more interesting. Rather than recognizing any preexisting claim on relief, the General Court instead recognized that the ship's master had acted in good faith and was therefore not responsible for the individual's relief. But—if not the ship's master—who was responsible? The answer was simple for "servants" (a broad category embracing essentially all individuals, employed or enslaved, who worked for someone else and were therefore marked by various degrees of unfreedom in the eyes of contemporaries)—"their masters shall provide for them." This varied little from the Augustinian vision of relationally determined responsibilities that had long informed the colony's model of relief—particularly surrounding familial duties. It was more interesting that "others shall be relieved at the charge of the province." This reflected the act's major innovation. It made the province's provision for the unsettled refugees of King Philip's War general. The province, thus, took responsibility for relieving the deserving poor within its boundaries who lacked legal claims to relief on any person or jurisdiction therein.[15]

Altogether, Massachusetts' settlement and relief legislation between 1675 and 1701 added up to much more than just responses to particular crises. These acts redefined the incentives shaping individuals' and townships' behavior and, over time, how they defined communities' boundaries. Repealing previous requirements that towns remove warned sojourners lest they gain settlement rights meant that towns could welcome newcomers' economic contributions without taking on any commiserate responsibilities. Towns' strategies for managing their relief-fund CPRs' appropriations and provisions problems no longer stood in tension. Meanwhile, the province's commitment to relieve unsettled paupers freed them of any potential guilt that might result from looking upon destitute, unrelieved deserving poor. They could now look upon provincial poor relief as a fiscal commons that placed them in the opposite situation from Buchanan's Samaritan—they knew someone else would certainly step in. Townships could abandon their duty to relieve their poor with impunity.

A number of towns, thus, embraced policies of warning all newcomers indiscriminately. This policy was on full display just south of Massachusetts during the 1780s. "Seeing . . . mention made of your want of Mechanicks" in Hartford, "A Mechanic" wrote of having "had at first a strong inclination to come and settle there" before hearing of "great difficulty in getting to be an inhabitant there, without [the] landed property" that then stood beyond his reach. Hearing that "several honest industrious men have been warned out of town, as soon as they have established themselves in business," he questioned whether anyone could gain settlement rights there. Given the incentives governing Massachusetts and Connecticut towns' decisions about granting settlement to newcomers in the 1780s, our mechanic's concerns were rather naïve. "A Citizen" writing to the *American Mercury* agreed. He aimed "to inform the Mechanic . . . that he has entirely mefconceived . . . the people of this town in their treatment of Strangers." Our citizen explained that the town had decided "to warn out every stranger indiscriminately" with the goal of "wounding . . . feelings as little as possible" by adopting the only policy befitting the new democratic age. This was almost certainly a bootleggers-and-Baptists argument—Massachusetts' and Connecticut's settlement and relief laws made warning every stranger the most fiscally prudent strategy for all towns—but a savvier mechanic would have known that his state or current settlement would handle his relief anyway, freeing him to ignore whatever warnings came his way and listen to his interlocutor "repeat[ing] the invitation . . . to mechanics" who were "much wanted here of almost every trade" (*American Mercury*, April 18, 1785, 3; *American Mercury*, April 25, 1785, 3).

The incentives behind Hartford's strategy applied across New England. Towns in Massachusetts and its neighbors with similar laws could now enjoy the economic growth that came with new settlers without any responsibility for their upkeep—they could minimize relief appropriations while welcoming new settlers who would aid with the provision problem of their budgetary CPRs. They thus grazed the fiscal commons with impunity. As Benton (1911) notes, towns all around New England, from Wenham to Canton to Lynn to all of Vermont's Connecticut Valley towns, warned newcomers without discrimination—the state could deal with their charges.

War again proved a driver of institutional change in the late-eighteenth century when Massachusetts and its neighbors revised their settlement and poor-relief systems to limit towns' increasingly rampant overgrazing of state fiscal commons as well as changing norms about mobility and community boundaries. Dayton and Salinger's (2014) two-tiered model of local and provincial poor relief came to full fruition during the depression following the French and Indian War, when the General Court granted Bostonians' longtime wishes with a 1767 law to make it easier for towns to police their boundaries. This legislation dictated that strangers could claim settlement rights only if they had communicated a desire to settle legally in a town—undetected residence would no longer allow an individual to claim settlement. Though Boston town officials warned all strangers nearly indiscriminately between the Seven Years War and the American Revolution anyway, this reform made it easier for towns to abandon the practice under duress. The Revolutionary War was one such time of duress, ensuring that local officials' efforts were otherwise occupied—as were the colonies' lower orders. And historians agree that few warnings were issued during it (Herndon 2001; Dayton and Salinger 2014). But the number of warnings increased in the postwar years, albeit unevenly. The deep postwar depression left communities managing their budgetary CPRs differently depending on interjurisdictional policy differences. In Massachusetts, warnings remained low through the 1780s. Town officials had responded to the depression's tightened belts by finding cheaper ways to determine individuals' legal settlements than warnings rendered superfluous by the 1767 provision requiring strangers to notify towns of their intention to claim inhabitancy. Warnings only spiked to new heights in the Bay State the year after state legislators passed a law in 1789, allowing individuals to claim settlement and therefore relief through two years of unnotified, uncontested residence (Dayton and Salinger 2014).[16] With restrictions on mobility increasingly inimical to cultural norms formed by the Revolution as well as a long period of meaningless warnings and provincial relief, Massachusetts and its neighbors all moved to reform their settlement laws in the late-eighteenth and early-nineteenth centuries.

At the same time, cultural and economic changes on the heels of the American Revolution exacerbated the situation. By the Revolutionary era, the nation's population was exploding—doubling every twenty years. Meanwhile America was transitioning toward a more liberal–individualist ethos. Though American colonists had always been more mobile than their European peers, further increased mobility was a consequence—as well as a source—of this transition. This was the era when the restless American, whom Tocqueville saw "carefully build[ing] a house in which to spend his old age" and moving before its completion, came of age. This restlessness that prompted Americans to settle "in a place that he soon leaves in order to carry his changing desires elsewhere" was not compatible with limits on mobility (Tocqueville [1835/1840] 2012, 944).

Moreover, state boundaries were coming to surpass town lines as borders of community responsibility and mobility. This was on display across the boundary in Connecticut. There, Benton (1911) would note with some disgust, warning out would remain a legal possibility into the twentieth century. Yet, by 1792, legislation affirmed the legal right of "any Inhabitant . . . within this State . . . to remove with his Family into any other Town in this State . . . without being liable to be removed." Connecticuters like "A Mechanic" could move unhindered and unwarned within the state, gaining settlement through six years' residence in a new locale.[17] Thereafter only international and interstate migrants could be warned, highlighting both American society's increased mobility and increasingly state-defined community boundaries in the years after the Revolution—along with decades of toothless warnings and provincial poor relief that facilitated movement (Dayton and Salinger 2014).

In the early months of 1794, representatives of Massachusetts towns in the General Court moved to reform its settlement regime in light of towns' rampantly overgrazing the state fiscal commons—poor relief accounted for three-quarters of the state's budget by 1793 (*Acts and Resolves* 1895, 677)— and changing cultural norms about mobility. The resulting legislation "repeal[ed] all laws heretofore made respecting such settlement" and put an end to warning out within the state. But it maintained many legacies of the earlier system. It and a follow-up act "providing for the relief . . . and removal of the poor" left responsibility for these tasks to impoverished strangers' in-state legal settlements (to which they were returned) or the state government if they had none. And the dozen different ways it allowed newcomers to establish legal inhabitancy preserved much of the previous regime's spirit regarding community boundaries. Presence at a township's incorporation continued to make one a part of its corporate body. Another of the act's provisions indicated that "Any person that shall be admitted an Inhabitant by any Town . . . at any legal meeting . . . shall thereby gain settlement." Selection for public service whether "in the Office of Clerk, Treasurer, Selectman, Overseer of the poor, Assessor, Constable or Collector of Taxes" or as "settled ordained Ministers of the Gospel" could also gain someone settlement (*Acts and Resolves* 1895, 439–42, 479–93). The latter reflected the continuing identification between town and parish, which would survive an 1820 challenge in the state's Supreme Judicial Court before a constitutional amendment finally abolished "the churches established by law in this government" in 1833 (Cushing 1969). It also reflected how the town's minister—like other public officials—could rely upon an income stream backed with taxes anyway, leaving little risk of his destitution (*Acts and Resolves*, 1895, 439–42).

Concern with the risk that an individual would worsen towns' appropriations problem and, with his contribution to the community's provision problem, shined through the remaining ways the 1794 act allowed people to gain settlement. Under it, any American citizen with a "freehold, in the Town . . . of the clear yearly income of Three Pounds . . . [for] three years successively . . . gain[ed] a settlement therein." Similarly, a citizen with an estate in a town assessed "at Sixty pounds, or the Income at three pounds twelve shillings . . . for . . . State, County, Town or District Taxes for . . . Five years successively" gained legal settlement. Thus, having a landed stake in a community and adding to its economic base qualified an individual for the fast track to settlement rights. "Any minor who shall serve an apprenticeship to any lawful trade for the space of four years, in any Town or District, and actually set up in the same therein, within one year after" completing it, found himself in a similar position—gaining settlement if he "continue[d] to carry on the same for the space of Five years." The General Court's specification that "being hired as a journeyman, shall not be considered as setting up a Trade" demonstrates another way that economics defined citizenship during the Revolutionary era—rather than defining the artisan's position within a community via his income, this highlighted the distinction between independent proprietorship and the dependent status contemporaries associated with employment relations. Such dependencies left individuals to pursue the slow track to settlement rights. Any citizen aged twenty-one or older could attain inhabitancy by residing in a township for ten years, during which he paid "all State, County, Town or District Taxes duly assessed on such person's poll or estate for five years." Outside of landed, propertied, or artisanal independence, men's economic route to settlement thus ran through tax assessments. Over time, one's contribution to the provision problem of the community's budgetary CPR entitled one to claim town membership and thereby a right to appropriate relief funds in times of duress. Finally, women's and children's settlement rights remained largely determined via their familial relationships, highlighting their dependent status legally under the doctrine of coverture and meaning that their rights, too, were mediated through the same economic lens (*Acts and Resolves*, 1895, 439–42).

Despite—or perhaps because it retained these inequities—the Settlement Act of 1794 tweaked towns' and individuals' incentives to create a new balance in which a largely localist model poor-relief system could once again function effectively. Towns retained the right to grant legal settlement via vote. And individuals of different wealth or station in life faced different obstacles in obtaining legal settlement rights, largely dependent upon their contribution to the provision problem of the town's budgetary CPR. But towns no longer possessed the power to exclude individuals unless they became public charges before establishing legal inhabitancy. As such, they could no longer simply graze the fiscal commons by warning all newcomers, shifting responsibility for relief of an ever-growing portion of Massachusetts's population to the state government. But the act made no attempt to turn back the clock to the purely localist model that had prevailed when individuals' geographic mobility had been far lower and towns could—and did—block settlements. Rather, it prevented communities from being swamped by the appropriations problem of relieving a large pool of newcomers by making settlement predicated on relatively long periods of residency, graduated by an individual's economic contribution to meeting the provision problem and likelihood of needing aid from the community.

Building upon long-standing English traditions, seventeenth-century Massachusetts towns developed a Tocquevillian model of localist poor relief. This system depended upon boundary rules delineating towns' legal inhabitants from strangers and the deserving poor from the undeserving to manage their relief-fund CPRs. Towns screened heterogeneously endowed would-be settlers based on their likely costs and contributions to their relief funds—much like David Beito's (2000) mutual-aid societies adopted pseudo-actuarial assessment structures. At the same time, they took advantage of shared cultural norms about work that largely helped them escape the "Samaritan's dilemma" theorized by James Buchanan (1975; Skarbek 2016). New England Puritans, however, were familiar with the Good Samaritan's moral. Minimizing the number of unsettled and, therefore, unaided poor was a complex problem in a system where each town had little economic incentive to welcome the impoverished stranger. It was only because towns were nested within larger provincial (later, state) institutions that they successfully coordinated a solution to this problem—creating a channel to settle the unsettled and limiting towns' ability to host strangers without offering them settlement rights.

During the final quarter of the seventeenth century, a series of wars wrought humanitarian crises for large, defensible towns like Boston, which their counterparts could little ignore. Consequently, their representatives approved a series of ad-hoc responses that, in sum, transformed Massachusetts' settlement and poor-relief regime—separating physical residence from legal settlement and creating provincially funded poor-relief provisions. In combination, these changes created a fiscal-commons situation that towns grazed with impunity, shifting more and more responsibility for poor relief to the provincial level over the eighteenth century. After these developments—and the American Revolution—changed cultural norms about mobility, towns' representatives in the General Court finally passed a new settlement act in 1794 that retained much of the previous laws' spirit regarding community boundaries but prevented towns from grazing the fiscal commons by doing away with warning out. This roundabout history highlights an easily forgotten lesson of Ostrom's (1990) work—that effective CPR-management systems emerge through iterative processes of trial and error, which can take centuries.

Massachusetts towns' experiences attempting to manage poor-relief CPRs highlight a few other key lessons for social scientists and contemporary debates. Most simply, colonial and early national settlement laws belie the commonplace that Americans enforced no restrictions on immigration prior to the 1880s—the federal government did not, but state and local authorities did well into the nineteenth century (Hirota 2017). More significantly, it highlights the intimate relation between communities' welfare provisions and their boundary rules.

While appropriations and provisions problems are always the two fundamental concerns for CPR management (Ostrom 1990), budgetary CPRs place them in a direct tension. Prospective residents are would-be contributors to both the appropriations and provisions problems—potentially costly recipients of public services and potentially lucrative taxpayers. Milton Friedman's famous claim that "It's just obvious that you can't have free immigration and a welfare state" might be an overstatement (1997, 55). But there is a clear trade-off between free migration and sustainable social spending.

While Friedman's famous quotation depicts this trade-off in purely economic terms, colonial New Englanders enforced boundary rules to manage their fiscal commons not only by screening would-be settlers economically but also for their adherence to the community's religious and cultural norms. Sociocultural heterogeneity can limit the solidarity underlying welfare spending and voluntarist aid (Putnam 2007), as displayed recently in Essen, Germany, where a food bank controversially balked at serving a majority of its limited provisions to Syrian refugees while its traditional appropriators shrank from waiting in line with "groups of young migrant men [who] . . . sometimes elbowed their way to the front" (Bennhold 2018). This relationship does not merely reflect the xenophobia of fallen man. Those outside the sociocultural mainstream—be they Quakers meeting in colonial Massachusetts, migrants at Essen's food bank, or vegan gadflies like Gipf-Oberfrick's Nancy Holten—do not share the cultural assumption of wider society that ease cooperation in CPR-management systems (Ostrom 1990), whether by swearing oaths to seal a deal, standing in line politely, or allowing town meetings to proceed without proposing futile motions against cowbells. Recognizing these concerns in addition to purely economic ones might contribute to more productive discussions of migration, welfare provisions, and civil society.

NOTES

1. I would like to thank this volume's editors and contributors, especially Sarah Wilford, for their helpful comments on previous drafts of this paper as well as Lyndsey Johnson for her comments, edits, and companionship.

2. Citizenship in the Swiss confederation remains defined by citizenship in one's municipality and canton of origin or naturalization, reflecting a historical tie between locally provided social assistance and municipal citizenship that was sundered only in 1977 (Argast 2009; Garber 2017; Roberts 2017).

3. Social, economic, and cultural historians have spilled much ink debating how capitalistic Revolutionary-era New England was—see Lamoreaux (2003) for an informative overview of this debate. But historians who argue that America was born capitalist and those contending that precapitalist models of moral economy persisted through the Revolution agree that New England was well on its way toward industrial capitalism by the Jacksonian era. Tocqueville, himself, recognized this fact in his oft-cited chapter on "the manufacturing aristocracy that we see arising before our eyes" ([1835/1840] 2012, 985).

4. Specifically, CPR scholars have shown emphatically that metaphorical models based on the tragedy of the commons, prisoners' dilemma, and the logic of collective action assume away possibilities for deliberation and cooperation among individuals, which can allow them to escape the tragic outcomes baked into these models' assumptions without pure privatization or outside-regulation strategies (Runge 1981; Gardner, Ostrom, and Walker 1990; Ostrom 1990; Raudla 2010).

5. Small close-knit communities with political institutions famously designed around town meetings clearly had (3) collective-choice arrangements and (4) effective provisions for monitoring. From the beginning, the provincial government clearly (7) recognized towns' power to (5) enforce settlement rules with sanctions. Finally, it established (6) clear procedures for resolving disputes between towns and individuals.

6. New Haven's Fundamental Agreement mandated that "church members onely shall be free burgesses" and its General Court opened its first session by resolving "thatt the worde of God shall be the onely rule . . . ordering the affeyres of gouernment in this plantatõ." Even the dissident founders of Portsmouth, Rhode Island—despite their own religious exile and colony's fame for respecting religious liberty—expected submission "to the Government that is or shall be established, according to the word of God" (*Records of the Colony and Plantation of New Haven* 1857, 17, 21; Benton 1911, 64, 100).

7. The specific example quoted is from a law passed by Plymouth's General Court in 1671. Almost identical language appeared in Connecticut's laws from 1673, 1702, 1750, 1759, 1784, and 1796; Massachusetts' landmark 1692 legislation; a law New Hampshire passed in 1719; and Vermont's Act of 1787. The principles informing this definition appear likely to have

predated any colony-level legislation on the topic (Benton 1911, 50, 54–55, 65–66, 69, 71, 91, 107).

8. In 1692 the General Court formally codified (*Acts and Resolves*, v. 1, 1869, 64–68) a wide range of common law principles about the governance of townships that had slowly accreted through specific decisions with an act that reads much like Tocqueville's ([1835/1840] 2012) chapter on "Town Powers in New England."

9. On the other hand, Boston showed that not all skilled laborers could await open arms when its selectmen ordered that "Wm Anderson at John Faireweath^rs, Tayl^r and John Hunt & Steephen Millard Butchers . . . be returned to the Countie Court, not admited Inhabitants. Alsoe W^m. Nowell & Thomas Rand Booke binders are to be returned as aboue, alsoe John Tudall" (*Boston Town Records*, v. 7, 1881, 64).

10. Instead, "if necessitje require," it ordered that these unauthorized strangers "shalbe releived & majntajned by those y^t were the cawse of their coming in" (*Records of Massachusetts*, v. 4, 1854, 230).

11. This act was initially passed on a temporary basis but was declared "a constant lawe" the following May (*Records of Massachusetts*, v. 1, 1853, 196, 228).

12. In September 1638, the Court ordered that "cunstables of each towne . . . informe the Court of Assistants, wch is to consider . . . fines" for "newe comers, if any bee admited w^thout license." Nine months hence, it created "Speciall Courts for trjall of strange^rs causes" to expedite them—displaying its overarching concern of minimizing their presence. The same concern had already been on display six years before it limited towns' entertainment of strangers, when the Court ordered "that noe man within the limitts of this jurisdiccõn shall hire any pson for a serv^t for lesse time then a yeare, vnles hee be a settled housekeep" (*Records of Massachusetts*, v. 1, 1853, 88, 241, 264).

13. Boston's rate for local and provincial expenses totaled £691. 2s in 1674, £3,386. 11s 8d in 1675, and £6,063. 18s in 1676, so taxes for the first two years of the war were 4.9 and 8.7 times the prewar baseline (*Boston Town Records*, v. 7, 1881, 90, 96–97, 102, 104, 113–14, 125).

14. In October 1690, Boston's selectmen approved a rate of £412. 4s 2d "for the poore and other occasions of this Towne." They used almost identical language in June 1691 for a rate of £435.7s before ceasing to bother to specify how much the rate would be in April 1693 and April 1694 (*Boston Town Records*, v. 7, 1881, 203–204, 206, 208, 214–15, 218, 231).

15. Though this act specifically articulated the principle of provincial relief only in reference to maritime migrations, three months later the General Court officially extended it to all "indigent persons . . . not belonging to any town . . . within this province" (*Acts and Resolves*, v. 1, 1869, 451–53, 469–70).

16. In Rhode Island, on the other hand, Herndon (2001) found warnings beginning to wax after hostilities ceased and spiking to new heights (in absolute terms) during the postwar depression of the 1780s, though rapid population growth meant that—outside of the 1784 spike—per capita warnings were relatively stable after 1775.

17. Connecticut residents' freedom to move within the state was predicated on their good behavior and economic independence because their new towns could prosecute them for vagrancy or return them to legal settlements if they flagrantly violated state law or were embarrassed and needed relief within six years of arrival in a new locale (Benton 1911, 72–73).

REFERENCES

Acts and Resolves of the Province of the Massachusetts Bay, Vol. I, 1692–1714. 1869. Boston: Wright & Potter.
Acts and Resolves of Massachusetts, 1792–1793. 1895. Boston: Wright & Potter.
American Mercury. 1785.
Argast, Regula. 2009. "An Unholy Alliance: Swiss Citizenship between Local Legal Tradition, Federal Laissez-Faire, and Ethno-National Rejection of Foreigners, 1848-1933." *European Review of History* 16 (4): 503–21.

Augustine, of Hippo, Saint. [397] 2012. *De Doctrina Christiana*. Translated by J. F. Shaw. Mineola, NY: Dover.

Beito, David T. 2000. *From Mutual Aid to the Welfare State: Fraternal Societies and Social Services, 1890-1967*. Chapel Hill: University of North Carolina Press.

Bennhold, Katrin. 2018. "Germans First? A Food Bank Bars Migrants, Setting Off a Storm." *New York Times*.

Benton, Josiah H. 1911. *Warning Out in New England*. Boston: W. B. Clarke.

Boettke, Peter J., Christopher J. Coyne, and Peter T. Leeson. 2011. "Quasimarket Failure." *Public Choice* 149 (1–2): 209–224.

Boston Town Records, Vol. 7. 1881. Boston: Rockwell and Churchill.

Buchanan, James M. 1975. "The Samaritan's Dilemma." In *Altruism, Morality, and Economic Theory*. Edited by Edmund S. Phelps, 71–86. New York: Russell Sage Foundation.

Buchanan, James M., and Yong J. Yoon. 2004. "Majoritarian Exploitation of the Fiscal Commons: General Taxes–Differential Transfers." *European Journal of Political Economy* 20: 73–90.

Cray, Robert E. Jr. 1988. *Paupers and Poor Relief in New York City and Its Rural Environs, 1700-1830*. Philadelphia: Temple University Press.

Cushing, John D. 1969. "Notes on Disestablishment in Massachusetts, 1780-1833." *William and Mary Quarterly* 26 (2): 169–90.

Dayton, Cornelia H., and Sharon V. Salinger. 2014. *Robert Love's Warnings: Searching for Strangers in Colonial Boston*. Philadelphia: University of Pennsylvania Press.

Friedman, Milton. 1997. "Milton Friedman at 85." Interview with Peter Brimelow. *Forbes* 160 (14): 52–55.

Garber, Megan. 2017. "In Switzerland, You Can Be Denied Citizenship for Being Too Annoying." *The Atlantic*.

Gardner, Roy, Elinor Ostrom, and James M. Walker. 1990. "The Nature of Common-Pool Resource Problems." *Rationality and Society* 2 (3): 335–58.

Herndon, Ruth Wallis. 2001. *Unwelcome Americans: Living on the Margin in Early New England*. Philadelphia: University of Pennsylvania Press.

Hirota, Hidetaka. 2017. *Expelling the Poor: Atlantic Seaboard States and the Nineteenth-Century Origins of American Immigration Policy*. Oxford: Oxford University Press.

Innes, Stephen. 1995. *Creating the Commonwealth: The Economic Culture of Puritan New England*. New York: W. W. Norton.

Jakee, Keith, and Stephen Turner. 2002. "The Welfare State as a Fiscal Commons: Problems of Incentives versus Problems of Cognition." *Public Finance Review* 30 (6): 481–508.

Jones, Douglas Lamar. 1975. "The Strolling Poor: Transiency in Eighteenth-Century Massachusetts." *Journal of Social History* 8 (3): 28–54.

Kelso, Robert W. 1922. *The History of Public Poor Relief in Massachusetts, 1620-1920*. Cambridge, MA: The Riverside Press.

Lamoreaux, Naomi R. 2003. "Rethinking the Transition to Capitalism in the Early American Northeast." *Journal of American History* 90 (2): 437–61.

Lemke, Jayme S. 2016. "Interjurisdictional Competition and Married Women's Property Acts." *Public Choice* 166 (3): 291–313.

Lipford, Jody W., and Bruce Yandle. 2014. "Grazing the State and Local Fiscal Commons: Do Different Tax Prices Lead to More or Less Grazing?" *Public Finance Review* 42 (4): 466–86.

Loiacono, Gabriel. 2015. "William Larned, Overseer of the Poor: Power and Precariousness in the Early Republic." *The New England Quarterly* 88 (2): 223–51.

Ostrom, Elinor. 1990. *Governing the Commons: The Evolution of Institutions for Collective Action*. Cambridge: Cambridge University Press.

Putnam, Robert. 2007. "E Pluribus Unum: Diversity and Community in the Twenty-First Century." *Scandinavian Political Studies* 30 (2): 137–74.

Raudla, Ringa. 2010. "Governing Budgetary Commons: What Can We Learn from Elinor Ostrom?" *European Journal of Law and Economics* 30 (3): 201–221.

Records of the Colony and Plantation of New Haven, from 1638 to 1649. 1857. Edited by Charles J. Hoadly. Hartford, CT: Case, Tiffany and Co.

Records of Massachusetts, Vol. I, 1628-1641. 1853. Boston: William White.

Records of Massachusetts, Vol. II, 1642-1649. 1853. Boston: William White.

Records of Massachusetts, Vol. IV—Part I, 1650-1660. 1854. Boston: William White.

Records of Massachusetts, Vol. V, 1674-1686. 1854. Boston: William White.

Roberts, Elizabeth. 2017. "Vegan Denied Swiss Citizenship for Her 'Loud' Views on Animal Rights." *CNN*.

Runge, Carlisle Ford. 1981. "Common Property Externalities: Isolation, Assurance, and Resource Depletion in a Traditional Grazing Context." *American Journal of Agricultural Economics* 63 (4): 595–606.

Skarbek, Emily C. 2014. "The Chicago Fire of 1871: A Bottom-Up Approach to Disaster Relief." *Public Choice* 160 (1–2): 155–80.

———. 2016. "Aid, Ethics, and the Samaritan's Dilemma: Strategic Courage in Constitutional Entrepreneurship." *Journal of Institutional Economics* 12 (2): 371–93.

Smith, Billy G. 1988. "Poverty and Economic Marginality in Eighteenth-Century America." *Proceedings of the American Philosophical Society* 132 (1): 85–118.

Tocqueville, Alexis de. *Democracy in America*. [1835/1840] 2012. Edited by Eduardo Nolla. Translated by James T. Schleifer. Indianapolis, IN: Liberty Fund.

Wagner, Richard E. 1992. "Grazing the Federal Budgetary Commons: The Rational Politics of Budgetary Irresponsibility." *Journal of Law and Politics* 9: 105–119.

Chapter Seven

Polycentricity and Transnational Environmental Governance

A Comparison of Literatures

James Heilman

Transnational environmental governance is populated by a diversity of governing units across many different issue areas. The most complex is climate change in which different aspects of the problem are governed by different groupings of governance organizations. States have negotiated to create the United Nations Framework Convention on Climate Change, the International Panel on Climate Change, the Kyoto Protocol, The Copenhagen Accords, and finally the Paris Agreement. They have also tried to address the issue through the Reducing Emissions from Deforestation and Forest Degradation (REDD+), the United Nations Environment Program, the United Nations Development Program, and other international organizations (IOs). Governance of climate change is not populated by only public organizations. Private organizations certify firms for reducing greenhouse gas (GHG) emissions and for engaging in sustainable forestry. At the subnational level, alliances of municipalities draw up action plans for combatting climate change (Betsill and Bulkeley 2006). Within the international relations (IR) literature, all of this activity has earned climate change governance the classification of a complex regime (Keohane and Victor 2011). To those not given to granting intellectual monikers, climate change governance might just be called a mess. While it is certainly the messiest or most complex issue area of transnational environmental governance, it is not the only one with a diversity of governance units acting to solve environmental problems. A mix of public and private organizations can be observed in a wide range of issue areas, from the management of food systems, such as fisheries and agriculture, to the management of waste systems, such as household garbage to electronics recycling. It is this diversity that has led scholars in IR and in the polycentric governance tradition to describe and analyze transnational environmental governance as a polycentric system.

In this chapter, I seek to answer two questions that arise when we bring these bodies of literature into conversation, as well as literature on public choice, and then use the literature review to raise questions that future research could answer. The first question is whether transnational environmental governance is just a mess with a diversity of governing units or if it is a polycentric system. By transnational environmental governance, I mean governance of environmental issues that span across at least two states, such as air pollution that is produced in one country but spreads to other countries on air currents and so is addressed through transnational governance. Polycentricity is not simply the presence of many governing units. It has core features that are shared by scholars of polycentricity, which enables us to analyze if a system of governance is generating the public goods that are made possible by a polycentric system and which might not be provided or produced under a centralized system of governance. I find evidence in the IR literature that issue areas in environmental governance do display properties of polycentricity.

Polycentric systems tend not to be static. They result in institutional change. Recent IR literature has tried to make sense of institutional change within transnational environmental governance. The second question I seek to answer is if the mechanisms of institutional change that are present in the literature on polycentricity, and the public choice literature, are present in the literature on institutional change in environmental governance. I find evidence in the IR literature that competitive mechanisms do drive institutional change, but other factors, not typically in the polycentricity or public choice literature, are also described.

In this chapter, I will begin the next section by reviewing definitions of polycentricity to highlight that a profusion of governing units is not the only characteristic of polycentricity. I will then examine the extent to which transnational environmental governance fulfills the criteria of polycentricity. In the second section, I will review mechanisms that produce institutional changes within polycentric systems and compare these to the mechanisms of change within transnational environmental governance. In the last section, I will argue that, by comparing IR, polycentricity, and public choice literatures, I open up questions for future research. The final section will focus on what the features of club economies as opposed to public economies are, what the constitutional constraints that could exist at the transnational level of governance are, what effect issue linkage has in a polycentric system, and what drives preference formation within a polycentric system.

A DIVERSITY OF GOVERNING UNITS OR POLYCENTRICITY?

Governance of environmental issues, such as transboundary air pollution, fisheries conservation, and climate change, often involve multiple governing agencies operating at different and overlapping geographic scales. These agencies can be created by sovereign states or private organizations, or they can be created by a combination of both types of actors. The presence of multiple sites of authority providing and producing the public good of environmental sustainability lends the study of the transnational environmental governance to polycentric analyses. I will explain why the complex system of transnational environmental governance fits within the conception of polycentric governance. I will cover the actors involved, the geographic scales at which they operate, and the interactions between these actors in order to defend the position that polycentric analyses can help us understand why and how overlapping governance arrangements emerge and change to provide public goods of environmental governance.

While transnational, or global, governance is a widely interpreted concept, in this chapter I adopt the definition used by Rosenau: "Global governance is conceived to include systems of rule at all levels of human activity—from the family life to the international organization—in which the pursuit of goals through the exercise of control has transnational repercussion" (Rosenau and Czempiel 1992, 13). Dingwerth and Pattberg (2006) argue this definition is widely used in the IR literature and is "rooted in the tradition in which governance has been introduced with regard to domestic political systems" (190). This connection between traditions focusing on domestic political systems and traditions focusing on international political systems is particularly useful for this chapter because I am connecting literatures from both scales of political systems. The definition also has an agentive feature that accords with public choice understandings of collective decision making. Those actors within a system of rule are pursuing goals through mechanisms of control, such as law, coercion, or persuasion. Buchanan reminds us that we must do politics without romance (Buchanan 1979). We must assume that governors have their own goals and preferences and they do not adopt the good of the public, whatever that may be, once they become governors.

One system of rule that has been used to characterize transnational environmental governance is a polycentric system. Within polycentric governance systems, public goods are provided and produced by multiple organizations. Just as for governance, there is no clear-cut definition of polycentricity, but analyses of polycentricity do share core assumptions. They comprise a system "of (1) many autonomous units formally independent of one another, (2) choosing to act in ways that take account of others, (3) through processes of cooperation, competition, conflict, and conflict resolution" (V. Ostrom [1991] 2014, 46). Elinor Ostrom argued that there are benefits to be gained from such a system. "Polycentric systems tend to enhance innovation, learning, adaptation, trustworthiness, levels of cooperation of participants, and the achievement of more effective, equitable, and sustainable outcomes at multiple scales" (E. Ostrom 2010, 552). If there are multiple autonomous units, then there is the possibility that multiple actors are creating the same rules, complementary rules, or conflicting rules. Whereas Wilson ([1885] 1956) saw this redundancy and competition as inefficient, Vincent Ostrom (1973) saw it as enhancing the capacity for government to serve the interests of its constituents. Polycentrism enables a community that faces heterogeneous problems to have heterogeneous governance organizations to address those problems.

McGinnis highlights that polycentricity also distinguishes between the provision of public goods by governance organizations and the production of public goods. "*Production* refers to the physical processes by which a public good or service comes into existence, while *provision* is the process by which this product is made available to consumers (McGinnis 1999, 3, emphasis original). This implies that the actor providing the public good need not be the actor producing the good. There can be competition between providers or producers. This competition creates a quasi-market for public goods. The benefits of this market for the community are that, if one actor is better at providing or producing a public good or service than other actors, then members of the community can choose to "buy" the public good or service from this provider/producer. Any decision made at the collective level is going to have external costs and decision-making costs for the individual. When individuals are given a range of public goods and services, they can choose the ones that have the lowest external and decision-making costs for themselves.

The conception of polycentricity advanced above accords with the conception in the IR literature. A recent volume tries to make sense of the extent to which the complex system of climate changes governance is polycentric. In order to do so, the authors identify five core features of polycentric systems of governance (Jordan et al. 2018). Local action, mutual adjustments, experimentation, trust, and overarching rules are these features. Each of these connects to Ostrom's insight that, even though the governance units are autonomous, they take account of each other. Putting aside the importance of local action for later, the fact that units mutually adjust to each other, generate trust within their communities, and adhere to overarching rules means that they are part of the same system of rules. Experimentation improves governance insofar as it enables people within the system to supply better public goods and services.

As the Jorden et al. edited volume argues, these features of polycentricity are present in the structure of transnational climate change governance. This is a field of governance populated with many governance units spanning from the municipal to the international level and including private governance units that engage in carbon offset accounting. It is not hard to extend this analysis to other issue areas of transnational environmental governance, such as forestry (Cashore, Auld, and Newsom 2004), fisheries (Gulbrandsen 2009), organic farming, and coffee production (Auld 2014), among many others. In each of these issue areas, there are multiple authoritative actors operating at different geographic scales to provide and produce public goods. But the presence of multiple governing units is not enough to make a polycentric system.

Overlapping sites of authority, mutual adjustment, experimentation, and economies of scale are just as important as the presence of a diversity of governance units. This raises a set of questions that scholars of environmental governance must reckon with before they use the concepts of polycentricity to analyze governance of an issue area. Is there only a diversity of governing units, or is there a diversity of governing units with overlapping authority taking account of each other? How many features of polycentricity are the actors engaged in? Polycentricity gives IR scholars a new toolkit of concepts with which to analyze transnational governance. Before the tools can be applied though, IR scholars first need to establish if they are analyzing a polycentric system or not.

Simply recognizing the diversity of actors providing and producing public goods has broadened the scope of understanding the dynamics of transnational environmental governance. Much of the literature in the 1970s until the early 1990s focused on the role of states (for seminal works, see Keohane and Nye 1977; Waltz 1979; Onuf 1989; Wendt 1992; Baldwin 1993). Nonstate actors, such as firms, nongovernmental organizations (NGOs), scientists, and lawyers, were largely ignored. The provision of public goods came from IOs created by states that were given the responsibility of achieving policy goals defined by states. The United Nations Environment Program, the Ozone Secretariat, and the United Nations Framework Convention on Climate Change are examples of such IOs.

Since the 1990s, many analyses have been done on how private organizations and private–public partnerships also provide and produce public goods (Wapner 1995; Cutler, Haufler, and Porter 1999; Haufler 2001; Hall and Biersteker 2002; Bartley 2007). Private organizations, such as the Forest Stewardship Council (FSC) and the International Federation of Organic Agriculture Movements (IFOAM), produce rules for voluntary adoption by firms involved in production and trade within their respective issue areas. The rules are like industry standards that are produced by industry organizations, such as the International Electrotechnical Commission (for more on nonenvironmental industry standards, see Mattli and Buthe 2011; Murphy and Yates 2009). For this reason, I call these types of private governance units standard-setting organizations (SSOs). The rules produced by these SSOs provide the public good of sustainable or fair production practices.

Typically, when a firm commits to following the rules, it is certified by a third party that monitors the firm's compliance. If the third party is satisfied that the firm is in compliance with the SSO's standards, the firm can put a certification label on its products and thereby communicate to other firms in a supply chain or directly to consumers that the firm is in compliance.

Private–public partnerships are a combination of the two forms of governance described above. These partnerships generally involve an IO and some private organizations that work together to provide and produce public goods. The Small Grants Program of the Global Environmental Facility (GEF) is an example of such an arrangement (for more on public–private partnerships, see Andonova 2010). The GEF was established in 1991 and is funded by thirty-nine countries. The GEF is an example of a publicly funded organization that seeks to disperse funds to state and nonstate actors that are working to achieve public governance goals. The organization provides funds to government agencies, civil society organizations, private sector companies, and research institutions to help them meet the goals of international environmental conventions and agreements.

It is this diversity of actors that is often first cited as a reason to think of transnational environmental governance as complex. As mentioned though, complexity is not polycentricity. Multiple governance units are not enough to constitute a polycentric system, although this recognition is still important. Elinor Ostrom pointed out that recognizing this diversity within the issue area of climate change governance can make us aware that much more is being done by many communities at different scales to address the problems of climate change than if we focused on only international treaties signed by the majority of powerful states (E. Ostrom 2010). She also noted that this diversity is important beyond giving us hope that at least some groups are doing something about such a pressing transnational problem. For Ostrom, the diversity of actors opened the possibility of experimentation, learning, and mutual adjustments.

There is evidence that polycentric governance is happening in different issue areas of transnational environmental governance. A brief review of the organizations involved in different issue areas demonstrates why the concept of polycentric governance is useful for analyzing the political processes of transnational environmental governance. Without these concepts, analyses of environmental governance could miss the importance of competing, overlapping, redundant, and complementary governance organizations and be tempted to misdiagnose the allocation of resources to environmental governance as inefficient.

Green (2010) examined the emergence of a focal SSO in the carbon accounting industry. Carbon accounting became important in the lead-up to the Kyoto Protocol because carbon offset exchanges were proposed as one possible means of encouraging firms to reduce their GHG emissions. In order to know how many tons of GHG emissions a firm had cut out so that these savings could be sold as carbon credits on an exchange, accounting procedures needed to be established. Green uses a supply and demand theory to explain the emergence of the Greenhouse Gas Protocol, a set of carbon accounting standards developed by the World Resources Institute and the World Business Council on Sustainable Development. There was a demand for some accounting standards from firms who knew that, at some point in the near future, there could be public regulation of GHG emissions. They wanted a set of standards in place sooner rather than later so that they could plan for the future. These standards could have been supplied by an international organization, such as a climate change secretariat, but there was no public focal institution that was capable of supplying these standards. Instead, the two NGOs were capable of working with civil society and firms to develop the standards. In another article, Green (2013) provides evidence that other carbon accounting SSOs frequently use the standards developed by the GHG Protocol to certify firms for reducing GHG emissions. This indicates that, within the carbon accounting industry, SSOs are converging on a set of standards. The dynamics of competition in the provision of this public good have enabled private governance units to mutually adjust to each other.

Consumers and firms can also "vote with their feet" (Tiebout 1956). If a certification matters to consumers, they will choose to buy the certified version of the product instead of the noncertified version. Similarly, if firms think certification provides them with a benefit, they will seek certification. This introduces the competitive mechanism to governance that is important to polycentrism. The option of choosing between substitutes offers constituencies a mechanism by which they can communicate their governance preferences. Few studies have looked at the full range of certification labels that firms can voluntarily adopt. Most studies in environmental politics are case studies of single SSOs or case studies of an economic sector with at least one SSO.

Two studies (Green 2014; van der Ven 2015) that have looked at the full breadth of transnational environmental SSOs (those SSOs that focus on environmental issues and operate in at least two countries) have found that, when the SSOs are categorized according to the industry they target with their standards, all SSOs have at least one competitor within their industry. Some industries are characterized by much more competition than others. For example, according to van der Ven (2015), at the high end of competition, the food industry has fourteen SSOs, whereas at the low end, the waste management industry has only two SSOs. The fact that no industry has only one SSO does show that competition is present across industries, although more work would need to be done to know if these SSOs are in direct competition.

Constituencies not only choose between competitors who are providing or producing the same type of public good but also between different types of public goods. For example, one brand of coffee could seek both organic certification and shade-grown certification. The first communicates farming practices free of pesticides; the second communicates that the coffee planta-tion is not clear-cutting forests to grow coffee. In both cases, the environ-mental benefits are interpreted as public goods because the benefits created are not just for the grower but also for communities, such as people living in the area of production or even everyone on the planet. The soil and water are kept clean of pesticides, which benefits everyone who must make use of that soil and water. Soil erosion is limited by the presence of trees for shade-grown coffee, which benefits others living in the area who will not see the quality of their soil reduced by arid conditions or landslides. Those same trees also reduce carbon dioxide, thereby mitigating climate change caused by GHGs, which affect the global climate. Once these private goods, the coffee beans that are packaged and sold, with their certification labels reach the market, consumers have the option of choosing coffee that carries both of the certifications or just one. When firms learn which certifications consu-mers prefer, they will meet the market demand. The effect is that consumer demand could direct the provision of one public good instead of the other or both public goods.

Communicating preferences for public good provision and production through the mechanism of market competition will not be available to governance solutions at the IO level. Usually there are no competing treaties for an environmental problem that states choose from. Instead, states work toward designing one treaty for an issue. States can learn about the prefer-ences of constituencies through the private provision of public goods. Trea-ties that build upon successful private certification schemes are likely to receive support, at least among some constituencies. The private governance system enables states to scale up successful attempts to provide and produce public goods. To date, there is no evidence of this occurring. Instead, the flow of legalization has gone in the opposite direction. Green (2013) argues that 79 percent of standards for carbon accounting developed in the Kyoto Protocol have been adopted by SSOs that certify firms for reducing or offset-ting GHG emissions.

These studies show that, within different issue areas of transnational envi-ronmental governance, there is not just a proliferation of governance units; these units are autonomous and account for each other. One of the obvious differences between polycentrism in transnational environmental govern-ance and polycentrism in a federalist democracy like the United States is that the former lacks the federalist structure of local, state, and national governments legally bound together by an overarching constitution that is present in the latter. Perhaps the closest analogous feature to a constitution in transnational environmental governance is the presence of a focal institution. Such an institution provides the rules and norms that other governance organizations adhere to, just as state and local governments must not violate the US Constitution in their provision and production of public goods.

Not all issue areas of transnational environmental governance have a focal institution. There is a range of complexity across issue areas. Within the IR literature, important axes of disagreement among actors have been identified. IOs and private organizations could agree or disagree over the nature of the problem, what the solution should be, the means of achieving the solution, and the relative benefits that will accrue to actors when the problem is solved (Zellie and van Asselt 2017). The more disagreement that is observed, the more likely that there will be a complex regime of governance instead of a focal institution that delegates governance functions to different organizations. Explaining what gives rise to the degrees of complexity within environmental governance has been the focus of much recent IR literature. Some of these explanations give confirmation to the expectations of polycentricity scholars, whereas others highlight the difficulty of using polycentric concepts at the transnational level.

IS INSTITUTIONAL CHANGE DRIVEN BY
MECHANISMS OF POLYCENTRICITY?

Through the 1970s and 1980s, the importance of institutions of transnational governance was debated in the IR literature. Realists argued that world politics could be understood in terms of state power. If institutions existed, they did so to serve the interests of the most powerful states (Mearsheimer 1995). If there was institutional evolution, realists expected this to be driven by changes in interests of the powerful states, not by processes endogenous to the institutions themselves. Contrasting their position were the liberal institutionalists who argued that institutions were not epiphenomenal (Keohane and Martin 1995). Institutions provided rules for cooperation and means of monitoring agreements. They made cooperation more likely and made it possible for states to realize new interests through negotiating and cooperating within institutions. The realist versus institutionalist debate was a major focus of IR literature, especially in the 1980s and early 1990s. Much of this literature ignored the interests and effects of nonstate actors. It was not until ideas of social constructivism (Onuf 1989; Wendt 1992) were imported into IR that nonstate actors were included in analyses of transnational governance. Social constructivists focused on the effects of norms, identities, and ideas on the emergence and evolution of institutions of transnational governance.

At the same time, Elinor Ostrom was trying to understand how communities devise governance arrangements for common-pool resources. At the time *Governing the Commons* (E. Ostrom 1990) was first published, there was not much crossover of ideas between the IR literature and the studies of common-pool resources. Both were interested in explaining institutional emergence and evolution, but the IR literature was focused on transnational institutions, whereas the common-pool resource literature was focused more on substate institutions. As explained above, the two literatures did not remain isolated from each other.

Current explanations for the institutional complexity of transnational environmental governance borrow from both the prior debates in the IR literature and understandings of institutional emergence and evolution that would sound familiar to scholars of polycentricity. A brief explanation of some recent literature that borrows from these schools of thought will help us to recognize interesting insights and questions that both IR and polycentricity scholars should address.

One of the most important questions for IR scholars has been why institutions emerge in the first place, especially institutions of private governance. For IR scholars, it is surprising that states would cede power to nonstate actors by allowing them to create rules for transnational governance. Given the state-centric focus of past debates in IR, it is no surprise that the role of state institutions is highlighted in some explanations. Whether or not a focal institution exists is given significant weight in Green's (2014) understanding of the emergence of private authority. Green includes a role for state preferences and focal international institutions. Consensus or disagreement among states and the presence or absence of focal international institutions affect the form of private governance that emerges. When states agree on preferences and have a focal institution to work through, they can delegate functions to PROs. When they have different preferences for solving environmental problems and lack a focal institution to work through, then PROs can provide the solutions in the form of private standards. Demanders, suppliers, and public governance institutions interact to determine whether or not PROs are created and the form they take.

The framework of suppliers and demanders in the explanation of the emergence of private authority is not unique to Green. In order for firms or NGOs to successfully create a new PRO, there must be demanders and suppliers of private governance (Mattli and Woods 2009). Buthe (2010) splits the demanders into two categories, those groups that want private regulation to be instituted in order to achieve some social or environmental goal and those firms that will demand that they be the targets private regulation. There must be a group that wants to supply new standards, and there must be a group that wants to adhere to a set of standards. Without either group, private governance would not occur. Instead, we would have either public governance agencies stepping in or no governance at all.

The fact that actors not part of the state apparatus would self-organize to devise rules of governance would not at all be surprising to polycentricity scholars. Elinor Ostrom (1990) explains how individuals can address governance problems without government. "Instead of presuming that the individuals sharing a commons are inevitably caught in a trap from which they cannot escape, I argue that the capacity of individuals to extricate themselves from various types of dilemma situations *varies* from situation to situation" (E. Ostrom 1990, 14). In the last section, I will explain how these contradictory reactions to the presence of nonstate governance open up insights that both schools of literature can benefit from.

A question unresolved in Green's framework is why a focal institution does or does not exist in the first place. Zelli and van Asselt's (2017) attempt to answer this is by proposing a framework that divides problems into conflicts over absolute or relative goods, conflicts over values or means, and problems of communication or distorted incentives. An important factor in understanding common-pool resource governance for Elinor Ostrom is the biophysical conditions of the resource itself. Zelli and van Asselt make this a key component of their explanation for the structure of institutional complexity within an issue area. Resources that are more like public goods pose benign problems because they are treated as absolute goods. These types of goods have low subtractability (E. Ostrom 2005, 25–26). The benefits that Canadian citizens derive from a healthy ozone layer do not impinge on the benefits that Australians also receive. Other problems are more like private property or common-pool resources; they have high subtractability and so are classified as delivering relative goods. Rules that enable Canadian fishermen to extract a certain amount of fish could limit the catch of fish for American fishermen.

One of the key insights of polycentricity is that in a heterogeneous community, there will be conflicts over values. Therefore, communities need heterogeneous solutions to their heterogeneous problems. This is not unique to polycentricity. Explaining how a collectivity with conflicts over values is able to effectively function is one of the key features of *The Calculus of Consent*. Buchanan and Tullock ([1962] 2004) offered a theory for how a collectivity with heterogeneous preferences and unknown preferences that would be known at a later date could construct a constitutional democracy. IR literature has also taken notice of the difficulty of value conflicts. Zelli and van Asselt (2017) do not offer a resolution to a conflict over values; they merely highlight the effect this has on the structure of governance of an environmental issue area. When there is a conflict over values, what some actors see as a problem, others might not. This conflict combined with a relative valuation of a good, instead of an absolute valuation is likely to produce no focal institution. The actors trying to solve the governance problem will not agree on what the problem is nor on the distribution of benefits, and so they will not agree on what the institution should do. However, when there is conflict only over the means of solving the problem, not whether or not there is a problem, and when a good is valued absolutely, then actors are likely to agree on establishing a focal institution to solve the governance problem.

A key part of Ostrom's study of the commons is understanding endogenous changes to institutions. Studies in IR literature looking at the evolution of SSOs have also sought to understand this process, although not through the same conceptual apparatuses used by Ostrom. Fransen (2012) and Auld (2014) focus on how interactions within SSOs enable endogenous preference and value formation. The interaction of actors within institutions can change the actor's preferences for governance outcomes, thereby driving institutional evolution. Their key insight is that the actors involved develop new preferences by interacting within an SSO or by competing with other SSOs. These actors will negotiate over the standards the SSO should produce, how those standards should be monitored and enforced, and what other actors should be allowed to be members of the SSO and have decision-making power over producing new standards. It is the process of negotiating that enables the actors to learn new preferences.

The explanations provided by Fransen (2012) and Auld (2014) for endogenous evolution shows that polycentric systems of transnational environmental governance enable preference and value discovery. Hayek argued that one of the most important aspects of a market system of private goods is the discovery process (Hayek 2002). Entrepreneurs discover new goods and services and new ways of organizing production, which generate new profit opportunities. Without a competitive market of private goods and the price system, this discovery process would not take place. Similarly, without a polycentric system of governance, the discovery process that leads to new governance organizations or new means of providing and producing public goods might not occur.

What if there are discovery opportunities that are being missed by policy entrepreneurs? Abbott (2017) has argued that in order to take advantage of the potential benefits of a polycentric system, orchestration organizations are needed. Orchestrators could nudge the public economy of a polycentric system to generate the benefits of competition or share knowledge gained through experimentation. Orchestration is a function performed by IOs that is intended to enhance environmental governance provided by all of these different actors at different scales (Abbott and Hale 2014; Abbot et al. 2015). "Orchestration is valuable for structuring and coordinating intermediary relationships where mutual adjustment is insufficient" (Abbott 2017, 10). Orchestration organizations are supposed to catalyze initiatives, track progress, showcase successes, and report achievements. They do not have the power to coerce other governance units but instead use "persuasion, material and ideational support, and reputational incentives to encourage organizations to reduce overlaps, manage conflicts, fill governance gaps, collaborate, and otherwise govern more effectively" (Abbott 2017, 10). The presence of these types of organizations could distort markets to serve the interests of the orchestrators. Keeping Buchanan's warning in mind that we must not assume that public agencies work only to satisfy the public's interests, the orchestrator will not necessarily orchestrate for the good of the public. The orchestrator will have its own preferences it wants to pursue. Nevertheless, governance within a polycentric system could prefer to have an orchestrator that does facilitate learning across units.

Bringing the literatures from IR, polycentricity, and Ostrom's work on the commons together enables us to see the ways in which they complement each other but also the ways in which they differ. There is evidence that competitive mechanisms present in polycentric systems do drive institutional change in transnational environmental governance. The actors in the system of rule are also able to endogenously change their preferences and so change their institutions. Other factors such as the nature of the problem and the presence or absence of a focal institution also affect institutional change in transnational environmental governance. The next section will work through avenues of future research that are opened up by comparing the different bodies of literature reviewed in this chapter as well as insights from the public choice literature.

PATHS FOR FUTURE RESEARCH

As has been described, a particular feature of transnational environmental governance is that there is not just one SSO for each issue area; there are usually at least two. Just as different public governing units in a polycentric system compete with each other, so do SSOs. Polycentricity enables local public economies to function (McGinnis 1999). A polycentric system allows governance entrepreneurs to engage in a discovery process. Demand for different or better public services is met by the emergence or adaptation of local public governance organizations.

While transnational environmental governance does not lend itself to local public economies at the scale of a municipality, the presence of many SSOs raises the question of what constitutes the features of an international public economy. Here, IR scholars could benefit from the public choice literature on community policing (E. Ostrom and Whitaker 1973; McGinnis 1999; Boettke, Lemke, and Palagashvili 2016). The costs and benefits of SSOs are typically studied in isolation of each other except for a few studies that look at the performance of all transnational environmental SSOs. In transnational environmental governance, there are often multiple SSOs competing with each other and are nested within a hierarchy of governance organizations that include public and hybrid organizations. Does this give rise to a transnational public economy? How does this differ from other types of public economies like community policing? Just as Oatley cautioned scholars of international political economy against reducing explanations of international economic governance outcomes to variations in national economies (Oatley 2011), scholars of polycentricity, public choice, and transnational environmental politics should investigate if there are transnational variables that affect the functioning of a transnational public economy.

What if the polycentric structure of transnational environmental governance not only generates public economies but also club economies? While much of the IR literature has focused on the public goods produced by transnational environmental governance, two authors have argued that SSOs also produce club goods. The costs and benefits of establishing club goods was first presented by Buchanan (1965). The club goods literature has grown beyond Buchanan's initial paper and has found applications in transnational private governance studies. Potoski and Prakash (2009, 2012) have been the leaders of bringing theories of club goods into the IR literature. Club goods differ from public goods. Both have a low subtractability of use, which means that the benefits one person receives from the good does not detract much from the benefits another person receives. This is different than a private good, which gives benefits only to the owner of the good. The difference between club and public goods is in the ease with which people can gain access to the benefits from the good. Those that produce club goods have less difficulty of excluding potential beneficiaries than do producers of public goods. For example, membership at a country club is a club good. Membership can be limited by fees and rules but once a member, a person can enjoy the same benefits as other members. A public park is a public good. Membership is hard to limit because any member of the public community can access the park, but the benefits one person receives from going to the park does not severely affect another person's enjoyment of the park.

Potoski and Prakash argue that private environmental governance creates governance clubs that produce club goods for their members (i.e., the firms that are certified for adhering to environmental standards established by the club). Clubs are a means of erecting barriers to market entry. They can be rent-seeking organizations. Certification schemes have erected market entry barriers for third-world fishermen who want to sell their products in industrialized countries (Kalfagianni and Pattberg 2014). The cost of certification has been too high for the former, and so they cannot afford to enter markets in which certified seafood is in demand. This benefits fishermen from industrialized countries that can afford to pay the cost of certification. This difference in capacity to pay certification costs generates benefits to members of fisheries SSOs similar to how public regulations that increase the cost of market entry return benefits to dominant firms in a market. Lower costs of membership might dilute the benefits of membership by increasing market competition. More certified suppliers would be selling to consumers demanding certified products, such as MSC-certified seafood. If there are features of clubs and club goods in transnational environmental governance, then how might a transnational club economy differ from a transnational public economy? Taking the distinction between these types of goods seriously could help us better understand the mechanisms of institutional change in environmental governance. Are the mechanisms of institutional change different in a club economy than in a public economy?

Two important features of polycentric systems are the presence of overarching rules, usually in the form of a constitution, and the capacity of people to vote with their feet. These features have unique characteristics within transnational environmental governance. There are no constitutions at the transnational level. The difficulty of making a constitution in a pluralist or heterogeneous society has been a focus for public choice scholars working on issues of constitutional democracy. Within this field, Buchanan and Tullock's *The Calculus of Consent* provides a methodologically individualistic approach to analyzing constitutional democracies. However, it would be hard to imagine how something like Buchanan and Tullock's unanimity rule would be used by policymakers or communities at the transnational level because the decision-making costs for each individual would be too high (Buchanan and Tullock [1962] 2004, 43). From a public choice perspective, this could be an argument for limiting the number and capacities of IOs since the external cost and decision-making cost to each individual of collectivizing decision making at the international level is so high. Yet states want to use IOs to either solve transnational problems or return benefits to members of their state, such as government officials, firms, and NGOs. It is inconceivable that IOs will cease to be part of transnational governance in the near, or even long-term, future. For scholars of public choice, this raises the question of what constitutional constraints should be placed on constitutional democracies when they act at the international level. These constraints should be constructed with knowledge that other actors will not have the same constraints. Constitutional democracies must bargain with authoritarian regimes at the international level. This has become an even more important feature of world politics because China has risen as a competitor to the United States in many issue areas and Russia has reemerged as a global competitor of the United States.

Even if each state had constitutional constraints at the international level, they most likely would not have the same constraints. They would each be playing by a different set of national rules. The constitutional constraints could not simply be aggregated up to work as a transnational constitution. While there are no constitutions at the international level, there are issue areas in which the rules of a focal institution structure the behavior of organizations that provide and produce public goods within the same issue area. For example, the Kyoto Protocol established GHG emission reduction targets for each country that signed on to the treaty and established rules for how countries could meet their reduction targets. Other governance organizations, such as the GEF, followed these rules and targets when they created projects to reduce GHG emissions. Given the lack of a constitution that binds different governing agencies together, scholars of polycentricity should investigate how polycentric systems can function at the transnational level without explicit constitutions. The hierarchical relationship between the GEF and the Kyoto Protocol could be likened to the relationship between a provincial and national government. What is different and similar about the hierarchical relationship between public governing units within a state and between governing units at the international level? Understanding how transnational polycentric governance functions without a constitution and how the lack of a constitution affects the hierarchical relationship between governing units at the international level would be interesting to scholars of IR, polycentricity, and constitutional political economy.

The global community that can be constituents of transnational polycentric systems of governance presents a problem for one of the important dynamics that enable a polycentric system to meet the demands of its constituents. How can polycentricity function when constituents might not be able to vote with their feet? A global problem like climate change certainly makes voting with one's feet difficult, at least until they have the capacity to move to another planet or moon. While this might be the most extreme example of the difficulty of creating overlapping sites of authority, the difficulty remains even when we reduce the geographic scale of the problem. Bangladeshis are likely to be much more affected by climate change than Canadians or Russians. Climate change might increase the growing season in the latter two countries, and new sea lanes through the arctic ice have already been opened for both countries. These are benefits that will not accrue to Bangladesh. Instead, Bangladesh might be inundated as sea levels rise, causing massive migration both within the country and out of the country. Where will refugees of climate change go? Moving between countries is not as easy as moving between municipalities.

Linking the issue of climate change governance to refugee governance introduces another set of questions that polycentricity scholars should investigate. Global governance is rife with issue linkage, and this affects the provision of public goods in a polycentric system. The preferences an actor has to provide or produce a public good are part of a larger hierarchy of preferences. We must recognize that the governor is an agent with their own preferences. In global governance this is especially important for states that have the capacity to pursue multiple preferences and use one issue area to achieve goals in another. Imposing environmental standards could be a means of protecting a domestic industry from rules of free trade or of forcing standards to diffuse when they cannot be agreed upon in trade governance organizations. This would come as no surprise to economists. Buchanan and Tullock (1975) argued that agreements on regulatory standards are a way for established firms to limit competition from smaller firms. We should distinguish between cases where actors are engaging in issue linkage and cases where they are not. Governance failures may come about when governors are trying to use one organization to accomplish goals on a related issue. Similarly, the practice of issue linkage could further increase the external costs to individuals. Giving collective decision-making power to a government organization that is pursuing multiple goals at the same time means that the governance organization is not simply trying to provide or produce the demanded public good; it is also trying to satisfy its own preferences or the preferences of its most influential constituents. This is something that is missed in the literature on orchestration. Orchestration organizations must be given their own agency. Scholars studying orchestrators should not assume that orchestrators are motivated only by the public good.

Not only might preferences of governors create linkages between different governance organizations; so might the ideas of governors and constituents. In transnational environmental governance, sustainable development has become a permanent feature of solutions to all environmental problems. What effect do such ideas or norms have upon transnational public economies and club economies? They could act as rhetorical devices, used by powerful actors to legitimate some set of rules that accord with the actor's preferences. But they also might generate new demands for governance or new ideas for how to provide and produce public and club goods. They could open a new range of discovery possibilities.

This gets into the question of the source of individual preferences. The social constructivist strand of research in IR has long been focused on this question, attributing the origin of preferences to shared norms, understandings, identities, and repeated interactions between individuals (Onuf 1989; Wendt 1992). This issue can also be found in the public choice literature. Chamlee-Wright and Storr (2010) explore how the expectations of residents of New Orleans regarding the capabilities and intentions of the government response to Hurricane Katrina generated decisions about how residents would react. By differentiating between expectations of government capabilities and intentions, the authors are better able to understand why citizens chose the rebuilding strategies that they did.

IR scholars could better explain the mix of governance units, the goods they provide and produce, and the institutional evolution by better understanding what generates the demand for these units and goods in the first place. The idea of environmental sustainability is one potential motivating factor, but the actual effects of sustainability is an empirical question. While the phrase frequently occurs within environmental governance units, it could just be a rhetorical strategy to gain support of environmental activists who care about sustainability. Recognizing that environmental sustainability is one possible factor that makes possible a range of responses to environmental problems leads to the question of what other ideas might also motivate the creation of governance units and public or club goods.

Comparing the IR literature with the polycentricity and public choice literature brings to the fore questions of how transnational public and club economies function, of the constitutional constraints that should exist for governments when they negotiate at the international level, of the constitutional constraints that could be placed on transnational environmental governance units, of the effects that issue linkage has on polycentric systems, and of the factors that generate and influence the preferences that individuals in a polycentric system pursue. As discussed, there has already been a sharing of ideas from the polycentric literature to the IR literature. IR has been a field of study that has changed itself by borrowing ideas from other fields (Waever 1998). Continuing to import ideas from the public choice and polycentricity literatures will enable IR scholars to better understand the emergence of transnational environmental governance units and their interactions and why there are or are not governance successes within the field.

REFERENCES

Abbott, Kenneth W. 2012. "The Transnational Regime Complex for Climate Change." *Government and Policy: Environment and Planning C*, 30 (4), 571–90.

———. 2017. "Orchestrating Experimentation in Non-State Environmental Commitments." *Environmental Politics*, 26 (4).

Abbott, Kenneth W., Philipp Genschel, Duncan Snidal, and Bernard Zangl, eds. 2015. *International Organizations as Orchestrators*. Cambridge: Cambridge University Press.

Andonova, Liliana B. 2010. "Public-Private Partnerships for the Earth: Politics and Patterns of Hybrid Authority in the Multilateral System." *Global Environmental Politics*, 10 (2): 25–53.

Armitage, Derek. 2008. "Governance and the Commons in a Multi-level World." *International Journal of the Commons*, 2 (1): 7–32.

Auld, Graeme. 2014. *Constructing Private Governance: The Rise and Evolution of Forest, Coffee, and Fisheries Certification*. New Haven, CT: Yale University Press.

Auld, Graeme, Steven Bernstein, and Benjamin Cashore. 2008. "The New Corporate Social Responsibility." *Annual Review of Environment and Resources*, 33: 413–35.

Baldwin, David A., ed. 1993. *Neorealism and Neoliberalism: The Contemporary Debate*. New York: Columbia University Press.

Bartley, Tim. 2007. "Institutional Emergence in an Era of Globalization: The Rise of Transnational Private Regulation of Labor and Environmental Conditions." *American Journal of Sociology*, 113 (2): 297–351.

Betsill, Michelle M., and Harriet Bulkeley. 2006. "Cities and the Multilevel Governance of Global Climate Change." *Global Governance*, 12: 141–59.

Boettke, Peter J., Christopher J. Coyne, and Peter T. Leeson. 2011. "Quasimarket Failure." *Public Choice*, 149 (1–2): 209–24.

Boettke, Peter J., Jayme S. Lemke, and Liya Palagashvili. 2016. "Re-Evaluating Community Policing in a Polycentric System." *Journal of Institutional Economics*, 12 (2): 305–25.

Buchanan, James M. 1965. "An Economic Theory of Clubs." *Economica* 32: 1–14.

————. 1979. "Politics without Romance: A Sketch of Positive Public Choice Theory and Its Normative Implications," Inaugural lecture, Institute for Advanced Studies, Vienna, Austria. IHS Journal, Zeitschrift des Instituts für Höhere Studien 3: B1–B11.

Buchanan, James M., and Gordon Tullock. 1975. "Polluters' Profits and Political Response: Direct Controls Versus Taxes." *The American Economic Review*, March: 139–47.

————. (1962) 2004. *The Calculus of Consent: Logical Foundations of Constitutional Democracy*. Indianapolis, IN: Liberty Fund, Inc.

Bullock, Graham. 2017. *Green Grades: Can Information Save the Earth?* Cambridge, MA: MIT Press.

Buthe, Tim. 2010. "Private Regulation in the Global Economy: A (P)Review." *Business and Politics*, 12 (3): Article 2.

Cashore, Benjamin, Graeme Auld, and Deanna Newsom. 2004. *Governing through Markets: Forest Certification and the Emergence of Non-State Authority*. New Haven, CT: Yale University Press.

Chamlee-Wright, Emily, and Virgil Henry Storr. 2010. "Expectations of Government's Response to Disaster." *Public Choice*, 144 (1): 253–74.

Cutler, A. Clair, Virginia Haufler, and Tony Porter, eds. 1999. *Private Authority and International Affairs*. Albany: State University New York Press.

Dingwerth, Klaus, and Philip Pattberg. 2006. "Global Governance as a Perspective on World Politics." *Global Governance*, 12 (2): 185–203.

Dorsch, Marcel J., and Christian Flachsland. 2017. "A Polycentric Approach to Global Climate Governance." *Global Environmental Politics* 17 (2): 45–64.

Fransen, Luc. 2012. *Corporate Social Responsibility and Global Labor Standards: Firms and Activists in the Making of Private Regulation*. New York: Routledge.

Green, Jessica F. 2010. "Private Standards in the Climate Regime: The Greenhouse Gas Protocol." *Business and Politics* 12 (3).

————. 2013. "Order Out of Chaos: Public and Private Rules for Managing Carbon Markets." *Global Environmental Politics* 13 (2): 1–25.

————. 2014. *Rethinking Private Authority: Agents and Entrepreneurs in Global Environmental Governance*. Princeton, NJ: Princeton University Press.

Gulbrandsen, Lars H. 2009. "The Emergence and Effectiveness of the Marine Stewardship Council." *Marine Policy*, 33 (4): 654–60.

Gulbrandsen, Lars H., and Graeme Auld. 2016. "Contested Accountability Logics in Evolving Nonstate Certification for Fisheries Sustainability." *Global Environmental Politics*, 16 (2): 42–60.

Hale, Thomas, and Charles Roger. 2014. "Orchestration and Transnational Climate Governance." *Review of International Organizations*, 9: 59–82.

Hall, Rodney Bruce, and Thomas J. Biersteker. 2002. "The Emergence of Private Authority in the International System." In *The Emergence of Private Authority in Global Governance*, edited by Rodney Bruce Hall and Thomas J. Biersteker, 3–22. Cambridge: Cambridge University Press.

Haufler, Virginia. 2001. *A Public Role for the Private Sector: Industry Self-Regulation in a Global Economy*. Washington, DC: Carnegie Endowment for International Peace.

Hayek, Friedrich A. 2002. "Competition as a Discovery Procedure." *The Quarterly Journal of Austrian Economics* 5 (3): 9–23.

Jordan, Andrew, Dave Huitema, Jonas Schoenefeld, Harro van Asselt, and Johanna Forster. 2018. "Governing Climate Change Polycentrically: Setting the Scene." In *Governing Climate Change: Polycentricity in Action?*, edited by Andrew Jordan, Dave Huitema, Harro van Asselt, and Johanna Forster, 3–25. Cambridge: Cambridge University Press.

Kalfagianni, Agni, and Philipp Pattberg. 2014. "Exploring the Output Legitimacy of Transnational Fisheries Governance." *Globalizations*, 11 (3): 385–400.

Keohane, Robert O., and Lisa Martin. 1995. "The Promise of Institutionalist Theory." *International Security* 20 (1): 39–51.

Keohane, Robert O., and Joseph Nye. 1977. *Power and Interdependence*. Boston: Little, Brown.

Keohane, Robert O., and Elinor Ostrom. 1995. *Local Commons and Global Interdependence: Heterogeneity and Cooperation in Two Domains*. London: SAGE Publications Ltd.

Keohane, Robert O., and David G. Victor. 2011. "The Regime Complex for Climate Change." *Perspectives on Politics* 9: 7–23.

Klein, Benjamin, and Keith B. Leffler. 1981. "The Role of Market Forces in Assuring Contractual Performance." *Journal of Political Economy*, 89 (4): 615–41.

Marx, Axel. 2014. "Legitimacy, Institutional Design, and Dispute Settlement: The Case of Eco-Certification Systems." *Globalizations*, 11 (3): 401–416.

Mattli, Walter, and Tim Buthe. 2011. *The New Global Rulers: The Privatization of Regulation in the World Economy*. Princeton NJ: Princeton University Press.

Mattli, Walter, and Ngaire Woods. 2009. *The Politics of Global Regulation*. Princeton, NJ: Princeton University Press.

McGinnis, Michael D. 1999. "Introduction." In *Polycentricity and Local Public Economies: Readings from the Workshop in Political Theory and Policy Analysis*, edited by Michael D. McGinnis, 1–30. Ann Arbor: University of Michigan Press.

Mearsheimer, John J. 1995. "The False Promise of International Institutions." *International Security* 19 (3): 5–49.

Murphy, Craig N., and JoAnne Yates. 2009. *The International Organization for Standardization (ISO): Global Governance through Voluntary Consensus*. New York: Routledge.

Oatley, Thomas. 2011. "The Reductionist Gamble: Open Economy Politics in the Global Economy." *International Organization*, 65 (2): 311–41.

Onuf, Nicholas G. 1989. *World of Our Making: Rules and Rule in Social Theory and International Relations*. Columbia: University of South Carolina Press.

Ostrom, Elinor. 1990. *Governing the Commons: The Evolution of Institutions for Collective Action*. Cambridge: Cambridge University Press.

———. 2005. *Understanding Institutional Diversity*. Princeton, NJ: Princeton University Press.

———. 2010. "Polycentric Systems for Coping with Collective Action and Global Environmental Change." *Global Environmental Change*, 20, 550–57.

Ostrom, Elinor, and Gordon Whitaker. 1973. "Does Local Community Control of Police Make a Difference? Some Preliminary Findings." *American Journal of Political Science* 17 (1): 48–76.

Ostrom, Vincent. 1973. *The Intellectual Crisis in American Public Administration*. Tuscaloosa: University of Alabama Press.

———. (1991) 2014. "Polycentricity: The Structural Basis of Self-Governing Systems." In *Choice, Rules and Collective Action*, edited by P. D. Aligica and F. Sabetti, 45–60. Colchester, UK: ECPR Press.

Ostrom, Vincent, Charles M. Tiebout, and Robert Warren. 1961. "The Organization of Government in Metropolitan Areas: A Theoretical Inquiry." *American Political Science Review* 55 (4): 831–42.

Potoski, Matt, and Aseem Prakash. 2009. *Voluntary Programs: A Club Theory Perspective*. Cambridge, MA: MIT Press.

———. 2012. "Green Clubs: Collective Action and Voluntary Environmental Programs." *Annual Review of Political Science* 16: 399–419.

Rosenau, James N., and Ernst-Otto Czempiel. 1992. *Governance without Government: Order and Change in World Politics*. Cambridge: Cambridge University Press.

Sandler, Todd. 2013. "Buchanan Clubs." *Constitutional Political Economy*, 24: 265–84.

Tiebout, Charles M. 1956. "A Pure Theory of Logical Expenditures." *Journal of Political Economy* 64 (October): 416–24.

Van der Ven, Hamish. 2015. "Correlates of Rigorous and Credible Transnational Governance: A Cross-Sectoral Analysis of Best Practice Compliance in Eco-Labeling." *Regulation & Governance* 9: 276–93.

Vogel, David. 1997. *Trading Up: Consumer and Environmental Regulation in a Global Economy*. Cambridge, MA: Harvard University Press.

Waever, Ole. 1998. "The Sociology of a Not So International Discipline: American and European Developments in International Relations." *International Organization* 52 (4): 687–727.

Waltz, Kenneth. 1979. *Theory of International Politics*. New York: McGraw-Hill.

Wapner, Paul. 1995. "Politics beyond the State: Environmental Activism and World Civic Politics." *World Politics*, 47 (3): 311–40.

Wendt, Alexander. 1992. "Anarchy Is What States Make of It: The Social Construction of Power Politics." *International Organization* 46 (3): 391–425.

Wilson, Woodrow. (1885) 1956. *Congressional Government: A Study in American Politics*. New York: Meridian Books.

Zelli, Fariborz, and Harro van Asselt. 2017. "The Institutional Fragmentation of Global Environmental Governance: Causes, Consequences, and Responses." *Global Environmental Politics*, 13 (3): 669–93.

Chapter Eight

Dispute Avoidance through International Regulatory Cooperation

A Public Choice Approach

Inu Manak

While tariffs are often the main area of focus in trade liberalization, overall levels of tariff protection have declined significantly over time. In contrast, regulatory barriers to trade, which are domestic rules and requirements on goods and services, have grown. As states utilize tariffs less because of multiple rounds of reductions in multilateral trade negotiations, they have opted for more opaque means of protectionism. But while regulatory barriers to trade have gained attention in recent years, with efforts to include provisions to address this problem in a number of recent trade agreements, there have not been as many formal trade disputes on these issues as one might expect.

Of the 561 requests for consultations made to the World Trade Organization (WTO), only 78 unique requests make reference to the Technical Barriers to Trade (TBT) and Sanitary and Phytosanitary (SPS) Agreements, which are the deepest multilateral efforts to address behind-the-border barriers.[1] Beyond formal disputes, the TBT and SPS Agreements also established committees made up of representatives of WTO members that monitor the implementation of the agreements. In these committees, states can openly raise concerns about another state's regulatory measures. While the number of these concerns has grown over time, totaling 993 unique concerns from 1995 to 2018, less than 5 percent of these concerns escalate into formal disputes. How do so many of these regulatory trade frictions avoid turning into full-fledged disputes?

The literature identifies several factors. While some scholars suggest that the costs to litigation itself are a significant deterrent to escalating disputes (Guzman and Simmons 2002; Sevilla 1998), particularly for developing countries (Bown and Hoekman 2005), others highlight the probability of winning (or the strength of the legal case), although difficult to measure, as a more important factor (Busch and Reinhardt 2000; Johns and Pelc 2011). While there must be some economic stakes involved to raise a dispute, the evidence is mixed on whether the overall trade value is a significant determinant for filing (Bown and Reynolds 2014; Allee 2004). Others have focused on the domestic political determinants for filing, such as filing disputes in election years when there's broader support for free trade (Chaudoin 2014) or the level of industry interest in pushing for a dispute (Hudec 1990; Shaffer 2003; Brutger 2017). Still others have suggested that many cases simply get solved in consultations (Busch and Reinhardt 2001) or through exacting side payments and issue linkages (Guzman and Simmons 2002; Davis 2004).

Despite the extensive literature on dispute settlement, less attention has been paid to the role of the committees and the forum for regulatory cooperation they provide as a mechanism for dispute avoidance. This regulatory cooperation function allows states to engage in dialogue and apply pressure to other states to adjust their regulatory measures. Wolfe (2013) argues that the technical nature of TBT and SPS issues favors a more substantive discussion that can facilitate resolution as opposed to the broader trade-offs and bargaining that may happen in other trade disputes. This is similar to one of the arguments put forward by Horn, Mavroidis, and Wijkstrom (2013), who also show that concerns raised about regulatory actions within the TBT and SPS committees are "akin to an informal form of resolution of trade conflicts" (730). In fact, the evolution of the committees over time has led them to be increasingly viewed as a forum for multilateral review of regulatory measures states take, whether implemented or in draft form (Puig and Al-Haddab 2011).

The committees, however, are not just a forum of state-to-state interaction but also provide space for the de facto participation of industry as well. Recognizing this more complex dynamic of interaction reminds us to be cognizant of what Buchanan (1949) referred to as the "individualistic view," which focuses on individuals and the institutions within which they interact, as opposed to the "organismic view," which treats the state as a single homogeneous actor, which acts to maximize a predetermined notion of social welfare. Among the insights from the vast public choice literature, which is grounded in Buchanan's individualistic view, is that interest groups often work to pursue the interests of their members. These studies have highlighted the importance of interest groups in understanding policy outcomes (Sloof 1998; Drazen 2002; Persson and Tabellini 2000), how the size of interest groups matters (Potters and van Winden 1996; Olson 1965; Stigler 1971;

Becker 1983), how interest groups buy protection (Grossman and Helpman 1996), and the incentives for individuals to partake in collective action (Olson 1965). A common thread throughout these studies is that interest group pressure or rent seeking, more broadly, produces a social cost (Tullock 1967), but this is in part due to the fact that many of these studies focus on the role of money in the form of campaign contributions or similar means to buy influence (van Winden 1999). However, there is a strand of literature that addresses the informational role of interest groups (Austen-Smith 1996; Lohmann 1995; Milner and Rosendorff 1996; Grossman and Helpman 2001), pointing to the fact that some interest group behavior can actually be welfare enhancing. Building on this literature, this chapter argues that the regulatory cooperation function of the WTO's committees is utilized by industry interests to push governments to reach settlements in order to avoid a lengthy dispute, thus producing a welfare-enhancing outcome.

This chapter examines how the institutional design of regulatory cooperation in this forum shapes and constrains behavior and also gives individual actors the ability to utilize the institutional environment to alter domestic rules to their advantage, ultimately, allowing states to avoid disputes. I argue that industry groups in particular are better able to push for the resolution of potential disputes through these international institutions due to two conditions: (1) the ability to have their voice heard and (2) decision-making rules that favor greater commitments among states to respond to foreign concerns. Furthermore, the successful utilization of these institutions by industry stakeholders not only sets a precedent for action but also generates momentum for the cycle to be repeated.

The findings lead to three main implications. First, the design of these institutions affects who can participate. Industry groups currently play a significant role in these processes, which has been a potent criticism against these efforts. As a result, states should be conscious of this as they replicate regulatory cooperation in other trade agreements. Second, while the public choice literature generally sees interest groups as reducing social welfare by concentrating benefits on their members at the expense of nongroup members, this paper shows that, counterintuitively, interest group pressure can be welfare enhancing by pushing governments to avoid lengthy disputes and to adjust potentially trade restrictive regulations. Third, regulatory cooperation provides another way of thinking about dispute settlement more broadly, moving away from more judicial models. In fact, it highlights the continued relevance of diplomacy in the WTO, suggesting alternative paths forward for the organization as the future of the formal dispute settlement system is increasingly called into question.

This chapter proceeds as follows. First, the chapter provides a brief explanation of what international regulatory cooperation is. Second, I give an overview of the relevant literature and offer a theory of dispute avoidance through regulatory cooperation. Third, the chapter examines a case study of a dispute that was successfully avoided through the WTO's SPS committee. The final section concludes with implications of this research.

INTERNATIONAL REGULATORY COOPERATION

As tariff barriers have significantly been reduced through several rounds of multilateral trade liberalization, countries have become more concerned with nontariff barriers (NTBs), which may impede the free flow of goods and services across borders. An NTB can take many forms, and there is no definitive list or description of what an NTB could entail (Pauwelyn, Guzman, and Hillman 2012). A prominent NTB is a domestic regulation that may restrict trade, such as when the US government required that certain muscle cuts of beef and pork sold in the United States bear a label explaining where the animal was "born, raised and slaughtered." This regulatory mea sure was successfully challenged by Canada and Mexico at the WTO.[2] As the ability to utilize tariffs as a policy instrument to restrict imports has declined, particularly among developed countries,[3] states have reverted to utilizing more opaque measures, such as regulations, to protect domestic industry (Kono 2006).

However, not all regulations are protectionist, and it is important to distinguish between regulatory protectionism as described above and regulatory divergence, which has gained increasing attention in trade negotiations.[4] Regulatory protectionism is covered by the general obligation of nondiscrimination outlined in the WTO agreements and, more specifically, by the General Agreement on Tariffs and Trade (GATT), Articles III and XX, as well as the TBT and SPS Agreements. Regulatory divergence is something different, with the main distinguishing characteristic being that the regulation is not necessarily crafted with protectionist intent, though it can have a trade restrictive effect. For example, countries can have divergent rules for the brightness of headlamps for cars or different testing requirements for makeup products that contain sun protection factor (SPF). Addressing these differences that may emerge has been the focus of international regulatory cooperation efforts and, I argue, an important contributor to dispute avoidance.

Since regulation often occurs in silos, it can be incredibly challenging to prevent regulatory divergence. As this problem has grown in importance, however, governments have looked for innovative ways to address it. The most comprehensive attempt, which has not been replicated elsewhere, is the effort by the European Union to create a single market.[5] But outside of a state or a supranational authority, how can regulatory convergence be achieved? There are two general ways to do this for regulations that are already in place: harmonization and mutual recognition or equivalence agreements.

Harmonization is when two (or more) countries decide to adopt the same regulation or standard. This can be quite difficult because it usually requires one of the countries to rewrite its domestic regulation. Countries can also pursue a mutual recognition agreement (MRA), which is typically very cumbersome and takes many years to negotiate. The goal of an MRA is to reduce duplicative testing by having the product tested once in the exporting market by recognizing another country's conformity assessment procedures (i.e., through accreditation systems) or results of conformity assessment (i.e., certificates, inspections, or test results).[6]

Regulatory cooperation can also be achieved through an equivalency agreement. The basic idea behind equivalence is that the parties to the agreement expressly acknowledge that the outcomes of their independent regulatory schemes achieve the same goal, regardless of variation in how they get there.[7] The United States and the European Union entered into an equivalence agreement on organic produce in 2012, for example, which allows products certified as USDA organic or meeting the requirements of the European organic designation to be sold in either market without additional testing by a conformity testing body.

For regulations that are not yet in place, however, states can also engage in dialogues on new and ongoing regulatory issues and choose to address these problems through unilateral actions. These actions tend to be the result of a process of consultations between states, both formal and informal, that allow for many of these issues to be addressed before a regulation is adopted. Thus, discussions often occur at the draft stage, which makes it easier to achieve a resolution of the issue since the rule has not yet been implemented. The aim of these bilateral and multilateral dialogues is to allow states to discuss regulatory differences *before* they emerge, given the difficulty of altering rules once they become law. The previously mentioned TBT and SPS committees are the most prominent example of this type of forum.[8] Through "specific trade concerns," which will be explained in detail below as well as discussions on regulatory practices, the committees have given countries a multilateral venue for regulatory cooperation to address regulatory outliers before they have a chance to become disputes. This form of regulatory cooperation is the focus of this chapter.

A THEORY OF DISPUTE AVOIDANCE THROUGH REGULATORY COOPERATION

International trade is governed by multilateral institutions (the WTO), plurilateral agreements (e.g., Information Technology Agreement), and regional

trade agreements (e.g., North American Free Trade Agreement). These varying forms of engagement establish rules by which states interact. Over time,
these rules have expanded to include issues that were once outside of trade
pacts altogether. Two of these issues are a specific form of nontariff barrier[9]
called technical barriers to trade (TBT) and sanitary and phytosanitary standards (SPS). TBT are the various domestic rules, requirements, and standards
to which producers must adhere to sell goods on the market. SPS are the
various plant, animal, and human health and safety standards that regulate
the domestic product market. If a company is selling something abroad, it
must make a product that meets the specifications of the jurisdiction in which
it is selling that good. Since regulatory regimes emerge within states and not
across states, it is not hard to see how there are numerous divergences in
rules for any given product. Essentially, regulations are generated domesti-
cally, but they affect the choices of foreign producers.

If these differences cannot be resolved, however, they can escalate to
formal disputes. As noted earlier, however, despite the growing number of
concerns over regulatory trade barriers, the number of formal disputes filed
at the WTO on these issues has been limited. To put this in perspective, let's
briefly look at notifications of measures with a potential impact on trade
made to the WTO by its membership.

Looking only at TBT and SPS notifications, it is apparent that they have
been trending upward since the organization's founding with 364 and 189
TBT and SPS notifications in 1995, respectively, to 1,787 and 922 notifications in 2017. The total number of all regular notifications over that time
period is 25,030 TBT notifications and 15,727 SPS notifications, though the
growth in membership does account for some of this. These figures overstate
the universe of potential cases, however, since a majority of these notified
measures may not significantly restrict trade or have little to no impact on
trade that they are never challenged.

However, from these notifications, WTO members can raise what are
called "specific trade concerns" in the TBT and SPS committees. These
concerns are raised from one member to another, asking for clarification or
adjustment of a measure to fall in line with their WTO obligations. To explain, when a WTO member considers that a notified (and sometimes not yet
notified) measure is potentially trade restrictive, it either verbally or in writing identifies the measure of concern and the country maintaining it and
requests clarification on its application. The state maintaining the measure
has a chance to respond to the specific trade concern (either right away or in
subsequent meetings). Some concerns have long staying power in that they
are repeatedly brought up at different meetings. Other concerns are resolved,
whereas some become the subject of a formal dispute (with varying levels of
progress within the dispute system). The number of specific trade concerns
(STCs) raised has increased over time, but what is surprising is the relatively

few that turn into full-fledged disputes. Of the well over 900 concerns that have been raised since 1995, less than 5 percent have escalated to a formal dispute. In fact, a large number of these concerns (approximately one-third) are resolved within the committees (Horn, Mavroidis, and Wijkstrom 2013) or dropped.

So why do so many cases drop off the radar or result in regulatory cooperation to the extent that they avoid a formal dispute? Horn, Mavroidis, and Wijkstrom (2013) argue that the committees provide a less political forum to discuss trade frictions as opposed to formal dispute settlement through consultations and litigation due to the highly technical nature of these issues in particular. While the TBT and SPS committees serve a number of different functions, one important feature is the role of the committees in dispute avoidance. Some have suggested that the work of the TBT and SPS committees plays an important role in facilitating regulatory cooperation (Wijkstrom 2015; Mavroidis 2016; Bollyky 2017). Wijkstrom (2015) describes the work of the TBT committee as "essentially a catalyst for dialogue at the multilateral level. It is a technical, expert-driven setting with two tracks—the Committee is a forum for (i) the development of guidance (soft law, informal, best-endeavor in nature) and (ii) peer review of trade measures" (2). Though there is no explicit obligation for regulatory cooperation under the TBT Agreement, it is implicit. This is in contrast to the SPS Agreement, which in Article 3 and Article 4 calls on members to pursue harmonization and equivalence where possible. Through consensus, WTO members have put forward a number of guidance documents that have worked to improve the transparency of domestic regulatory action and the adoption of best practices. In addition, through raising STCs, members have effectively developed a system of regulatory peer review.

But looking at the international relations literature more broadly, why would we see this level of cooperation among states? Some argue that cooperation is simply a product of interaction between states and can be explained by conventional military power, market power (Drezner 2008; Simmons 2001), the flexibility to make side payments and through issue linkage (Guzman and Simmons 2002; Davis 2004), and the willingness to make credible commitments (Fearon 1995, 1997). More recently, a growing body of literature draws on interdisciplinary theories of competition to argue that a mixture of market forces, imitation, and reputational concerns drives states to converge on the same set of policies (Gilardi 2012).

States may also use international institutions as cover to carry out domestic reforms, thus creating a binding constraint to domestic actions (Dai 2005; Vreeland 2003; Mansfield, Milner, and Rosendorff 2002; Moravcsik 2000; Vaubel 1986; Putnam 1988). In some ways, certain forms of regulatory cooperation could be said to contain elements of a binding constraint, where to affect domestic regulatory change, states refer to their international obligations. It is important to keep in mind, however, that this raises questions about the appropriate sphere of action for government (Buchanan 1999), not least because this action happens in an arena outside of complete state control.

Another strand of literature has brought our attention to recurrent processes and actors beyond and below the state that may wield influence in shaping international outcomes. These theories build on the work of Gourevitch (2002) and argue that institutions provide the opportunity structures for political change, which can act as both targets and constraints (Sikkink 2005). While a policy change could be the result of a one-time action by stakeholders, a so-called boomerang effect (Keck and Sikkink 1999), change can also occur because of multiple actions over an extended period, reflecting a spiral (Risse, Ropp, and Sikkink 1999).

In the realm of regulatory politics, some authors have noted that transnational advocacy networks wield a substantial amount of power and have been able to collaborate on setting global standards (Bach and Newman 2010; Farrell and Newman 2015; Kahler and Lake 2009), sometimes, through the creation of epistemic communities (Haas 1992) that are able to push an agenda for convergence in certain issue areas. This body of research focuses its attention on various actors in the chain of decision making, such as regulators (Bach and Newman 2007), civil society and NGOs (Carpenter 2007; Charnovitz 1996), and industry (Egan 2001). These studies show that these autonomous substate actors are able to influence domestic policy change through transnational networks and coalition building.

But these actors face several constraints. The first constraint is access. Some institutions are relatively open or closed, which affects the influence that stakeholders can have on the decision-making process (Sikkink 2005). Second, the degree to which their participation is institutionalized will have a significant impact on their perceived legitimacy (Risse-Kappen 1995). Third, these actors must understand the institutional structure in which they're operating and work within those rules while being mindful of the power of states within those institutions (Krasner 1995). Understanding the difficulty that stakeholders face in effecting change reminds us that the institutional structure is a key factor that can determine whether policy changes are possible or not. Therefore, some have argued that the complementarity of domestic and international institutions is central to determining the influence any actors can have (Büthe and Mattli 2011). For example, states that do not have an open regulatory system that allows for comments on proposed regulations may be less likely to have stakeholders that get involved at the international level to offer their opinions on another state's regulations. However, the nature of interest groups matters as well because the more diffuse they are, the more difficult it can be to wield influence (Stigler 1971).

Building on this body of literature, I elaborate on how the institutional design of regulatory cooperation shapes and constrains behavior and also gives individual actors the ability to utilize the institutional environment to not only alter domestic rules to their advantage but also avoid escalating trade tensions to formal disputes. To do so, I combine the literature in international relations scholarship with the public choice approach. The public choice approach can be described as "a body of analysis that allows us to relate the behavior of individual participants in market activity, as buyers, sellers, investors, producers, entrepreneurs, to the results attained for the whole community, results that are not within the purposes of knowledge of the participants themselves" (Buchanan 1999, 47). Bringing these economic models of interest groups into political science analysis is useful not only for the questions it raises about the political process but also for the framework of inquiry it provides (Mitchell and Munger 1991). With regard to interest group behavior, this is particularly salient because the general assumption in the public choice literature is that interest group influence produces a social cost (Tullock 1967; Stigler 1971; Grossman and Helpman 1996; van Winden 1999) even though it may at some point play an important informational role (Austen-Smith 1996; Lohmann 1995; Milner and Rosendorff 1985; Grossman and Helpman 2001; Chalmers 2013). So public choice not only focuses our attention on who participates in the policymaking process at a more granular level but also asks us to question the incentives for participation and outcomes it produces.

As the earlier discussion on international regulatory cooperation made clear, the process of cooperation can take various forms and involves a large number of actors. Breaking down these interactions, instead of viewing the phenomenon as just a government-to-government exercise, provides a more detailed picture of what regulatory cooperation actually entails and why it can be a useful means to avoid disputes. Since many countries are considering including regulatory cooperation chapters in new trade agreements, it is worth taking a look at how the existing structures have influenced actor behavior and, ultimately, policy outcomes. While some may argue that theories that examine the relationship between the domestic and international levels of analysis account for this, the conventional approach has been to aggregate domestic preferences to the state level, as if individuals are just parts of a larger whole (Buchanan 1999; Oatley 2011). However, public choice brings the individual to the center of analysis. This helps us build a better picture of competing interests within the state, the incentives of various actors and how policy can alter their behavior, and the ultimate policy preferences they support (Smith 1991).

Public choice also helps us better understand why certain policies are adopted by evaluating who is affected (and may engage in rent seeking), how the decision rules interact with those affected by policy, and who controls the agenda. This approach is closely related to international relations theories that are interactive. However, instead of focusing on the intended outcome of institutional arrangements, it zeroes in on the interactive process that arrangements create. While public choice may be generally skeptical about the value produced by the interaction of interest groups and government, I show that there is room for broadening our understanding of instances in which interest group pressure can be welfare enhancing. Part of the challenge in public choice lies in the fact that it largely focuses on processes within a single state, rather than in interactions between states. However, the processes it identifies are still valuable for making sense of this interaction, and it is worthwhile to test if these mechanisms can neatly be transposed from the domestic to international sphere. I utilize both IR theory and the public choice approach to make my argument and show that, in international regulatory politics, interest group pressure produces the opposite effect of what public choice theory would predict.

I argue that industry groups can enhance welfare through dispute avoidance and are better able to push for the resolution of potential disputes through regulatory cooperation mechanisms due to two conditions: (1) voice and (2) the impact of specific decision-making rules that structure interaction between actors and yield varying levels of commitments among states. The institutional rules thus shape and constrain behavior at both the domestic and transnational level. Access is the first step in the process, and the second step is the rules that determine how influential that access can be. Essentially, if states do not make credible commitments to take stakeholder views into account, there is no guarantee of influence. Furthermore, the degree to which states institutionalize this interaction in the formal rules will mitigate their impact (Risse-Kappen 1995). Governments can then reference these binding constraints as cover for adjusting domestic policy that otherwise would be untenable (Vreeland 2003). The successful utilization of these institutions by industry interests not only sets a precedent for action but, in doing so, generates the momentum for the cycle to be repeated. It is this process that then allows for domestic regulatory adjustment and, ultimately, dispute avoidance.[10]

Voice: Who Gets Heard

Hirschman (1970) describes voice "as any attempt at all to change, rather than to escape from, an objectionable state of affairs, whether through individual or collective petition . . . through appeal to a higher authority with the intention of forcing change" or "to mobilize public opinion" (30). As noted earlier, the first key obstacle for stakeholders to influence international institutions is simply having a seat at the table. Without access, exercising voice will not be as effective. In a bilateral setting, the number of potential actors will be smaller, and as a result, it is expected that governments will exert greater control over setting the agenda. However, in a multilateral forum, other governments can allow for the representation of unexpected voices, which once airing their concerns, may be harder to ignore. Thus, more actors in the process can dilute the voice of protectionist interests. It is important to note, however, that there can be negative returns to too much voice, verging on harassment (Hirschman 1970). In addition, influence may be determined by a group's "logistic power function," that is, how much it spends relative to others, and political talent (Tullock 1980). But institutional structures can also be organized in such a way to give opportunities for voice to opposing parties and thus allow for a broader range of input (Ostrom 2015). Therefore, who gets heard in an institution matters for both how it works and the day-to-day outcomes it produces.

Additionally, a variety of voice serves another important function in that it helps reduce the information problem that prevents governments from addressing regulatory barriers in the first place. For example, the WTO has set up an ePing[11] system, which takes all the notifications governments must supply on new or proposed regulations on TBT and SPS issues and makes them available to the public. This is a useful tool for businesses and NGOs to search for specific rules and sign up for alerts the moment a new notification is posted. This process gives relevant groups information to bring to their governments about potential barriers to trade since governments do not have the ability to make an assessment on the impact of each regulation that foreign governments put forward. As a result, this system helps broaden the scope for participation for actors that are well attuned to their export interests and can thus bring such issues to the attention of their government to address in the WTO's TBT and SPS committees.

These institutional features can therefore lower the information costs to participation and address the problem of rational ignorance (Kufuor 2000, 7). It is therefore expected that institutions that employ transparency mechanisms that provide information to the broader public and stakeholders will also see greater participation by stakeholders in these institutions, in particular, export interests, which are usually the first to notice and experience a trade barrier.

Decision-Making Rules and Credible Commitments

The way decision-making rules are structured within an institution and the commitment governments make to be bound by various aspects of these rules are an important part of understanding not only how the decision rules interact with those affected by policy and who controls the agenda but also why certain outcomes may not be as permissible. For instance, some organizations will require members to take a vote to adopt new international standards. In the International Standards Organization (ISO), which is the leading body for globally accepted standards, decisions are taken by consensus, absent "sustained opposition," which does not require unanimity, and also through a two-thirds majority vote on some stages of the decision-making process (ISO/IEC Directives, Part I 2018). Voting rules are important to consider because they structure the choices available to the voting individual (Buchanan and Tullock 1999).

Institutional rules and adherence to them can be observed directly. For example, within the TBT and SPS committees, when a government raises an STC, which is basically pointing out to another country that a proposed or existing regulation may be in violation of their WTO obligations, the responding country *must* supply an answer to the country raising the concern. So if an interest group really wants clarification or to put pressure on a foreign government to explain its potentially trade-restrictive practices, getting your own government to raise a concern at the committees is one way to go about this. Therefore, one can expect that stakeholders (export interests in particular) regularly try to bring these issues to their trade ministry's attention. But also, the commitment made by the responding government is an important one. If the regulation in place is, in fact, trade restricting and requires adjustment to avoid litigation, then the government can provide an explanation for why it has to adjust its policy to its constituents. [12]

Transparency mechanisms also generate credible commitments as well. For instance, the Canada-U.S. Regulatory Cooperation Council (RCC), a bilateral forum for dialogue on regulatory cooperation that was established in 2011, has open stakeholder sessions as well as multiple calls for comments and proposals from the public. Though some official submissions are not made public, the stakeholder sessions are often recorded or livestreamed. [13] This allows stakeholders to hold the government accountable to some extent because, if their views are not taken into account or are blatantly ignored, they can choose not to take part in future efforts. Since governments rely on outside interests to identify areas of regulatory divergence and to help push for cooperation, losing this support would weaken their efforts at international regulatory cooperation.

In addition, transparency in participation also helps stakeholders connect with each other and, in some instances, form coalitions. Building coalitions among actors across states can serve to "frustrate or promote" the objectives of states (Krasner 1995). In the extreme, this could lead to the development of private foreign policy to effect change, especially by entities that have no territorial interest, for example, MNCs (Nye and Keohane 1971). On the other hand, it can also provide an opportunity for widely dispersed export interests to build concentrated relationships with like-minded individuals across borders as economic interdependence leads to "changing jurisdictional boundaries" (Newman and Posner 2011). Some have argued that generating a "winning coalition" is a central obstacle transnational actors must overcome (Risse-Kappen 1995, 25), though it is not clear that coalitions are necessary for impact.

The next section explores a case study of the WTO's SPS committee, showing how a potential trade dispute was avoided through the committee's regulatory cooperation mechanism and, importantly, the role of industry in facilitating resolution. The TBT committee operates in a similar fashion and therefore is not explored separately. In addition, for the purposes of this study, since SPS concerns are reported as "resolved" by the WTO membership, it is easier to identify those concerns that do, in fact, get settled.[14] Though there are various aspects of regulatory cooperation at the WTO that could be examined,[15] I focus on the work of these committees because they are often cited as forums to effectively address these concerns on a multilateral level. While there are other cases of regulatory cooperation that could be explored, such as the RCC or the Trans-Tasman Agreement, there are particularities to these cases that may not be generalizable given the close history of the countries involved. As the regulatory cooperation forums in the Canada-European Union Comprehensive Economic and Trade Agreement (CETA) and the Comprehensive and Progressive Agreement for Trans-Pacific Partnership (CPTPP) have not yet had enough time to function, it is too early to evaluate these processes. It is important to note that the TBT and SPS committees are not representative of all forms of international regulatory cooperation but do reflect the principles that are carried over in other agreements.

CASE STUDY: THE WTO'S TBT AND SPS COMMITTEES

The TBT and SPS Agreements went into force on January 1, 1995. They cover government measures that take the form of technical regulations (such as regulations, standards, and testing procedures) or that concern food safety and plant or animal health, respectively. These agreements are in addition to the general disciplines outlined by the GATT and form an important part of WTO members' rights and obligations. The TBT and SPS Agreements address nontariff measures, which have grown in importance as tariffs have been reduced over the years. Both agreements require members to notify the WTO Secretariat of any new TBT or SPS measures that may affect trade with other members.[16]

Notifications of these measures have increased over time: there were 553 unique notifications in 1995, while in 2017, 2,709 notifications were filed with the Secretariat.[17] Following notification, a 60-day comment period allows other states to ask questions about the intended measure and offer feedback or note concerns. The committees are an exercise of one of the core features of the TBT and SPS Agreements, that is, transparency. The TBT and SPS committees, which usually have three formal sessions a year, "provide a regular forum for consultations" (SPS Agreement, Article 12.1) and give states the "the opportunity of consulting on any matters relating to the operation of this Agreement or the furtherance of its objectives" (TBT Agreement, Article 13.1).

Since WTO members must make notifications of TBT or SPS measures and other members have a right to ask questions about these measures, a strong dialogue has developed within the committees to not only provide clarification on measures but also to address regulatory divergence. As a result, members can comment on draft regulations before they become law and offer their input. However, in instances where a measure has already been implemented or is flagged as having the potential to be discriminatory, a member can raise an STC. The country to which the issue is raised, the responding party, *must* give a response to the member raising the concern. Sometimes, while one member will raise an STC, others might join in and offer additional questions or explanations of how the measure might affect them as well. Often, coalitions are built with other states to raise concerns ahead of scheduled committee meetings (Doherty 2018).

There are two additional items to note regarding the work of the committees. First, as compared to formal WTO litigation, which is typically between the largest markets bringing disputes against each other, participation in the committees is much broader. In fact, over 78 percent of the entire WTO membership has submitted notifications to the committees, including many developing countries, and roughly over half of the membership has raised an STC. Second, though these committees can be attended only by government officials (and invited observers who cannot make comments), there is evidence of private sector buy-in on the committee work. For example, Wijkstrom (2015) notes that between the years 2013 and 2014, "57 of the 89 new trade concerns brought to the TBT Committee, delegations explicitly mention the private sector in connection with raising the matter," and furthermore, "large companies tend to know about draft measures before their governments and try to resolve the matter themselves first" but ask the government for help if the issue cannot be privately resolved (4).

Within the Office of the United States Trade Representative (USTR), both the TBT and SPS divisions monitor WTO notifications independently, but the SPS division engages in active outreach to industry to get their input on specific measures on a regular basis. One of the reasons for more active engagement on SPS is simply the nature of SPS measures, which tend to be about market opening or closing measures, whereas TBT measures tend to be more complex. However, regardless of whether it is a TBT or an SPS measure, the USTR will continue to raise a concern in subsequent committee meetings so long as industry wants them to, particularly if a measure is in a draft stage and could still be revised before implementation (Weiss 2018). It is worth noting that it is often difficult to identify the specific industries involved because there is no public record of their involvement and specific firms are not referenced in the committees when concerns are raised. Much of the details are thus filled in through discussions with current and former government officials. Below, I examine a specific trade concern that was raised by the United States on regulatory measures by China to imports of various food, illustrating a high level of industry involvement in attaining adjustment and reconsideration of the proposed measure, which was helped along by the way discussion of these issues is structured within the SPS Committee.

China's Lack of Transparency for Certain SPS Measures

In June 2016, the United States raised a concern over China's lack of transparency for certain SPS measures. This had been raised many years earlier, in 2004, but China's 2015 Food Safety Law prompted reengagement on the issue. A number of measures related to the implementation of the 2015 Food Safety Law were not notified directly to the WTO. When the US representative to the SPS Committee raised the concern in June, she stated: "The United States urged China to notify this measure, as well as all SPS measures that could impact international trade, in order to allow its trading partners to comment on them, and to take these comments into account upon finalizing the measures" (G/SPS/R/83 para. 4.51). A lack of an official notification of the measure to the WTO combined with a relatively short timeline for implementation of the measure would not allow exporters enough time to adjust nor give affected countries enough time to figure out whether the measure's impact would be more trade restrictive than necessary to achieve its objective and offer alternatives.

General frustration with China's restrictive and oftentimes arbitrary food safety laws has been a long-standing problem for industry in many countries. A top shareholder of Australia's baby formula company Bellamy's Organic noted that it was "concerning the Chinese can really be in such a powerful position over our economy that they can turn things off seemingly at random" (Niesche 2017). A report by the US Chamber of Commerce (2016) noted that the 2015 food safety law "is much stricter than the previous versions" and that agricultural exporters continue to be hampered by, among other things, "non-tariff barriers such as slow and unpredictable and frequently inequitable approval processes," recommending further bilateral cooperation to address these concerns (24, 52).

One particular measure at issue required that imported food products bear a certificate "with an attestation that the imported food meets Chinese laws, regulations, and standards" (G/SPS/R/86/ para.3.44) and that these certificates would need to include both product and shipment details. One issue of contention was that the rule required the competent domestic agency to issue certificates, which would be a challenge in any decentralized regulatory market that relies on producer self-certification. The US government made clear that such a requirement was "outside of the purview of the United States Food and Drug Administration" (G/SPS/R/87 para. 4.49) and asked China to consider "replacing the official certification requirement with a less trade restrictive measure that recognized the primary responsibility of food business operators for compliance, which would be consistent with domestic Chinese requirements, as well as with Codex[18] principles and guidelines" (G/SPS/R/87 para. 4.50).

Initially, the certification requirement had been brought to the attention of various embassies in Beijing by the Chinese General Administration of Quality, Supervision, Inspection and Quarantine (AQSIQ), the agency responsible for developing the measure. This began a process of bilateral consultations between the United States and China to resolve this issue (which other countries undertook as well) in addition to consultation with industry stakeholders, such as the US Chamber of Commerce, and other associations on the ground in Beijing (Doherty 2018).

USTR official Julia Doherty described consultations in Beijing as "very active," including bilateral consultations with other affected countries to share information on the potential impact of the measure. In addition, since China is such a large market, US exporters are actively engaged in regular monitoring of such developments and provide information back to their governments about how a particular measure will affect their trade (Doherty 2018). Both the US Information Technology Office and the American Chamber of Commerce were involved on the ground in Beijing on this particular issue. In fact, industry often played a facilitative role in ongoing discussions. For example, in congressional testimony before the U.S.-China Economic and Security Review Commission, Michael Robach, vice president for food safety at US agrifood company Cargill stated that "[o]rganizations such as ours, such as GFSI, have been effective partners for enabling meaningful dialogue between industry and the U.S. and the Chinese governments" (Robach 2018, 150).

There was also a significant amount of direct outreach from the US government to encourage industry comments, such as in September 2017, when the US Department of Agriculture's Foreign Agricultural Service put out a report on the updated food safety law and requested that US industry and other interested parties submit comments to the USDA as soon as possible in order to facilitate the submission of their comments at the WTO (USDA 2017). These and other comments received either directly to the USTR or the American Embassy in Beijing all served to assist the government in providing a clear explanation for the impact of the proposed rules on

US exporters, which would then be used in coordinating efforts with other countries in approaching China to adjust both bilaterally and in the SPS Committee. Michael Ward, a senior agricultural attaché at the American Embassy in Beijing, noted the challenges US exporters faced with regard to China's 2015 food safety law and argued that the WTO committees were one way the United States could voice its concerns in addition to coordinating comments to the Chinese government among a coalition of countries (Caporal 2018).

The pressure was maintained on China in SPS Committee meetings through 2016 and 2017.[19] In July 2017, Israel noted that it was particularly concerned about "the significant and unnecessary barriers to trade the mea sure would cause," and the European Union "underlined the ambiguity of some of the provisions and the difficulties this would pose for custom authorities" (G/SPS/R/87 para. 4.51–52). Throughout 2017, some countries stated their appreciation for China's openness to bilateral meetings and receptivity to their concerns. In July 2017, the representative for China explained that a revised measure had been notified to the TBT Committee and "stated that the notified measure had included Members' suggestions and comments and welcomed further feedback on the notification to the TBT Committee" and added that "China looked forward to a strengthened communication and cooperation with members" (G/SPS/R/87 para 4.53). The revised notification appeared to add clarity to what would be considered a competent domestic authority, suggesting that certifying agencies or companies providing information on conformity with Chinese law would simply need authorization from the authorized domestic government agency to issue certificates (G/TBT/N/CHN/1209).[20] Though this may not fully solve the problem raised by the United States, it at least provided additional clarification and showed that China was taking member concerns into account.

China's willingness to listen to the concerns of other countries was welcomed by other countries and did seem to generate a result in the end. In November 2017, a month after the measure was initially slated to be implemented, China announced that it would delay implementation by two years (until September 2019) in order to take information provided by other WTO members into account. This policy shift was seen as a positive and hopeful development for the United States (Doherty 2018). Australia also applauded the announcement of the two-year transition period, with Steven Ciobo, the Trade, Tourism and Investment Minister, adding that Australia was "committed to being a reliable food supplier to China, and will work closely with the food export industry and Chinese authorities to ensure all import requirements are met" (Callick 2017).

While it was unclear whether the measure would be dropped entirely, the countries raising concerns in the SPS Committee successfully pushed for significant amendments to China's rule. The coalition of states that worked together to share information from industry consultations helped build a clear picture of the impact of the measure and its trade-disruptive effects if implemented as written. This was then communicated through both the SPS Committee and directly through bilateral talks with China to push for delays in implementation. In the November 2017 SPS Committee meeting, "the United States welcomed the clarifications provided by China and the opportunity to work with China on the matter" (G/SPS/R/88 para. 3.59). In the end, the SPS Committee provided an important forum to apply concerted pressure to China and achieve a policy change. This would not have been possible without the requirement that China could not ignore requests for clarification, making the peer effects all the more effective.

Ultimately, the work of committees changes the way countries approach regulation because the main focus of the committees is on how to improve implementation at the national level (Doherty 2018). However, regulatory adjustment in the largest markets, such as the United States, European Union, China, and India, is rare (Weiss 2018). Through dialogue in the committees, members can look at best practices within the SPS Committees in national offices and identify ways to improve external communications, public consultation, and transparency. In addition, for less-developed countries, there are efforts by the WTO through providing technical development assistance, which can help to build capacity in this area. The primary goal is to focus on ways to prevent or to reduce trade concerns, which is why there is such a focus on good regulatory practice and the need to improve the quality of regulation more generally. In the meantime, the specific trade concerns allow one outlet for WTO members to address regulatory divergence or regulatory protectionism where bilateral talks fail.

IMPLICATIONS: THE ROLE OF REGULATORY COOPERATION IN INTERNATIONAL AGREEMENTS

This chapter began with a simple question of why so many regulatory trade frictions between states do not lead to formal disputes. To explore this, I focused on the TBT and SPS committees at the WTO, arguing that their regulatory cooperation function essentially provides a path to dispute avoidance. Furthermore, the structure of cooperation also gives industry stakeholders a significant role in bringing their issues to governments but also having their specific concerns heard by other states. The findings lead to two main implications.

First, the design of these institutions affects who can participate. As a result, states should be conscious of this as they replicate regulatory cooperation in other trade agreements. Second, regulatory cooperation provides another way of thinking about dispute settlement more broadly, moving away from more judicial models. In fact, it highlights the continued relevance of diplomacy in the WTO as well as the special role of industry groups, suggesting alternative paths forward for the organization as the future of the formal dispute settlement system grows increasingly into question. I address each in turn.

In constructing new institutions for international regulatory cooperation, it is worth asking how the interests of those affected can be taken into account, especially since regulation resides predominately in the domestic sphere. Within states, it is well known that regulatory politics is a complex affair and, though democratic societies may aim for representation of the *public* or *citizenry*, policy rarely achieves this. Buchanan (1999) acknowledged this particular challenge in a discussion of the behavior of the political economist, where he notes that, while she should be "ethically neutral," the key problem is that the test regarding whether to recommend policy A over policy B "is consensus among members of the choosing group, not objective improvement in some measurable social aggregate" (195). As a result, the policy choice becomes an inherently normative one and largely shaped by the decision makers, regardless of various input. Therefore, the structure of these initiatives should be sensitive to these issues. Given this starting point, below, I offer some general principles for thinking about such institutions.

The first element to keep in mind in applying the public choice approach to international affairs offers a word of caution because, as Risse (2006) points out, the absence of a global *demos* makes international governance particularly difficult. However, Hoekman and Sabel (2017) argue that the choice presented by critics as being between democracy or open markets is false since there is not a single global regulator that creates or enforces international economic rules. International regulatory cooperation in particular is often built on a sectoral basis and through a cooperative dialogue where states retain the ultimate authority in deciding whether they will participate or not. Furthermore, they argue that "outcomes will differ from those parties would have taken in autarky and reflect both economic interdependence and differences in values and institutional approaches" (16). In essence, the dialogue fostered by regulatory cooperation can generate more sensitivity to different approaches.

But whether or not regulatory cooperation is perceived as legitimate or democratic will largely depend on who gets to participate in this dialogue. A major challenge, as highlighted by Majone (1991), is that it is not easy to identify all dominant actors or "problem owners" so the community needs to be "sufficiently open and competitive so that interesting new ideas may emerge" (457). This is always going to be difficult to apply internationally, for the reasons mentioned earlier. For instance, what if some stakeholders simply have greater capacity to be heard? Will they play an outsized role in shaping international rules? In addition, it is important to keep in mind that regulatory cooperation after the fact, that is once a rule is in place, is often very difficult to achieve. That is why there has been an increased focus on good regulatory practice and consultation at the earliest stage possible of regulatory development. However, this also poses a potential problem in that not all regulations can be notified in advance nor would it be politically feasible to allow interests outside of the state to comment.

For instance, in the United States, draft legislation, unlike draft regulations, cannot be notified to the WTO. So when the United States was taking up the issue of banning clove cigarettes, WTO members that later challenged this law could do so only once the law was adopted (the matter was complicated by the fact that there was a short ninety-day implementation period after the law was signed, giving them little time to provide comments). If Indonesia submitted an opinion on the legislation before it was adopted, this could have had more adverse effects or caused policymakers to dig their heels in further on this issue (Weiss 2018). Therefore, it is sometimes better to solve these issues in the appropriate state-to-state forums to avoid political friction.

Second, the role of private actors, such as firms, has always been controversial, but this paper has shown that industry influence can actually be welfare enhancing when it comes to resolving regulatory trade barriers. Industry is a key player in both informing new regulation and revising old rules because they are often the first to experience the impact of rule changes or inertia. One way to improve the legitimacy of private actor engagement, however, is by increasing transparency in the process. This was done successfully with a bilateral regulatory cooperation initiative, the Canada-U.S. RCC, where stakeholder engagement was extended to the broader public.

In the WTO, participation is a far trickier process. As a member-driven organization, the topic of allowing nonstate actors greater participation always generates pushback. However, as the specific trade concerns at the TBT and SPS committees reveal, industry is already heavily involved in the process. It is therefore worth considering how this can be made more transparent in the future. A possible yet perhaps controversial proposal is to give private standing to nonstate actors in raising concerns within the committees. This would have to be thought through carefully in order to balance capacity to participate with having a stake in the issue. Also, it might help quell concerns over an outsize role of industry in the process. Speaking more generally about the WTO, Esty (1998) argues that NGOs offer a source of "analytic competition" whose inclusion would improve responsiveness and representativeness of the organizations (123). He suggests that fears of special interest manipulation are misplaced and there should be formal procedures for NGO participation in the WTO.

The way this participation is structured matters as well. In a meeting between Prime Minister Justin Trudeau and President Obama in March 2016, both leaders recognized the need to have more consumer voices in the RCC process. One reason for their limited impact may simply be because the RCC builds off the existing domestic procedures of notice and comment and therefore stakeholders that already have been navigating this space for a long time are better situated to participate. Examining international standard-setting institutions, Büthe and Mattli (2011) argue that the complementarity of domestic institutions to private standard setting organizations largely determines their success in having their voice heard. This problem is reflected in comparing the work of the Canada-U.S. RCC and the U.S.-Mexico High Level Regulatory Cooperation Council, which was founded at the same time but did not produce any results. A key reason for this was Mexico's national regulatory structure, primarily the fact that taking decisions on this matter is outside the authority of the presidency and that the Comisión Federal de Mejora Regulatoria (COFEMER), within the Ministry of the Economy, which is responsible for regulatory improvement, does not really have the authority to make regulatory changes or push regulators to cooperate (Weiss 2018). Without the domestic capacity to adjust regulations or encourage international regulatory cooperation, countries with similar national structures will find it difficult to shape and reform regulations to align with international standards.

Third, decision-making rules matter. As noted above, transparency is an important part of this and affects how states behave in these institutional environments. For example, a recent study of the UN Human Rights Council finds that, if decisions are taken by consensus, it can diffuse the burden of judgment on any single state, thus making it easier for states to pass tougher resolutions (Nooruddin and Prasad 2018). Also, whether states must provide a response to another country's request for clarification (as with STCs) will have an impact on interactions within these institutions because a requirement to provide additional information puts a spotlight on the potentially offending state to explain its reasoning behind a specific measure it has taken. This public "naming and shaming" function can thus serve to pressure states to adjust or rethink their potentially trade distorting measures. On the other hand, if the process is entirely voluntary and dependent on regulators (as in the Canada-U.S. RCC), regulators have all the leeway to decide what issues they will take up; they may just choose the easiest or most convenient issue for them, which may leave some difficult problems unaddressed (Weiss 2018).

The Canada-U.S. RCC, for example, has been criticized for its lack of institutionalization, making it subject to the whims of whoever is in power. In fact, since President Trump has been in office, the work of the RCC appears to have come to a standstill. Ultimately, we will have to see where it goes, but it may be one of the reasons why countries are pushing to include a regulatory cooperation chapter in new trade agreements. In CETA, the level of commitment might be stronger because the chapter does not include a clause on the nonapplication of dispute settlement, unlike the TPP. Therefore, it is possible that violations of the regulatory cooperation chapter could hypothetically lead to a legal challenge, heightening government's willingness to cooperate.

Finally, with regard to the WTO, the work of the TBT and SPS committees reveals an alternative dispute resolution process that the committees are able to facilitate through regulatory cooperation. By raising concerns on regulatory measures in the committees, states are not only able to engage in a dialogue to better understand why a rule is being proposed in the first place but also work diplomatically to resolve disputes before they arise. This role should not be understated, especially at a time when the WTO finds itself in crisis of legitimacy following sharp criticism from the United States, which has single-handedly blocked the appointment of new jurists to the highest adjudicatory body in the organization, the Appellate Body.

While formal dispute settlement through litigation has its value, it is important to keep this in perspective.

From 1995 to 2017, WTO members have filed just 561 requests for consultations, of which only 308 have gone on to form a panel. Of these 308, only 235 have resulted in a panel report (the remaining are either settled or simply not pursued), and roughly 66 percent of these disputes are then appealed. This is over a span of twenty-two years. There are still many cases that never even make it to a request for consultation and not necessarily because of issues over cost and capacity.

As this chapter has shown, many disputes can be successfully avoided before they reach that stage. This reminds us that, while plenty of scholarship and news coverage is often focused on contentious litigation, the role of the WTO is actually far broader than that. Through the TBT and SPS committees, it has been an effective mechanism for dispute avoidance, and this model should be considered for expansion in the work of other committees as well. This would not only generate more dialogue and cooperation between its membership but also keep the work of the WTO at a level with lower political stakes.

In thinking about ways to reform the regulatory cooperation function of the TBT and SPS committees and expanding it, it is worth emphasizing that dispute avoidance in the TBT and SPS committees is further facilitated by the industry stakeholders that not only bring these issues to their governments but also submit detailed data and research on the impact such measures will have. Industry thus remains central to the consultative process. In the case of the United States, one former official noted that the USTR will continue to raise a concern in subsequent committee meetings so long as industry wants them to (Weiss 2018). Given the fact that participation is de facto limited to industry stakeholders, it is worth thinking about how this can be expanded to include other groups. In the SPS Committee, the FAO/WHO Codex Alimentarius Commission (Codex), the FAO International Plant Protection Convention (IPPC), and the World Organization for Animal Health (OIE), often referred to as the "three sisters," have observer status in the committee meetings. While there is no equivalent in the TBT Committee, the World Health Organization has also been quite vocal in the committee on regulatory measures related to smoking. The WTO membership should seriously consider ways to increase both participation and transparency in this process so as to avoid criticisms of negotiating in the shadows.

In conclusion, the form regulatory cooperation takes is important not only for existing institutions but also for those that have not yet been created because it is increasingly being considered in new trade agreements, which will shape how these issues are addressed in the years to come (Lester and Manak 2017). However, each case should be evaluated separately because the needs, level of trust between countries, and the goals of each initiative vary widely. So before throwing in a chapter on regulatory cooperation in every "modern" trade agreement, we should ask whether it belongs there given the specific context. Wolfe (2016) notes that "[a] trade agreement cannot in itself achieve regulatory alignment . . . but it can create an enabling framework" (29). We should therefore be mindful of the forces we enable.

NOTES

1. The core GATT principle of national treatment provides a basic constraint on domestic regulation because it requires all domestic regulations to be nondiscriminatory in terms of their impact on imported goods. The TBT and SPS agreements elaborate on this principle and expand into deeper, behind-the-borders barriers through mechanisms such as the encouragement of the use of international standards as a basis for regulation and a requirement that certain regulations be based on science.

2. Not all aspects of the measure were found to be in violation of the WTO Agreements (i.e., ground beef), but in general, the dispute was considered to fall in favor of the complaining parties, Canada and Mexico. See United States – Certain Country of Origin Labelling (COOL) Requirements, WT/DS384/AB/R / WT/DS386/AB/R, adopted 23 July 2012, DSR 2012:V, p. 2449.

3. Many developing countries still actively utilize their "binding overhang," the difference between applied and bound MFN tariff rates. See Busch and Pelc 2014.

4. For a detailed discussion of this distinction, see Lester and Manak (2017).

5. For a detailed history of this process, see Michelle Egan (2001).

6. Though countries do not adjust their internal regulations, MRAs require that the parties identify acceptable conformity assessment bodies that can assess whether a product meets the requirements of the destination market. It is important to stress that this form of regulatory cooperation does not result in convergence of any kind. The International Standards Organization defines conformity assessment as "The process for demonstrating that [product] features meet the requirements of standards, regulations and other specifications" of a specific jurisdiction and conformity assessment bodies as an organization "that can undertake conformity assessment techniques and activities. They can come in any organizational form and ownership, and can be commercial in focus or not-for-profit entities. They can be government agencies, national standards bodies, trade associations, consumer organizations, or private or publically owned companies." See ISO, "Conformity Assessment Tools to Support Public Policy,"

https://www.iso.org/sites/cascoregulators/01_3_conformity-assessment-bodies.html (accessed August 4, 2018).

7. These types of agreements do not require states to agree to a set of acceptable conformity assessment bodies.

8. For example, the bilateral Canada–U.S. Regulatory Cooperation Council, established in 2011. This has been loosely emulated in the Canada–European Union Comprehensive Economic and Trade Agreement; the Trans Pacific Partnership (TPP) also contains a chapter on regulatory coherence, but the agreement has not yet been implemented; and the United States was pushing for a chapter on regulatory cooperation in the Transatlantic Trade and Investment Partnership (TTIP) with the European Union.

9. Some examples of nontariff barriers are quotas, subsidies, antidumping and countervailing duties, export restraints, technical barriers to trade, and health and safety regulations.

10. Though it could be argued that international coordination in and of itself could serve as a form of collusion (Vaubel 1986), I argue that the expansion of participation beyond state actors dilutes this problem and weakens the ability of states to control the agenda and, ultimately, the outcomes.

11. See World Trade Organization, International Trade Centre, and the United Nations Conference on Trade and Development, SPS and TBT Notification Alert System, http://www.epingalert.org/en (accessed March 24, 2018).

12. A similar argument has been put forward by Milner, Mansfield, and Rosendorff (2002) in explaining how governments agree to trade openness.

13. Due to the sensitive nature of some submissions, including business information, submissions are not made public. However, they can be requested through a freedom of information request, but segments will be redacted.

14. Horn, Mavroidis, and Wijkstrom (2013) suggest that items could also be considered as "resolved" if they are not brought up again after three subsequent meetings.

15. See, for instance, Celine Kauffmann and Nikolai Malyshev, "International Regulatory Cooperation: The Menu of Approaches," E15 Task Force on Regulatory Systems Coherence, International Centre for Trade and Sustainable Development (October 2015).

16. These notification systems have become digitized and easier to access over time.

17. Generally, the trend has been a steady upward increase, with a few exceptions.

18. The Codex Alimentarius Commission is an international food standard–setting agency, which is referenced in the SPS Agreement, along with the International Office of Epizootics (IOE) and the framework of the International Plant Protection Convention as recognized international standard–setting bodies that can be referenced in domestic regulation and improve harmonization among members.

19. See SPS Information Management System, STC 184, Lack of Transparency for Certain SPS Measures, http://spsims.wto.org/en/SpecificTradeConcerns/View/121 (accessed March 24, 2018).

20. Thanks to Huan Zhu for translating the official notification document.

REFERENCES

Allee, Todd. "Legal Incentives and Domestic Rewards: The Selection of Trade Disputes for GATT/WTO Dispute Resolution." Manuscript. University of Illinois (2004).

Austen-Smith, David. "Interest Groups: Money, Information, and Influence." In *Perspectives on Public Choice*, edited by D. C. Mueller. Cambridge: Cambridge University Press, 1996.

Bach, David, and Abraham L. Newman. "The European Regulatory State and Global Public Policy: Micro-Institutions, Macro-Influence." *Journal of European Public Policy* 14, no. 6 (2007): 827–46.

———. "Transgovernmental Networks and Domestic Policy Convergence: Evidence from Insider Trading Regulation." *International Organization* 64, no. 3 (2010): 505–28.

Banks, Jeffrey S., and Barry R. Weingast. "The Political Control of Bureaucracies under Asymmetric Information." *American Journal of Political Science* (1992): 509–24.

Becker, Gary S. "A Theory of Competition among Pressure Groups for Political Influence." *The Quarterly Journal of Economics* 98, no. 3 (1983): 371–400.

Bollyky, Thomas. "The Role of Regulatory Cooperation in the Future of the WTO." RTA Exchange. Geneva: International Centre for Trade and Sustainable Development (ICTSD) and the Inter-American Development Bank (IDB) (2017).

Bown, Chad P., and Bernard M. Hoekman. "WTO Dispute Settlement and the Missing Developing Country Cases: Engaging the Private Sector." *Journal of International Economic Law* 8, no. 4 (2005): 861–90.

Bown, Chad P., and Kara M. Reynolds. *Trade Flows and Trade Disputes.* Washington, DC: The World Bank, 2014.

Brutger, Ryan. "Litigation for Sale: Private Firms and WTO Dispute escalation." Unpublished manuscript. web.sas.upenn.edu/brutger/files/2017/02/Litigation_For_Sale_2-3-17_Full_VERSION-2h4f1bv. pdf (2017).

Buchanan, James M. "The Pure Theory of Government Finance: A Suggested Approach." *Journal of Political Economy* 57, no. 6 (1949): 496–505.

———. *The Collected Works of James M. Buchanan, Volume 1: The Logical Foundations of Constitutional Liberty.* Indianapolis, IN: Liberty Fund, Inc., 1999.

Buchanan, James M., and Gordon Tullock. *The Collected Works of James M. Buchanan, Volume 3: The Calculus of Consent: Logical Foundations of Democracy.* Indianapolis, IN: Liberty Fund, Inc., 1999.

Busch, Marc L., and Eric Reinhardt. "Bargaining in the Shadow of the Law: Early Settlement in GATT/WTO Disputes." *Fordham International Law Journal* 24 (2000): 158.

Büthe, Tim, and Walter Mattli. *The New Global Rulers: The Privatization of Regulation in the World Economy.* Princeton, NJ: Princeton University Press, 2011.

Callick, Rowan. "Beijing's Touch Food Import Checks on Hold." *The Australian* (October 2, 2017). LexisNexis.

Caporal, Jack. "USDA Official Sees Mounting Challenges for Agricultural Exporters to China." Inside U.S. Trade. Published February 23, 2018. Accessed July 15, 2018. https://insidetrade.com/daily-news/usda-official-sees-mounting-challenges-agricultural-exporters-china.

Carpenter, R. Charli. "Setting the Advocacy agenda: Theorizing Issue Emergence and Non-emergence in Transnational Advocacy Networks." *International Studies Quarterly* 51, no. 1 (2007): 99–120.

Chalmers, Adam William. "Trading Information for Access: Informational Lobbying Strategies and Interest Group Access to the European Union." *Journal of European Public Policy* 20, no. 1 (2013): 39–58.

Charnovitz, Steve. "Participation of Nongovernmental Organizations in the World Trade Organization." *University of Pennsylvania Journal of International Law* 17 (1996): 331.

Chaudoin, Stephen. "Audience Features and the Strategic Timing of Trade Disputes." *International Organization* 68, no. 4 (2014): 877–911.

Dai, Xinyuan. "Why Comply? The Domestic Constituency Mechanism." *International Organization* 59, no. 2 (2005): 363–98.

Davis, Christina L. "International Institutions and Issue Linkage: Building Support for Agricultural Trade Liberalization." *American Political Science Review* 98, no. 1 (2004): 153–69.

Doherty, Julia. Interview by Inu Manak. Conducted over telephone. Washington, DC, March 21, 2018.

Drazen, Allan. *Political Economy in Macroeconomics.* Princeton, NJ: Princeton University Press, 2002.

Drezner, Daniel W. *All Politics Is Global: Explaining International Regulatory Regimes.* Princeton, NJ: Princeton University Press, 2008.

Egan, Michelle. *Constructing a European Market: Standards, Regulation, and Governance.* Oxford: Oxford University Press, 2001.

Esty, Daniel C. "Non-Governmental Organizations at the World Trade Organization: Cooperation, Competition, or Exclusion." *Journal of International Economic Law* 1 (1998): 123.

European Commission, Agriculture and Rural Development. "U.S.-European Union Organic Equivalence Agreement Frequently Asked Questions and Answers." Published 2012. Accessed March 24, 2018. https://ec.europa.eu/agriculture/organic/sites/orgfarming/files/docs/body/faqs-eu-us-equivalence-2012_en.pdf.

Farrell, Henry, and Abraham Newman. "The New Politics of Interdependence: Cross-National Layering in Trans-Atlantic Regulatory Disputes." *Comparative Political Studies* 48, no. 4 (2015): 497–526.

Fearon, James D. "Rationalist Explanations for War." *International Organization* 49, no. 3 (1995): 379–414.

———. "Signaling Foreign Policy Interests: Tying Hands versus Sinking Costs." *Journal of Conflict Resolution* 41, no. 1 (1997): 68–90.

Frey, Bruno S., and Heinz Buhofer. *Integration and Protectionism: A Comparative Institutional Analysis.* Verlag Rüegger, 1986.

Gilardi, Fabrizio. "Transnational Diffusion: Norms, Ideas, and Policies." *Handbook of International Relations* 2 (2012): 453–77.

Gourevitch, Peter. "The Second Image Reversed: The International Sources of Domestic Politics." *International Organization* 32, no. 4 (1978): 881–912.

———. "Domestic Politics and International Relations." In *Handbook of International Relations*, edited by W. Carlsnaes, T. Risse, and B. A. Simmons, 309–28. London: SAGE Publications, Ltd., 2002. doi:10.4135/9781848608290.n16.

Grossman, Gene M., and Elhanan Helpman. "Electoral Competition and Special Interest Politics." *The Review of Economic Studies* 63, no. 2 (1996): 265–86.

———. *Special Interest Politics.* Cambridge, MA: MIT Press, 2001.

Guzman, Andrew, and Beth A. Simmons. "To Settle or Empanel? An Empirical Analysis of Litigation and Settlement at the World Trade Organization." *The Journal of Legal Studies* 31, no. S1 (2002): S205–35.

Haas, Peter M. "Introduction: Epistemic Communities and International Policy Coordination." *International Organization* 46, no. 1 (1992): 1–35.

Hirschman, Albert O. *Exit, Voice, and Loyalty: Responses to Decline in Firms, Organizations, and States.* Vol. 25. Cambridge, MA: Harvard University Press, 1970.

Hoekman, Bernard M., and Charles Sabel. "Trade Agreements, Regulatory Sovereignty and Democratic Legitimacy." (2017).

Horn, Henrik, Petros C. Mavroidis, and Erik N. Wijkstrom. "In the Shadow of the DSU: Addressing Specific Trade Concerns in the WTO SPS and TBT Committees." *Journal of World Trade* 47 (2013): 729.

Hudec, Robert E. *The GATT Legal System and World Trade Diplomacy.* Lexis Publications, 1990.

International Standards Organization. ISO/IEC Directives, Part 1 Consolidated ISO Supplement—Procedures Specific to ISO (2018). Accessed August 1, 2018. https://www.iso.org/sites/directives/current/consolidated/index.xhtml.

Johns, Leslie, and Krzysztof J. Pelc. "On the Strategic Manipulation of Audiences in WTO Dispute Settlement." Department of Political Science, University of California (2011).

Kahler, Miles, and David A. Lake. "Economic Integration and Global Governance: Why So Little Supranationalism?" *The Politics of Global Regulation* (2009): 242–75.

Keck, Margaret E., and Kathryn Sikkink. "Transnational Advocacy Networks in International and Regional Politics." *International Social Science Journal* 51, no. 159 (1999): 89–101.

Kono, Daniel Y. "Optimal Obfuscation: Democracy and Trade Policy Transparency." *American Political Science Review* 100, no. 3 (2006): 369–84.

Krasner, Stephen D. "Power Politics, Institutions, Transnational Relations." *Cambridge Studies in International Relations* 42, no. 1 (1995): 257.

———. "State Power and the Structure of International Trade." *World Politics* 28, no. 3 (1976): 317–47.

Krugman, Paul R. "What Do Undergrads Need to Know about Trade?" *The American Economic Review* 83, no. 2 (1993): 23–26.

Kufuor, Kofi Oteng. "Public Choice Theory and the Failure of the ECOWAS Trade Liberalisation Scheme." *World Competition* 23 (2000): 137.

Lester, Simon, and Inu Manak. "Addressing Regulatory Trade Barriers in Mega-Regional Trade Agreements." In *Mega-Regional Trade Agreements*, edited by Thilo Rensmann, 337–63. Springer 2017.

Lohmann, Susanne. "Information, Access, and Contributions: A Signaling Model of Lobbying." *Public Choice* 85, no. 3–4 (1995): 267–84.

Majone, Giandomenico. "Professionalism and Mutual Adjustment." In *The Public Sector*, edited by Franx-Xaver Kaufmann, 451–68. New York: Walter de Gruyter, 1991.

Mansfield, Edward D., Helen V. Milner, and B. Peter Rosendorff. "Why Democracies Cooperate More: Electoral Control and International Trade Agreements." *International Organization* 56, no. 3 (2002): 477–513.

March, James G., and Johan P. Olsen. "The New Institutionalism: Organizational Factors in Political Life." *American Political Science Review* 78, no. 3 (1983): 734–49.

Mavroidis, Petros. "Regulatory Cooperation: Lessons from the WTO and the World Trade Regime." International Centre for Trade and Sustainable Development, E15 Initiative. January 2016.

Milner, Helen V., and B. Peter Rosendorff. "Trade Negotiations, Information and Domestic Politics: The Role of Domestic Groups." *Economics & Politics* 8, no. 2 (1996): 145–89.

Mitchell, William C., and Michael C. Munger. "Economic Models of Interest Groups: An Introductory Survey." *American Journal of Political Science* 35, no. 2 (1991): 512–46.

Moravcsik, Andrew. "The Origins of Human Rights Regimes: Democratic Delegation in Postwar Europe." *International Organization* 54, no. 2 (2000): 217–52.

Newman, Abraham L., and Elliot Posner. "International Interdependence and Regulatory Power: Authority, Mobility, and Markets." *European Journal of International Relations* 17, no. 4 (2011): 589–610.

Niesche, Christopher. "Regulation Hampers Australia-China Trade." *The New Zealand Herald* (July 16, 2017). LexisNexis.

Nooruddin, Irfan, and Shubha Kamala Prasad. "States in Glasshouses: The Effect of Domestic Insurgency on How Countries Vote in the UN Human Rights Council." Working Paper (2018).

Nye, Joseph S., and Robert O. Keohane. "Transnational Relations and World Politics: An Introduction." *International Organization* 25, no. 3 (1971): 329–49.

Oatley, Thomas. "The Reductionist Gamble: Open Economy Politics in the Global Economy." *International Organization* 65, no. 2 (2011): 311–41.

Olson, Mancur. *Logic of Collective Action: Public Goods and the Theory of Groups (Harvard Economic Studies v. 124)*. Cambridge, MA: Harvard University Press, 1965.

Ostrom, Elinor. *Governing the Commons*. Cambridge: Cambridge University Press, 2015.

Pauwelyn, Joost H. B., Andrew Guzman, and Jennifer A. Hillman. *International Trade Law*. Wolters Kluwer Law & Business, 2012.

Peltzman, Sam. "Toward a More General Theory of Regulation." *The Journal of Law and Economics* 19, no. 2 (1976): 211–40.

Persson, Torsten, and Guido Tabellini. *Political Economics: Explaining Public Policy.* Cambridge, MA: MIT Press, 2000.

Potters, Jan, and Frans van Winden. "Models of Interest Groups: Four Different Approaches." In *Collective Decision-Making: Social Choice and Political Economy*, edited by Norman Schofield, 337–62. Dordrecht: Springer, 1996.

Puig, Gonzalo Villalta, and Bader Al-Haddab. "The Transparency Deficit of Dispute Settlement in the World Trade Organization." *Manchester Journal of International Economic Law* 8 (2011): 2.

Putnam, Robert D. "Diplomacy and Domestic Politics: The Logic of Two-Level Games." *International Organization* 42, no. 3 (1988): 427–60.

Risse, Thomas. "Transnational Governance and Legitimacy." In *Governance and Democracy: Comparing National, European and International Experiences*, edited by Arthur Benz and Ioannis Papadopoulos, 179–99. Oxon: Routledge, 2006.

Risse, Thomas, Stephen C. Ropp, and Kathryn Sikkink, eds. *The Power of Human Rights: International Norms and Domestic Change*. Vol. 66. Cambridge: Cambridge University Press, 1999.

Risse-Kappen, Thomas, ed. *Bringing Transnational Relations Back In: Non-State Actors, Domestic Structures and International Institutions*. Vol. 42. Cambridge: Cambridge University Press, 1995.
Robach, Michael. Testimony for Hearing before the U.S. China Economic and Security Review Commission (April 26, 2018). Accessed July 20, 2018. https://www.uscc.gov/sites/default/files/transcripts/April%2026%2C%202018%20Hearing%20Transcript.pdf.
Scheve, Kenneth F., and Matthew J. Slaughter. "What Determines Individual Trade-Policy Preferences?" *Journal of International Economics* 54, no. 2 (2001): 267–92.
Sevilla, Christina R. *Explaining Patterns of GATT/WTO Trade Complaints*. No. 98. Weatherhead Center for International Affairs, Harvard University, 1998.
Shaffer, Gregory C. *Defending Interests: Public-Private Partnerships in WTO Litigation*. Washington, DC: Brookings Institution Press, 2003.
Sikkink, Kathryn. "Patterns of Dynamic Multilevel Governance and the Insider-Outsider Coalition." *Transnational Protest and Global Activism* (2005): 151–73.
Simmons, Beth A. "The International Politics of Harmonization: The Case of Capital Market Regulation." *International Organization* 55, no. 3 (2001): 589–620.
Sloof, Randolph. *Game-Theoretic Models of the Political Influence of Interest Groups*. Boston: Kluwer, 1998.
Smith, Rodney T. "Canons of Public Choice Analysis of International Agreements." In *The Political Economy of International Organizations: A Public Choice Approach*, edited by Roland Vaubel and Thomas D. Willett, 46–57. Boulder, CO: Westview Press, 1991.
Stigler, George J. "The Theory of Economic Regulation." *The Bell Journal of Economics and Management Science* (1971): 3–21.
Tullock, Gordon. *The Selected Works of Gordon Tullock, Vol. 6: Bureaucracy*. Indianapolis, IN: Liberty Fund, Inc., 2005.
———. "Efficient Rent Seeking." In *Toward a Theory of the Rent Seeking Society*, edited by J. M. Buchanan, R. D. Tollison, and G. Tullock, 97–112. College Station: Texas A&M University Press, 1980.
———. "The Welfare Costs of Tariffs, Monopolies, and Theft." *Economic Inquiry* 5, no. 3 (1967): 224–32.
U.S. Chamber of Commerce. "Cultivating Opportunity: The Benefits of Increased U.S.-China Agricultural Trade." Published 2016. Accessed July 20, 2018. https://www.uschamber.com/sites/default/files/documents/files/cultivating_opportunity_full.pdf.
Van Winden, Frans. "On the Economic Theory of Interest Groups: Towards a Group Frame of Reference in Political Economics." *Public Choice* 100, no. 1–2 (1999): 1–29.
Vaubel, Roland. "A Public Choice Approach to International Organization." *Public Choice* 51, no. 1 (1986): 39–57.
Vreeland, James Raymond. *The IMF and Economic Development*. Cambridge: Cambridge University Press, 2003.
Weiss, Jeffrey. Interview by Inu Manak. Conducted in person. Washington, DC, March 23, 2018.
Wijkstrom, Erik. "The Third Pillar: Behind the Scenes, WTO Committee Work Delivers." International Centre for Trade and Sustainable Development, E15 Initiative. August 2015.
Wolfe, Robert. "Does Sunshine Make a Difference: How Transparency Brings the Trading System to Life." *Handbook of Global Economic Governance* (2013): 40–56.
———. "Canadian Trade Policy in a G-Zero World: Preferential Negotiations as a Natural Experiment." In *Redesigning Canadian Trade Policies for New Global Realities*, edited by Ari Van Assche, Stephen Tapp, and Robert Wolfe, 1–41. Montreal: Institute for Research on Public Policy, 2016.

Chapter Nine

The Role of Experts and Intellectuals in Designing the Postconflict Iraqi Constitution

Jozef Andrew Kosc

> To act on the belief that we possess the knowledge and the power which
> enable us to shape the processes of society entirely to our liking, knowledge
> which in fact we do *not* possess, is likely to make us do much harm.
> —F. A. Hayek (1974, n.p.)

What happens when exogenous "experts" are called to draft a new postconflict constitution? Due to the foreign policy prerogatives of powerful states, this is a vital question to ask today. As long as states continue to engage in nation-building exercises, the technocratic design of new constitutions intended to stabilize warring societies will continue to serve as the single "most pressing problem in modern constitutional design" (Pildes 2008, 200–201). In recent years, international and national bodies have attempted to usher in constitutional transformation with varying degrees of success in Libya, Somalia, and South Sudan, while talks of constitutional design for a war-torn Syria have emerged at the highest levels of diplomacy. Since the publication of Arend Lijphart's seminal "Consociational Democracy" (1969), a small but inordinately influential literature has emerged to tackle the question of post-conflict constitution making. This literature has influenced policy decisions and will continue to do so. What has been the impact of experts drawing from this literature in crafting real-world constitutions?

In the political economy literature, there exists already a long-standing debate between various proponents and critics of exogenous expert involvement in institutional design. James M. Buchanan (1959) suggested an advisory role for the expert. Though Buchanan's expert is merely one player among equals at the negotiating table, as an expert, the economist ought to facilitate agreement, or "consensus," between competing views. In seeking consensus, the economist may be forced to "discriminate between reasonable and unreasonable men" (1959, 135). F. A. Hayek was more critical of exogenous social scientists involved in institutional design (what he called the "scientistic error," and elsewhere, "rational constructivism"), arguing that they suffer from a lack of local knowledge that is necessary to construct functioning institutions (1974, 1973, 1988). More recent contributions to this debate include Coyne (2008), on the role of American experts planning and executing liberal state-building efforts, as well as Levy and Peart (2017), whose work attempts to construct ethical procedures for expert involvement in economic decision making. The latest and most ambitious contribution to the debate comes from Roger Koppl (2018). Koppl's framework seeks to identify which "market structures tend to generate more reliable expert opinions and which market structures tend to generate less reliable expert opinions" (42). He identifies a series of models, characteristics, and conditions of expert involvement in decision making, each of which lowers or heightens the risk of "expert failure" (190). To date, Koppl offers the single most comprehensive theory of expert involvement in institutional decision making. His theory is untested, and he welcomes the application of his framework to novel studies (237).

This chapter will apply and test Koppl's (2018) theory to the case of constitution making in postconflict and occupied Iraq (2003–2005). The case is selected due to the unusual and extraordinary strength of the relevant variable—an entirely new and exogenous heavily expert-influenced postconflict constitutional settlement. The heuristic merits of a *small-c* case study where the relevant "variable is at an extreme value" are well-known in the social sciences (George and Bennett 2005, 81). Additionally, although much has already been written about the controversial constitution of Iraq, surprisingly little attention has been paid to the critical role of experts in shaping the document. And yet it is in this respect that the Iraqi case is most unique. From late 2003 until late 2005, numerous constitutional scholars and political scientists were involved in the constitution-making process. Other perspectives were tabled by various public intellectuals as well as political actors. The various players of the Coalition occupant had their own expert views on the matter. Altogether, the Iraqi constitution was one of recent history's most debated constitutional settlements—both in sheer scope of perspectives presented and in the level of international expertise involved. As an expert-influenced postconflict constitution, it approximates the quality of an ideal type (Hamoudi 2014, 11). And yet, in the end, the consociational settlement is also deemed a policy failure (Younis 2011).

The chief aim of this chapter will be to analyze and illustrate the conditions and characteristics of expert involvement in postconflict constitution making that contributed to expert failure. First, I will outline the academic literature on postconflict constitutional design. Second, I will delve into the public intellectual discourse surrounding the Iraqi constitution before exploring the blueprints envisioned by some of the most important experts involved in the constitution-making process. I will subsequently analyze the widely held views of nonexpert Iraqis at the time. In the next section, I make the case for a "thin" account of expert failure while suggesting avenues of future scholarship for mounting a "thick" case. Subsequently, I analyze the impact of the aforementioned experts on the realities of constitution making, using Koppl's (2018) framework to investigate the conditions that may have contributed to expert failure. The Iraqi case provides support for Koppl's framework as being plausible for understanding postconflict constitution making, suggesting that expert involvement may have a severely limiting role on the universe of plausible constitutional documents and work contrary to citizens' own constitutional preferences. The final section summarizes findings and offers concluding lessons.

POSTCONFLICT CONSTITUTIONAL DESIGN: COMPETING SCHOOLS OF THOUGHT

In order to understand the influence of experts on the Iraqi constitution-making process, it is first necessary to map the academic universe from which experts have drawn their ideas. Presently, the two major and competing schools of thought are those of *integration* and *accommodation*. Differences in focus lie in articulating contrasting constitutional structures as paramount for maintaining peace among warring parties or between conflicting interests.

The integration approach seeks to promote a "single public identity coterminous with the state's territory" (McGarry, O'Leary, and Simeon 2008, 41). Integrationists prefer a single centralized state without internal boundaries and are skeptical of territorial decentralization (especially autonomous ethnic regions or enclaves). Insofar as they support federalism, it is only as an institutional guard on the abuses of power, and they are strongly opposed to ethnic-based federalism as opposed to mere geographic federalism. Legislatures ought to be representative of individual citizens within ridings and not of ethnic blocs. The executive government (either a single-person presidency or a prime minister supported by a majoritarian parliament) should likewise seek to function as a unifying power, rising above sectarian interests. Meritocracy is the means through which bureaucrats and justices govern and hold public office, as opposed to sectarian-based quotas or affirmative action (McGarry, O'Leary, and Simeon 2008, 45–50, 70–71).

Similarly, integrationists condemn sectarian political parties and support issue-based and nationwide political parties. They prefer electoral systems (majority runoff, the alternative vote system, or single-member plurality) that tend to favor moderate or centrist parties (those that must appeal to a wide base to secure victory). Most critically, integrationists prefer a single public *national* identity and a *nation-building* government as well as a universal bill of rights that emphasizes the rights of individual citizens (McGarry, O'Leary, and Simeon 2008, 70–71).

Accommodationists support "the recognition of more than one ethnic, linguistic, national or religious community in the state" (McGarry, O'Leary, and Simeon 2008, 52). Whereas integrationists attempt to unify citizens under a single national identity, accommodationists aim to "secure the coexistence of different communities within the same state" (McGarry, O'Leary, and Simeon 2008, 52). They accept territorial decentralization (for example, ethnically homogeneous regions), pluralist federalism, and regional bills of rights that emphasize not only individual rights but also the collective rights of sectarian groups (McGarry, O'Leary, and Simeon 2008, 70).

Accommodationists do not see meritocracy as the sole means through which bureaucrats and justices may gain and hold public positions, and they stress quotas, affirmative action, or descriptive systems of representation for different communities. Legislatures are to be broadly representative of different sectarian groups; some accommodationists support explicit power-sharing quotas ("corporate consociationalists"), while others are conscious of shifting concepts of subnational identity and therefore prefer proportional representation in the legislature ("liberal consociationalists"). Accommodationists champion the existence of identity-based, sectarian, or subnational political parties (McGarry, O'Leary, and Simeon 2008, 70–71).

Within the accommodation school, there are two main subdivisions that translate into competing policy visions: the *centripetalism* of Donald Horowitz and his disciples and the *consociation* of Arend Lijphart and his followers (Choudhry 2008, 28). The key differences lie in their respective approaches to executive formation, electoral systems, and federalism. Consociationalists prefer an executive government comprised of power-sharing coalitions of different sectarian or ethnic parties (either through a diverse parliamentary cabinet or a rotating or multiple-person presidency). Centripetalists prefer a majoritarian and unifying executive—one that is closer to the integrationist model—albeit one that is comprised of an interethnic coalition of "moderate" politicians. Consociationalists seek proportional representation (either single transferable vote or party list) as an electoral system. Centripetalists prefer the complex alternative vote system and distribution rules for regions in elections (the Nigerian model). Centripetalists are willing to accept federalism to accommodate large minorities situated in homogeneous geographic regions but otherwise remain skeptical of federal states. Consociationalists are broadly supportive of different types of pluralist federalism, in the interests of permitting minority groups to retain a degree of semiautonomy or self-governance from the central state (McGarry, O'Leary, and Simeon 2008, 53–56, 58–63, 70–71).

The competing schools of thought (integration versus accommodation as well as consociationalism versus centripetalism) influenced the thoughts and policy visions of the various experts involved in discussing and later enacting the constitution-making process in Iraq. Drawing from this literature, the real-world public intellectual discourse on the Iraqi constitution was largely divided along the very same axes as the academic debates.

THE IRAQI CONSTITUTION IN
PUBLIC INTELLECTUAL DISCOURSE

In the follow-up to the constitutional design process as well as in the years immediately following the ratification of the 2005 constitution, many approaches were outlined, offered, and justified as appropriate for Iraq's social and political needs. Proponents and critics mostly sided with one of the aforementioned competing schools of thought. But there was also significant support for outright partition of the Iraqi state. The different views can be summarized as follows.

Proponents of Integration

The most prominent and influential supporter of integration before and after the constitution-making process was Kanan Makiya. An intellectual leader of the Iraqi National Congress (INC), an umbrella for anti-Hussein opposition parties in the 1990s, Makiya was incredibly influential in the run-up to the invasion of Iraq. As early as August 2002, Secretary of Defense Donald Rumsfeld met privately with prominent leaders of the INC and other opposition parties to discuss the future of a post-Hussein Iraq (Allawi 2007, 82; Al-Ali 2014, 42). Bush administration officials would continue to court Makiya's vision at meetings of prominent Iraqi exiles and opposition groups over the next few months (in December 2002 in London; February 2003, in Salahuddin; and in Baghdad after the invasion, in April 2003) (Diamond 2006, 34; Lukitz 2011, 84). But Makiya's vision for the constitutional settlement was first publicly documented in his paper, "A Model for Post-Saddam Iraq" (2003).

Here, Makiya (2003) outlines a vision of a liberal and democratic Iraq. Federalism is supported but only as "an extension of the principle of the separation of powers" and an institutional check against majoritarian abuses (8). This is a natural guard against the type of abuses perpetrated under the Hussein regime. Makiya argues *against* an ethnically based federalism for two reasons. First, since Iraq comprises many distinct ethnic and religious groups (not only Kurdish and Arab but also Armenian, Chaldean, Turkoman, and others), a federalism that distinguishes between only a Kurdish region and a mainland Arab region would be undemocratic, unfairly discriminating against Iraq's other ethnic groups. Second, an ethnic federalism that would be extended to include all of Iraq's distinct ethnic and religious groups would be impractical since many minority groups are widely dispersed across different territories. His solution lies with a federalism that is purely geographic or territorial (Makiya 2003, 8–9). As with most integrationists, he champions individual religious freedoms and cultural pluralism but rejects the accommodationist public state recognition of citizens according to their religious or sectarian identity (the "confessional system in Lebanon") (10–11).

Like Makiya, Adeed Dawisha and Karen Dawisha (2003) offered an integrationist blueprint for the new Iraqi state before the constitution-drafting process had even begun. Federalism ought to be territorial, based on the existing eighteen administrative provinces of Iraq, whereas state revenues from "strategic assets," such as oil, ought to be managed by the central government. The central state ought to employ revenue-sharing policies to distribute wealth between rich and poor provinces (Dawisha and Dawisha 2003, 38–39). The authors reject the "dangerous" prospects of a Bosnia-style power-sharing executive government, which they see as merely institutionalizing sectarian disputes. On the other hand, they recognize that an all-powerful executive threatens the balance of power. They therefore propose a "weak but unified" executive branch comprised of both a majoritarian prime minister (with real powers) and a largely ceremonial president elected by a legislative upper house. An indirectly elected president would prevent the office from falling into the hands of a sectarian politician (supported, in the case of Iraq, by the 60 percent majority of eligible Shi'ite voters). Instead of a president, they also propose the reinstatement of the Hashemite monarchy under the form of a constitutional monarchy, wherein the limited sovereign functions as a unifying and historically legitimate head of state (41–44). Instead of accommodation-style quotas for minorities and sectarian groups in the legislature, the authors recommend using multimember districts (MMDs), in which diverse ridings have a greater opportunity to elect diverse politicians. The national legislature ought to comprise both local "district representatives," elected in MMDs, and politicians elected through a party list system. The authors explain the advantage of an otherwise complex system of voting: "it would allow voters to have direct and personal contact with their local representatives while also encouraging the development of nationwide parties with national, rather than regional or sectarian, agendas" (45). Political parties that did not register candidates in most districts would be barred from running in the party-list half of the election. Sectarian parties, such as those of Kurdistan, would be forced to form "truly nationwide" mandates or risk having political representation limited to seats won in MMDs (44–45).

The Dawishas (2003) mix their integrationist proposals with some accommodationist elements that are appropriate for the case of Iraq. While they support a meritocratic civil service, they make room for quotas in the upper house of the parliament. In addition to elected provincial representatives, they believe that half of the upper house should also comprise representatives from religious communities, tribes, and professional associations (46–48).

A third and final early champion of integration was Andreas Wimmer (2003). Observing the onset of sectarian identity politics early in the occupation, Wimmer recognized that full-fledged democracy "will likely be dominated by the micropolitics of clientelistic alliance building . . . and by the macro-politics of ethno-religious party competition" (120). Citing Horowitz (1985, 342–49), he worries that the nascent ethno-religious parties will adopt increasingly radical positions in order to appeal to their sectarian voting bloc, on the whole eschewing the chances of a lasting, peaceful settlement. He does not think that accommodation-style power sharing would work, as "Iraq lacks a political culture of moderation and compromise" (120–21). Instead, he recommends a wide swathe of policy prescriptions that oscillate from textbook integration to strong centripetalism. First, he champions a strong, unifying executive government (a prime minister or president), elected through a majoritarian nationwide electoral system that also requires a majority of votes in provinces (similar to the Nigerian constitution). He also prescribes the alternative vote system for electing the legislature since this system forces politicians to court citizens outside of their immediate sectarian affiliation. Political parties also ought to organize across different provinces (so that they are not limited to ethnically homogeneous ridings) (122).

Like Makiya, Wimmer (2003) supports a territorial federalism (one that does "not correspond with ethnic boundaries") and believes that the Kurdish territory ought to be split into two provinces instead of a powerful super province (a region) (124). He also echoes Makiya's call for fiscal federalism, in which the central government would have control over oil revenues alongside distributive powers. The rationale for such proposals is common sense; it would reduce incentives for sectarian struggles over revenues and for sectarian struggle over disputed territories (such as Kirkuk and Mosul) alongside the border between Kurdistan and mainland Iraq (124). While Wimmer does not champion the creation of an Iraqi nationalism, he is not opposed to the emergence of a reconstructed Ba'ath Party nor does he think that the Coalition should "be afraid of Iraqi nationalists" (126). Indeed, Coalition authorities (or international bodies, such as the UN) ought to invest in programs that foster the creation of an Iraqi civil society (127).

Many other integrationist voices followed these initial proposals. Among them, Salamey and Pearson (2005) wade into the debate prior to the ratification of the final constitution but following the establishment of the provisional constitution (the TAL) as the rule of law for the occupation period. Other integrationists reiterated these and similar proposals in the aftermath of the broadly consociational settlement of 2005, calling for formal and drastic reforms of the constitution (Baker and Hamilton 2006; Daloglu 2006; International Crisis Group 2006; Said 2006; Visser 2006). But the proverbial damage, in their eyes, was already done, and these proposals had little impact (if any at all) on the realities of the constitution.

Proponents of Accommodation (Centripetalism)

The centripetalist perspectives offered were quite similar to the integrationist models already outlined. Indeed, if approaches to postconflict constitutional design were to be outlined on a scale, as McGarry, O'Leary, and Simeon (2008) have elsewhere illustrated, centripetalism (with its unifying electoral systems that privilege secular, liberal moderates) would lie closest to integration (68).

Dawn Brancati (2004) writes before the Coalition Provisional Authority (CPA) and the appointed Iraqi Governing Council (IGC) have concluded with the drafting of the provisional TAL. As an accommodationist, she supports the establishment of ethnically based federal regions (three regions, one for the Kurds, Shi'a, and Sunnis, respectively) (15). She proposes a decentralized federalism, in which strong regions have general autonomy over cultural, economic, and political issues. Oil revenues ought to be managed by the central government in Baghdad, which should nevertheless distribute greater funds to regions that produce more oil. Unlike integrationists, she believes that this would create greater stability, whereas a more equitable distribution of revenues may result in resentment and violence in regions that believe they ought to have a greater share in revenues (14). Her argument against a territorial federalism, comprised of the existing eighteen governorates, is quite original; she believes that more regions, with greater heterogeneity of population, would give rise to a greater plurality of ethnic and sectarian political parties in more regions of the country. Sectarian parties would also have an incentive to stir discord across the nation, whereas in an ethno-federalist state, they would be limited largely to their particular region (17–18).

As a centripetalist, Brancati (2004) is aware of the potential threat of civil war and even secession that may result from ethno-federalism. To counter this possibility, she proposes the establishment of "cross-regional voting laws," which would force political parties to run candidates in different regions, and "to win a certain percentage of the vote in these regions to be elected to the federal government" (16). She presents the Nigerian model, which is often touted as ideal by centripetalists (16). Another way to curtail the threat of interethnic conflict is to support an integrationist-style executive government (a unifying president, elected directly through a nationwide, cross-regional vote) (16–17). To protect against abuses of regional minorities (for example, Shi'a in the Sunni region) and small minorities (Turkomans, Assyrians, and others), she believes in a strong federal judiciary, in which abuses occurring in regions may be brought before the federal court (17).

Much later in the constitution-drafting process, Horowitz (2005) enters the debate. Writing just before the December 2005 Iraqi national elections and after both the provisional TAL and the final constitution have already been ratified, he decries the settlement as "probably the weakest federation in the world" (n.p.). He does not put forward his own vision for constitutional reforms but offers a scathing critique of the final settlement. Like Makiya (2005) in his ex post facto assessment and that of many other integrationists, Horowitz (2005) objects to the very limited list of executive powers, the inordinate amount of constitutional powers delegated to governorates and the sole Kurdish region, and control over oil resources by regional governments. He also notes the incomplete nature of the settlement: "[t]he upper house, to represent provinces and regions, is mentioned in the constitution but is not even to be brought into existence until after the next legislative elections" (n.p.). Horowitz (2005) predicts that, without a stronger central government, Iraq will fracture into three de facto states: an increasingly independent Kurdistan, an Iranian-backed Shiite region, and a Sunni heartland that is the home of insurgents and radical Islamists.

Proponents of Accommodation (Consociationalism)

Those advocating for a consociational Iraqi constitution were few in number but, as will be revealed, inordinately influential in their views. Here, we find, chiefly, the political scientists Brendan O'Leary and John McGarry. What is curious about both major proponents of the consociational model is that they were conscripted to work as constitutional advisers for the Kurdistan Regional Government (KRG) and the Kurdistan National Assembly (KNA) during the negotiations over the TAL (O'Leary, McGarry, and Salih 2006, 342–43). O'Leary (2006) does not hide that his prescriptions were "heavily focused on Kurdistan's interests" (79). In the same piece, he asks: "What sort of federation will most effectively make Iraq both democratic and pluralist? What model of federation best suits Kurdistan?" (48). Although these scholars also believed that power sharing served the interests of the entire federation of Iraq, there are nevertheless ethical concerns that may be tabled when a constitutional proposal seeks that which "best suits" a *minority population* within the context of designing a constitution for an entire polity.

O'Leary's (2006) position, although written in the aftermath of the constitutional negotiations—largely to defend the consociational settlement from its numerous detractors—is itself based on influential talks he had given very early during the Coalition occupation, first in Washington, DC (September 2003), and later in Oslo (November 2003) (87). As a disciple of Lijphart, whom he thanks in his notes (87), O'Leary is a firm consociationalist. "The answer," he writes, lies in "power-sharing within a 'pluralist federation' for Iraq and 'federacy' arrangements for Kurdistan—elements of which are already embedded in the potential interim constitution" (48). He supported an ethnically based federalism of three distinct regions (one for each of the Sunni, Shi'a, and Kurds), although he has elsewhere advocated for five regions (two for the Shi'a in the south of Iraq, one for the Kurds in the north, one for the Sunni in the Iraqi heartland, and Baghdad as its own region) (68, 88). He rejects outright the integrationist or centripetalist model of territorial federalism based on the existing eighteen governorates in Iraq. This model, he claims, would lead to the disintegration of the KRG and would prompt a war between the KRG and mainland Iraq (68).

Perhaps predictably, he supports a decentralized federalism with very strong regional governments. These regions ought to have general autonomy, in addition to bilingual bureaucracies. What is quite unique and extreme about O'Leary's (2006) proposal, even among fellow consociational thinkers, is that he also believes that different regions should have their own regional constitutions, regional bills of rights, and regional supreme courts. He does not provide a justification for this beyond stating that it is necessary due to "Iraq's deep diversity" (77).

In line with the consociational school of thought, O'Leary (2006) supports executive power sharing (through a collective presidency); although, here, he wishes to see the three-person council established in the TAL expanded to include even more members and, ideally, based on proportional representation of different sectarian groups (what is known as the d'Hondt method) (56). He also supports a legislature that is bicameral, "one chamber of the citizens as a whole and one that represents the regions or federative units" (51). This in itself is not, strictly speaking, a consociational proposal. The upper house ought to be elected through proportional representation (77). The lower house should be elected according to proportional representation or through a nationwide party-list system or a party-list system using regional ridings, "with compensation at the federal level for any disproportionality at district levels" (76). The parliament should also reserve special seats for very small minorities (76). He explicitly rejects distributive or cross-regional party requirements for federal elections (the Nigerian model, supported by integrationists like Wimmer and centripetalists like Brancati) on grounds that such an electoral system would privilege nationwide Arab parties to the detriment of Kurdish parties (76–77).

Opposed to a strictly meritocratic civil service, O'Leary (2006) supports proportional representation of different sectarian groups or else quotas for such groups both in the federal bureaucracy and in the judiciary (73). Finally, and perhaps most uniquely, he supports the TAL's treatment of the KRG as a unique "federacy," not on par with Iraq's other governorates but as a unique "semisovereign entity." The unique KRG region must have a veto on constitutional amendments proposed in Baghdad as well as, ideally, the right to "opt out" of any unappealing legislation passed by the federal parliament. The region should also have the right to maintain its own "regional guards," who would work alongside the federal military in policing borders. There also ought to be a provision that prevents the federal military from being deployed in the KRG without the express permission of the KRG (78–79).

John McGarry (2006) does not add much beyond the prescriptions of O'Leary (2006). He summarizes his position forcibly with the following: "[t]he choice that Iraq faces is . . . not between a nation-state model and a pluri-national state model, but between a pluri-national federation and division into two or more states" (111). What is remarkable about McGarry is that he takes as his model of "decentralized federalism and power-sharing" in Iraq the example of Canada—a multinational state that has seen peace since confederation in 1867 and has witnessed very little violence in its stable and prosperous history. He seems to be aware of the dangers of a comparison between two such radically different societies but nevertheless makes the case (110).

Elsewhere, McGarry (2007) presents a novel argument against the vision of an integrationist Iraqi constitution, in which "there is no guarantee that a centralized Iraq would evolve in the benign neutral way envisaged or implied in integrationist accounts" (175). He cites the specter of a Shi'a-controlled centralized theocracy that works against secular values (175). He concludes his analysis by portraying himself as a pragmatic proponent of consociation as the best imperfect bargain available: "liberal consociation offers a more reasonable and even-handed response to Iraq's complex reality than the alternatives on offer" (184).

Proponents of Partition

There were several notable proponents of the outright partition of Iraq. The first of these, in chronological order, was Leslie H. Gelb, an influential journalist. Gelb's (2003) "three-state solution" of partitioning Iraq into the "Kurds in the north, Sunnis in the center and Shiites in the south" was unique in having been written as early as November 25, 2003 (n.p.). This proposal came in the direct aftermath of the November 15th Agreement, during which Ambassador L. Paul Bremer III and Secretary of Defense Donald Rumsfeld agreed on and announced a timeline for constitution making and the transfer of sovereignty (Arato 2009, 110–13). Gelb's rejection of the Bush administration's then newly announced plan rested on a (grossly oversimplified) historical account of Iraq as "artificially and fatefully made whole from three distinct ethnic and sectarian communities" (n.p.). The concept of a unified Iraq was, in his eyes, "unnatural" (n.p.).

Gelb's (2003) essay proposes a two-stage process toward partition, beginning with the establishment of a "loose confederation" of autonomous regions, whose borders would be "drawn as closely as possible along ethnic lines" (n.p.). Baghdad would belong to the Sunni central region. Minority populations in Baghdad would either arrange political "deals" (presumably some sort of local power sharing, although this is not specified) with regional governments or else would migrate to live in other regions (n.p.). The United States should be prepared to both fund and offer military protection for all cross-regional migration. Although a "loose confederation" would be preferable to the creation of three separate and new states, if violence continued to escalate between sectarian groups and between the newly created regional governments, then full partition should be supported as a second step (n.p.). Gelb concluded that, in such a case, the Iraqis "would all have to live with simple autonomy, much as Taiwan does with respect to China" (n.p.).

Peter W. Galbraith was another proponent of partition whose views were ultimately quite influential. Galbraith (2006), who was a professor at the National War College prior to the invasion of Iraq and during the first few months of the occupation, reveals himself in his memoirs as one of the chief constitutional advisers to the Kurdish parties alongside McGarry and O'Leary (the latter whom he refers to in his book). Like Gelb (2003), Galbraith's (2006) support for partition rested, first, on his oversimplified interpretation of Iraqi history. At the beginning of his memoir, he argues that there has never been a single, voluntary Iraqi nation. He claims that the "main error" of the Coalition was the "unrealistic and futile commitment to preserving the unity of a state that was never a voluntary creation of its people, and that has been held together by force" (12). Elsewhere, he writes: "I don't believe it is possible over the long run to force people living in a geographically defined area to remain part of a state against their will. . . . I believe a managed amicable divorce is in the best interests of the peoples of Iraq" (162). Toward the end of his book, he compares support for a united and single nation of Iraq to the "doomed effort" of US and European support for Yugoslavia in 1991 (207).

Galbraith's (2006) second reason for supporting partition is grounded in his analysis of Iraq's demography. He writes that the "three main constituent communities" in Iraq are relatively geographically homogeneous, residing in territories that correspond, "more or less, with the three Ottoman valiyets from which Iraq was created" (100). But whereas Gelb (2003) discusses migration, Galbraith (2006) admits that he does not have a policy solution for Baghdad (nor does he discuss other heterogenous areas beyond the capital city) (222). The only exception is Kirkuk, long contested between the Kurds and mainland Iraq, for which he seems to support the creation of a citywide semiautonomous government—complete with its own consociational arrangements (202). Galbraith's unique focus on Kirkuk is notable. As will be explained in the next section, Galbraith's loyalties ultimately lay with Kurdish authorities, and his concerns for the rest of Iraq were marginal at best. His third and final reason for supporting partition was the claim—a plausible one—that "not one" Kurdish leader "wanted a unified Iraq" (99).

There were two other notable proponents of partition in all-but-name, including Michael E. O'Hanlon of the Brookings Institution and Joseph R. Biden, Jr., who served as a US Senator at the time. O'Hanlon (2006) believed that the United States should help facilitate a confederacy of three or four regions, with only an equitable program of per capita oil revenue sharing holding them together. In his view, a confederacy, unlike formal partition, would still leave open the opportunity for national integration at some point in the future. In the short term, a "safe passage" program would open doors for the "voluntary ethnic relocation" of Iraqi citizens to their preferred region (n.p.). Such a program would include the government-overseen "swapping" of residential private property (n.p.). Meanwhile, Biden teamed up with Gelb (Biden and Gelb 2006) to offer a radical federalist vision of "three largely autonomous regions" connected nationally by a small list of central government powers and a Baghdad that "would become a federal zone" (n.p.). What is most curious and notable about their support for a soft partition (what they called a "strong regionalism") is that it is partly justified by the finished constitution—already drafted into law by that point. They note: "the Iraqi Constitution, in fact, already provides for a federal structure and a procedure for provinces to combine into regional governments" (n.p.). The integrationist nightmare scenario is therefore the solution, according to Biden and Gelb. Both of these ambitious proposals were offered to the public in the aftermath of the constitution-making process (in the summer of 2006), and as such, their impact was largely inconsequential in the absence of constitutional reformation.

THE VIEWS OF APPOINTED EXPERTS

Having outlined the public intellectual discourse surrounding the Iraqi constitution, I turn now to some of the most critical experts involved in the constitution-making effort.

L. Paul Bremer III

The chief American expert overseeing the drafting of the TAL was Ambassador Bremer. His role in overseeing the process flowed from his overall position as head of the CPA, from which he managed all aspects of state building until the nominal transfer of sovereignty to the government of Ayad Allawi in June 2004. According to Galbraith (2006), Bremer was at first a proponent of a soft integrationist vision. During a meeting with Kurdish leaders on January 27, 2004, he was willing to accede to the asymmetric existence of the KRG as a "federal unit" but wanted a strong central government in Baghdad with broad powers over borders, the economy, security, and natural resources. He also sought the integration of the Kurdish peshmerga into the new Iraqi Army and the disbandment of an independent KRG judiciary (which had already existed prior to the Coalition invasion) (Galbraith 2006, 163–64). Diamond (2006) also notes Bremer's initial support for an integrationist constitution, reflecting the initial preferences of the Bush administration (162). In his memoirs, Bremer reflects on this initial view: "[w]e were willing to support the Kurdish demand for federalism—but only in the context of a unified Iraq, with a central government exercising authority over key national issues such as defense, foreign policy, and Iraq's natural resources" (Bremer and McConnell 2006, 270). His position was grounded in a cautious view of constitution making; since the TAL was only an "interim" settlement, Bremer wanted to leave "sensitive issues" to the negotiators of the permanent constitution (Bremer and McConnell 2006, 271).

However, Bremer's seeming preferences for an integrationist settlement quickly dissolved in favor of the hardline consociational desires of the Kurdish and Shi'a parties, which included broad demands for a semiautonomous KRG with many of the powers initially reserved for the federal government as well as the ability to form future regional governments (Bremer and McConnell 2006, 292–308). Reflecting in hindsight on the process, Bremer notes that he was well pleased with the TAL having "embedded the concepts of balance of power in government" (Bremer and McConnell 2006, 392). Once the consociational view was enshrined by the TAL, Bremer spent little time shifting the official position of the occupation. Accommodation-style federalism was highlighted as a key theme of the CPA public relations campaign to promote the provisional settlement (Diamond 2006, 110).

Bremer's memoirs provide numerous clues as to why he did not firmly hold to an integrationist nation-building vision. First, Bremer's two-track method of constitutional negotiation reflected an accommodation-style analysis of Iraq as a divided society. He had assigned his Governance Team to work with Arab members of the IGC while he engaged Kurdish parties one on one. The full IGC membership had not "seriously begun to focus on a unified draft" until a mere ten days before the deadline for ratification (Bremer and McConnell 2006, 269, 292). He refers to this approach as "divide and conquer" (Bremer and McConnell 2006, 295).

Second, his governance style reflected an analysis of Iraqi society as divided between competing sectarian groups—a view that was espoused chiefly by the aforementioned expert proponents of an accommodation-style settlement. From the beginning, Bremer governed the CPA through a sectarian framework. Operating under the jurisdiction of UN Security Council Resolution 1483, Bremer established the Interim Governing Council (IGC) on July 13 as an appointed body of twenty-five Iraqi officials who would assist in the drafting of the TAL. Bremer's chief criteria for appointing the IGC was sectarian identity; this is reflected in his justification for failing to appoint anyone from three of the preexisting provinces of Iraq to the IGC, which was that there were already ten Shi'ite members from the south (Bremer and McConnell 2006, 97–98). Jawad (2013) notes that "[t]his was the first time in the history of Iraq that appointments were made on sectarian and ethnic bases" (8). Al-Ali (2014) notes: "each of the council's members had an ethno-sectarian identity foisted upon them . . . even Hamid Majid Mousa of the Communist party was counted as a Shia member, despite being obviously non-sectarian" (77). Arato (2009) argues that Bremer launched a "trend toward ethnicization," which manifested itself time and time again through the "establishment of ethnic-religious quotas whenever governmental structures were [henceforth] negotiated" (50).

Noah Feldman

The first academic adviser to enter the scene was Noah Feldman, a professor of law, whose tasks included advising Bremer on constitutional issues, and second, albeit in an unofficial capacity, assisting the drafters of the TAL (Feldman 2006, 70). Feldman's mandate lasted from April to July 2003 (Diamond 2006, 49), many months before the formal process of constitution making had begun in late November 2003, and so his impact was minimal. However, his views may have been instrumental in shaping the initial preferences of Bremer and other CPA officials. Feisal al-Istrabadi, another important expert whom I will turn to later, also recalls that he called Feldman a number of times during the drafting of the TAL and that his advice was "extremely helpful," although by then, Feldman was no longer formally involved in the constitution-making efforts (interview with al-Istrabadi, May 9, 2016, n.p.).

In his memoir, Feldman (2006) is critical of the Coalition's failure to establish an absolute monopoly over violence in the aftermath of the invasion. In his eyes, an insufficient number of Coalition troops created a power gap and conditions of general anarchy. In such conditions, confessional identity groups became prescient for survival and collective security (73–75, 78–80). This pragmatic view has the support of the broader academic literature (Dodge 2012, 34–35). Feldman's (2006) support for consociational power sharing as the "best case scenario" on offer in Iraq stems from this analysis (47). Elsewhere, his other views reflected strong consociational biases or else an antipathy toward the integrationist view of Iraq history. He did not think that a national civil society existed beneath the edifice of Ba'ath Party Iraq, and he was skeptical of the prospects of establishing a new Iraqi identity (a crucial claim of integrationists) (74, 78). Reflecting on the final constitutional text, however, he was critical of the way in which American interests sidelined significant Sunni demands for a more centralized state, pushing through the final constitutional settlement with only the support of Kurdish and Shi'ite parties (136).

Larry Diamond

Larry Diamond, an established and well-regarded political scientist, was hired by then-US National Security Advisor Condoleezza Rice to assist Bremer and the CPA on political transition and constitutional formation (Diamond 2006, 14–16). As part of this mandate, which lasted from January to April 2004, he would closely advise the IGC constitutional committee, which was formally tasked with drafting the TAL. Diamond is unique among the experts involved in constitution making in that he does not come out clearly in favor of any one school of constitutional design, preferring instead an issue-by-issue approach to different questions. He was critical of an early draft of the TAL that promised a strong executive government. On this issue, he reveals an accommodationist preference: "the country would be better off with a system in which power was diffused among multiple centers, some with veto power, rather than concentrated in one office or branch . . . the draft appeared to give sweeping decree authority to the presidency council" (141). On the question of judicial independence and the technocratic composition of bureaucratic bodies, he stood on the side of the integrationists stating that "I felt, appointments should be made on professional, not political, grounds" (149).

On the question of Kurdish regional autonomy under a federal arrangement, Diamond (2006) appears torn but ultimately stands on the side of accommodation. In his eyes, "federalism made eminent sense," and "it was hard to see how Iraq's deep regional, ethnic, and sectarian divisions could be managed . . . without constitutional guarantees of autonomy" (163). And yet he was also cognizant of the fact that Iraq "had always been highly centralized, and for many Iraqis, the unitary state was a bedrock principle of their nationalist identity" (163). Diamond's support for a Kurdish region did not extend, however, to the prospect of additional regions (the type seen as admissible by consociationalists like O'Leary and McGarry and some of the proponents of partition). In a telling paragraph, he reflects on sympathies for the integrationist fear of regionalism: "I shared [Feisal] Istrabadi's concern [on the right of provinces to form regions in the model of Kurdistan]. . . . I worried that if the divisions were consolidated mainly along Kurdish, Sunni and Shiite lines, Iraq could meet the same fate [disintegration]" (168). Later, in the afterword of his book, while reflecting on the final constitutional arrangement, he writes: "a political structure consisting mainly of three ethnic regions would doom Iraq to disintegration and probably civil war" (356).

Altogether, a close reading of Diamond (2006) suggests that he was a moderate proponent of the accommodation power-sharing school. Reflecting on the TAL, before the drafting of the permanent constitution had begun, he feared going "down the road of unraveling the pluralist power-sharing spirit of the interim constitution," which would "have alarming implications for the country's stability and unity" (201). He adds a critique of outright partition: "I remained hopeful that the steep slide to separation . . . could be averted" (201). Toward the end of his memoir, he formally outlines the academic debates between consociational power sharing versus the moderation-seeking centripetalism, which no doubt played out in his own mind during the constitution-making efforts (317), even citing Lijphart versus Horowitz in an endnote (373, endnote 4). He suggests that "both approaches favor federalism and devolution of power as tools for managing conflict in a deeply divided society" and that "both approaches avoid constitutional arrangements that simply empower the majority at the expense of the minority" (317). Notably, he neglects to include the integrationist model in his personal literature review.

Brendan O'Leary and John McGarry

I have already outlined the strong consociational views of Brendan O'Leary and John McGarry, both of whom acted as constitutional advisers to the KRG during the drafting of the TAL. O'Leary (2006) does not hide the fact that his consociational model underpinned the text of the TAL, and indeed, he argues that consociationalists (whom he refers to as "pluri-nationalists") "consolidate this success in the final constitution" (69). He further adds that it is "imperative that they do so; otherwise Iraq will not function and an implosion and civil war may follow" (69). Elsewhere, he notes that "the TAL provides the necessary basis for a flourishing federation" (49). Indeed, where he is critical of the TAL, it is only insofar as it does not offer enough consociational power sharing; he writes: "the TAL has consensual features in its federal design, although others remain to be established" (55).

Clearly articulating his intentions for the final constitutional settlement, O'Leary, alongside his colleagues Karna Eklund and Paul R. Williams (2006), authored an article titled "Negotiating a Federation in Iraq," which functions as a blueprint for KRG negotiators during the process of drafting the final constitution. In this piece, the authors argue that members of the constitution-drafting committee ought to consolidate the consociational victories of the TAL (137–38). A year later, McGarry (2007) offers an ex post facto defense of the Iraqi constitution as a consociational model, against both integrationist critics (Makiya, the International Crisis Group, and others), centripetalist critics (Horowitz), and those who support partition (such as Biden and Gelb). In this piece, he argues bluntly: "if Iraq's next generation is to be free of conflict, the 2005 constitution needs to be defended and . . . developed in a liberal consociational direction" (171). A year after that, both O'Leary and McGarry (2008) return to offer a glowing review of the 2005 constitution, which they consider to be a model of consociationalism.

Peter W. Galbraith

Although Galbraith's ideal solution—as aforementioned—was one of partition, he reveals in his memoir that his voice was critical in supporting a *consociational* Iraqi constitution. Galbraith began advising Kurdish leaders from the near onset of the occupation, in April 2003. He first presented various federal and consociational models (those of Canada, Bosnia, and the United States) to Kurdish prime ministers Barham Salih and Nechirvan Barzani, after which he authored a memo outlining the central tenets of a beneficial consociational arrangement for Kurdistan. Galbraith claims authorship of many ideas that underlay the official Kurdish position in constitutional negotiations. Among these, he proposed Kurdish regional control over natural resources as well as a Kurdish regional police and military. He also proposed a Kurdish supremacy clause, in which the regional constitution would overshadow the national constitution of Iraq in the event of any conflict between the two (Galbraith 2006, 159–61).

Much later, in February 2004, with formal discussions over the TAL under way, Galbraith contributed to the "Kurdistan Chapter," the official constitutional position of the KNA presented to Bremer and the CPA. This *maximalist* vision of Kurdish autonomy saw the supremacy of the KNA over legal and political affairs of the Kurdish region, with the exception of "a few matters assigned to the federal government (notably foreign affairs)" (Galbraith 2006, 166). The borders of the KRG were declared to be those already controlled by Kurdish authorities on the day of March 18, 2003 (the day prior to the invasion of Iraq). The document also called for a regional military (the Iraqi Kurdistan National Guard), answerable only to the KRG, although deployable outside the region at the request of Baghdad (subject to KRG approval). The conventional Iraqi military could deploy inside KRG territory only with the express approval of the KNA. The document also calls for regional control over natural resources (including the management and control of commercial production for future oil fields). As a compromise to Baghdad, the federal government could continue to oversee the commercial production of existing operational oil fields, including in the contested city of Kirkuk. Federal taxes would also have to be approved by the regional government before being imposed on the region's citizens (Galbraith 2006,

166–69). Galbraith (2006) admits that the goal of Kurdish leaders at the time (including the two presidents and two prime ministers), whom he was paid to advise, was simply to "preserve the de facto independence of Kurdistan" (159). Whereas other leaders at the constitutional bargaining table saw the "opportunity to build a new Iraq," his clients had a much simpler goal: "a document that took the least away from them" (162).

Unlike McGarry and O'Leary (2008), who believed that consociational federalism was to the benefit of both the Kurds and the whole nation of Iraq, Galbraith speaks very little of Iraq beyond those elements that directly concern the Kurds. He offers no comments on the Iraqi constitution beyond those that concern the asymmetric federal structure of the KRG. He shares common ground with integrationist critics who believe that a consociational and decentralized federal settlement might lead to the breakup of the nation. But Galbraith sees partition as a *positive* development and warms to the idea of federalism as a roadside stop toward disintegration. He reflects, toward the end of his memoir: "Iraq's three-state solution could lead to the country's dissolution. There will be no reason to mourn Iraq's passing . . . Kurdistan's full independence is just a matter of time . . . And if Iraq's Shiites want to run their own affairs, or even have their own state, on what democratic principle should they be denied?" (206).

Adnan Pachachi and Feisal al-Istrabadi

Two major proponents of integrationist nation building were Adnan Pachachi and Feisal al-Istrabadi, both members of the liberal nationalist Iraqi Independent Democrats party at the time, with the former being its head (al-Istrabadi 2009, 1644). Pachachi had served as Iraq's Foreign Minister from 1965 to 1967 and returned to Iraq in April 2003 at the behest of the White House. He later became the chair of the TAL drafting committee. Feisal al-Istrabadi was Pachachi's legal adviser as well as a translator of early constitutional drafts from Arabic into English. Al-Istrabadi represented Pachachi on the drafting committee and worked closely with the CPA Governance Team on the day-to-day drafting of the TAL. He was also the main author of the TAL's liberal bill of rights (interview with al-Istrabadi, May 9, 2016, n.p.).

Al-Istrabadi identifies himself as a nationalist when reflecting on his role in helping draft the TAL (2009, 1645). This view is corroborated by Diamond (2006). On certain issues, Pachachi and al-Istrabadi represented a maximalist integrationist position. They argued, for instance, that only the federal government should have control over the management of natural resources. The provincial or regional control of resources would simply help ignite the prospects of a civil war, especially since certain geographic territories (such as central Iraq) had no oil (al-Istrabadi 2005–2006, 292). The federal government should also have sole ownership and control over the disbursement of revenues from the sale of oil. This view stood in opposition to the views of the Kurdish parties, for instance, who wanted an equal regional "joint ownership" of resources (al-Istrabadi 2009, 1644–45).

On other issues, Pachachi and Istrabadi were softer in their views than the other integrationist experts whose views had contributed to public intellectual discourse. Al-Istrabadi notes that he was willing and open to accede to an accommodation-style asymmetrical federation for the KRG (a softer view than that of Makiya, the Dawishas, or Wimmer) since he did not wish to take away from the Kurds the de facto independence that they had experienced since 1991 (2009, 1630). Elsewhere, he writes about the ethic that underlay his support for a Kurdish region and yet also bolstered his opposition to consociational-style regional-based federalism for mainland Iraq: "[t]he author expressed the view that an interim constitution should only preserve the status quo with respect to federalism—i.e., recognize only the KRG as a federated region—allowing a permanent constitution to deal with the issue for the rest of the country" (2009, 1648). Al-Istrabadi later reflected that the drafters of the TAL did not have any legitimacy to make radical changes to the status quo on issues of federalism since the drafters were not elected and there would be no public referendum on the TAL (interview with al-Istrabadi, May 9, 2016, n.p.).

Al-Istrabadi remained critical of the constitution-making process long after his formal role had ended. Once the permanent constitution was ratified, al-Istrabadi (2007) recommended both reopening constitutional negotiations in order to resolve outstanding issues (including what he called "ambiguities respecting the ownership, management, and distribution of Iraq's oil") and starting a formal process of reconciliation and political dialogue with nationalist insurgents (16). When I spoke with al-Istrabadi (May 9, 2016, n.p.), he reflected: "We so weakened the [Iraqi] state between the TAL and the permanent constitution as to give rise to the situation we have now in Iraq, where the Kurds are on the cusp of independence, and it is very difficult to see how you get the rest of the country put back together."

Zalmay Khalilzad

The Afghan-born Khalilzad Zalmay was an experienced diplomat and a member of the US National Security Council (Gordon and Trainor 2012, 9). In December 2002, President Bush appointed him as his "Special Presidential envoy to the Free Iraqis" (Khalilzad 2016, 151). His role was to meet with Iraqi opposition leaders in exile and discuss possibilities for the post-Saddam future. In this role, Khalilzad first met with leaders at a conference in London later that month (151–60). Later, in February 2003, only a few short weeks before the invasion of Iraq, Khalilzad made a covert trip to Salahuddin in Iraq, where he met with Kurdish leaders (159–67). In the immediate aftermath of the Coalition invasion, Khalilzad was given jurisdiction over the appointment of an Interim Iraqi Authority (IIA) and held meetings with local leaders in April toward that end, first in Nasiriyah and later in Baghdad. However, President Bush changed his mind on the quick transfer of sovereignty to an interim government, and with the appointment of Bremer as the head of the CPA, Khalilzad left the scene (170–71, 174–75). He returned to Iraq as the US Ambassador to Baghdad two years later in June 2005, at the invitation of President Bush. His initial tasks were threefold: to prod the Iraqi parties toward drafting the permanent constitution; to ensure that the December 2005 elections went smoothly; and subsequently, to assist with the formation of the new government following the first free elections (226, 233, 238).

Like every other aforementioned expert proponent of consociation, Khalilzad (2016) approached Iraq with an (oversimplified) historical lens that highlighted Iraq's three major sectarian groups as the key focus of analysis. In his memoir, he reveals this view:

> Iraq . . . had suffered from an excessively strong and oppressive state under Saddam. For those who had suffered most under that regime—the Shia Arabs and the Kurds—the principal constitutional goal was to limit the power the central government could exert over their communities. For the Sunni Arabs, who felt entitled to ownership of Iraq, the issue was how to establish a strong state and keep Iraq together—under their control. (Gordon and Trainor 2012, 239)

Although the new Iraqi political elite—appointed by the Coalition in a sectarian manner in order to represent sectarian interests—may have held such positions, instrumentalizing their ethno-confessional identity for the sake of political power (Dodge 2012, 34–35; Makiya 2016, 297–319), the vast majority of nonexpert Iraqis did not. Undoubtedly, with such a view, Khalilzad (2016) was led to support an accommodation-style constitution. First and foremost, he saw the role of the United States as bringing "Iraq's leaders together to negotiate a power-sharing deal" (233).

Khalilzad arrived in Baghdad just three short weeks before the planned August 15 deadline to submit the permanent constitution to the transitional national assembly for a vote of approval (238). That deadline came and went, and Khalilzad continued to negotiate over constitutional questions until October 11, just four days before the October 15 national referendum on the constitution (244, 250). He recalls that he spent the final days of constitutional formation meeting with the leaders of Iraqi political parties over meals, where negotiations over outstanding issues took place in small groups (242). Even his approach to constitutional formation was accommodationist in style since he "tried to build consensus step by step, with individual blocs or parties" before discussing the main issues with the drafting committee as a whole (245). This was not unlike the approach previously applied by Bremer in negotiating the TAL.

Khalilzad supported centripetalist initiatives that would bring together sectarian parties under moderate banners. For instance, he supported the "supermajority provision" of the constitution, under which the prime minister and president were to be elected by a two-thirds majority of the national assembly. In his own words, this would "require Iraqis to work toward inclusive politics" (243). He had also initially planned to facilitate the creation of moderate cross-sectarian political parties in time for the December 2005 elections while asking (but failing to receive permission) for President Bush to covertly fund liberal and centrist parties in advance of the election (251–52). In his memoirs, reflecting on the state of American foreign policy years later in 2016, he continues to believe that the "biggest shortcoming" of US state-building efforts writ large is the failure to support explicitly liberal political parties (316–17).

His moderate centripetalist sympathies also led him to support "phasing in federalism provisions" (240). The final constitution included two such initiatives. First, in what Khalilzad calls the "ultimate compromise," the constitution itself would not establish the criteria by which any number of provinces could form a regional government. These would be established in a future law, which would have to be enacted by the national assembly within six months from the formation of government in early 2006 (248). Second, the constitution allowed for an amendment process (250). According to Khalilzad, these provisions allowed discontented Sunni parties to mobilize electoral support before the December 2005 elections in an attempt to change the settlement on federalism in the future (248). However, Khalilzad ultimately sided with a consociational approach on issues of federalism, and many of his centripetalist ideals were abandoned. He supported the Kurdish maximalist demands for semiautonomy, including maintaining the Peshmerga as an independent security force, ownership of natural resources, and an "equitable share of revenues from Iraq's hydrocarbon revenues" (241). He also concluded that he "could not take away the right of other Iraqis to form federal regions along the lines of the KRG" (248). His initial plan to facilitate cross-sectarian political parties was scrapped because he came to believe that "such an effort would be premature" and "Iraqis were not ready to organize based on issues rather than identity" (251).

In the aftermath of constitutional formation, following the December 2005 elections, Khalilzad continued to influence the political process in ways that seemed both centripetalist and consociational in outlook. He vetted various potential leadership candidates for the prime ministerial office and helped push the ostensibly sovereign national assembly into electing Nouri al-Maliki, whom Khalilzad believed was a moderate and a nationalist (262–65). However, he was also instrumental in facilitating the consociational government and cabinet of 2006, in which the president was a Kurd, the prime minister was a Shi'a Arab, and the speaker was a Sunni Arab, while the ministerial portfolios were allocated on a partisan basis (256–57). During his remaining time as US Ambassador to Iraq, he worked to strengthen local governments, seeing as his justification the "federal nature of the Iraqi government and the delegation of authority to regional and provincial bodies [in the constitution]" (269).

THE VIEWS OF NONEXPERT IRAQIS

Dodge (2007) cites numerous polls taken during and after the constitution-making process to reveal that a clear *majority* of Iraqi citizens preferred a constitution that was reflective of integrationist, nation-building principles. Polls taken by the Iraqi Center for Research and Strategic Studies revealed that 64.7 percent of citizens polled preferred a "politically centralized unitary state as opposed to a federation" (28). The same poll found that 67 percent preferred fiscal as well as administrative centralization. Polls conducted by Oxford Research International in February, March, and June 2004 and November 2005 concluded with similar results. In the February 2004 and November 2005 polls, the question was asked: "Which structure should Iraq have in the future?" Approximately 70 percent of respondents opted for "one unified Iraq with a central government in Baghdad." The same polls revealed mass opposition to decentralization—with only 3.8 percent polled in 2004 supporting partition and only 9 percent supporting partition in 2005. Only 12 percent of KRG citizens polled in 2004 and 20 percent polled in 2005 sought partition (28).

Other polls cited by Marr (2007) in the same volume reveal similar trends. In a US State Department Office of Research poll conducted in October 2004, over 50 percent of Kurds identified as Iraqi nationals either primarily or alongside their Kurdish identity. In another poll conducted by the International Republic Institute in April 2005, over 50 percent of Arab Iraqis identified most closely with Iraqi nationalism, while only 12 percent identified with their ethnic group and 20 percent with their religious identity (54, footnote 4).

In the same volume, McGarry (2007) responds to these polls by citing the results of the Iraqi popular referendum on the constitution (which took place in October 2005): 79 percent of Iraqis who participated in the referendum supported the final constitutional text, with levels of support reaching close to 100 percent in the three Kurdish provinces (174). But the referendum statistics are a red herring; citizen support for *any* constitutional document in a time of civil war and a general lack of state capacity cannot be equated with citizens' particular constitutional preferences (which the aforementioned polls have already illustrated as largely reflective of the integrationist model). McGarry (2007) also fails to cite the other relevant statistics regarding the constitutional referendum; the Sunni-majority al-Anbar and Salahuddin provinces almost unanimously rejected the document. A majority, but not more than two-thirds of the population in Nineveh province, likewise voted against the text (Jawad 2013, 14). Al-Istrabadi (2009) suggests that the constitution was "likely rejected by the majority of the non-Kurdish political class and almost certainly rejected by the majority of Iraq's non-Kurdish citizens" (1651).

The nationalist sympathies of the majority of Iraqis have been expressed multiple times *since* the ratification of the constitution. Indeed, so foreign to ordinary Iraqis was the concept of a sectarian federated Iraq, made possible by the consociational constitution, that in the aftermath of the constitutional settlement, once the dust had settled, "[m]any suspected that dividing Iraq was the goal of the neoconservatives in the first place" (al-Istrabadi 2009, 1652). A national poll conducted in March 2007 suggests nearly 60 percent support for a unified Iraq, against partition or a federated state with multiple semiautonomous regions. The same poll cites earlier support rates for a "single, unified country with a central government in Baghdad" of 70 percent in 2005 and nearly 80 percent in 2004 (ABC News/USA Today/BBC/ARD 2007, 8).

Mass opposition of Iraqis to regional-based sectarian federalism was expressed *politically* in early 2009, after the Islamic Supreme Council for Iraq (ISCI) political party, known as the Supreme Council for the Islamic Revolution in Iraq (SCIRI) until 2007, expressed desire to create a super region of nine Shi'a-majority provinces in southern Iraq, governed from Basra. Despite the obvious benefits that such a region would have offered Iraq's Shi'a population (the proposed boundaries of the new region would have included 80 percent of Iraqi oil reserves), the proposal failed to gather enough support for a mere referendum in Basra province, the condition of which was the support of just 10 percent of eligible voters' signatures (al-Istrabadi 2009, 1631–32; Younis 2011, 8). Finally, Iraq has seen a number of nationwide protests against the perceived incompetence and corruption of sectarian governance since 2011 (Al Jazeera 2011), throughout 2012 and 2013 during the so-called Iraqi Spring (Al Jazeera 2012; Wyer 2013), and almost unabated since the summer of 2015 (Abdulrazaq 2018; Aldouri 2017).

ASSESSING EXPERT FAILURE

We now turn to the central question of this chapter. Did the Iraqi constitution-making process result in expert failure? Koppl (2018) offers two slightly different definitions of expert failure. The first is what I will refer to as a "thick," or substantive, account of expert failure, which is one in which experts "fail when [or because] they give bad advice" (189). There is a growing literature that discusses the ill-fated Iraqi constitution and the troubling social and political pathologies that have developed in its wake, including institutionalized sectarianism (Dodge 2005; Dodge and Simon 2003; Rayburn 2014), corruption (Al-Ali 2014), weak state capacity and governmentality (Dawisha 2013), and the rise of a distinctly Shi'ite brand of authoritarianism under former prime minister Nouri al-Maliki (Dodge 2012). At least one account explicitly traces policy failure to the consociationalism of the constitution (Younis 2011).

While it is not the goal of this chapter to develop a novel "thick" account of expert failure in Iraq, at the time of writing, several new geopolitical developments have once again thrust the viability of the Iraqi constitution into the public eye. Years of Shi'a–Sunni sectarian violence, culminating in the rise of the Sunni extremist Islamic State of Iraq and Syria (ISIS), has highlighted the inability of consociationalism to thwart sectarian violence (indeed, one may ask whether a heightened sense of identity politics contributed to the emergence of such militant forms of Islamism). More so, in the aftermath of years of atrocities committed by both Sunni and Shi'ite extremists against small and powerless ethnic minorities (Assyrians, Chaldeans, and Yazidis, among others), one can question whether more attention ought to have been paid to the integrationist case presented by these weakest members of Iraqi society (so quickly brushed aside in favor of the narratives and preferences of the dominant three sectarian groups). In the aftermath of the 2017 Kurdish referendum on secession (Rasheed and Jalabi 2017), one may pose the question, as Makiya (2005) once did: "[w]hat is wrong with pursuing the Constitution to its logical conclusion: the breakup of Iraq?" (n.p.). Finally, in the aftermath of the 2018 national elections, which have favored technocratic, nationalist, and antisectarian political platforms (Sullivan 2018), one might finally begin to draw greater attention to the desires of the vast majority of nonexpert Iraqis.

Koppl's (2018) second definition describes the failure of experts as "any deviation from a normative expectation associated with the expert's advice" (189). I will refer to this standard as a "thin" account of expert failure. The application of this thin account to Iraq is as follows. The exact legal and normative goals of postconflict constitution making in Iraq were codified on May 22, 2003, through UN Security Council Resolution 1483, which recognized the occupation of Iraq by Coalition forces and bestowed upon "the Authority" (the Coalition Provisional Authority) certain "authorities, responsibilities, and obligations" granted to occupation regimes under international law (UN Security Council 2003, 2). This included, chiefly, the responsibility to facilitate "the right of the Iraqi people freely to determine their own political future" (UN Security Council 2003, 1). Expert failure in the case of

Iraqi postconflict constitution making would therefore necessarily be defined as any constitutional settlement that did not represent the political view—the "normative expectation" (Koppl 2018, 189)—of the majority of nonexpert Iraqis at the time of constitutional formation.

According to this "thin" standard, the case of postconflict constitution making in Iraq was *undoubtedly* one of expert failure. The majority preferences of the native nonexpert Iraqi population have already been outlined. Despite these preferences, largely sympathetic toward the integrationist nation-building view, the realities of constitution making were inordinately influenced by only one type of expert vision. Younis (2011) observes that the constitution of Iraq is clearly a consociational document. Three major elements of a consociational settlement—federalism, a parliamentary system with a power-sharing executive government and proportional representation—are featured prominently in the case of Iraq (although the system of proportional representation is the result of the electoral law, not the constitution) (4–8, 11–13).

Nor do some of the key experts attempt to hide their intellectual legacy in various glowing ex post facto assessments. In an extraordinary judgment, McGarry and O'Leary (2008) defend the new social contract as a *model* of consociationalism (347, 367). Almost every major component of the constitution, in their eyes, is fully "consistent with liberal consociational principles" (347). Elsewhere, McGarry (2007) writes that the 2005 constitution, precisely because it is "consistent" with consociationalism, "needs to be defended and, particularly where it is incomplete or vague, developed in a liberal consociational direction" (171). Haider Ala Hamoudi (2014), a consociationalist who was appointed in 2009 to assist in constitutional revisions (a process that did not result in any revisions), heaps even greater praise on the text, as a model of "best constitutional processes," a "remarkable story," and a "symbol of national unity" (11–12). Undoubtedly, it is clear that the consociational preferences of academic advisers and Coalition officials translated into the document.

CHARACTERISTICS THAT LED TO EXPERT FAILURE

The Iraqi case of constitution making contains most of Koppl's (2018) conditions that contribute to the plausibility of expert failure. Koppl's theory (2018) suggests "two dimensions of expert power" that contribute to or detract from the likelihood of expert failure. The first dimension measures the freedom of nonexperts. As a general rule, the "greater the freedom of nonexperts to ignore the advice of experts, the lower is the chance of expert failure, *ceteris paribus*" (189). Put in other words, this first dimension measures the power of nonexperts to decide policy without regard for expert opinions. The second dimension measures market competition in the realm of expertise. As a general rule, the "more competitive is the market for experts, the lower is the chance of expert failure, *ceteris paribus*" (189). I will analyze the Iraqi case through the lens of these two central theoretical insights.

In addition to these two axes, Koppl offers some additional characteristics that may increase the plausibility of expert failure in relevant cases. Not all of these additional characteristics are relevant in cases of constitution making. Some are relevant only in unique instances of expert involvement (for instance, the involvement of particular regulated industries or regulated professions) (205–14). I will also analyze the Iraqi case through the lens of some of these secondary characteristics that are relevant in cases of constitution making.

The Monopoly of Expertise

The model of expert involvement during the drafting of the TAL undoubtedly fits the criteria of a "rule of experts," in which experts decide for nonexperts and there is no market competition among experts (Koppl 2018, 190). Diamond (2006) notes that Bremer and the CPA staff, from the beginning, expressed a strong preference for a constitution drafted by an *appointed* group of representative Iraqi experts, as opposed to an elected committee (49). This preference reflected and was influenced by the consensus opinion of the academic literature on postconflict state building, which notes the dangers of "rushed national elections which could strengthen extremists and diminish prospects for democracy and peace" (48). Diamond himself, in his role as adviser, supported this view; he cites the cases of postconflict Angola and Liberia, where rapid elections had the unintended effects of fueling sectarian violence, as weighing on the minds of CPA officials (80).

Of course, these views were rejected by the Iraqis. At the London meeting with Iraqi opposition parties (December 2002) as well as the Salahuddin meeting with Kurdish opposition parties (February 2003), Khalilzad encountered universal interest in an Iraqi-led interim government seizing the reins of power either prior to the Coalition invasion or immediately afterward. There was vehement opposition to a US-led state-building project (Khalilzad 2016, 166, 167). Later on, Bremer's appointed IGC at first unanimously rejected the two-step process of constitution making and its needlessly binding timelines declared by the Coalition in the November 15 Agreement (Gordon and Trainor 2012, 34). Much later, Bremer recalls protests with "tens of thousands" demanding electoral representation (Bremer and McConnell 2006, 278).

Reflecting the preferences of the US government, the IGC's ten-person drafting committee was tasked with drafting the TAL. The IGC was appointed ostensibly to represent the views of nonexpert Iraqis. However, it was done so in a sectarian and unrepresentative manner. Diamond (2006) recalls that the IGC did not even have representatives from every Iraqi province (207). In practice, however, the CPA's appointed Governance Team (also referred to as the "working committee") conducted the vast majority of "day-to-day" drafting during the first few weeks of the process. Only a week before the deadline did Bremer convene the entire drafting committee and begin addressing this group as a whole (interview with al-Istrabadi, May 9, 2016). The strange situation during the early days of the CPA occupation was that not a single official charged with the drafting of the TAL had been elected to hold their position in the drafting committee, despite the fact that the Coalition had helped facilitate "dozens" of elections for civil society groups and "over five hundred separate elections at municipal and provincial levels to reconstitute Iraq's Olympic Committee" (Bremer and McConnell 2006, 286). The drafting of the TAL was therefore a closed-door monopoly in which experts decided on behalf of nonexperts.

The drafting of the permanent constitution was supposed to function according to the "quasi-rule of experts," in which experts decide for nonexperts, but "compete among themselves for the approval of nonexperts" (Koppl 2018, 194). An example of such a model is that of representative democracy (190). This process was intended to give more power to nonexperts since the constitutional committee was comprised of fifty-five members of the transitional national assembly, which had been elected in the January 2005 elections. Later, American officials extralegally appointed an additional fifteen Sunni members to the committee in order to improve representation of Iraqi constituents (Al-Ali 2014, 85). These officials were supposed to represent the heterogeneous views of nonexpert Iraqi constituents while drafting the constitution. Finally, the process was intended to culminate with conditions of relative "autonomy" (in which nonexperts are free to reject the advice of experts) (Koppl 2018, 195) since the expert-designed constitution was ultimately put forward to a vote by national referendum on October 15, 2005.

However, in practice, the process played out similarly to the drafting of the TAL, with an expert monopoly over decision making. There was very little consultation with nonexpert constituents, and the closed-door process was closely monitored by the US Embassy. Historian Al-Ali (2014) argues that Khalilzad and other American officials had "cut and pasted" the TAL's provisions into the working document, overriding any shifts toward a more centralized and powerful federal state that may have been negotiated during the drafting process (91). During these final weeks, the draft that emerged "deleted all the changes that had been introduced by the constitutional committee and reintroduced the TAL's original wording" (95). Al-Istrabadi (2009) notes that "there was very little discussion of the substance of what the draft text [of the constitution] contained and little reason to have confidence that many in the electorate knew what they were voting for" (1650). The vote was truly an "informed" one only in the KRG, where political elites had mobilized support (1650).

The Lack of Market Competition

Koppl (2018) fleshes out his definition of market competition by drawing attention to three conditions of competitiveness. The first is *rivalry* between experts, which necessarily requires freedom on the part of the client to select among competing expert solutions. The second is what Koppl calls "synecological redundancy," or *multiple experts* with *different views* (the absence of homogeneity among expert opinions). Finally, "it is unlikely that the full range of relevant expert opinions will be available to clients if entry is controlled" (205). Therefore, the third condition is that there must be "free entry" of experts into the market for expert ideas (205).

Wimmer (2003) very shrewdly observed an almost unilateral preference for consociational power sharing among the elite coterie of academic advisers, Coalition officials, and the newly empowered Iraqi elite even in the earliest stages of constitution making (121). At various points in his memoir, Diamond (2006) reflects on Pachachi and al-Istrabadi as the sole proponents of a nation-building integrationist view on various constitutional issues, ranging from the limitations of federalism, the structure and the independence of the judiciary, the structure of the executive, the right to form semi-autonomous regions, and the various questions associated with control over natural resources (144, 149–50, 152, 167, 169). And apart from Galbraith, whose support for partition operated purely in the realm of ideations, there were no expert advisors supporting the partition of Iraq. The drafting of the TAL therefore suffered from very little rivalry among experts and, similarly, little synecological redundancy, with most experts parroting similar views.

The drafting of the permanent constitution could have included a strong market competition among experts since the elected members of the constitution-making committee were supposed to represent the heterogeneous views of nonexpert Iraqis. However, in practice, this process had *even less* market competition than the drafting of the TAL. Writing in the aftermath of the TAL ratification, al-Istrabadi believed that all of the "substantive" debates that occurred during the drafting of the TAL were fair game for renegotiation during the drafting of the permanent constitution (al-Istrabadi 2005–2006, 301–2). However, there is reason to believe that this was never the intention of the Coalition occupiers.

In separate conversations with British Prime Minister Tony Blair as well as with Larry Diamond, Bremer revealed his desire for the TAL to function as a model for the permanent settlement (Bremer and McConnell 2006, 269; Diamond 2006, 16). Such an interpretation makes sense when considering the distinct timelines for drafting both constitutions; the provisional text was drafted over a four-month period, whereas the permanent settlement was drafted in under six weeks (Al-Istrabadi 2009, 1652). Perhaps because of these intentions, the White House frontloaded the appointment of expert advisers during the first part of constitution making; once the TAL was in place, there was no need for someone like Diamond or Feldman. Only someone like Khalilzad was necessary to prod along compromise.

Negotiations therefore suffered from the absence of any expert integrationist proponents. Whereas al-Istrabadi and Pachachi proved a foil against the total domination of the accommodation camp during the drafting of the TAL, there were no such experts representing these views during the drafting of the permanent constitution. When I interviewed al-Istrabadi (May 9, 2016), he recalled that he was not even consulted by anyone from the permanent constitution-making committee nor, to his knowledge, were any of his colleagues, despite having obvious positions of importance during the drafting of the TAL. Nor was there any apparent reason to include any integrationist advisers since the secular liberal parties as well as the Sunni parties who had supported such views during the drafting of the TAL were not well represented in the permanent constitution-drafting committee. This was the result of the well-known Sunni boycott; three major Sunni political parties (the Iraqi Islamic Party, the Association of Muslim Scholars, and the Sunni Endowments) boycotted the January 2005 elections for the transitional national assembly. Despite American machinations to include an additional fifteen Sunni representatives in the committee, the committee remained largely unrepresentative of a majority of the Iraqi population (Arato 2009, 210, 216–17). According to Galbraith (2006), the result was that "the same Shiites and Kurds who sat on the Governing Council were the main players in the negotiations on the permanent constitution" (170). This is also a conclusion reached by al-Istrabadi (2009, 2012). The process therefore had even less rivalry and synecological redundancy than the drafting of the TAL.

Finally, it should be obvious that neither the drafting of the TAL nor the drafting of the permanent constitution allowed for the "free entry" of expertise into the decision-making process. McGarry and O'Leary (2008) observe that the number of different visions outlined for the Iraqi constitution in the public intellectual discourse far outnumbered the largely homogeneous views expressed by appointed experts. At least in terms of the sheer number of voices supporting integration, the nation-building approach was "arguably the most popular prescription in the West, among supporters of the 2003 invasion . . . as well as among the invasion's critics, in the Democratic Party in the U.S., and among a broad swathe of European political opinion" (345). They are also correct in observing that the "consociational approach tacitly underlay the decision by the Coalition Provisional Authority (CPA) to appoint the IGC in the summer of 2003, and was more prominent in the 2005 Constitution" (345).

In making these two observations, the authors inadvertently testify to the existence of a dissonance between the vast majority of wisdom (both endogenous Iraqis and international) advocating for an integrationist solution as well as many others advocating for partition and the *selective wisdom* that permeated the constitution-making process. Although the consociational view was always a minority view in the overall public discourse, it was certainly a majority among those experts whose views were ultimately critical. If entry into the market of relevant expertise had not been controlled by the CPA and, later, by the US Embassy, perhaps many of the varied voices advocating different visions of the Iraqi constitution in the public square would have found themselves in positions of influence against the overrepresented views of the advocates of consociation.

Monopsony and the White House as "Big Player"

During the drafting of the TAL, the Bush administration and the White House enforced a monopsony on the market of expertise. Monopsony, which refers to the existence of a single buyer in a market, contributes to expert failure because "[i]t makes even nominally competing experts dependent on the monopsonist and correspondingly unwilling to give opinions that might be contrary to the monopsonist's interests or wishes" (Koppl 2018, 214). The White House, through the CPA, was the sole client of the appointed experts, even if the experts, through the IGC, were drafting a constitution *on behalf of* the Iraqi people. Even those experts who were hired by the Kurdish parties (such as Galbraith, O'Leary, and McGarry) to maximize Kurdish interests were, in an indirect way, working for the CPA since the CPA had constructed and enforced the entire process of constitution making as state building.

The power of the sole client in influencing the drafting of the TAL cannot be disputed. The White House and the CPA initially favored the maximalist integrationist vision presented by the Dawishas, Makiya, and Wimmer. Early preferences for an integrationist symmetrical federalism, based on the preexisting eighteen provinces of Iraq (without any reference to a special region for the KRG), as well as a preference for a strong central government with many powers, are attested to both by Galbraith (2006, 165) and Bremer and McConnell (2006, 289–90). Such preferences were reflected in the initial drafts of the TAL and in the initial ascendancy of integrationist experts like al-Istrabadi and Pachachi. Diamond recalls that, after arriving in Baghdad in early January 2004, he was provided with an early, very capacious draft of the TAL that had been put together under the IGC drafting committee. The committee itself was chaired by Pachachi. This early document did not include any references to federalism nor to the distinct questions of the Kurdish region and included a strong executive government consisting of a three-person presidency council (Diamond 2006, 140–41). The Bush administration later expressed preference for a "strong—almost presidential—prime minister," with few checks and balances on governing authority (Diamond 2006, 153). This preference of the Americans was included in both the TAL and the final constitution (with the presidency council relegated to "largely a ceremonial body") (Diamond 2006, 153).

The initial preferences of the White House soon gave way, however, to the primacy of deadlines. Arato (2009) observes that the Bush administration was primarily interested in a rapid transfer of sovereignty to an Iraqi government in order to positively influence President Bush's domestic US reelection campaign in 2004 (129). Crucially, Bremer himself was chiefly driven by internal timelines, which seem to have mattered more than the substance of many constitutional issues. He recalls a National Security Council (NSC) meeting on February 13, 2004, in which Secretary of Defense Rumsfeld, Secretary of State Colin Powell, and even President Bush showed flexibility on deadlines, but Bremer held firm. He did not want to compromise the integrity of the overall state-building timeline, fearing that Iraqis would doubt US intentions over the occupation and strike out against US soldiers (Bremer 2006, 289–90).

In such circumstances, Bremer and the White House shifted strategies. Eklund, O'Leary, and Williams (2006) reveal that it was ultimately Bremer who "heavily steered, if not dictated" the TAL in its final consociational form (117). In his memoirs, Bremer reveals that, by late February 2004, he had approved most of the consociational demands of the Kurdish and Shi'a parties, which had divided the committee and were stalling consolidation (Bremer and McConnell 2006, 292–96). And it was Bremer (with the backing of Condoleeza Rice from the White House) who had approved the final, most contentious draft of the TAL (Bremer and McConnell 2006, 297–308).

The White House could not be said to form a monopsony during the drafting of the permanent constitution since the draft was ultimately put forward to a vote by national referendum on October 15, 2005. Thus, the Iraqi citizenry could be said to be an additional client and beneficiary of the constitution-making process. However, the White House continued to function as a "Big Player" in the decision-making process, influencing the direction of the process. Koppl (2018), citing Koppl and Yeager (1996, 368), defines a "Big Player" as "anyone who habitually exercises discretionary power to influence the market while himself remaining wholly or largely immune from the discipline of profit and loss" (215). Since Iraq had been sovereign since June 2004 and the constitution of Iraq would influence Iraqi citizens in perpetuity (and not the citizens of America), the White House could not be said to either benefit extensively from a substantively decent document or to bear the burden of a poorly designed constitution. The potential costs and profits to the United States were minimal. And yet the Bush administration continued to exert both overt and covert influence in methods that were planned in advance.

Bremer notes the intentional inclusion of timelines and deadlines in the TAL, which would be binding on the process of drafting the permanent settlement in order to "structure and concentrate political activity" after the CPA had left (Bremer and McConnell 2006, 293). Al-Istrabadi (2009) observes that the major concern of the Bush administration was to apply pressure toward the rapid consolidation of a permanent constitution in order to positively influence the Republican Party in the eyes of domestic American voters during the US midterm elections of 2006 (1642). As during the drafting of the TAL, the White House was primarily concerned with meeting these deadlines for the sake of domestic political gain, and any substantive support for a particular vision of the constitution seems to have swiftly fallen apart to make room for prompt consolidation. Galbraith (2006) reveals how, in July 2005, Secretary of Defense Rumsfeld traveled to Baghdad with a single message: to stress the absolute unwillingness of the administration to accept a postponement of the constitutional deadline. This was contrary to the provisions of the TAL, which had in fact allowed for an extension (190). Al-Istrabadi (2009) adds that "[a]t key junctures, when the Iraqi participants wanted additional time, the United States intervened to insist upon a shortened timetable" (1654).

The White House also expressed more direct influence over the settlement due to the involvement of the US Embassy. According to Khalilzad (2016), all Iraqi parties quickly accepted the regional status of the KRG and the concept of Iraq as a federation. They also universally acceded to the consociational structure of the executive government (243). This was similar to the near-universal support for executive power sharing expressed during the drafting of the TAL (Bremer and McConnell 2006, 292). However, the issue of the nature and structure of federalism within mainland Iraq bitterly divided the committee (Khalilzad 2016, 247). The influence of Khalilzad as an expert interlocutor was therefore *critical* in pushing through a document that not everyone had agreed upon. He admits as much, suggesting that he was disappointed with the fact that the constitution did not have the support of the Sunni Arab committee members (249). However, he was ultimately "exasperated with their obstinacy" and worked to push through the consociational settlement (248). According to Galbraith (2006), Khalilzad "summoned Iraq's top leaders to the capital's Green Zone, initiating three weeks of non-stop talks that produced the Kurdish-Shiite deal that is the basis of the Iraqi Constitution" (192). Al-Istrabadi (2009) speculates that, if it had not been for American pressure during a time when sectarian tensions were high as a result of the ongoing civil strife in Iraq, the transitional national assembly would have opted for a very different constitution: "[w]hilst many of the provisions protecting Kurdish autonomy might remain intact, there is little doubt that there would be a much more robust federal government" (1651).

The Lack of Democratic Processes and the Failure to Consult Informed Citizens

In Koppl's (2018) model, a "well-informed" citizenry does not have any impact on "disciplining" expert opinion if the model of expert involvement does not allow for nonexpert power in decision making (91). Citing Buchanan and Tullock ([1962] 1999) and the findings of public choice theory, he does not believe that democratic processes can somehow constrain the rule of experts. Instead, Koppl argues that "the rule of experts is inconsistent with pluralistic democracy" (91). The logical inverse of this observation is that democratic involvement in decision making can be found only in other models of expert involvement (such as the quasi-rule of experts or the rule of nonexperts). The lack of democratic processes is therefore a benchmark for observing the rule of experts. Koppl's observation takes on a uniquely perverse meaning in the Iraqi case.

Diamond (2006) recalls that, by January 2004, the CPA, the US Agency for International Development (USAID), and the National Endowment for Democracy had funded many local Iraqi initiatives. To these were added the efforts of the National Democratic Institute for International Affairs and the International Republican Institute, both of which were funding local political initiatives, town halls, and discussion groups. Among these meetings were conferences organized by Iraqi intellectuals and academics (such as Ghassan Al Atiyyah) on behalf of native Iraqi think tanks and political initiatives, such as the Iraqi Foundation for Development and Democracy and the Iraqi Higher Women's Council. At least one of these academic conferences convened to discuss the specific topic of constitution making (Diamond 2006, 125–31). By the time the constitution-drafting process had begun in late November 2003, the Coalition had also overseen the creation of over *six hundred* provincial, citywide, and local government councils. However, none of these councils were directly and democratically elected, and they remained, on the whole, underfunded, without resources or any real power (Diamond 2006, 115–17). *None* of these local governance bodies, discussion forums, or endogenous think tank initiatives were involved in any part of the drafting of the TAL (Diamond 2006, 197), reflecting Koppl's observation that democracy cannot coexist with the rule of experts.

To add insult to injury, USAID set up over 15,000 public discussions with over 300,000 Iraqi citizens in the aftermath of the TAL drafting process (Diamond 2006, 209). The purpose of these meetings was to "sell it [the TAL] to the Iraqi people" (Diamond 2006, 182). However, there is no evidence of any attempt to integrate the findings of these discussions into the drafting of the permanent constitution, which occurred a year later, once again, behind the closed doors of the Green Zone. It was as if all of these bodies were put up to give the *veneer* of informed citizen participation throughout the entire process of constitution making.

Limiting "Unreasonable" Views

Koppl (2018) offers an interesting critique of Buchanan's (1959) political economist as expert–adviser, which is helpful in understanding expert failure in the Iraqi case. In Koppl's view, since the expert–adviser filters "reasonable" from "unreasonable" positions, presumably through the lens of his or her academic worldview, he or she establishes a set of epistemic constraints on plausible institutional design. The result is that "the theorist is no longer one among equals" but ultimately "decides for the polity which opinions count. Opinions the theorist cannot imagine are thereby excluded and do not count" (2018, 79). Koppl does not elaborate further on how experts may limit or shape unreasonable views within his framework of expert failure. Considering his preference for nonexpert decision making, one can assume that he would be critical of experts cultivating epistemic limitations on plausible institutional solutions. In the model of "self-rule" or "autonomy," nonexperts "may freely accept or reject . . . [the experts'] advice" (195). In cases where nonexperts are empowered to ignore expert opinions on what is reasonable or unreasonable, the decision for making such judgments lies ultimately with the nonexpert decision makers. Expert judgments on reasonableness become significant and problematic in models of expert monopoly over decision making, as in the case of Iraq, where such judgments restrict the realm of plausible institutional solutions without concern for the judgments of nonexpert citizens. One can observe in the Iraqi case that certain views that were supported by the public intellectual discourse (and may or may not have found popularity with nonexpert Iraqi citizens) were never seriously considered by any of the appointed experts-as-advisers involved in constitution making. I will not judge the merits of these views but, instead, will focus on the logic of epistemic exclusion at work.

Partition was, from the beginning, one such view that was discarded as "unreasonable." In fact, many experts sought explicitly to combat the *threat* of partition. Bremer, reflecting on the views of the White House NSC principals (including Vice President Dick Cheney, Secretary of State Powell, Secretary of Defense Rumsfeld, CIA Director George Tenet, General Pete Pace, and National Security Advisor Condoleezza Rice), notes that the administration wanted to avoid the secession of the KRG, which they believed might lead to "the breakup of Iraq, civil war, and escalating regional instability" (Bremer and McConnell 2006, 278–79). Partition is also considered "unreasonable," if not ethically dubious, by the academic consensus. McGarry,

O'Leary, and Simeon (2008) refer to partition as the impractical product of a bygone era and as a problematic moral equivalent to such ghastly methods as forced assimilation and ethnic expulsions (85). The process of constitutional design in Iraq could therefore be said to suffer from the epistemic limitations of what was considered to be reasonable not only in the realm of geopolitics but also by the academic literature of postconflict constitutional design.

According to Koppl (2018), the most likely model of expert involvement in institutional design to result in expert failure—that of the "rule of experts"—is one in which experts decide for nonexperts and there is no market competition among experts (190). These conditions were represented in the drafting of the TAL, a process that also suffered from a market monopsony, with the CPA and White House as the sole clients of expertise. While the drafting of the permanent constitution was intended to approximate the conditions of the "quasi-rule of experts," in the end, the same characteristics of expert monopoly and an even greater lack of market competition among expertise took hold. This second stage of the constitution-making efforts suffered also from the continued inordinate influence of the Bush administration as an economic "Big Player." In addition, both stages of the constitution-making process suffered from a lack of insight from informed citizens and the restriction of plausible constitutional arrangements deemed "unreasonable" by appointed experts. Undoubtedly, all of these conditions contributed to a "thin" account of expert failure in Iraq, one in which the views of the majority of nonexpert Iraqi citizens were not reflected in the constitutional settlement, and may have also contributed to a "thick" account of expert failure, one in which the consociational settlement was poorly designed and contributes to policy failure. Despite the wealth of options considered for Iraq by the public intellectual discourse and the majority preferences of the nonexpert Iraqi population, the realities of constitution making were inordinately influenced by only one type of expert vision.

In hindsight, the preponderant influence of consociational expert thought on the Iraqi constitution is unsurprising. Accommodation-style power sharing is a well-enshrined and popular policy prescription for postconflict settlements. Hartzell and Hoddie (2007) examine thirty-eight separate cases of post–civil war settlements, from 1945 until 1999, and find only one case that did not apply some sort of power-sharing solution (21). And yet the popularity of accommodation-style constitutions does not translate into the universality of their success. For every successful case, there is a failed case of consociationalism (see, for instance, Leenders 2012). Moreover, Hartzell and Hoddie observe a critical difference between the well-proven use of power-sharing institutions in post–civil war settlements and the use of these institutions to "stabilize" other postconflict situations. The latter is a distinct and relatively untested phenomenon, observed in recent cases such as Iraq and Afghanistan, where civil war did not exist prior to invasion and more conventional conflict (2007, 150, footnote 19). The high degree of success in using power-sharing settlements to resolve civil wars does not ipso facto translate into the success of such institutions in other postconflict situations. Feldman (2006) understood these nuances of postconflict constitutional design and wrote that "[t]he best political scientists, constitutional theorists, and area experts are regularly wrong . . . and when the divergent views of a range of scholars are amalgamated, they may be even more wrong than any one of them would be in isolation" (71). This statement, unfortunately fortuitous in the Iraqi case, suggests a few broader lessons.

A significant lesson is the inherent risk of monopsony, under which experts at every level hesitate to express views that don't reflect the preferences of the powerful (Koppl 2018, 214). Involving multiple states in postconflict nation-building efforts under a multilateral occupation authority is unlikely to make much of a difference. Despite the involvement of multiple states in the overall war and occupation, monopsony over the process of constitution making undoubtedly existed in the select few hands of the White House and the CPA leadership. In the absence of an endogenous nonexpert constitution-making effort, some foreign actor must always and ultimately be in charge of overseeing the process that—regardless of the characteristics of that process—did not generate naturally among the native population. That monopsony is unavoidable—indeed, a defining feature—in all cases of foreign-led postconflict constitution making, suggests that there will always be an inherent risk of expert failure in institutional design. This fact should weigh heavily on state actors deciding to engage in postconflict constitution making and, in many cases, should force them to reconsider the very practice.

However, I recognize that the phenomenon of postconflict constitution making is unlikely to go away anytime soon. Thus, I conclude that, if states *do* engage in such efforts, they ought to at least minimize the conditions that are likely to contribute to expert failure. Ensuring that these conditions are met will conversely increase the likelihood of a constitutional settlement that is accepted and respected by the nonexpert citizens of a nation. This very fact should incentivize states to adopt Koppl's (2018) criteria since constitutional provisions that are respected by local populations and therefore have popular legitimacy are a proven indicator of successful and lasting constitutional settlements (Ginsburg, Elkins, and Melton 2007, 1146).

When powerful states draw from the verifiable expertise of academics in assisting a nation-building and constitution-making project, they ought to ensure that a *wide array* of thinkers with radically different intellectual visions are called upon. By creating conditions wherein there is a "free entry" of experts into the process of constitutional design, states can increase the likelihood of endogenous native intellectuals participating in institutional formation as well as increase the likelihood of the involvement of international experts with underrepresented views. Additionally, states ought to employ multiple experts with different views, increasing what Koppl (2018) refers to as "synecological redundancy" (205). There should also be rivalry between appointed experts, ensuring that the client state has the opportunity to select among competing expert visions of constitutionalism. Finally, and perhaps most importantly, the process of constitution making should ultimately be decided by nonexperts. By incorporating electoral representation into every aspect of the constitution-making process, consulting with informed citizens, and educating nonexperts as to the preferences of experts *prior to* national referendum by nonexpert citizens, states can ensure conditions that approach "self-rule" or "autonomy," under which expert failure is the least likely to take place (Koppl 2018, 190). The real world of constitutional design should not be a laboratory for prescriptive struggles over expert or intellectual supremacy but should always strive to represent the will of the people.

REFERENCES

ABC News/USA Today/BBC/ARD Poll. *Ebbing Hope in a Landscape of Loss Marks a National Survey of Iraq.* Published March 19, 2007. https://abcnews.go.com/images/US/1033aIraqpoll.pdf.

Abdulrazaq, Tallha. "Iraq Protests Reveal an Inconvenient Truth about Sectarian Politics." *The Arab Weekly*, July 22, 2018. https://thearabweekly.com/iraq-protests-reveal-inconvenient-truth-about-sectarian-politics.

Al-Ali, Zaid. *The Struggle for Iraq's Future: How Corruption, Incompetence and Sectarianism Have Undermined Democracy.* New Haven, CT: Yale University Press, 2014.

Aldouri, Saad. "What to Know about Iraq's Protest Movement." Chatham House, The Royal Institute of International Affairs. June 6, 2017. https://www.chathamhouse.org/expert/comment/what-know-about-iraq-s-protest-movement.

Al-Istrabadi, Feisal Amin Rasoul. "A Constitution without Constitutionalism: Reflections on Iraq's Failed Constitutional Process." *Texas Law Review* 87, no. 7 (June 2009): 1627–55.

———. Interview with author, May 9, 2016.

———. "Islam and the State in Iraq: The Post-2003 Constitutions." In *Constitutionalism in Islamic Countries: Between Upheaval and Continuity*, edited by Rainer Grote and Tilmann J. Röder. Oxford: Oxford University Press, 2012.

———. "Rebuilding a Nation: Myths, Realities, and Solutions in Iraq." *Harvard International Review* 29, no. 1 (Spring 2007): 14–19.

———. "Reviving Constitutionalism in Iraq: Key Provisions of the Transitional Administrative Law." *New York Law School Review* 50 (2005–2006): 269–302.

Al Jazeera and Agencies. "Iraqis Protest against 'Sectarian Policies.'" December 23, 2012. https://www.aljazeera.com/news/middleeast/2012/12/20121223311030429167.html.

———. "Tensions Flare in Iraq Rallies." February 25, 2011. https://www.aljazeera.com/news/middleeast/2011/02/2011224192028229471.html.

Allawi, Ali A. *The Occupation of Iraq: Winning the War, Losing the Peace.* New Haven, CT: Yale University Press, 2007.

Arato, Andrew. *Constitution Making under Occupation: The Politics of Imposed Revolution in Iraq.* New York: Columbia University Press, 2009.

Baker, James A. III, and Lee H. Hamilton. *The Iraq Study Group Report.* New York: Vintage Books, 2006.

Biden, Joseph R. Jr., and Leslie H. Gelb. "Unity through Autonomy in Iraq." *New York Times*, May 1, 2006. https://www.nytimes.com/2006/05/01/opinion/01biden.html.

Brancati, Dawn. "Can Federalism Stabilize Iraq?" *Washington Quarterly* 27, no. 2 (2004): 5–21.

Bremer, L. Paul III, and Malcolm McConnell. *My Year in Iraq: The Struggle to Build a Future of Hope, with Afterword*. New York: Simon & Schuster, 2006.

Buchanan, James M. "Positive Economics, Welfare Economics, and Political Economy." *The Journal of Law & Economics* 2 (1959): 124–38.

Buchanan, James M., and Gordon Tullock. *The Collected Works of James M. Buchanan*. Volume 3, *The Calculus of Consent: The Logical Foundations of Constitutional Democracy*. Indianapolis, IN: Liberty Fund, [1962] 1999.

Choudhry, Sujit. "Bridging Comparative Politics and Comparative Constitutional Law: Constitutional Design in Divided Societies." In *Constitutional Design for Divided Societies: Integration or Accommodation?*, edited by S. Choudhry, 3–40. Oxford: Oxford University Press, 2008.

Coyne, Christopher J. *After War: The Political Economy of Exporting Democracy*. Palo Alto, CA: Stanford University Press, 2008.

Daloglu, Tulin. "End Sectarian Violence." *Washington Times*, April 17, 2006. https://www. washingtontimes.com/news/2006/apr/17/20060417-094715-3749r/.

Dawisha, Adeed. *Iraq: A Political History*. 3rd ed. Princeton, NJ: Princeton University Press, 2013.

Dawisha, Adeed, and Karen Dawisha. "How to Build a Democratic Iraq." *Foreign Affairs* 82, no. 3 (May/June 2003): 36–50.

Diamond, Larry. *Squandered Victory: The American Occupation and the Bungled Effort to Bring Democracy to Iraq, with Afterword*. New York: Owl Books, 2006.

Dodge, Toby. *Iraq: From War to a New Authoritarianism*. Abingdon, UK: Routledge, for The International Institute for Strategic Studies, 2012.

———. *Iraq's Future: The Aftermath of Regime Change*. Abingdon, UK: Routledge, for The International Institute for Strategic Studies, 2005.

———. "State Collapse and the Rise of Identity Politics." In *Iraq: Preventing a New Generation of Conflict*, edited by Markus E. Bouillon, David M. Malone, and Ben Rowswell, 23–39. Boulder, CO: Lynne Rienner Publishers, 2007.

Dodge, Toby, and Steven Simon (eds.). *Iraq at the Crossroads: State and Society in the Shadow of Regime Change*. Oxford: Oxford University Press, for The International Institute for Strategic Studies, 2003.

Eklund, Karna, Brendan O'Leary, and Paul R. Williams. "Negotiating a Federation in Iraq." In *The Future of Kurdistan in Iraq*, edited by Brendan O'Leary, John McGarry, and Khaled Salih, 116–42. Philadelphia: University of Pennsylvania Press, 2006.

Feldman, Noah. *What We Owe Iraq: War and the Ethics of Nation Building*. 3rd ed. Princeton, NJ: Princeton University Press, 2006.

Galbraith, Peter W. *The End of Iraq: How American Incompetence Created a War without End*. New York: Simon & Schuster, 2006.

Gelb, Leslie H. "The Three State Solution." *New York Times*, November 25, 2003. https:// www.nytimes.com/2003/11/25/opinion/the-three-state-solution.html.

George, Alexander L., and Andrew Bennett. *Case Studies and Theory Development in the Social Sciences*. Cambridge, MA: Belfer Center for Science and International Affairs, John F. Kennedy School of Government, Harvard University, 2005.

Ginsburg, Tom, Zachary Elkins, and James Melton. "Baghdad, Tokyo, Kabul: Constitution Making in Occupied States." *William and Mary Law Review* 49 (2007): 1139–78.

Gordon, Michael R., and General Bernard E. Trainor. *The Endgame: The Inside Story of the Struggle for Iraq, from George W. Bush to Barack Obama*. New York: Pantheon Books, 2012.

Hamoudi, Haider Ala. *Negotiating in Civil Conflict: Constitutional Construction and Imperfect Bargaining in Iraq*. Chicago: University of Chicago Press, 2014.

Hartzell, Caroline A., and Matthew Hoddie. *Crafting Peace: Power-Sharing Institutions and the Negotiated Settlement of Civil Wars*. University Park: Pennsylvania State University Press, 2007.

Hayek, F. A. *The Fatal Conceit: The Errors of Socialism*. Chicago: University of Chicago Press, 1988.

———. *Law, Legislation and Liberty*. Volume I, *Rules and Order*. Chicago: University of Chicago Press, 1973.

———. "The Pretence of Knowledge." Lecture to the memory of Alfred Nobel, December 11, 1974. www.nobelprize.org/nobel_prizes/economicsciences/laureates/1974/hayek-lecture.html.

Horowitz, Donald L. *Ethnic Groups in Conflict*. Berkeley: University of California Press, 1985.

———. "The Sunni Moment." *Wall Street Journal*, December 14, 2005. https://www.wsj.com/articles/SB113452228580321836.

International Crisis Group. "The Next Iraqi War? Sectarianism and Civil Conflict." *Middle East Report*, No. 52, February 27, 2006. https://www.crisisgroup.org/middle-east-north-africa/gulf-and-arabian-peninsula/iraq/next-iraqi-war-sectarianism-and-civil-conflict.

Jawad, Saad N. "The Iraqi Constitution: Structural Flaws and Political Implications." *LSE Middle East Centre Paper Series*, November 1, 2013.

Khalilzad, Zalmay. *The Envoy: From Kabul to the White House, My Journey through a Turbulent World*. New York: St. Martin's Press, 2016.

Koppl, Roger. *Expert Failure*. Cambridge: Cambridge University Press, 2018.

Koppl, Roger, and Leland Yeager. "Big Players and Herding in Asset Markets: The Case of the Russian Ruble." *Explorations in Economic History* 33, no. 3 (1996): 367–83.

Leenders, Reinoud. *Spoils of Truce: Corruption and State-Building in Postwar Lebanon*. Ithaca, NY: Cornell University Press, 2012.

Levy, David M., and Sandra J. Peart. *Escape from Democracy: The Role of Experts and the Public in Economic Policy*. New York: Cambridge University Press, 2017.

Lijphart, Arend. "Consociational Democracy." *World Politics* 21, no. 2 (January 1969): 207–25.

Lukitz, Liora. "The Shi'is in Post-Saddam Iraq: A Common Political Front, but Different Tactics?" In *Post-Saddam Iraq: New Realities, Old Identities, Changing Patterns*, edited by Amnon Cohen and Noga Efrati, 53–103. Eastbourne, UK: Sussex Academic Press, 2011.

Makiya, Kanan. "A Model for Post-Saddam Iraq." *Journal of Democracy* 14, no. 3 (July 2003): 5–12.

———. "Present at the Disintegration." *New York Times*, December 11, 2005. https://www.nytimes.com/2005/12/11/opinion/present-at-the-disintegration.html.

———. *The Rope*. New York: Pantheon Books, 2016.

Marr, Phebe. "Iraq's Identity Crisis." In *Iraq: Preventing a New Generation of Conflict*, edited by Markus E. Bouillon, David M. Malone, and Ben Rowswell, 41–54. Boulder, CO: Lynne Rienner Publishers, 2007.

McGarry, John. "Canadian Lessons for Iraq." In *The Future of Kurdistan in Iraq*, edited by Brendan O'Leary, John McGarry, and Khaled Salih, 92–115. Philadelphia: University of Pennsylvania Press, 2006.

———. "Liberal Consociation and Conflict Management." In *Iraq: Preventing a New Generation of Conflict*, edited by Markus E. Bouillon, David M. Malone, and Ben Rowswell, 169–88. Boulder, CO: Lynne Rienner Publishers, 2007.

McGarry, John, and Brendan O'Leary. "Iraq's Constitution of 2005: Liberal Consociation as Political Prescription." In *Constitutional Design for Divided Societies: Integration or Accommodation?*, edited by S. Choudhry, 342–68. Oxford: Oxford University Press, 2008.

McGarry, John, Brendan O'Leary, and Richard Simeon. "Integration or Accommodation? The Enduring Debate in Conflict Regulation." In *Constitutional Design for Divided Societies: Integration or Accommodation?*, edited by S. Choudhry, 41–88. Oxford: Oxford University Press, 2008.

O'Hanlon, Michael E. "Voluntary Ethnic Relocation in Iraq?" Brookings Institution, August 27, 2006. https://www.brookings.edu/opinions/voluntary-ethnic-relocation-in-iraq/.

O'Leary, Brendan. "Power-Sharing, Pluralist Federation, and Federacy." In *The Future of Kurdistan in Iraq*, edited by Brendan O'Leary, John McGarry, and Khaled Salih, 46–91. Philadelphia: University of Pennsylvania Press, 2006.

O'Leary, Brendan, John McGarry, and Khaled Salih (eds.). *The Future of Kurdistan in Iraq.* Philadelphia: University of Pennsylvania Press, 2006.

Pildes, Richard H. "Ethnic Identity and Democratic Institutions: A Dynamic Perspective." In *Constitutional Design for Divided Societies: Integration or Accommodation?*, edited by S. Choudhry, 173–201. Oxford: Oxford University Press, 2008.

Rasheed, Ahmed, and Raya Jalabi. "Iraqi Court Rules Kurdish Independence Vote Unconstitutional." *Reuters*, November 20, 2017. https://www.reuters.com/article/us-mideast-crisis-iraq-kurds/iraqi-court-rules-kurdish-independence-vote-unconstitutional-idUSKBN1DK0Q6.

Rayburn, Joel. *Iraq after America: Strongmen, Sectarians, Resistance*. Stanford, CA: Hoover Institution Press, 2014.

Said, Yahia. "Federal Choices Needed." *Al-Ahram Weekly*, 784, March 2–8, 2006. http://weekly.ahram.org.eg/Archive/2006/784/sc6.htm.

Salamey, Imad, and Frederic Pearson. "The Crisis of Federalism and Electoral Strategies in Iraq." *International Studies Perspectives* 6 (2005): 190–207.

Sullivan, Michael D. "I Fought against Muqtada al-Sadr. Now He's Iraq's Best Hope." *Foreign Policy*, June 18, 2018. https://foreignpolicy.com/2018/06/18/i-fought-against-muqtada-al-sadr-now-hes-iraqs-best-hope/.

UN Security Council. *Resolution 1483* (2003). http://unscr.com/en/resolutions/doc/1483.

Visser, Reidar. "Iraq's Partition Fantasy." *Open Democracy*, May 19, 2006. https://www.opendemocracy.net/conflict-iraq/partition_3565.jsp.

Wimmer, Andreas. "Democracy and Ethno-Religious Conflict in Iraq." *Survival* 45, no. 4 (2003): 111–34.

Wyer, Sam. "Political Update: Mapping the Iraq Protests." Institute for the Study of War, January 11, 2013. www.understandingwar.org/backgrounder/political-update-mapping-iraq-protests.

Index

About the Contributors

Dr. Donald J. Boudreaux, professor of economics at George Mason University, senior fellow in the F. A. Hayek Program for Advanced Study in Philosophy, Politics and Economics, and Martha and Nelson Getchell Chair for the Study of Free Market Capitalism, Mercatus Center at George Mason University.

Dr. Christopher J. Coyne, F. A. Harper Professor of Economics at George Mason University, and associate director of the F. A. Hayek Program for Advanced Study in Philosophy, Politics and Economics, Mercatus Center at George Mason University.

Dr. Charles Delmotte, postdoctoral fellow in the Classical Liberal Institute at New York University and Edison Fellow, Antonin Scalia Law School at George Mason University.

Dr. Malte F. Dold, postdoctoral research fellow in the Economics Department at New York University.

James Heilman, PhD student in political science at the University of Massachusetts Amherst.

Dr. Bobbi Herzberg, distinguished senior fellow in the F. A. Hayek Program for Advanced Study in Philosophy, Politics and Economics, Mercatus Center at George Mason University.

Bob Kaminski, PhD student in history at the University of Chicago.

Jozef Andrew Kosc, PhD student in international development at the University of Oxford.

Inu Manak, PhD student in government at Georgetown University.

Alexander Schaefer, PhD student in philosophy at the University of Arizona.

Jan P. Vogler, PhD student in political science at Duke University.

Dr. Sarah J. Wilford, Centre for the Study of Governance and Society, King's College London.